Lecture Notes in Computer Science   12789

More information about this subseries at http://www.springer.com/series/7409

Xiaowen Fang (Ed.)

HCI in Games

Experience Design and Game Mechanics

Third International Conference, HCI-Games 2021
Held as Part of the 23rd HCI International Conference, HCII 2021
Virtual Event, July 24–29, 2021
Proceedings, Part I

Springer

Editor
Xiaowen Fang
DePaul University
Chicago, IL, USA

ISSN 0302-9743 ISSN 1611-3349 (electronic)
Lecture Notes in Computer Science
ISBN 978-3-030-77276-5 ISBN 978-3-030-77277-2 (eBook)
https://doi.org/10.1007/978-3-030-77277-2

LNCS Sublibrary: SL3 – Information Systems and Applications, incl. Internet/Web, and HCI

This Springer imprint is published by the registered company Springer Nature Switzerland AG
The registered company address is: Gewerbestrasse 11, 6330 Cham, Switzerland

Foreword

Human-Computer Interaction (HCI) is acquiring an ever-increasing scientific and industrial importance, and having more impact on people's everyday life, as an ever-growing number of human activities are progressively moving from the physical to the digital world. This process, which has been ongoing for some time now, has been dramatically accelerated by the COVID-19 pandemic. The HCI International (HCII) conference series, held yearly, aims to respond to the compelling need to advance the exchange of knowledge and research and development efforts on the human aspects of design and use of computing systems.

The 23rd International Conference on Human-Computer Interaction, HCI International 2021 (HCII 2021), was planned to be held at the Washington Hilton Hotel, Washington DC, USA, during July 24–29, 2021. Due to the COVID-19 pandemic and with everyone's health and safety in mind, HCII 2021 was organized and run as a virtual conference. It incorporated the 21 thematic areas and affiliated conferences listed on the following page.

A total of 5222 individuals from academia, research institutes, industry, and governmental agencies from 81 countries submitted contributions, and 1276 papers and 241 posters were included in the proceedings to appear just before the start of the conference. The contributions thoroughly cover the entire field of HCI, addressing major advances in knowledge and effective use of computers in a variety of application areas. These papers provide academics, researchers, engineers, scientists, practitioners, and students with state-of-the-art information on the most recent advances in HCI. The volumes constituting the set of proceedings to appear before the start of the conference are listed in the following pages.

The HCI International (HCII) conference also offers the option of 'Late Breaking Work' which applies both for papers and posters, and the corresponding volume(s) of the proceedings will appear after the conference. Full papers will be included in the 'HCII 2021 - Late Breaking Papers' volumes of the proceedings to be published in the Springer LNCS series, while 'Poster Extended Abstracts' will be included as short research papers in the 'HCII 2021 - Late Breaking Posters' volumes to be published in the Springer CCIS series.

The present volume contains papers submitted and presented in the context of the 3rd International Conference on HCI in Games (HCI-Games 2021) affiliated conference to HCII 2021. I would like to thank the Chair, Xiaowen Fang, for his invaluable contribution in its organization and the preparation of the Proceedings, as well as the members of the program board for their contributions and support. This year, the HCI-Games affiliated conference has focused on topics related to experience design in games, user engagement and game impact, game mechanics, serious games, gamification for learning and Mixed and Virtual Reality games.

I would also like to thank the Program Board Chairs and the members of the Program Boards of all thematic areas and affiliated conferences for their contribution towards the highest scientific quality and overall success of the HCI International 2021 conference.

This conference would not have been possible without the continuous and unwavering support and advice of Gavriel Salvendy, founder, General Chair Emeritus, and Scientific Advisor. For his outstanding efforts, I would like to express my appreciation to Abbas Moallem, Communications Chair and Editor of HCI International News.

July 2021   Constantine Stephanidis

HCI International 2021 Thematic Areas
and Affiliated Conferences

Thematic Areas

- HCI: Human-Computer Interaction
- HIMI: Human Interface and the Management of Information

Affiliated Conferences

- EPCE: 18th International Conference on Engineering Psychology and Cognitive Ergonomics
- UAHCI: 15th International Conference on Universal Access in Human-Computer Interaction
- VAMR: 13th International Conference on Virtual, Augmented and Mixed Reality
- CCD: 13th International Conference on Cross-Cultural Design
- SCSM: 13th International Conference on Social Computing and Social Media
- AC: 15th International Conference on Augmented Cognition
- DHM: 12th International Conference on Digital Human Modeling and Applications in Health, Safety, Ergonomics and Risk Management
- DUXU: 10th International Conference on Design, User Experience, and Usability
- DAPI: 9th International Conference on Distributed, Ambient and Pervasive Interactions
- HCIBGO: 8th International Conference on HCI in Business, Government and Organizations
- LCT: 8th International Conference on Learning and Collaboration Technologies
- ITAP: 7th International Conference on Human Aspects of IT for the Aged Population
- HCI-CPT: 3rd International Conference on HCI for Cybersecurity, Privacy and Trust
- HCI-Games: 3rd International Conference on HCI in Games
- MobiTAS: 3rd International Conference on HCI in Mobility, Transport and Automotive Systems
- AIS: 3rd International Conference on Adaptive Instructional Systems
- C&C: 9th International Conference on Culture and Computing
- MOBILE: 2nd International Conference on Design, Operation and Evaluation of Mobile Communications
- AI-HCI: 2nd International Conference on Artificial Intelligence in HCI

List of Conference Proceedings Volumes Appearing Before the Conference

http://2021.hci.international/proceedings

3rd International Conference on HCI in Games
(HCI-Games 2021)

Program Board Chairs: **Xiaowen Fang**, *DePaul University, USA*

- Amir Zaib Abbasi, Pakistan
- Abdullah Azhari, Saudi Arabia
- Barbara Caci, Italy
- Darryl Charles, UK
- Benjamin Ultan Cowley, Finland
- Khaldoon Dhou, USA
- Kevin Keeker, USA
- Xiaocen Liu, China
- Haipeng Mi, China
- Keith Nesbitt, Australia
- Daniel Riha, Czech Republic
- Owen Schaffer, USA
- Fan Zhao, USA
- Miaoqi Zhu, USA

The full list with the Program Board Chairs and the members of the Program Boards of all thematic areas and affiliated conferences is available online at:

http://www.hci.international/board-members-2021.php

HCI International 2022

The 24th International Conference on Human-Computer Interaction, HCI International 2022, will be held jointly with the affiliated conferences at the Gothia Towers Hotel and Swedish Exhibition & Congress Centre, Gothenburg, Sweden, June 26 – July 1, 2022. It will cover a broad spectrum of themes related to Human-Computer Interaction, including theoretical issues, methods, tools, processes, and case studies in HCI design, as well as novel interaction techniques, interfaces, and applications. The proceedings will be published by Springer. More information will be available on the conference website: http://2022.hci.international/:

General Chair
Prof. Constantine Stephanidis
University of Crete and ICS-FORTH
Heraklion, Crete, Greece
Email: general_chair@hcii2022.org

http://2022.hci.international/

Contents – Part I

User Engagement and Game Impact

Game Mechanics

Contents – Part II

Gamification and Learning

Mixed and Virtual Reality Games

Experience Design in Games

Toward a Theory-Driven Model of Emotional Interaction Design in Mobile Games Research

Weiwen Chen[✉], Xiaobo Lu, and Xuelin Tang

Department of Information Art and Design, Academy of Arts and Design,
Tsinghua University, Beijing, China
chenww19@mails.tsinghua.edu.cn, luxb@tsinghua.edu.cn

Abstract. The rapid development of mobile information technology provides good opportunities for the maturity and growth of mobile games. In busy modern life, mobile games are playing an increasingly important role in people's social connection. In addition to entertainment functions, mobile games in the near future have the potential to become a new method of teaching, by which users can learn a variety of knowledge in a lively and interesting way. What factors contributed to the birth of an excellent mobile game? Obviously, the emotional factors in interaction design play a vital role. Emotion-based interaction design can evoke various positive emotions of players, such as the sense of accomplishment, satisfaction, flow experience, awe, and other psychological experiences. Thus, it is of importance to analyze the emotional factors in mobile game interaction design and discuss emotional interaction design principles and methods. The purpose of this paper to establish an emotional interaction design model, which could provide the theoretical basis for improving mobile game design theory, expanding mobile game functions and value, meeting users' more advanced emotional needs and guiding mobile game development and design practice. This paper first discusses the emotional design theory proposed by Professor Don Norman. And then it analyzes the intersection and integration of interaction design and psychology, human factors engineering, aesthetics, and other disciplines. Corresponding to the three levels of emotional design: visceral, behavioral, and reflective, it puts forward an emotional interaction design model consisting of user interface design, interaction operation design, and interaction experience design. Finally, it improves and applies the emotional interaction design model in mobile games through case studies.

Keywords: Mobile games · Emotional interaction design · User interface · Interaction operation · Interaction experience

1 Introduction

The essence of the game is not entertainment, it is a brilliant fusion of emotion and design process [1]. Many experts and scholars have different opinions on the definition of emotion. First of all, emotion belongs to the field of neurophysiology [2]. Because the brain's nervous system is stimulated by multiple external factors, it produces a series of physiological reactions that make people produce positive or negative emotions. This process may be spontaneous and unconscious [3]. Secondly, emotion is also

X. Fang (Ed.): HCII 2021, LNCS 12789, pp. 3–19, 2021.
https://doi.org/10.1007/978-3-030-77277-2_1

a keyword in psychology. Scholar Richang Cao defined emotion as a kind of psychological activity of people's attitude and behavior towards objective things [4]. All in all, emotions are the strong and complex feelings a person has towards objective factors in the surrounding environment.

Emotions play an extremely important role in the design. Cognitive psychologist Professor Donald Norman [5, 6] found that whether a person loves a product or not depends on the memories, pleasant feelings, and unconscious impulses that the design brings to her/him, which are directly related to emotions. The emotional system is an essential part of our lives, which affects people's feelings, behaviors, and thoughts, thereby helping people quickly choose between good and bad. Therefore, he believed that the emotional elements in design are more crucial than practical elements, which are the key to the success of a product.

In the same way, interaction design in the information age should not only satisfies basic interaction functions but also brings users an unprecedented emotional experience [7]. Bill Moggridge [8] once explained that technology is not the core of interaction design and emotional experiences the user obtains during the interaction are more important. Stephen P. Anderson [9] believed that in order to make a product stand out from many competing products, the interaction must be seductive, which is closely related to the aesthetics of the interface, playful interaction, and subtle details. Van Gorp [10] and others argued that because emotions can affect people's decision-making, attention, and the construction of meaning in life, emotion-based design can better serve users and allow them to obtain a good user experience. It is feasible to integrate emotional design methods into interactive experience design, which focuses on the aesthetic appearance of the interface and the natural and engaging interaction process. Junjie Zhao [11] demonstrated that interaction design based only on operational logic cannot meet the deep-seated emotional needs of users, and emotional interaction will be the main trend of human-computer interaction in the future, which is manifested in three aspects: emotionalization of interactive interfaces, interactive operations, and interactive functions and features.

It can be seen in researches that interaction design is no longer satisfied with usability, and pays more attention to giving users an aesthetic, pleasant, and meaningful interactive experience. As one of the most popular categories of electronic games, mobile games are characterized by their strong interactivity [12]. Compared with games based on computers and consoles, the process of interaction between players and mobile games is more flexible and faster. In addition to basic ways such as click, drag, zoom in, and zoom out, users can also connect mobile phones with external hardware devices, voice interaction, and gravity sensing [13]. In fact, the experience and interaction design of a mobile game itself is an emotional process [14]. According to Eric Walsh [15], the games are fundamentally designed as an experiential process to bring an emotional impact to the player, which are not limited to fun and engagement, and could be the encouragement of reflection on philosophical issues, creation of new concepts, improvements on empathy, or further connect the inner world in players with the outer world. So how do we mobilize the player's emotions in the game interaction process, improve the game experience, and resonate with the players? Studies in HUD design method proposed a player-centered model including player roles, plot guidance, and task systems. They designed interaction and visual forms that conform to player habits and psychological expectations and dug deeper into their social, respectful, emotional, and other more complex high-level needs [16]. Haoqi Miao [17] analyzed the emotional elements corresponding to each layer in the mobile game interface, so as to summarize interactive interface design principles: the visual and auditory interface design based on the visceral level, functional operation design based on the behavioral layer, and emotional resonance design based on the reflective layer. Similarly, some scholars analyzed the emotional interaction factors at the audio-visual level, behavioral level, and content level in game interaction design, and established an emotional factor model of game interaction design [18].

2 Theory-Driven Model of Emotional Interaction Design

2.1 Three Levels of Emotional Design Theory

From user's first sight of the appearance and shape of the product to the process of using it, emotional factors have large impacts on users' cognition and preference. As a result, Professor Donald Norman [5] proposed three levels of emotional design: visceral design, behavioral design, and reflective design. Visceral design corresponds to the appearance, texture, tactile impression, material, and color of the product, which directly and quickly affects human senses and emotions. At the visceral level, human vision, hearing, and perception play a leading role. The behavioral design aims at how users feel when using the product. There are four elements of excellent behavioral design: function, understandability, usability, and physical feel. A good behavioral design should be human-centered and make users psychologically satisfied. The reflective design has risen to the value and meaning level, which is closely related to society, cultural identity, and the spiritual connotation of products. For a person, the reflective design can arouse the private memory in the mind, reflect on what one has done, build a sense of identity and meet the inner emotional appeal. Generally speaking, the emotional design theory focuses on analyzing and constructing design methods for creating excellent products from three different levels, enhancing the external and internal attractiveness of the product, giving the product its soul, and capturing the instantaneous emotions of users, which build a bridge between users and products, arouse resonance between people and man-made objects, bring people unforgettable memories, and sublimate the value of design to a higher level.

2.2 Emotional Interaction Design Model

The connotation and territory of design are continuously extended and expanded. Nowadays, design is no longer limited to the design of physical objects and it is more focused on the dematerialized products such as systems, interactive interfaces, frameworks, and service processes [19]. In order to make it convenient for users to find valuable information from massive amounts of data, interaction design has emerged as a distinctive design concept [20]. There are many information products with strong usability, complete functionality, and good performance, but the user experiences are not satisfactory. The reason is that the final service objects of interaction design are all living people with emotions and cognitive abilities [21]. All users want to have a wonderful experience and get a sense of accomplishment and identification. Imagine that smooth communication does make people feel good, but the highest level of communication between people is to exchange feelings, souls and find resonance, which is also the deeper goal of interaction design. Interaction design should not only utilize the basic interaction design principles, such as aesthetics, usability, correctness but also consider the user's emotional factors in the interaction process, which can make human-computer interaction become as natural, vivid, and emotional as human-to-human interaction does, bringing users an unparalleled emotional experience and meeting higher needs of the user according to Maslow's hierarchy of needs [22] (see Fig. 1).

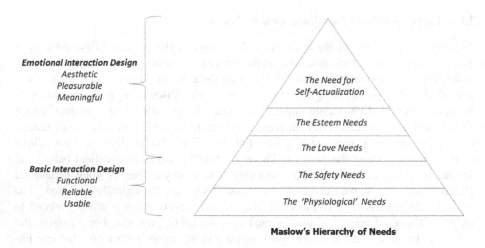

Fig. 1. The target levels of Interaction Design

Corresponding to the three levels of emotional design, emotional interaction design also has three different levels, which are user interface design, interaction operation design, and interaction experience design.

The first is the visceral design of the user interface, which is the basic composition of information products and the medium of human-information interaction. This level refers to the arrangement and selection of colors, layout, and size of texts, icons, buttons, and other visual elements on the interfaces, and the application of background music or vibration effects, acting on the user's vision, hearing, and touch, which is to meet the user's instinctive needs. Just like when people interact with each other, the other person's appearance, facial expressions, voice, and body movements will affect the people's cognition and judgment. A good user interface design can leave a good first impression on users, bring positive feedback, and encourage users to interact more with the product. Although this level is the most basic, the user interface is the first step for users when they contact with the product [23]. If the layout is appropriate, the patterns are exquisite, the color matching is reasonable, such an interface will definitely enhance the user's primary experience, improve product identity, and pave the way for the next level of the emotional interaction design.

The second is the behavioral design of the interaction operation. This level refers to the construction of the interactive logic framework, the design of interactive gestures, and the realization of interactive effects, acting on the emotional response of the user during the real-time interaction. Just like people communicate emotionally with others through body movements such as shaking hands, hugging, and using languages. A good interaction operation design is functional, convenient, and reliable, which can prevent users from thinking too much, improve the efficiency of information exchange, bring users a smooth operating experience, and quickly achieve user goals [24]. Then, the application of a variety of interactive gestures, voice, expressions, physiological signals, and other multi-modal and multi-channel interaction ways allow users to choose the best operation that suits their own habits.

The last is the reflective design of the interaction experience. This level refers to the culture, spirit, and meaning the product wants to convey through the application of its content, function, and rhetoric, acting on users' needs for love, self-esteem, and self-actualization. Just like the connections between people, the metaphysical spiritual pursuits such as the attitude toward life, the way of looking at the world, and the belonging of social values determine the closeness of the relationship between people. A good interaction experience design can convey positive ideas, strengthen connections, evoke memories, satisfy users' emotional appeals such as the sense of social belonging, the sense of life accomplishment, and the sense of value realization, which will accumulate user stickiness and loyalty [25].

According to the research on the characteristics and methods of emotional interaction design, this paper establishes an emotional interaction design model, through which it then explores the emotional factors that affect the interaction design in mobile games from those three levels (see Fig. 2).

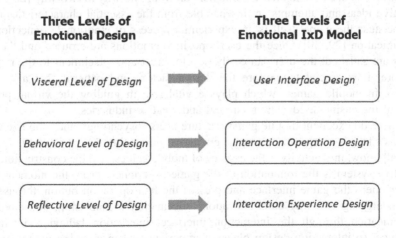

Fig. 2. Three levels of the emotional interaction design model

3 Emotional Interaction Design in Mobile Games

Mobile games refer to game software that runs on mobile devices. Since the birth of the Tetris, the first game running on mobile phones in 1994, mobile games have experienced 27 years of development history. With the development of Internet technologies, the types of mobile games have undergone earth-shaking changes, and the interaction operations have also varied from simple button interaction to screen touch interaction to multi-channel, multi-sensory interaction. As mobile games have the advantages and features of portability, mobility, and flexible operation, they are in sharp contrast with the large-scale online games and stand-alone games based on computers and platforms, making up for fixed shortcomings, such as slow running speed, poor effects, time-consuming, complicated operations, and unsatisfactory gaming experience due to some subjective and objective factors like insufficient configuration, time and technology [26]. Nowadays, people's leisure time has become more precious because of the accelerating pace of life and the increasing pressure of life. Taking a break from mobile games has become the primary choice for many young people and office workers to entertain, communicate emotions with friends and family, exercise logical thinking and reaction ability, relax the body and mind, and other important emotional needs.

Obviously, making full use of the advantages of mobile games is not only crucial for business, but also for education. One of the main functions of the game is to learn knowledge, master skills, and increase experiences. Compared with the boring learning process in the past, educational games based on mobile devices can attract learner's attention and improve their enthusiasm for learning [27]. Similarly, the cultural and creative industry has also learned from the methods of mobile games, empowering traditional display media and spaces to make the transmission of information more vivid and efficient; breaking the estrangement of tradition and modern and participants and creators to bring new life to the traditional culture, change the participation process from passive to active, and alter communication from one-way to two-way [28]. These innovative ideas and attempts are inseparable from the essential characteristics of the game because the game itself is an experiential process of emotional connection and communication [29, 30]. Once the user's positive emotions are aroused and the deep appeals are satisfied, the user can easily develop trust and attachment to the product. Therefore, it is crucial to explore the design factors and patterns that affect user emotions in mobile games, which plays a vital role in guiding the virtual product design of the business, education, cultural and creative industries.

So how do excellent mobile games capture users' psychology and mobilize users' emotions? This is inseparable from the emotional interaction design in mobile games. As we all know, interactivity is the essence of mobile games, and the construction of an interactive system is the foundation of the game experience. From the moment when the user opens the game interface and presses the first operation button, the user has been undergoing two-way communication, information transmission, and emotional communication through the interaction interface, interaction behavior, interaction experience, so interaction design plays an important role in affecting user cognition, awakening user emotions, and improving user experience. Based on the emotional interaction design model proposed in the previous paragraph, this paper analyzes the emotional factors of interaction design in many excellent mobile games and summarizes visceral design of the user interface, behavioral design of the interaction operation, and the reflective design of the interaction experience. The emotional interaction design model of mobile games provides a theoretical basis and guidance for designing educational, creative, entertained, and other mobile virtual product practices, and provides new ideas, methods, and paths for enhancing the experience and charm of digital products.

3.1 Visceral Design of the User Interface

The response of the visceral level is the natural and spontaneous behavior that people make to the external environment. Humans obtain surrounding information through looking, smelling, hearing, tasting, and touching, and then they quickly make judgments after comprehensive processing by the brain. These feelings are inseparable from people's emotions and affect people's cognition and memory. People are more inclined to things that are physically attractive to themselves and can bring good emotions. Therefore, the shape, color, size, and other external characteristics of a product play a vital role in emotional design. For mobile games, the first image of its user interface determines its "destiny" [31].

The visceral layer of the emotional interaction design model is the design of the user interface. As mentioned earlier, the emotional elements in the interaction interface include the colors, styles, and layout design of the visual and auditory elements that act on the human physiological senses. Correspondingly, in the interface of the mobile game, the modeling style of the character, the construction of the scene, the atmosphere effect of the music, and the layout of the icons constitute the elements of its visceral design.

The first is the style of the game's characters. The character's ratio, clothing, facial expressions, and action reflect the disposition of the game itself and establish the basic style and tone of the game. In the process of the game, the character becomes the user's comparison and mapping of the real world itself in the virtual world. By controlling the actions of the character, the user unconsciously connects herself/himself with the character to express the will and emotion. To a large extent, the design of game characters determines the type and scope of user groups and the degree of their preference. For example, the mobile game "Onmyoji" which is based on the myths and legends of the Heian period in Japan is extremely good at creating characters. It deconstructs and reconstructs natural and artificial elements by drawing inspiration from traditional Japanese clothing and crafts styles. There are kinds of game characters designed with a distinctive personality, gorgeous clothes, and different postures, giving each character a different temperament, attracting a large number of young users who are keen on Japanese styles.

And then is the construction of the game scene. The use of warm and cold main colors in the scene, the outline of thick and thin lines, and the creation of spatial depth can bring a deep impression to the player in a short time, causing a positive or negative emotional experience. The physical attributes of color itself, such as hue, brightness, and saturation, have objective and intuitive effects, which can bring people direct psychological feelings. Colors also have symbolic functions in visual expression.

On the one hand, warm colors, which symbolize light and warmth, awaken people's joy and cheerful emotions; on the other hand, cold colors, which symbolize peace and stability, arouse people's soft and soothing emotions. Such association preferences are people's indirect psychological induction of colors [32]. For example, the scene construction of "Journey" is impressive. The expansive golden desert, the humid and dark blue underground passage, and the holy and cold white mountain top not only restore the colors of the natural environment itself but also symbolize the emotional feelings at different stages in life, making people think deeply about the thoughts, attitudes, and philosophies that the game wants to express (see Fig. 3).

Fig. 3. Different scenes in "Journey" bring players different emotions

Next is the use of sound effects. Music has an unshakable position in our emotional life. The volume, level, strength, and weakness of the sound, the speed of the rhythm, and the ups and downs of the melody will all give people different psychological feelings [33]. "Florence" is an interactive storybook-style mobile game whose designer uses different music to express the changes in feelings. It is worth mentioning that the construction of the game scene is inseparable from the coordination of colors and music. "Florence" perfectly combines colors and music to highlight the plot and character emotions. For instance, in the first chapter of the game, the blue-gray tone of the screen and the slow and quiet music indicate the boring life of the girl. As the plot progresses, the color of the picture becomes brighter after the girl encounters love and the background music gradually changes from soft to high-pitched (see Fig. 4).

Fig. 4. The color of the picture changes as the plot progresses

Finally, the layout matters as well. The user interface is a collection of icons, text, and other elements arranged through humanized rules for displaying information [31]. Because the mobile phone interface is small and the screen size is fixed, the conditions for information display are very limited. As a result, the designer needs to prioritize the information in the limited interface and then builds a vivid interface that is easy for players to operate and can effectively transmit information through the application of symbols and simulations. "Machinarium" is a puzzle-solving game. In order to provide players with absolute freedom of operation, the designer hides the operation box used to provide information and indicates necessary clues and tips through the objects in the scene and the dialogs between the game roles; when the protagonist enters the prison, the screen becomes constricted, occupying only one-third of the entire dark interface. This symbolic layout is not only vivid but also gives players a great sense of depression, suffocation, and loneliness (see Fig. 5).

Fig. 5. The menu is hided during the playing

3.2 Behavioral Design of the Interaction Operation

The design of the behavioral level is related to the use, whose elements are functionality, understandability, usability, and physical feel. For information products, the way of human-computer interaction directly affects user experience. Good human-computer interaction design principles can clearly show product functions, conform to human instincts and thought habits, enhance understandability and usability and allow users to have a relaxed and happy operating experience.

The second layer of the emotional interaction design model is the design of the interaction operation. The emotional elements in the interaction operation include the construction of the interaction logic framework, the design of interactive gestures, and the realization of interaction effects. Correspondingly, in the behavioral level of mobile games, the presentation and realization of interaction logic, the design of interaction gestures and body movements, interaction rhetoric, and the interaction dimensions constitute the elements of its operation design. These four elements are intertwined with each other.

The construction of the interaction logic framework is the foundation. If there is no logical and clear interaction framework, it is difficult for players to experience a smooth sense of operation. A good interaction logic is closely related to the layout of icons which belongs to the visceral level. The arrangement of icons first needs to be related to the type of game and the operating habits of the player in order to improve the ease of use of the interface. That is the reason why competitive, role-playing, and gunfighting mobile games are generally operated horizontally. According to the display of the operating hot zone, users are accustomed to placing the left and right fingers in the lower left and right corners of the screen respectively, so they can control the character to move back and forth [17]. As a result, the buttons for adjusting the angle of view and skill release need to be placed in this area.

The design of the icon needs to consider its functionality and understandability. In mobile games whose touch screen interface plays the potential of emotional interaction, the interactive patterns on the game interface are no longer just imaginary, abstract symbols with interactive functions, but the bridge between the player and the game. Interactive gestures are the mapping of real behaviors. For example, sliding represents throwing, casting, swinging, and other actions in the physical world; clicking represents pressing, squeezing, pushing and other actions; expanding or narrowing the distance between the fingertips represents actions such as zooming in or out. "Florence" reindividualizes abstract symbols, more precisely, it transforms the player's operating behavior into an emotional experience in the game.

The jump of game scenes and the presentation of information levels must conform to logic and laws; instant information feedback is also of great significance. If the operation is wrong, it requires a warning sign to appear or display a corresponding prompt. For example, in "Machinarium", the player clicks on suspicious objects and clues on the screen to proceed with the next operation. If the target selection is wrong, the character will shake his head as a reminder, so the user can understand that her/his operation is wrong and change the thinking and goals.

In terms of emotional interactive rhetoric, "Florence" is a fantastic example that uses poetic interactive design methods such as simulated reality, symbolic mapping, and unity of contrast. It makes use of psychology and affects human emotions to give players a sense of participation and intense flow experience in the game. Firstly, the interactive elements on the interface guide the player to interact with the game by simulating the behavior of people in their daily lives. For example, at the beginning of the first chapter of the game, the vibration of the alarm clock, the ringing of the mobile

Fig. 6. Interaction operation simulates reality

phone, and the action of brushing teeth all simulate daily behaviors and reactions in real life. Players can subconsciously operate and interact without too much thinking (see Fig. 6). Then is the use of symbolism. In the fifth chapter of the game, in the dialogue between the girl and the boy, the designer uses puzzles to indicate the psychological changes between them. Players need to assemble the dialog boxes by playing puzzles, and the number of puzzles gradually changes from eight pieces to six pieces to only one piece at the end. This interactive process from difficult to easy symbolizes the relationship between the hero and the heroine from alienation to closeness (see Fig. 7).

Fig. 7. The number of puzzles symbolizes the relationship

The interaction dimension is the space where the interaction behavior is operated. In mobile games, most of the operation behaviors occur on a two-dimensional plane, so gesture design is extremely limited, and the senses that act are limited to vision and hearing. With the development of VR, AR, and MR technology, the interaction dimension has expanded from a two-dimensional plane to a three-dimensional space. For example, "Pokémon Go" combines virtual images with real-life scenes [34].

3.3   Reflective Design of the Interaction Experience

Reflection is a kind of conscious indirect cognition behavior that the user transforms and associates certain potential information and characteristics contained in things, and projects them into life experience. The interaction experience that an excellent emotional interaction design brings to users determines the user's overall impression of the product. It is an extension of the visceral level and the behavioral level, which connects cognition and emotion, explains the connotation and meaning of the product, and then promotes customer stickiness.

The third level of the emotional interaction design model is the reflective design of the interaction experience. The emotional elements in the interaction experience include the content, function, and application of rhetoric of the product. Correspondingly, in the interaction experience of mobile games, storylines, social functions, positive feedback and additional connotations constitute the emotional elements of the interaction experience.

The first is the narrative design of the storyline. The story is composed of characters, plots, scenes, and other basic narrative elements, which is a kind of memory behavior of human life, history, and nature. A good story can bring the audience into its woven world, bring strong and profound emotional stimulation to the audience, and immerse the audience in emotional satisfaction. In short, the story itself is the carrier of emotion. The lightweight features of mobile games make their lifespan short and players cannot engage for a long time, but with the design of the storyline, the game itself becomes an interactive storybook, bringing players an immersive narrative experience. This is because the story can create an emotional connection between the character and the player, so that the player would feel that she/he is substituting into the game character, creating an empathy connection. The story lays the foundation for meanings and provides a framework for the player's actions [35]. For one, the player has the initiative to tell the story. With the progress of the plots, the player will gradually understand the background and characters in the game and feel more and more about the role. This emotional connection evokes the player's inner emotions and resonates. For another, the story allows the player to reflect on what they did in real life, project the emotions in life into the game, and give life to the character. This is a two-way communication interaction process which has transformed the identity of the player and the meaning of the game in a real sense.

Then comes the realization of social functions. Sociality is the essence of humans, and the source of human happiness is completely intertwined with others [36]. Positive social connections will arouse positive emotions, and on the contrary, people will feel depressed. Research has shown that the games that can cultivate people's optimism are those that are the most social because people are eager to share with others in order to gain encouragement and praise from others [37]. The traditional game interaction system makes players pay more attention to the object, that is, manipulating an object to achieve a goal, weakening its virtual identity. With the development of Internet technology, mobile games have increasingly taken into account the importance of social functions: the interface design has set up a chat window; the social system has divided into a friend system, a trade union system, a master-apprentice system, a marriage system, and other social systems; the game has established a more complex and active social network, and strangers can also establish trust relationships through cooperation. The mobility characteristics of mobile games have given them more powerful social functions. Nowadays, location-based games such as "Pokémon Go" mainly use the social concept of "services based on the actual location of users", which connects virtual and reality, promotes the emotional connection of people in real life and provides a new effective channel for strangers to socialize.

The third is positive feedback. The need for self-actualization is the highest human need, which can make people obtain the most sustainable and motivating positive emotions, such as self-worth, the sense of accomplishment, and satisfaction. Positive feedback in the game allows players to work harder, complete difficult challenges more successfully, and obtain more lasting emotional experiences. Firstly, the goal is the key factor, which is the driving force for people to move forward. The fastest way to improve the quality of people's daily life is to give people a specific goal, something that can be accomplished but also challenging [29]. Then, the reward mechanism is the basis for the effective establishment of a positive feedback loop. The reward is the recognition of the results of people's hard work, which positively reflects our ability and enables people to gain a sense of self-value. The reward mechanism, which has the traits of availability, continuity, periodicity, and accumulation in the game, can bring players tangible emotional rewards, mobilize the enthusiasm of the players, and make the players feel happy. As the game progresses, the level of the player increases and the time accumulates, rewards become more abundant, which means the growth of resources, experience, value, and abilities, enhancing the player's initiative in the operation and bringing them psychological satisfaction.

The last is the added value of the game. The function of the game is not only to bring entertainment value to users but also to bring meaning to life, which is also the added value of the game. The meaning is the feeling that we are in a magnificent environment; it is the belief that our actions are more important than personal achievements; it is the dream we all desire to achieve. There is no doubt that we are constantly struggling to find the meaning of life. The best way to add meaning to your life is to connect your daily actions with things beyond yourself [29]. In mobile games, the magnificent background helps to connect individuals with a strong sense of mission; the immersive environment arouses our curiosity and the sense of surprise; the realization of the final goal makes us aware of the sense of achievement and inspires participation; the devotion of the game progress evokes the most enthusiastic and satisfying positive emotions of players.

Referring to the emotional interaction design model proposed in Sect. 2, this chapter analyzes and studies the emotional factors of interaction design in some typical mobile game cases, and finally summarizes the emotional interaction design model in mobile games in detail (see Fig. 8). The three levels of emotional interaction design in mobile games are not progressive or separated but integrated. This is because users could gain interactive experience by interacting with the product interface. That is to say, the visceral level design of the user interface and the behavioral level design of the interaction operation determine the reflective level design of the interaction experience, and a good interaction experience will also enhance people's evaluation of the interactive process.

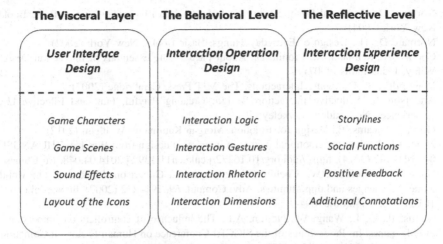

The Visceral Layer   The Behavioral Level   The Reflective Level

User Interface Design	Interaction Operation Design	Interaction Experience Design
Game Characters	Interaction Logic	Storylines
Game Scenes	Interaction Gestures	Social Functions
Sound Effects	Interaction Rhetoric	Positive Feedback
Layout of the Icons	Interaction Dimensions	Additional Connotations

The Emotional Interaction Design Model in Mobile Games

Fig. 8. The emotional interaction design model in mobile games

4 Conclusion

As a type of electronic games, mobile games pay more attention to entertainment and interactivity, and their interaction design pays more attention to the experience process and the emotional needs of players than general digital products, which has also become its drawback. In many people's impressions, games are easy to indulge and affect real life, but we can also promote the advantages of games and apply them to the interaction design of other digital products by studying the methods and experience of emotional interaction design in mobile games. To better meet people's spiritual needs and stimulate people's positive emotions, this is the true value of the game. Based on the emotional design theory proposed by Professor Donald Norman, this paper expounds the three levels of emotional interaction design, proposes an emotional interaction design model, and analyzes the methods of emotional interaction design in mobile games, and summarizes the emotional elements of interaction design in mobile games, hoping to provide theoretical guidance for the emotional expression of the interaction design of digital products such as video games in the future.

References

1. Werbach, K., Hunter, D.: For the Win: How Game Thinking Can Revolutionize Your Business. Wharton Digital Press, Philadelphia (2012)
2. Panksepp, J.: Affective Neuroscience: The Foundations of Human and Animal Emotions. Oxford University Press, New York (1998)
3. Ekman, P., Davidson, R.: The Nature of Emotion: Fundamental Questions. Oxford University Press, New York (1994)
4. Cao, R.C.: General Psychology (in Chinese). People's Education Press, Beijing (1979)

5. Norman, D.: Emotional Design: Why We Love (or Hate) Everyday Things. Basic Books, New York (2004)
6. Norman, D.: The Design of Everyday Things. Basic Books, New York (2002)
7. Cooper, A., Reimann, R., Cronin, D.: About Face 3: The Essentials of Interaction Design. Wiley, Indianapolis (2007)
8. Moggridge, B.: Designing Interactions. The MIT Press, Cambridge (2007)
9. Anderson, S.: Seductive Interaction Design: Creating Playful, Fun, and Effective User Experiences. New Riders, Berkeley (2011)
10. Gorp, T., Adams, E.: Design for Emotion. Morgan Kaufmann, Waltham (2012)
11. Zhao, J.J.: Look at the emotional factors in interaction design from WeChat. ZHUANGSHI **04**, 141–142 (2014). https://doi.org/10.16272/j.cnki.cn11-1392/j.2014.04.048. (in Chinese)
12. Coulton, P., Bamford, W., Chehimi, F., Edwards, R., Gilbertson, P., Rashid, O.: Mobile games: challenges and opportunities. Adv. Comput. **69**, 191–242 (2007). https://doi.org/10.1016/S0065-2458(06)69004-9
13. Cairns, P., Li, J., Wang, W., Nordin, A.I.: The influence of controllers on immersion in mobile games. In: Proceedings of the SIGCHI Conference on Human Factors in Computing Systems, CHI 2014, pp. 371–380. Association for Computing Machinery (April 2014). https://doi.org/10.1145/2556288.2557345
14. Tzvetanova, S.A.: A Design Methodology for Emotional Interface. The Hong Kong Polytechnic University School of Design, Hong Kong (2006)
15. Walsh, E.: How to Design for Impact in Games. Rensselaer Polytechnic Institute, New York (2018)
16. Dai, F.Q., Ji, T., Galli, F.: The explore of internet game's HUD design methods. ZHUANGSHI. **02**, 106–107 (2014). https://doi.org/10.16272/j.cnki.cn11-1392/j.2014.02.045. (in Chinese)
17. Miao, H.Q.: Research on Mobile Game Interaction Design Based on Emotional Design Concept. South China University of Technology, Guangzhou (2019). (in Chinese)
18. Zhang, Y.L., Zhang, T.X.: Emotional factors in internet game interaction design. Design **21**, 144–145 (2016). (in Chinese)
19. Black, A., Luna, P., Lund, O., Walker, S.: Information Design: Research and Practice. Routledge, New York (2017)
20. Colborne, G.: Simple and Usable Web, Mobile, and Interaction Design. New Riders, Berkeley (2017)
21. Bergemann, D., Morris, S.: Information design: a unified perspective. J. Econ. Lit. **57**, 44–95 (2019). https://doi.org/10.1257/jel.20181489
22. Maslow, A.H.: A theory of human motivation. Psychol. Rev. **50**, 370–396 (1943). https://doi.org/10.1037/h0054346
23. Blair-Early, A., Zender, M.: User interface design principles for interaction design. Des. Issues **24**, 85–107 (2008). https://doi.org/10.1162/desi.2008.24.3.85
24. Krug, S.: Don't Make Me Think: A Commonsense Approach to Web Usability. New Riders Press, Berkeley (2005)
25. Murray, J.H.: Inventing the Medium: Principles of Interaction Design as A Cultural Practice. The MIT Press, Cambridge (2012)
26. Montola, M., Stenros, J., Waern, A.: Pervasive Games: Theory and Design. Morgan Kaufmann, Waltham (2009)
27. Huizenga, J., Admiraal, W., Akkerman, S., Dam, G.T.: Mobile game-based learning in secondary education: engagement, motivation and learning in a mobile city game. J. Comput. Assist. Learn. **25**, 332–344 (2009). https://doi.org/10.1089/g4h.2015.0038

28. Michala, M., Alexakos, C., Tsolis, D.: Mobile applications and games for a digital educational program on art and culture in secondary school. In: 2018 9th International Conference on Information, Intelligence, Systems and Applications (IISA), pp 1–6. IEEE (July 2018). https://doi.org/10.1109/IISA.2018.8633697
29. McGonigal, J.: Reality is Broken: Why Games Make Us Better and How They Can Change the World. Penguin Press, London (2011)
30. Freeman, D.: Creating emotion in games: the craft and art of Emotioneering™. Comput. Entertain. **2**, 15 (2004). https://doi.org/10.1145/1027154.1027179
31. Johnson, D., Wiles, J.: Effective affective user interface design in games. Ergonomics **46**, 1332–1345 (2003). https://doi.org/10.1080/00140130310001610865
32. Birren, F.: Color Psychology and Color Therapy: A Factual Study of the Influence of Color on Human Life. Hauraki Publishing, San Francisco (2016)
33. Deutsch, D.: The Psychology of Music. Academic Press, New York (1998)
34. Rauschnabel, P.A., Rossmann, A., Dieck, M.C.: An adoption framework for mobile augmented reality games: the case of Pokémon Go. Comput. Hum. Behav. **76**, 276–286 (2017)
35. Zhou, T.: Understanding the effect of flow on user adoption of mobile games. Ubiquit Comput. **17**, 741–748 (2013). https://doi.org/10.1007/s00779-012-0613-3
36. Fonseca, X., Slingerland, G., Lukosch, S., Brazier, F.: Designing for meaningful social interaction in digital serious games. Entertain. Comput. **36**, 1875–9521 (2021). https://doi.org/10.1016/j.entcom.2020.100385
37. Penttinen, E., Rossi, M., Tuunainen, V.K.: Mobile games: analyzing the needs and values of the consumers. J. Inf. Technol. Theor. Appl. **11**, 5–22 (2010)

A Specific Measurable Model

How Can Test Results be Influenced by Interactive Prototypes and Design Manuscripts?

Xiang Gao, Nian Liu, Yong-Cheng Liu, Si-Si Yuan,
and Zhi-Peng Hu[✉]

Netease, Hangzhou, People's Republic of China
gaoxiang1@corp.netease.com

Abstract. In the development process of video games, both the iteration of original designs and the verification of new designs are quite frequent, therefore a large number of tests are of great importance. Sketches of designers are usually linear and static, while the interactive prototypes developed from them are non-linear and dynamic. Under this circumstance, the same design, using a design manuscript and an interactive prototype to make the player understand the game's interaction strategy, can lead to different test results. A controlled experiment has been conducted: for the same interaction design, the design manuscript as well as the interactive prototype were respectively demonstrated to two groups of players, so as to verify the impact of these two on the test results. In the meantime, this paper will provide game developers with a measurable model, which can help them make a choice between interactive proto-type and design manuscript in testing. For players, this model can also be used to measure whether the interaction design actually affects their feelings because of the design itself, or because of some static and dynamic effects.

Keywords: Interactive prototype · Design manuscript · Measurable model · Video games

1 Introduction

In the process of modern game development, the quality of interaction design is a significant factor that affects the quality of games. Game developers tend to conduct a large number of tests, during which the design manuscripts and interactive prototypes are commonly used in the industry. However, these two methods have sufficient difference both in the cost of development, and in people's dynamic and static senses. And these can also affect the result of the test, therefore, the option between interactive prototype test and manuscript test is of great importance.

A prototype is a working model built to develop and test design ideas. In web and software interface design, prototypes can be used to examine content, aesthetics, and interaction techniques from the perspectives of designers, clients, and users. Usability professionals often test prototypes by observing users as they perform tasks typical of the intended use of the product. By gathering data on user mistakes and comments,

© Springer Nature Switzerland AG 2021
X. Fang (Ed.): HCII 2021, LNCS 12789, pp. 20–33, 2021.
https://doi.org/10.1007/978-3-030-77277-2_2

designers and usability professionals can find usability problems at an early stage of the design, before substantial resources are invested in flawed designs (Walker et al. 2002). When used in various experiments, interactive prototypes should at least be operable, not just being an interface display.

A manuscript is a picture display of the designer's original scheme. For an interactive design, the designer usually has several design manuscripts to illustrate the logic of the design, which can be a wireframe diagram or a more beautified picture. The design manuscript can clearly show the overall layout of the design, including those of icons, decorative pictures and illustrative texts.

Studies on interactive prototype and manuscript in this paper are clearly different from those on the low-fidelity and high-fidelity prototypes, which are more discussed in the current industry. According to researchers (Virzi et al. 2020), low-fidelity prototypes should have the following features: (1) are an efficient way to search the design space (Virzi 1989); (2) are predictive of preferences in the actual product (Wiklund et al. 1992); (3) enhance user participation in the design process (Muller 1991); (4) enable visualization of possible design solutions (Muller 1991) and (5) provoke innovation (Moggridge 1993). Therefore, high-fidelity and low-fidelity differ more in the level of prototype development.

Nevertheless, in this paper, the difference between interactive prototype and manuscript lies more in its dynamic or static sense. Interactive prototype can be directly experienced when players manipulate the electronic equipment, and manuscript is only used as images for observation. This is the intrinsic difference between them: whether they are low or high fidelity is not the focus of this paper, and will not make a difference just due to the degree of fidelity.

2 Theory

2.1 Dynamic and Static Effects on Human Sense

In a whole process of game, most of the information acquired by the player comes from the visual information, through which the player interacts with others, and the logic of the game can also be remembered. This element of interactivity distinguishes games from many other forms of media, in which the physical body is "transcended" in order to be immersed in the narrative space (Blake 2009).

However, the content of dynamic visual information is different from that of static visual information. Players of dynamic visual information are more likely to be attracted by some moving and operable contents. Consequently, in game development, some dynamic effects are often adopted as hints of significant information on the interface. Static visual information is more about layout and aesthetics, and game designers can even enhance the gameplay by adjusting the game's level design, texture and color choices, as well as object placement if these decisions are based on the study of the player's visual attention in a 3D game environment (Seif EI-Nasr 2006).

There are two major influences on human's visual attention: bottom-up and top-down processing. Bottom-up processing is the automatic direction of gaze to lively or colorful objects as determined by low-level vision. In contrast, top-down processing is consciously directed attention in the pursuit of predetermined goals or tasks. Previous work in perception-based rendering has exploited bottom-up visual attention to control detail (and therefore time) spent on rendering parts of a scene (Cater et al. 2002).

It is significant to point out here that we sense image detail only in a 2° foveal region, relying on rapid eye movements, or saccades, to jump between points of interest. Our brain then reassembles these glimpses into a coherent, but inevitably imperfect, visual percept of the environment. In this process, we literally lose the sight of some unimportant details (Cater et al. 2003). In this paper, we demonstrate how properties of the human visual system, in particular inattentional blindness, can be exploited to accelerate the rendering of animated sequences by applying a priori knowledge of a viewer's task focus.

Considering that the intrinsic difference between interactive prototype and manuscript takes place in the different mechanisms of dynamic and static sense, when discussing the player's concentration, differences of spatial distribution and changes of visual attention over time (Dye et al. 2009) are quite obvious in these two schemes, which may lead to various test results. So, relevant experiments are necessary for further verification.

2.2 Performative and Interactive Design

Performative design pays more attention to the layout of design, and design itself is the content related to the layout or the demonstration of specific art style. Its focus can be divided into the following two points:

1. Whether the player is willing to accept the sensory experience of the layout, as well as its visual expressiveness.
2. Whether the player can use the buttons and entrances normally in this layout, and ensure that the player's actions will not be affected by the layout itself.

Interactive design concentrates more on the interactive logic. The design itself contains a logical jump, recognition, and some animation transitions that the player needs to understand. This type of design focuses on the following two points:

1. Can the player understand the interaction logic? Understanding is the player's ability to understand the designer's design logic through trials, based on the design content.
2. Whether the player accepts the interactive logic or not, which depends on whether the player is willing to use this logic to play the game once they understand it.

3   Design

The core argument of this research is not the merits of the two plans. What we are concerned about is the nature of interactive prototype and manuscript, as well as their possible effects on the test result. Therefore, we conducted two experiments: the first group used manuscripts to test the new and the old design, while the second group used interactive prototype. Here, it may occur that both in the tests of manuscript and interactive prototype, players' degree of preference is consistent, or they prefer the new or the old design. But this does not prove that testing through interactive prototype and manuscript has no difference. Considering this, what we need to analyze is the reason of players' preference.

In this research, we conducted a preference test of the main interface for UNO!™, a popular mobile game in more than 180 countries. The purpose is to examine the possible effects of interaction prototypes and manuscripts on the test results. Consequently, both the interactive prototype and manuscript contain two parts: the manuscript includes images of new main interface as well as that of the original main interface; the interactive prototype includes new main interface prototype and also the original main interface prototype.

In the old design, all the entrances are displayed in the main interface at the beginning of the game, as shown in Fig. 1. The player will complete the upgrade operation by clicking the relevant entrance. As the level increases, a new entrance will be unlocked, and the special effect of unlocking will be included in the interaction prototype (Fig. 2).

In the new design, when a player comes into the game for the first time, there is only one entrance in the main interface, as shown in Fig. 3. Clicking the entrance will upgrade the player's level, which is in line with the old design. Once upgrading the level, a new entrance will be unlocked, but the difference is that the main interface can be divided into two pages, as shown in Fig. 4 and Fig. 5, which can be switched by the green button on the left. And in the page shown in Fig. 4 contains a custom button. By clicking it, player can come into the interface shown in Fig. 6, where he or she can replace the entrance of classic mode with one of a favorable mode.

So, there were two tests. The first test was conducted to know how much players preferred the old or new version of the design by looking at the manuscript, while the second test was about to know how much players liked the old or new design through the interactive prototype. From these two tests, you can compare the influence of interactive prototype as well as the manuscript on test results of the same design.

4   Experiment

4.1   The Chosen Players

There were 10 players in the manuscript test, including 4 males and 6 females. And 4 players have a background of interactive design.

When it came to the interactive prototype test, there were 19 players, including 11 males and 8 females. And 9 players had played UNO!™ before.

All these players were Chinese. Before the experiment, we explained the relevant situation of our experiment to them and asked them to sign the consent. We promised to keep their personal information confidential. These players could also quit at any time they wanted during the experiment.

Fig. 1. The initial state of main interface in the old design

Fig. 2. The final state of main interface in the old design

4.2   Plans of the Experiment

During the manuscript test, we tried to take the test one by one. First, players could use a mobile device to look at the new interface (Fig. 3 to Fig. 6). After that, they would look at the old design (Fig. 1 and Fig. 2). During the process, we would attempt to offer them oral guide, which included the order of their observation, the meaning of each image, and the maneuverability of each button. The test lasted for ten to fifteen minutes.

Fig. 3. The initial state of main interface in the new design

Fig. 4. The first page of unlocked main interface in the new design

Similar to the manuscript test, at the beginning of interactive prototype test, we attempted to take the test one by one, and players could use a mobile device to experience the interactive prototypes of the new and the old design. In order to ensure that players' experience would not be affected by other factors, all the entrances of the old and new interface, as shown in Fig. 7 and Fig. 8, were permitted to click. At the same time, these players were divided into two groups with different order of experience (One group could experience from the new to the old prototype, while the other group took the contrary order). And players could explore their own actions in the

Fig. 5. The second page of unlocked main interface in the new design

Fig. 6. The customized page in the new design

testing process. When they were in doubt, we would provide them with specific guidance. The test lasted for fifteen to twenty minutes.

4.3 Further Interview

Further, we would compare the results of the two tests, so our focus was the same for the players who tested the interactive prototype or the manuscript. Therefore, in the player interview, we emphasized on two questions:

Fig. 7. Annotations of the entrances in the new design

Fig. 8. Annotations of the entrances in the old design

1. Which version of design do players prefer, the new or the old one?
2. Can players repeat the logic of the interaction shown in the new design without being reminded? Are there any possible problems in their retelling process?

In the first question, players would give out a specific preference, and we would record their reasons. This is crucial that we need to abstract from it the reasons players hold to prefer a certain design. That is where our conclusions come from.

In the second question, players would repeat the interactive logic of the new design. Considering that the design itself was complex, there would be great difference between the feelings of interaction prototypes with actual operation, as well as the manuscript with a static experience, which could make a difference in understanding the same design. So, we need to pay attention to the prominence of the difference itself, and the possible causes of the difference.

4.4 Tool for the Experiment

In this experiment, Android 8.0 mobile devices were used to test the manuscript and interactive prototype, and the interactive prototype was developed through Unity.

5 Results, Significance and Limitation

5.1 Analysis of the Results

According to the results above, most players preferred the old design, not matter which type of test (interactive prototype test or manuscript test) they had experienced. This could prove that the old design was more welcomed by players (Table 1).

Table 1. Preference of players

Type of test	Total players	Prefer more to new design	Prefer more to old design
Interactive prototype test	19	4	15
Manuscript test	10	1	9

Nevertheless, can this result prove that there is no difference in interactive prototype test as well as in manuscript test? We need to analyze more on these players' reasons for not preferring the new design (Table 2).

Table 2. Why did players dislike the new design?

Type of test	Total players	Cannot understand how to operate	Do not know the functions of buttons well	Information is partial	Layout is unreasonable	Do not know the relation between different interfaces
Interactive prototype test	19	2	2	10	2	2
Manuscript test	10	7	5	8	6	7

According to the results above, we can clearly notice that the gap between results of the interactive prototype test and manuscript test is quite obvious. When categorizing these reasons, we find that the static manuscript has played an important role in offering most players (80% of the total players in the test) a sense of "partial information" when experiencing the new design. When operating the interactive prototype, players could enhance their understanding of the interactive logic by experiencing the prototype repeatedly. But when it came to the manuscript test, the way for players to understand the logic was limited to the external guidance as well as their own imagination. And the imagination itself could provide the players with insufficient, and even wrong information. In the meantime, the difference of players' accommodation to the layout catches our attention. Here is the answer of a player from the interview,

> "There are merely few pictures in the manuscript, and I cannot click on them to see their interactive effects. So, I can only drive my attention to the overall layout."

Besides this player, several players also provide such feedback, which has great significance for us to measure the applicability of two test methods. The static monotonicity of manuscript can make more players focus on the layout of the content, while the use of interactive prototype can to some degree change this focus because of its persistently dynamic experience (Table 3).

Table 3. Deviation between players repeat and the designer's logic

Type of test	Total players	Have deviation compared with designer's logic	Have no deviation compared with designer's logic
Interactive prototype test	19	4	15
Manuscript test	10	9	1

The results above are of great importance. As we can see in the table, in the manuscript test, most of the players were not clear about the overall interaction logic of different interfaces, or even had obvious deviation when repeating the logic to researchers. For example, a player pointed out that,

> "I think that the green custom button can be used to flip the entrance, but I don't know its exact function by merely looking at the icon itself."

After providing them with the expanding image (Fig. 6), some players still cannot know that it is a custom interface. How can this take place? From the table below, we can partly summarize the reasons for the discrepancy occurred in players' understanding (Table 4).

Table 4. The discrepancy occurred in players' understanding of the game function

Type of test	Do not understand the function of custom button	Do not understand the switched order of interfaces	Believe that the switch button is used to play the video	Take the custom interface as something to choose the mode
Manuscript test	5	4	1	2

When we analyze these reasons, it is easy to find that the unclear logic shown in the manuscript test lies mainly in the function of specific buttons as well as the logic of interaction. In fact, the manuscript itself contains a lot of possible dynamic information that needs to be imagined by players. Nevertheless, the process of imagination can easily lead to a process of generating deviation.

5.2 Significance of the Research

From our own perspective, the research can provide game developers some thoughts when they need to choose between interactive prototype and manuscript for an interactive test. Compared with manuscript, interactive prototype can occupy a lot of development expenditure. However, because of their differences in offering people a dynamic or static sense, the interactive prototype as well as the manuscript can greatly affect the test results. Considering this, this research is going to build up a measurable model, which is aimed to measure what type of test is better to use interactive prototype or manuscript. And this can allow developers to choose a more suitable test method - whether they want to control the cost, or they pursue the accuracy of the results, this can offer great help.

5.3 Limitation of the Research

This research has the following limitations in the process:

1. Based on the interview results of the two tests, this research analyzed the reasons for players' preferences and further obtained some characteristics of the model. But there was no second verification for these characteristics.
2. Plans of designs selected in this research cannot cover all the directions of interaction design and lacks the verification of its various directions. Considering this, more work should be done further.

6 Conclusion

The premise of this research is that there is a difference in development expenditure between interactive prototype test as well as manuscript test, which is an objective experience obtained from long-term work.

6.1 Influences of Interactive Prototype and Manuscript on Player Tests

Interaction prototypes and manuscripts have an obvious impact on the results of player test. The influencing factors are as follows:

1. **A dynamic interactive prototype and a static manuscript can have an impact on the player's focus.** Static manuscript will let players pay more attention to details because of its static monotony, but this will also let them ignore the part of logical interaction, and pay more attention to the layout of the interface. With dynamic interactive prototypes, players focus more on the usability of the logic because of its abundance of dynamic interactions.

2. **A dynamic interactive prototype and a static manuscript can have an impact on the player's understanding of logic.** Some designs may involve transformations, animated transitions or complex logics. When looking that them, the player can still be confused about its logic of the action even after the static manuscript has been fully explained. This is much less of a problem for interactive prototype because it is operable and the player can generate a clear understanding of the logic in the process of repeatedly making mistakes.

3. **A dynamic interactive prototype and a static manuscript can have an impact on the player's psychological anticipation.** Since these two are not the final version of the game during the process of test, players will imagine in some directions. And this is more prominent in static manuscript test, where the majority of the player's understanding of logics comes from the imagination. Here, it is highly likely to generate wrong imagination, which will further affect the results of the entire test. Even when these players are told about the correct logic, they will still make such mistakes and finally influence the results. Nevertheless, this does not mean that negative emotions cannot take place in the interactive prototype tests. In this case, players conduct repeated operations back and forth, and this frequency is often not consistent with the one in the real game. This can probably cause players to feel bored, so as to affect the test results.

6.2 A Specific Measurable Model: How to Choose Between Interactive Prototype Test and Manuscript Test?

From the research above, we find out that the following factors can become the measurable criteria:

1. What Is the Type of the Design? Is That a Structural Layout or a Logical Interaction?
This is the core element of the designer's design. Static manuscript can do well in tests on the layout, structure, or even the beauty of the images related to the design. Because of its static nature, in the process of the test, players will pay more attention to the layout of the content.

If the design contains interactive logics such as the jump, transformation and animation, dynamic interactive prototype is much more suitable than static manuscript. Since the manuscript cannot express the dynamic logic clearly, the player tends to generate his or her own imagination of the design itself, which may conflict with the designer's original design intention. Thus, the dynamic interactive prototype is more recommended for testing interactive logics.

2. Operative or Sensory?
This is also a significant basis of measuring the suitable test methods. Although all the designs are related to the layout, but for the real players, all these layouts can affect their real in-game operation. Therefore, if the design itself can affect the players' operation, the static manuscript cannot tell you the exact feeling of players when using the designs in reality. Good-looking but not practical cannot be considered as features of a good design, so the interactive prototype test can offer a lot of crucial conclusions at this time.

3. Officially Launched or in the Process of Development?
Whether it's officially launched or in development is also an important factor. If the game has been launched, its players have built up considerable operating habits. At this time, whether it is an iterative design or a new design, what the designers have to consider is that the design itself do not greatly affect the operation habits held by the existing players. Therefore, it is necessary to invite old players to the test, during which the interactive prototypes can be more intuitive to see influences of the new interaction on old and new players.

4. Expenditure?
After taking the first, the second, and the third criteria into consideration, developers may have the capability to choose the specific test method. Nevertheless, the problem of expenditure is inevitable. For such a simple logic of clicking Page A to jump to Page B, designers can have many means to perform well, but for complex interactive logics, if game developers want to develop interactive prototypes, there would be a cost. Here, we think that if the potential cost is expected to be high, static manuscript for simple usability tests will bring many benefits for further tests. Although we have emphasized a lot of advantages held by interactive prototype test, the expenditure is still an important premise for our research. And this is also the point that developers should pay attention to.

The model as well as the influencing factors obtained in this paper are based more on experimental results and work experience, and abstracted through interview content and analysis. There will be a lot of follow-up verification work, and further research is still required on this topic.

References

Virzi, R.A., Sokolov, J.L., Karis, D.: Usability problem identification using both low-and high-fidelity prototypes. In: Proceedings of the SIGCHI Conference on Human Factors in Computing Systems, pp. 236–243 (April 1996)

Virzi, R.A.: What can you learn from a low-fidelity prototype? In: Proceedings of the Human Factors Society Annual Meeting, vol. 33, no. 4, pp. 224–228. SAGE Publications, Los Angeles (October 1989)

Wiklund, M.E., Thurrott, C., Dumas, J.S.: Does the fidelity of software prototypes affect the perception of usability? In: Proceedings of the Human Factors Society Annual Meeting, vol. 36, no. 4, pp. 399–403. SAGE Publications, Los Angeles (October 1992)

Muller, M.J.: PICTIVE—an exploration in participatory design. In: Proceedings of the SIGCHI Conference on Human Factors in Computing Systems, pp. 225–231 (March 1991)

Moggridge, B.: Design by story-telling. Appl. Ergon. **24**(1), 15–18 (1993)

Blake, A.: Game sound: an introduction to the history, theory, and practice of video game music and sound design. J. Des. Hist. **22**(3), 226–227 (2009)

El-Nasr, M.S., Yan, S.: Visual attention in 3D video games. In: Proceedings of the 2006 ACM SIGCHI International Conference on Advances in Computer Entertainment Technology, 22 pages (June 2006)

Cater, K., Chalmers, A., Ledda, P.: Selective quality rendering by exploiting human inattentional blindness: looking but not seeing. In: Proceedings of the ACM Symposium on Virtual Reality Software and Technology, pp. 17–24 (November 2002)

Cater, K., Chalmers, A., Ward, G.: Detail to attention: exploiting visual tasks for selective rendering. In: ACM International Conference Proceeding Series, vol. 44, pp. 270–280 (June 2003)

Dye, M.W., Green, C.S., Bavelier, D.: The development of attention skills in action video game players. Neuropsychologia **47**(8–9), 1780–1789 (2009)

HEROES: An Action Game Enabling Players with and Without Disabilities to Play Together

Milan Peschll and Helmut Hlavacs(✉)

Faculty of Computer Science, University of Vienna, Vienna, Austria
helmut.hlavacs@univie.ac.at

Abstract. The exclusion of impaired people from various areas of life is undeniable, leisure and entertainment (including games) being definitely among them. The paper focuses on the research of the current state of accessibility in gaming, non-mental disabilities (grouped into visual, auditory and physical) and the ways of compensating for them in real life and gaming. It results in the development of a game prototype with assisstive AI for physically challenged players, which is then subsequently tested in field on a mixed school with both challenged and unchallenged children and aims to breach the barrier of impaired players feeling "left out", bringing both groups of players together through making them realize their similarities, rather than their differences. The aim was to help and empower the player, not replace him.

Keywords: Accessibility in games · Blind gamers

1 Motivation

Despite living in a modern age with many possibilities, people with disabilities (estimated at least 25% of the entire population suffers from some sort or presence of disability) [1] still encounter the struggle with being left out in many of these possibilities and areas. One of the areas is leisure and entertainment, which includes gaming. Both research and personal experience have led us to the opinion that there is very little focus and room on the market when it comes to impaired gamers.

The personal experience goes back to a childhood friend, who was born physically challenged (partial paralysis of his whole right-side muscular apparatus), struggling or being totally unable to enjoy most of the games we used to play. We always tried to incorporate him in any multiplayer game we have played, but very often, he was unable to catch up and hence stripping him of most of the joy or the feeling of being a part of the game. Across all genres, no game was designed/would offer sufficient adjustments for impaired persons.

Sure, there are initiatives (of which many are already inactive, mainly due to financial reasons) that try to raise awareness and bring more spotlight to

© Springer Nature Switzerland AG 2021
X. Fang (Ed.): HCII 2021, LNCS 12789, pp. 34–44, 2021.
https://doi.org/10.1007/978-3-030-77277-2_3

this topic – such as The AbleGamers Charity[1] [2] or SpecialEffect, the gamers' charity[2] [3] – which have been successful to some extent, but the current situation is still nowhere near to ideal. Solutions (such as customized controllers) are only created as external byproducts of small companies/independent initiatives. Big companies making triple-A titles have little to no interest of considering impaired people [4] – many do not offer custom key re-mapping [4], have controls far too complex or lack assistive mechanisms to compensate for the person's disability.

Media (including Games) harness the power of creating the feeling of inclusion of impaired people [5]. The aim of this project is to create a game that is primarily considering challenged gamers, with suitable complexity and assistive AI mechanisms, that are gradually more and more powerful, making them at least a bit of an asset to the team, and hence harnessing this power mentioned above.

2 Research

2.1 Research on Disabilities

To come up with a proper concept for the game, thorough research on compensation methods for various disabilities was imperative. The goal was to create a game where anyone, no matter the (physical) disability would be able to enjoy it. For the sake of simplicity, we decided to group the disabilities into:

- **Visually impaired** - partial or full loss of vision
- **Auditory impaired** - partial or full loss of hearing
- **Physically impaired** - ranging from light stages of paralysis, undeveloped motorics to missing/fully dysfunctional limbs - meaning people who have at least some (nearly) "healthy" limb(s) - to heavy stages of paralysis, progressive muscle diseases, cerebral palsy etc.

Visually Impaired. Visually impaired players pose a great challenge, since (unlike the loss of smell or taste) the loss of vision strips the subject off a sense with enormous information processing capabilities [6]. We humans use a combined product of motor, sensory and cognitive skills to effectively navigate through space and most of the information used for this is gathered via our vision [7]. Hence it is logical, that by losing such a powerful source of information and the ability to efficiently process them, we have to compensate for it.

In (lighter) cases of only partial visual impairment (meaning the person is still able to see, but with some medical conditions) contrast sensitivity is in strong correlation with vision-related activities and vision-related quality of life [8]. This could mean, that in case of subject being not fully blind, opting for visuals of high-contrast should positively affect their ability to perceive obstacles and avoid them (such as game obstacles). But even for those, who have not lost

---

[1] www.ablegamers.org.
[2] www.specialeffect.org.uk.

their vision totally, graphical presentation of information might not be the most suitable option [9].

It is rather advised to compensate for the loss/impairment of vision by using other sensory channels, of which auditory capabilities are claimed the be among the most suitable [6,10], e.g. due to being present in the process of evaluating data during spatial localization [11,12]. The crucial part is, that in order for auditory cues to be helpful (especially when trying to detect and avoid obstacles), they have to be perceived withing a suitable time advance [13].

Auditory Impaired. As for auditory impaired people, alternative reactionary input, being mostly visual, is supposed to be among the best ways of compensation. [14] Voices, music, sounds and atmosphere can be imitated via distinct visual cues, such as subtitles or highlights (e.g. screen turning darker/red, flashing effects etc.) [14] The focus on players with impaired audition was not really strong for this project, since all inspirations and concepts we did not include any important game mechanics or features being solely presented via sound - meaning that this group does not need any compensation for their disability.

Physically Impaired. Since this was a group covering many different types and stages of physical disability, it needed thorough research. The significance of this group can be justified by the fact that cerebral palsy by itself is statistically one of the leading neurological impairment causes in childhood [15]. It is accompanied with damage to perception, congitive skills, communication, behavior or musculo-skeletal problems [16] which by its own suitably describes many struggles physically impaired people have to deal with. An that is only one of the many various physical disabilities.

To cover the wide variety of disabilities this group is focused on and come up with proper compensation methods, we have chosen the many stories provided by AbleGamers and SpecialEffect - featuring descriptions of the specific disabilities the players are suffering from and how they managed to work around, including also video footage. Here are some of them listed:

- **Steven Paschall** - suffered a stroke, lost control of his left arm, now plays with a modified XBOX-like controller using his right arm and his lips [2]
- **Mike "Brolylegs" Begum** - arthrogryposis and scoliosis, bound to crawl around or lie in a specialized wheelchair, currently being a professional Street Fighter V player beating non-impaired players with a PS4 controller operated by his mouth [2]
- **Randy "N0M4D" Fitzgerald** - arthrogryposis, playing games competitively by operating a modified controller with his mouth [2]
- **Callum** - paralyzed from shoulders down, playing games with his chin using a modified PS4 controller [3]
- **Ceyda** - cerebral palsy, playing games with a totally custom controller featuring mainly joysticks and over-sized buttons [3]
- **Joel** - spinal muscular atrophy, now being able to effectively play Rocket League against non-impaired players [2]

- **Giddeon** - stunted arm growth with very few fingers developed, now winning Forza 3 races with their special controller [2]

This shows that the most used, and hence probably most suitable, controllers for physically challenged people are either modified console controllers (Ps- and XBOX-like) or totally customized controllers, revolving around the same elements as the console ones do - joysticks for movement and (preferably over-sized) buttons for action.

The focus on researching ways of compensation for all of these groups was crucial, because, when considering accessibility as one of the primary goal, they have to be direction-setting and correspondent with the game concept. This way, we have found out that our game concept has to revolve around being able to be controlled mainly via any controller-like joystick, with additional features (if necessary) on easily accessible button.

3 Game Design

3.1 Game Concept

Based on the conducted research on disability compensation and the inspirations mentioned in the "Related Work" section, we had to look for rather "stripped-down" than "feature-rich" concepts. What this meant was that we would have to encompass enjoyability, appeal and the ability to include the challenged player/build team spirit and bonds within a concept with suitable game logic complexity ("How does the game work? How difficult is it to understand the concept? How long does this process take?") and controls complexity ("Is it easy/accessible to use to controls of the game effectively?"), resulting in high levels of accessibility without regards to as many types and levels of disability as possible.

Hence, in order to be able to create a project as complete as possible (meaning it is enjoyable, appealing, atmospheric etc.), we decided to utilize our previous skills in Adobe Illustrator (for graphics and animation) and Unity3D Game Engine (for the actual game development). The concept we opted for is a 2D level-based runner-like team-game (1–4 players) called "Heroes". The players control "animal-like" creatures with superhero costumes (since children idolize superheroes) to make them feel like they are "Heroes" instead of feeling left out. The concept includes these key features:

- **2D setup**
- **Reduced complexity via controller-like joystick controls**
- **Level-based game progression**
- **Automatic player movement via invisible area**
- **Non-excluding death system**
- **Team-focused collectible system**
- **Assistive AI for physically challenged players**

2D Setup & Controller-Like Joystick Controls. The 2D setup was chosen mainly due to three reasons. The first one being the fact that orientation in 2D space is very easily visualised and easy to harness for both impaired and non-impaired players, resulting in better accessibility. The second one were our previous graphic design experiences (both game and non-game related), which allowed us to create visually appealing 2D graphics, such as backgrounds, characters, enemies, obstacles, collectibles and their respective animations. The third one was the ability to fulfill the concept, strongly emphasized by Dr. Hlavacs, of the team "staying together at all costs and situations."

Reduced Complexity via Controller-Like Joystick Controls. The 2D setup is very easily combined with practical representation of all the research on suitable compensation & controls for physically challenged players. Navigation in a 2D runner-like game is very easy, intuitive and most importantly almost absolutely harnessable within the controls of a controller-like joystick. This allows to create the desired high levels of accessibility.

Level-Based Game Progression. We were discussing multiple options with Dr. Hlavacs, but the final choice was opting for a level-based game progression. This creates greater potential (when compared to e.g. a infinite-runner-like concept) for game variety - different levels, sequences, enemies, obstacles, music, graphics, environments etc. This allowed us the creation of a better, fuller and more potent base for a project that could be then further developed.

Automatic Player Movement Within an Area. When considering accessibility as one of the main building blocks of this project, the in-level progression system had to be carefully chosen to be as suitable as possible. Here, the creation of an invisible area that is automatically moved (just like the player in standard runner games) seemed to be the best option. It provided a great solution for fulfilling the concept of team "staying together at all costs and situations." The whole team is automatically moved through the level with the area, but is simultaneously (every player by him/herself) allowed to move freely (both horizontally and vertically) within it, to avoid enemies and obstacles and gather collectibles. This player movement is constrained by the area, so the player is unable to leave it via his/her own actions. This means that even if a player is heavily impaired, he/she will always move with the team and can never get off the screen and become separated, creating the feeling of always being a part of the team.

Non-excluding Death System. The death system functions the way that even if the player dies, he just becomes a "ghost" and is still visually present on screen, being moved with the area and having the ability to move around it freely, but without the possibility of interacting with anything. This again contributes to the concept of the team always staying together. All "dead" players are respawned if any "alive" team member collects a respawn collectible and the game ends only if the whole team is dead.

Team-Focused Collectible System. The collection system features the following collectibles:

- **Gold** - if collected, adds a point to the team score pool (no individual score)
- **Resurrect** - if collected, all "dead" team members are being respawned, if all team members are alive, the team is awarded with bonus points
- **Shield** - if collected, the player is awarded with a shield (consuming 1 collision with an enemy/obstacle)
- **Team shield** - if collected, every "alive" team member is awarded with a shield

The aim of this collectible system is to eliminate concurrency between the players as much as possible and rather motivate them to work together and take care of each other - the more daring players can try to collect bigger chunks of gold or team shields (which are usually harder to access) and hence provide the "weaker" team-members (e.g. the heavily impaired ones) with the same benefits - being respawned, adding to the team score or granting them a team shield, making them instantly a bigger asset to the team and creating the feeling of inclusion.

Assistive AI for Impaired Players. Despite capitalizing on the controller-like joystick controls, there are cases where reducing the complexity of the game and the controls might not be a sufficient way of compensation. Within this concept, mostly visually impaired (whether it is partial or full loss of vision) and heavily impaired (e.g. heavier stages of cerebral palsy/paralysis) persons would feel it.

The aim of the assistive AI's is to make these players feel as a part of the team by being as useful as possible. Hence, the 4 different, gradually more and more powerful, AI's (2 for visually challenged and 2 for physically challenged players) focus mostly on keeping the player alive by either notifying the player about the incoming danger, avoiding the danger independently of the player or a combination of both. The AI's features are:

- **Visually challenged AI 1** - designed for visually challenged, but not fully blind players, provides audio cues about incoming danger (enemy/obstacle), how to avoid it (in which direction) and about being safe (no incoming danger in front of the player)
- **Visually challenged AI 2** - designed for blind players, has the same features as Visually challenged 1, but additionally, if the dangerous element comes too close, it starts to avoid the danger by itself until the player is "safe"
- **Physically challenged AI 1** - visually cues the player via an " ! " exclamation mark that there is danger incoming and while a button is pressed and held, it automatically avoids any incoming danger until the player is "safe"
- **Physically challenged AI 2** - automatically avoids any incoming danger until the player is "safe"

All of these AI's are overridable by dedicated player controls - meaning, that if the wishes to play riskier (e.g. collect more collectibles) his controls input override the AI, making him able to be more useful to the team, but risking "death" on the other hand. This way, the players are being compensated for their disability by being assisted in avoiding obstacles/enemies, but do not become almighty and still have to try by themselves (creating space for their own involvement) if they want to perform better.

4   Implementation

4.1   Graphics

For the project to live up to our expectations (meaning it would be visually appealing, since the target audience are gamers, regardless of being physically challenged or not, mainly children), proper graphics were a necessity. We opted for a silhouette-oriented concept for Game Objects (characters, obstacles, enemies) in combination with colorful aspects - such as the background, collectibles etc., providing enough contrast between game object and the background, considering that higher contrast is critical for partially visually challenged players [8]).

Characters. Since the aim of the game is the inclusion of gamers with disabilities, the design of the characters was chosen to be animal-like silhouette figures with superhero costumes, to make the players, especially the challenged ones, feel rather like a part of a superhero team, than feeling left out. The game includes a team of up to 4 characters, of which everyone requires multiple states in the Unity3D animator - Idle, Walk (full animation), Fly, Dead, with Shield and signalizing danger (in case the player is using any AI help).

Collectibles. Collectibles ought to be very distinct - hence, while they are at the same layer in the game as players, enemies and obstacles, they are colorful (Gold - +1 point, purple - shield, green - unused, red - respawn dead members). The team shield collectible was created as a prefab in Unity3D by connecting 4 purple collectibles together.

Player - Common AI Traits. All of the AI's are there to pose as solutions to various disabilities and their different stages. They are based on the usage of "Raycasts" - invisible directional lines (red and blue) that continuously check for possible threats in front of the players. These are then used to either provide audio cues to assist the player and/or avoid obstacles automatically/with a press of a button. At least 3 "Raycasts" were used in every case to avoid any possible threat that is only partially in the way of the player (Fig. 1).

Very important is that every action of the AI (especially the ones that avoid obstacles by themselves) are overridable through specific player input (via controls), meaning that if the player wishes to risk more and try to be more helpful,

Fig. 1. In-game graphics (Color figure online)

he/she may, but is risking death. The aim is always to empower the challenged players, not replace them.

- **Player 1 (Red)** - Visually challenged AI 1
- **Player 2 (Blue)** - Visually challenged AI 2
- **Player 3 (Yellow)** - Physically challenged AI 1
- **Player 4 (Green)** - Physically challenged AI 2

Fig. 2. Raycasts for impaired player AI's (Color figure online)

Player - Visually Challenged AI 1 & 2. The "Visually challenged AI 1" poses a solution for visually challenged players, who arc not totally blind. According to the research above, visually impaired players have to be "notified" about incoming danger soon enough to be able to avoid it (Fig. 2).

If any of the three "Raycasts" collides with a dangerous object in front of the player, the cue tells the player in which direction to avoid the obstacle. After reaching safety a "Safe" audio cue is played. The audio cues were (for temporary means) created with FromTextToSpeech[3] [17] and for the collection of the "Gold" collectible a sound sample from "NoiseCollector" was used [18].

The "Visually Challenged AI 2" serves as the solution for blind players. It is an extension of the previous AI, using an extra set of "Raycasts" - the longer ones provide audio cues, while the shorter ones try to automatically save the player from danger, unless overriden.

Player - Physically Challenged AI 1 & 2. These AI's are grouped since they have the most of the code and logic in common. They both have 1 set of "Raycasts" that are identical to the shorter set of "Raycasts" from the previous AI - both in length and functionality.

However, the "Physically challenged AI 1" cues the player visually via an exclamation mark (" ! ") that appears in the front of the player. If the player presses and holds the button(s) for "avoiding" the AI starts to avoid the obstacles until the player is safe. If the player would happen to hold the button through the whole game, he/she would be consistently avoiding obstacles, since the AI does not break upon reaching safety.

The "Physically challenged AI 2" does everything the "Physically challenged AI 1" does, but automatically. This means, that the player does not have to provide any input and is being heavily assisted in avoiding enemies and obstacles. This is meant to assist the most heavily impaired players (such as the ones suffering from cerebral palsy etc.). The AI is effectively capable of avoiding both simple and more complex sequences of enemies and obstacles and currently manages to pass a 2.5 min long level all by itself.

5   Evaluation

The evaluation was based on in-field testing of the game at Joint School Mokrohájska 3, which is a mixed school of both impaired and non impaired children, with the impaired being of various disabilities. All the following arrangements were agreed on with the headmaster of the school.

The real process of testing first consisted of both impaired and non-impaired high-school students (1st and 2nd grade) placed into 2-man teams (1 impaired and 1 non-impaired). The impaired consisted mostly of visually impaired (heavily challenged or blind) and one physically challenged (paralyzed bottom half of the body with some motoric damage to the upper limbs). Later fully randomized

---

[3] www.fromtexttospeech.com.

teams were built, 2–4 players consisting of both non-impaired and impaired children.

The results were pleasantly surprising. The vast majority of the children have become very active and captivated and new children kept coming to the classroom in interest to join. They began to switch teams randomly in all variations - all non-impaired, mixed, all impaired. Additionally, e.g. if only 1 blind person from the team was left alive, everyone else (inside or outside of the team) began to navigate them to get a "respawn" collectible and to bring the others to the game.

Our observations show how this kind of cooperative game fosters playing together, and common fun experiences that the children can have together. It also shows that due to the AI support all gamers are equally competitive in the sense that they can equally contribute to the common goals.

6   Conclusion and Future Work

Certainly, there is still much room for improvement, if the project ought to be a fully-developed game. Among these is certainly adding more content (levels, enemies, mechanics and more dynamic elements), creating multi-language support (for the game content and the AI's - especially audio cues), gathering more feedback and conducting more scientific research and testing (involving more schools, private and public organizations), considering more disabilities, the list goes on and on.

The first refinement to the AI to be implemented will be the increase in its complexity. It will (in its logic) try to imitate how humans naturally asses avoiding obstacles (especially sets of them) in front of them, iteratively looking for the shortest path to avoid a sequence of obstacles.

To sum it all up, as the results of the preliminary in-field testing have shown, this prototype has very much lived up to its expectations. The goal was to aid the impaired players to tip the scales of balance between them and non-impaired players and hence reach a state where players would not differ, regardless of being physically challenged or not, but would rather focus on the joy and inclusion of everyone. To breach the barriers and the feeling of "being left out" and focus rather on the similarities than the differences between both groups was the aim - and the achievement.

References

1. Oliver, M.: Understanding disability (1996)
2. The AbleGamers Foundation: The Ablegamers charity. http://www.ablegamers. org/
3. TheSpecialEffect: Special effect, the gamer's charity. https://www.specialeffect. org.uk/
4. Griliopoulos, D.: Five tricks developers should use to help disabled gamers. http:// www.pcgamer.com/five-tricks-developers-should-use-to-help-disabled-gamers/

5. Repková, K.: Mediá a zdravotne postihnutie. http://dspace.specpeda.cz/bitstream/handle/0/507/261-269.pdf?sequence=1
6. Tou, J.T., Adjouadi, M.: Computer vision for the blind (1985)
7. Lahav, O., Mioduser, D.: Multisensory virtual environment for supporting blind persons' acquisition of spatial cognitive mapping, orientation, and mobility skills (2002). http://playpen.icomtek.csir.co.za/~acdc/assistive%20devices/Artabilitation2008/archive/2002/papers/2002_28.pdf
8. Ekici, F., Loh, R., Waisbourd, M., et al.: Relationships between measures of the ability to perform vision-related activities, vision-related quality of life, and clinical findings in patients with glaucoma. JAMA Ophthalmol. 133(12), 1377–1385 (2015). https://doi.org/10.1001/jamaophthalmol.2015.3426
9. Sherman, J.C.: The challenge of maps for the visually handicapped. http://mapcontext.com/autocarto/proceedings/auto-carto-2/pdf/chall-of-map-4-visual-handicap.pdf
10. Wiener, W.R., Welsh, R.L., Blasch, B.B.: Foundations of orientation and mobility (2010). https://books.google.sk/books?hl=en&lr=&id=nYENqA5LZKUC&oi=fnd&pg=PR7&ots=I3RQi04FPx&sig=NnkKfT1-9wHe2IABAnbwgpJYT1s&redir_esc=y#v=onepage&q&f=false
11. Veraart, C., Wanet, M.-C.: Sensory substitution of vision by audition (1985)
12. Easton, R., Greene, A., DiZio, P., et al.: Auditory cues for orientation and postural control in sighted and congenitally blind people. Exp. Brain Res. 118(4), 541–550 (1998)
13. Brambring, M.: Mobility and orientation processes of the blind. In: Warren, D.H., Strelow, E.R. (eds.) Electronic Spatial Sensing for the Blind. NATO ASI Series (Series E: Applied Sciences), vol. 99, pp. 493–508. Springer, Dordrecht (1985). https://doi.org/10.1007/978-94-017-1400-6_33
14. Barlet, M.C., Spohn, S.D.: Ablegamers includification (2012). https://www.includification.com/AbleGamers_Includification.pdf
15. Demeši, D.Č., et al.: Cerebral palsy in preterm infants (2016). http://www.doiserbia.nb.rs/img/doi/0042-8450/2016/0042-84501600019D.pdf
16. Okáľová, K.: Detská mozgová obrna (2008)
17. FromTextToSpeech: From Text to Speech. http://www.fromtexttospeech.com/
18. NoiseCollector: shortwaxcylinder_IR.wav. https://freesound.org/people/NoiseCollector/sounds/220243/

Gaze as a Navigation and Control Mechanism in Third-Person Shooter Video Games

Patricio Isbej and Francisco J. Gutierrez[✉]

Department of Computer Science, University of Chile, Beauchef 851, West Building,
Third Floor, Santiago, Chile
{pisbej,frgutier}@dcc.uchile.cl

Abstract. Gaze as an input mechanic, to this date, has not been widely adopted as a navigation and control mechanism in video games. However, recent advances in the development of affordable hardware, such as portable eyetrackers, have the potential to drive an increasing interest in the design of gaze-induced interaction metaphors in interactive systems. In order to bridge this gap, we designed a prototype third-person shooter video game controllable through traditional inputs (i.e., a console joystick), gaze-based controls (i.e., mediated through an off-the-shelf commercially available eyetracker), or hybrid mechanics. This paper reports the design rationale of the video game and the results of a proof of concept, aiming to comparatively measure user experience and playability of the video game under the influence of traditional and/or gaze-based navigation and control mechanisms. The obtained results show that users preferred hybrid controls for interacting with the game, as it improves performance and provides assistance and useful affordances for enhancing the overall experience. These results are quite promising and provide insights for designing novel gaming mechanics incorporating gaze as an active navigation and control input.

Keywords: Eye-tracking · Gaming experiences · Design · Empirical study

1 Introduction

In recent years, gaming has been flourishing as an exciting field of scholarship, both in academia and industry. While simultaneously bridging creative arts, cognitive sciences, and human-computer interaction, video games enact a thriving application domain encompassing entertainment and serious development (e.g., education and health).

Eyetracking is the procedure of measuring, through different means, the position and movement of eyes (i.e., gaze) as a way to accurately determine the observation focus of a subject [12]. This technique is used in gaze behavior research when an individual performs different tasks, such as interacting with video and

© Springer Nature Switzerland AG 2021
X. Fang (Ed.): HCII 2021, LNCS 12789, pp. 45–56, 2021.
https://doi.org/10.1007/978-3-030-77277-2_4

image content within a digital document, with a particular emphasis on identifying where such a user focuses his/her attention [3]. Moreover, eyetracking and gaze-controlled mechanisms can be used as methods for conveying natural human-computer interactions as a way to improve user experience. In particular, these approaches have been rapidly gaining the attention of the gaming research and development community [9].

The extensive use of eyetracking devices to augment user experiences in gaming scenarios can also be linked to the growth and increasing availability of affordable hardware solutions to provide accurate gaze detection. Among these products, Tobii, a commercial eyetracking device, also provides software development kits (SDK) for major video game engines (e.g., Unity and Unreal), which favors the development of new interaction mechanisms to increase immersion and player experiences in commercial video games. In that respect, more than 100 games—including a few AAA titles—have been developed over the past few years and incorporating eyetracking as an extension to standard gameplay [1].

Although there are currently some video games using gaze as an extension to standard gameplay, a recent literature survey [11] reports that most of the studies demonstrating the potential effectiveness of gaze as an interaction mechanism in video games lack of strong and rigorous empirical support. Therefore, the potentially new, useful, and reusable knowledge obtained by producing these novel interactions, is not necessarily translated into proper design guidelines to extend our current understanding in this application domain. For instance, while player performance in gaze-controlled video games is not necessarily better than controlling the same game with more standard devices (such as a joystick), users feel more engaged and overall report a better experience when playing these games [2,7,8]. However, this latter observation could also be explained by a latent novelty effect that needs to be controlled.

Building upon this line of research, this paper presents the design and development of a 2D top-down third-person shooter (TPS) video game, explicitly addressing gaze as a possible navigation and control input. In this game, we allowed the use of gaze as a proper interaction mechanism within the application, ranging from allowing the player to move the character to aiming and shooting. The particularity of this game is that it allows users to select what combination of traditional (i.e., controlling the game with a standard joystick) and gaze mechanics are used. Therefore, this design choice allows to empirically study player performance and player experience across four conditions:

- One variant of *only traditional controls*, for both navigation and aiming and shooting
- Two variants of *hybrid controls* (i.e., mixing gaze inputs and a traditional joystick) for navigation and/or aiming and shooting
- One variant of *only gaze-based controls*, for both navigation and aiming and shooting

The game presented in this paper was developed in Unity, coupled with Tobii 4C as eyetracking device. In order to formally assess player experience in each game variant, (1) we computed performance metrics (i.e., final score, time to complete the game tutorial, and time to complete the game) and (2) asked players to complete the Game Experience Questionnaire [4] at the end of the game session.

The rest of this paper is structured as follows. Section 2 reviews and discusses related work. Section 3 provides an overview of the video game, as well as presents the main design and development decisions. Section 4 describes the empirical setup for measuring player experience. Section 5 presents and discusses the obtained results, particularly by providing insights for infusing gaze-based interaction mechanics in video games. Finally, Sect. 6 concludes and provides perspectives on future work.

2   Related Work

One of the main issues that emerges when using an eyetracker to detect gaze is that the person makes involuntary eye movements to detect his/her surroundings. Therefore, when using an eyetracker as an input device, it inevitably introduces the risk of triggering involuntary actions from the user. This phenomenon, known in the literature as Midas Touch [5], must be accounted for when using an eyetracker for mediating the interaction with any kind of software. In order to overcome this problem, designers could introduce a supplementary event to confirm the action that the user intends to perform, such as clicking/tapping a button or a particular gesture made with the eyes (e.g., blinking). Likewise, partial slowdowns or standby events forcing the user to stare at the screen could be introduced to make sure that the performed action is actually intended and not a byproduct of the natural eye movement and/or blinking. In that respect, Velichkovsky et al. [10] proposed a method in which they attempt to solve the Midas Touch Problem: the authors differentiate events made by ambient fixation (i.e., an overall and panoramic exploration of the screen characterized by rapid movements made with the eyes using peripheral vision) and focal fixation (i.e., a fixed glance to a specific point in the screen where less ocular movements are performed).

Velloso and Carter [11], in a recent systematic mapping study covering video games and gaze-mediated interaction literature, identified several lines of analysis that illuminate further research in the topic. In particular, the authors (1) classified the different types of eye movement, (2) identified the entry types that are captured by eye tracking devices, and (3) proposed a taxonomy of game mechanics that can be developed in this application domain. In particular, these mechanics are: *navigation, aiming and shooting, selection and commands, implicit interactions*, and *visual effects*. Therefore, this contribution serves as a starting point for identifying plausible ways to introduce gaze-based mechanics in video games.

From the different mechanics identified in the work by Velloso and Carter, those that will be addressed in this paper are two: (1) navigation and (2) aiming and shooting. In particular, these mechanics define clear and independent ways in which users can control the actions of a video game character or his/her surroundings through gaze.

Following the same line of reasoning, Navarro and Sundstedt [8] used implicit interactions in a video game of the shoot'em up genre, where the player controls a spaceship and must shoot to asteroids and enemy ships. The player's spaceship enables two modes of attack: offensive and defensive. When the player glances at his own ship, the game assumes that he/she tries to avoid the enemies, so the game automatically adapts and changes its behavior to defensive mode. Conversely, when the player fixes his/her attention to the enemies (e.g., by staring at them), the game then adapts its behavior to offensive mode.

Dechant et al. [2] conducted an empirical evaluation of selection techniques in a first-person video game. The authors measured the time that it took a player to aim to random targets over the screen. This task was comparatively evaluated using five different techniques, three of them using an eyetracker (either as a sole input device or in a hybrid combination with more traditional controls, such as mouse and keyboard or joysticks). The conclusions of this work stated that the mouse outperformed the other devices, while using only the eyetracker gave the worst results. Furthermore, the authors found that eyetracking, when combined with traditional joysticks, was the preferred input mechanism according to users and even outperformed just using the joystick in certain configurations. There results serve as the first inspiration for designing the prototype game that is presented in this paper.

In summary, most of the literature covers first-person shooting games with specific targets. Therefore, there are several other video game genres where eyetracking and gaze interaction can be explored as input mechanics.

3   Game Design

The designed video game is a 2D top-down third-person shooter. This means that the main character is able to move in two axes (i.e., horizontally and vertically), while simultaneously aiming and shooting enemies. In this game, players have the options to use traditional controls, gaze controls, or a combination of both.

The goal of the game is that the player gets as many points as possible by shooting enemies that appear randomly in each stage (see Fig. 1). In order to provide smoother controls, and ease the interaction with the user's gaze, enemies are widely separated one from another and are static instead of randomly spreading all over the screen. This also obeys to limiting the potential negative effects of Midas Touch, as discussed by Velichkovsky et al. [10] in a prior work. Therefore, enemies are represented as towers (akin to defense fortresses), which are large enough to be easily recognized by the player.

As stated above, gaze controls are triggered by the use of an eyetracker that makes the user interact with the character represented on screen. In that respect, players can either navigate and/or control the game character by aiming and/or shooting the targets. Both mechanics (i.e., navigation and control) can both be set up independently upon launching a game session. Therefore, the video

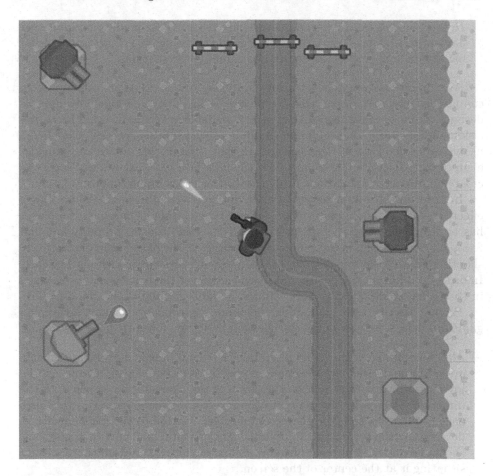

Fig. 1. Main interaction screen of the video game

game as a whole provides four different kinds of input setup, depending on the preferred interaction device (i.e., joystick or eyetracker):

- *Only traditional controls*: in this setup, both character movement and actions (i.e., aiming and shooting) are controlled using a traditional video game console joystick. In practical terms, this game mode serves as a benchmark for evaluating the effect of introducing gaze controls as input mechanics.
- *Only gaze controls*: in this setup, the player only interacts with the video game through his/her gaze, as captured and processed by the eyetracker. In this mode, both navigation and control actions are managed by the user's gaze. In practical terms, the player is able to fixate his/her view on a specific object on screen, and then use his/her gaze to move the character over the game stage.

- *Hybrid controls*: in this setup, players can either (1) use traditional inputs for navigating and gaze controls for aiming and shooting; or (2) gaze controls for navigating and traditional controls for aiming and shooting.

As support hardware for detecting, capturing, and processing gaze, we used a commercial off-the-shelf portable eyetracker: Tobii 4C. The rationale behind this design decision is that this device is widely available in the market and has a precision and accuracy acceptable enough for detecting subtle movements and being usable in a video game setting context. In that respect, this device also provides a supporting software development kit (SDK) which easily allows developers to create third-party applications using the eyetracker as input support.

In order to control for potential interruptions derived from the Midas Touch effect, the game contemplates a predefined time threshold in which the player has to stop navigating the screen with their gaze in order to properly aim and fixate his/her position in the game stage. Otherwise, the player risks of erratically shooting all over the screen when he/she pans out the screen with his/her gaze. In order to calibrate the device and teach the player the basic controls designed in the game, we designed a short tutorial at the beginning of the game session.

Having described the main design decisions regarding eyetracking device and game mechanics, we now detail the interaction schema for both game mechanics:

- *Map navigation*: In the game setup that uses traditional controls, movements are performed using the left analog sticks (or directional pad buttons) in the joystick, which map the current position of the character on screen with the direction selected by the player in the joystick. In the game setup that uses gaze as input control, the character on screen will follow the player's gaze as detected by the eyetracker. In order to make natural and smooth transitions, the game camera will be adjusted to follow the character at all times, always situating it at the center of the screen.
- *Aiming and shooting*: In the game setup that uses traditional controls, aiming will be detected with the right analog stick of the joystick and shooting will be mapped to the shoulder buttons (or triggers). In the game setup using gaze controls, the character will aim to the direction where the player is currently observing, as detected by the eyetracker. In order to confirm the action (as to limit potential Midas Touch effects), upon completing a certain time threshold, the character will visibly aim to a target on screen and start shooting in that direction.

4   User Study

In this section we summarize the main considerations taken in the study design for assessing player performance and player experience in the developed video game.

4.1 Participants and Materials

We recruited 24 volunteer participants, across both genders and ranging different experiences with video games (from casual gamers to hardcore gamers). For convenience reasons, participants were all undergraduate students in computer science at the University of Chile, aged between 22 to 32.

In order to control for hardware settings, all participants used the same equipment when interacting with the game. In particular, this consisted on:

- Tobii Eye Tracker 4C, for gaze controls
- Xbox One Joystick, for traditional controls
- LG 27MK400H-B Monitor, as screen display

4.2 Experimental Design

We followed a within-subjects experimental design, where all participants were exposed to both conditions: (1) playing the game with traditional controls and (2) playing the game with gaze-controlled mechanisms. In particular, given the nature of the second empirical condition (i.e., gaze controls) we split the assignment of subjects to one of the following three sub-conditions: (2-a) gaze controls *only* for navigation, (2-b) gaze controls *only* for aiming and shooting, and (2-c) gaze controls for both navigation *and* aiming and shooting.

In addition, we controlled for potential learning effects across conditions. Therefore, half of the study participants were randomly assigned to empirical condition (1) and then to one of conditions (2), whereas the other half was asked to first complete their assigned task in one of conditions (2) and then to complete condition (1).

As a result, we randomly assigned participants to one of the following six groups:

1. Complete condition (1) and then condition (2-a)
2. Complete condition (1) and then condition (2-b)
3. Complete condition (1) and then condition (2-c)
4. Complete condition (2-a) and then condition (1)
5. Complete condition (2-b) and then condition (1)
6. Complete condition (2-c) and then condition (1)

4.3 Procedure

First of all, we explained to all participants the context and scope of the study. In particular, they were asked to provide explicit, free, and informed consent to continue with the experiment. No participants declined to complete the trial.

Participants were told that they had to complete the game twice. Detailed instructions on the eye tracker calibration procedure were displayed on the game screen. Afterwards, a brief tutorial on the game mechanics had to be completed.

Once all the preparations were complete, participants played the game following the specific control mechanics assigned to their experimental group. The game automatically recorded performance metrics (namely score and time to complete each stage).

Finally, when the participant ended the game, he/she was asked to fill in the Game Experience Questionnaire [4] to formally assess their play experience. This instrument is considered as an industry standard and is widely used by researchers in player-computer interaction [6].

4.4 Ethical Considerations

Complying with the ethical procedures in empirical research with human subjects proposed by the American Psychological Association (APA), we required explicit, free, and informed consent to all participants. As compensation, we raffled a 10 USD giftcard among all participants who completed the study.

5 Results

In this section, we briefly summarize the obtained results by the end of the experiment.

5.1 Player Performance

As depicted in Figs. 2, 3, and 4, the game variant where gaze is used as a control mechanism for aiming and shooting, obtained the best results. This is explained by obtaining, in average, lower penalization in score (left bars) and lower time to complete the level (right bars). Likewise, when gaze is used for both navigation and controlling the game, the results are comparatively worse than in the other game variants.

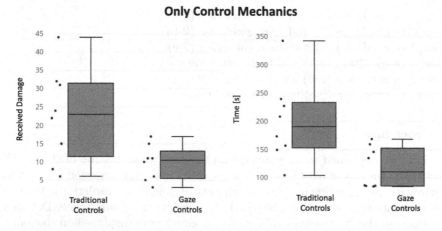

Fig. 2. Performance: traditional control vs gaze control for aiming and shooting

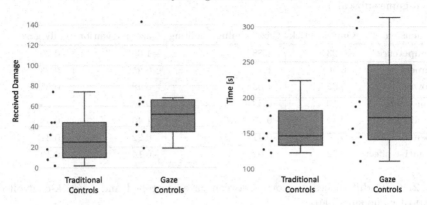

Fig. 3. Performance: traditional control vs gaze control for game navigation

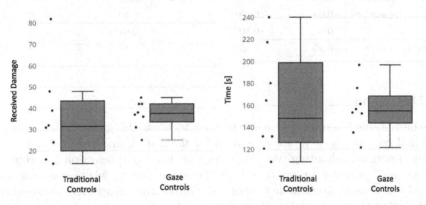

Fig. 4. Performance: traditional control vs gaze control for both navigation and aiming/shooting

5.2   Player Experience

Tables 1 and 2 show the difference of mean GEQ scores for each dimension, along in-game and post-game subscales. A positive value in the table indicates that the gaze-controlled game outperforms the joystick-control variant for each given dimension. Scores range from 1 to 5.

Table 1. GEQ differences in scores between gaze-controlled and joystick-controlled game (in-game subscale)

Dimension	Only joystick	Gaze: aiming/shooting	Gaze: navigation	Only gaze
Competence	−0.23	1.68	−1.65	−0.70
Immersion	0.56	1.10	0.25	0.33
Flow	0.62	1.03	0.48	0.35
Annoyance	0.10	−0.33	0.54	0.08
Challenge	0.39	−0.75	1.45	0.48
Positive affect	−0.17	−0.41	0.22	−0.31
Negative affect	0.32	0.92	−0.14	0.19

Table 2. GEQ differences in scores between gaze-controlled and joystick-controlled game (post-game subscale)

Dimension	Only joystick	Gaze: aiming/shooting	Gaze: navigation	Only gaze
Positive experience	0.43	1.38	−0.45	0.35
Negative experience	−0.09	−0.40	0.10	0.02
Tiredness	0.31	−0.50	0.63	0.81
Return to reality	0.26	0.00	0.42	0.38

5.3 Discussion

From the obtained results, participants tend to favor the game variant where traditional controls (i.e., joystick) is used for navigation and gaze controls are used for aiming and shooting. We can argue that this input selection is accepted as a "natural" way for interacting with the game scenes, where gaze can be effectively used as an acceptable support to improve the engagement and overall control during the play session. The other combinations can be interpreted as gaze being more a nuisance rather than effective support.

In particular, hybrid controls, whenever they are adapted to specific control mechanics during gameplay, effectively improve both performance and player experience. This is relevant when conceiving novel interaction metaphors and mechanisms in video games of the third-person shooter genre.

5.4 Study Limitations

While valuable, our results are not exempt from limitations. In that respect, our study sample, for convenience reasons, only reflects the reality of players in the controlled empirical setting. In order to overcome this concern, our next step in this research will consist on replicating the study with larger groups across different user groups in terms of age, gender, and gaming habits.

6   Conclusion and Future Work

In this paper we presented the design of a 2D top-down third-person shooting video game that can be controlled using traditional controls (i.e., console joysticks), gaze interaction (i.e., mediated with an off-the-shelf commercial standalone eyetracker), or a combination of both mechanisms. In order to understand the effectiveness of input controls for navigating and/or aiming and shooting in the game, we conducted a proof-of-concept user study.

The key take-aways of the contribution presented in this paper can be summarized as follows:

– For real-time video games, it is not recommended to use gaze controls for fine movements, precision shooting, and fast reaction events.
– The design of the game should address as much as clearance as possible for detecting and capturing eye movement and gaze, given that, by nature, people tend to perform involuntary erratic movements when transitioning between central and peripheral vision.
– For action video games, eyetracking and gaze controls are best suited as a supplementary support for entry methods, and not as a sole independent main control.

As future work, we intend to replicate this study with a larger sample of users as a way to corroborate and/or specialize the derived findings. Likweise, we aim to explore the introduction of eyetracking and gaze controls in other video game genres, as well as conceiving novel ways to promote engagement, immersion, and flow among video game players using the abovementioned mechanisms.

References

1. Tobii gaming. https://gaming.tobii.com/games. Visited 14 Nov 2020
2. Dechant, M., Stavness, I., Mairena, A., Mandryk, R.L.: Empirical evaluation of hybrid gaze-controller selection techniques in a gaming context. In: Proceedings of the 2018 Annual Symposium on Computer-Human Interaction in Play, pp. 73–85. CHI PLAY 2018. ACM, New York (2018). https://doi.org/10.1145/3242671.3242699
3. Duchowski, A.T.: A breadth-first survey of eye-tracking applications. Behav. Res. Methods Instrum. Comput. **34**(4), 455–470 (2002). https://doi.org/10.3758/BF03195475
4. IJsselsteijn, W.A., de Kort, Y.A.W., Poels, K.: The game experience questionnaire. Technische Universiteit Eindhoven (2013)
5. Jacob, R.J.K.: What you look at is what you get: eye movement-based interaction techniques. In: Proceedings of the SIGCHI Conference on Human Factors in Computing Systems, pp. 11–18. CHI 1990. ACM, New York (1990). https://doi.org/10.1145/97243.97246
6. Law, E.L.C., Brühlmann, F., Mekler, E.D.: Systematic review and validation of the game experience questionnaire (GEQ) - implications for citation and reporting practice. In: Proceedings of the 2018 Annual Symposium on Computer-Human Interaction in Play, pp. 257–270. CHI PLAY 2018. ACM, New York (2018). https://doi.org/10.1145/3242671.3242683

7. Nacke, L.E., Stellmach, S., Sasse, D., Lindley, C.A.: Gameplay experience in a gaze interaction game. arXiv e-prints arXiv:1004.0259 (Apr 2010)
8. Navarro, D., Sundstedt, V.: Simplifying game mechanics: gaze as an implicit interaction method. In: SIGGRAPH Asia 2017 Technical Briefs, pp. 4:1–4:4. SA 2017. ACM, New York (2017). https://doi.org/10.1145/3145749.3149446
9. Sundstedt, V.: Gazing at games: using eye tracking to control virtual characters. In: ACM SIGGRAPH 2010 Courses, pp. 5:1–5:160. SIGGRAPH 2010. ACM, New York (2010). https://doi.org/10.1145/1837101.1837106
10. Velichkovsky, B., Rumyantsev, M.A., Morozov, M.A.: New solution to the midas touch problem: identification of visual commands via extraction of focal fixations. Procedia Comput. Sci. **39**, 75–82 (2014). https://doi.org/10.1016/j.procs.2014.11.012
11. Velloso, E., Carter, M.: The emergence of eyeplay: a survey of eye interaction in games. In: Proceedings of the 2016 Annual Symposium on Computer-Human Interaction in Play, pp. 171–185. CHI PLAY 2016. ACM, New York (2016). https://doi.org/10.1145/2967934.2968084
12. Young, L.R., Sheena, D.: Survey of eye movement recording methods. Behav. Res. Methods Instrum. **7**(5), 397–429 (1975). https://doi.org/10.3758/BF03201553

Foresthlon: Investigating Gender Experience Through a Hybrid BCI Game

Roman Konečný[1] and Fotis Liarokapis[2,3]([⊠])

[1] Faculty of Informatics, Masaryk University, 60200 Brno, Czech Republic
374611@mail.muni.cz
[2] Research Centre on Interactive Media, Smart Systems and Emerging Technologies,
1011 Nicosia, Cyprus
f.liarokapis@cyens.org.cy
[3] Faculty of Engineering and Technology, Cyprus University of Technology,
3036 Limassol, Cyprus
fotios.liarokapis@cut.ac.cy

Abstract. Foresthlon is an adaptation of the well known Biathlon game where the player has to move in a forest as well as shoot at the target in order to win the game. A two-dimensional hybrid BCI game was designed and implemented in order to provide a new and exciting experience for the player without ruining gameplay. The main goal of the game is to run and hit all the targets as quickly as possible as the main indicator of how successful the attempt is the time the player was able to finish the game. A user study was performed with 30 participants to examine gender differences in terms of user-experience, cognitive workload, and performance. Results indicate that male participants performed slightly better than females, although there are no significant differences.

Keywords: Brain-Computer Interaction · Hybrid games · User studies

1 Introduction

Electroencephalography (EEG) is a neuroimaging technique discovered in 1929 [3] which is currently widely used by brain-computer interfaces (BCIs). The main advantages are the low cost, portability and ease of use. BCIs allow people to manifest their will without any kind of movement required in the process [30]. Although there have been a number of BCI games presented in the past, they typically suffer from low performance in terms of accuracy and speed [23]. A preliminary study suggested that brain activity follows a different pattern for different categorised computer games [2].

Partially supported by the project that has received funding from the European Union's Horizon 2020 research and innovation programme under grant agreement No 739578 (RISE–Call: H2020-WIDESPREAD-01-2016-2017-TeamingPhase2) and the Government of the Republic of Cyprus through the Directorate General for European Programmes, Coordination and Development.

© Springer Nature Switzerland AG 2021
X. Fang (Ed.): HCII 2021, LNCS 12789, pp. 57–74, 2021.
https://doi.org/10.1007/978-3-030-77277-2_5

Although we know from the literature that gender has an effect on EEG patterns [6,11], there is little research on games and BCIs. The importance of gender was previously investigated when interacting with a BCI game [27]. A study with 34 participants showed that females reported less concentration to a training task compared to males. Moreover, to make BCIs an interaction modality for games and other applications, they must enhance the user experience [5]. A user study with 30 participants using two inexpensive commercially available devices in different games showed that BCI systems with one channel is well suited for use with games utilising neurofeedback [8].

Biathlon is one of the most challenging winter games that combines cross-country skiing with rifle shooting. It has been an Olympic event since the Winter Games in Squaw Valley, United States, in 1960s and since then it has evolved a lot by introducing new techniques (i.e. sprint, pursuit, and mass-start) [13]. This paper presents a simplified adaptation of the Biathlon game where the player has to move in a forest. The game is called Foresthlon and to win the game the player has to shoot at different targets.

In particular, a two-dimensional (2D) BCI game was designed and implemented in order to provide a new and exciting experience for the player without ruining gameplay. This is of particular importance when designing BCI games. Although BCI games are mainly developed either for people with disabilities (i.e. paraplegics), the rest of them are usually experimental prototypes. However, Valve Corporation, which is one of the main manufacturers in VR, is currently working on a product aiming in connecting BCIs with games.

The main goal of the game is to run and hit all the targets as quickly as possible as the main indicator of how successful the attempt is the time the player was able to finish the game. To model interactions, attention levels of the player where used for the movement while meditation levels for shooting (Fig. 1). A user study was performed with 30 participants to examine gender differences in terms of user-experience, cognitive workload, and performance. Results indicate that male participants performed slightly better than females, although there are no significant differences.

Fig. 1. Attention for running and meditation for shooting [12]

The rest of the paper is structured as follows. Section 2, presents background work and Sect. 3 the details of the implementation of the BCI game. Section 4 describes the experiment and Sect. 5 illustrates the results. Finally, Sect. 6 concludes the paper.

2   Background

One of the first BCI gamification approaches was a two-dimensional navigation application of a virtual maze [26]. Since then there have been numerous BCI controlled games presented. A systematic review of EEG-based BCIs used in the video games has been recently published [10]. The survey examines the progress of BCI research with regard to games and shows that gaming applications offer numerous advantages by orienting BCI to concerns and expectations of a gaming application.

This paper covers only hybrid BCI (hBCI) games [19] which are focused on the combination of different signals including at least one BCI channel [17]. Early examples of hBCIs, combined multiple brain signals [1, 7], brain signals with heart signals [24], brain signals with muscular fatigue [15], and brain signals with eye gaze [22].

In terms of game hBCIs, one early approach described how techniques (such as context dependence, dwell timers, etc.) were implemented in an application to control the Massive Multiplayer Online Role Playing Game World of Warcraft [25]. Another hBCI, focused on controlling a penguin of a VR game through a BCI and a joystick [14]. An experiment with 14 participants showed that half of them achieved the required performance to test the penguin game and that the use of a secondary motor task did not deteriorate the BCI performance during the game.

Moreover, a 2D Tetris hybrid game featuring two modes (non-BCI and BCI input) which required users to meditate in order to change the game difficulty was evaluated by thirty participants [16]. Results showed that a one-sensor BCI device in games positively contributes to enjoy ability but raises mental demand without dropping performance.

More recently, a hybrid BCI paradigm was proposed by combining motor imagery (MI) and steady-state visually evoked potentials (SSVEPs) to control Tetris game [28]. A online control experiment with ten subjects showed that all subjects successfully completed the predefined tasks with high accuracy. Finally, a hybrid BCI gaming application based on the computer game Jewel Quest was presented with the aim of improving rare target classifications characterized by class imbalance and overlap [20].

3   Foresthlon BCI Game

3.1   Hardware

The NeuroSky Mindwave EEG headset has operating frequency between 0.05–0.5 Hz and estimates attention and meditation levels. It was used for a number of reasons. First of all, it uses a dry sensor, so no conductive gel is required.

Secondly, is easy to use and operate and comfortable for the players. The main downside of NeuroSky Mindwave is that not the whole area of the brain is covered. However, for the purpose of gaming and in particular for hybrid interaction is one of the best mediums existing [16].

The device includes three parts: (a) one EEG recording electrode that lies on the front of the forehead and records the activity of the frontal lobe, (b) one clip that is attached to one of the earlobes which acts as ground and reference, and (c) the ThinkGear ASIC Module (TGAM) which does a denoising and has a sampling frequency 512 Hz [18].

Moreover, it provides output from NeuroSky proprietary eSense meter, which can calculate attention and meditation levels using the brainwaves measurements. This output was used in this paper as the input source for the game together with keyboard inputs. It is worth mentioning, that the raw data is hard to analyze because they are very noisy and what can be obtained is the general alertness of the user [18].

For both attention and meditation eSense, the value is reported on a scale of 1 to 100. In this scale, 5 intervals are established and one special value is present. The special value is 0, indicating that the device is unable to calculate attention or meditation level with a reasonable amount of reliability. The intervals are as follows: 1 to 20, 20 to 40, 40 to 60, 60 to 80 and 80 to 100. Those intervals are not used in this research as the game uses the whole range of the scale. Both attention and meditation levels are refreshed once a second [12].

3.2   Implementation

In terms of software implementation, the industry standard Unity game engine was used for creating the game. Details of the implementation can be found on [12] and a summary is presented here. The code was written in C sharp programming language using Microsoft Visual Studio 2015. For editing and creating the graphics elements, GNU Image Manipulation (GIMP) was used. The game offers the following options:

- PreStart: Main menu screen when the game starts.
- Running: The player is currently running, attention level is used as a source for input.
- Shooting: The player is currently at the shooting range, meditation level is used as a source for input.
- Pause: The game is currently paused, menu is displayed.
- End: The player finished the game and the final screen is displayed.

Data from the NeuroSky MindWave headset are collected by the TGC-ConnectionController. It gets both attention and meditation level from the device and raises events to MovementInputController and ShootingInputController where the input is processed for the purposes of the game, but only for the current part of the game. That means that if the player is in the shooting part, only meditation level is processed and the same applies for the attention level while running. When in menu, no input is collected in the controllers. That allows to immediately store the input value for logging purposes [12].

Those three classes can be (with some modification to make them more generic, rather than specialized entities) used as an extensible interface which can be used in any game or program that should be controlled using Neurosky Mindwave headset. For the purposes of the Foresthlon application, it was decided to include this interface in the solution, but it can be extracted into separate DLL which can be used in other applications. The UML diagram is illustrated in Fig. 2.

The core class is the TGCConnectionController, which gets the data from the MindWave device. In the constructor of the class, the basic setup of the parameter (how frequently would the data be updated, which inputs would be used) is done, as well as the injection of IAttentionInputController, IMeditation-InputController, IRawDataInputController and IInputLogger instances [12].

The logger is always provided by the consuming application, the controllers can be the basic ones, or inherited classes from the base classes (AttentionIn-putController, MeditationInputController and RawDataInputController). TGC-ConnectionController is triggering events that are consumed by the input controllers, that can then be used within the application itself for controlling the application and logging the data.

3.3   Game Design

The gameplay consists of two parts that repeats 4 times. In the first part, the player runs forward to the shooting range as quickly as possible. When running, attention level is the input for the game as it sets the player's speed. In the second part of the game, the player is at the shooting range and the goal is to hit the target. If the player misses, the shooting can be repeated. Otherwise the player can continue in the game by running to the next shooting range [12].

Furthermore, to make the game easier, the player has unlimited ammo. As a result, shooting can be repeated infinite times. There is, however, a 2 s delay between shooting and next action. The distance between shooting ranges was set to 100 in-game meters. That means that the total distance the player needs to run is 400 m and can shoot at 4 shooting ranges. After the final successful shot, the game ends. As mentioned before, the main goal of the game is to run and hit all the targets as quickly as possible as the main indicator of how successful the attempt is the time the player was able to finish the game.

The running part of the game is pretty straightforward to include the attention level as the source of the input. The main game design consideration involved how the shooting operation will occur (which was based on the meditation level). At the shooting range, a box is displayed above the target which is separated into three parts and there is a moving circle inside this box. The middle part has a green color and the player is supposed to hit a defined key when the circle is inside the green area to make a successful shot.

Movement speed of the circle is set according to player's meditation level, so the more is the player meditated, the slower the circle moves in the box. After

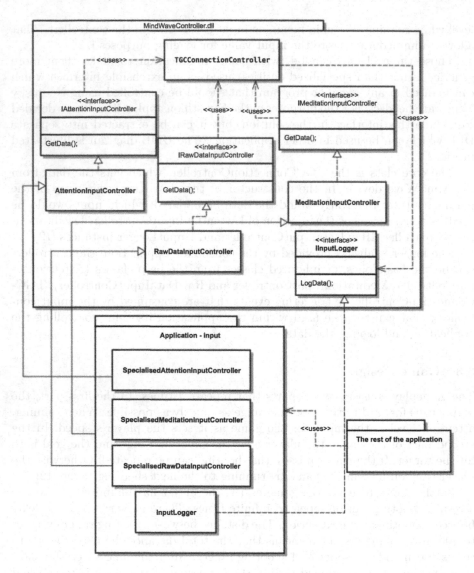

Fig. 2. UML diagram depicting the usage of the NeuroSky MindWave controlling interface in an application [12]

finishing the game, the player can see the final time as well as the ranked position on the leader-board. At this stage, the player can fill in his/her name, so the attempt can be saved into the leader-board and the log file (which includes time, number of attempts needed and input values throughout the run) [12].

3.4   Game Play

An effective way for a hBCI to combine all the control channels is to merge their individual decisions [17]. The running part of the game is simulated by emitting the background particles which, combined with the archer's running animation, makes the illusion of the moving archer. The speed of the archer is basically the speed at which the particles are emitted and the speed of the animation of the archer.

The movement speed is calculated from the input and its range is between 0 to 7 in-game meters per second. Once the player reaches the shooting distance (76.7 m after start of the game and after each shooting), a line is emitted and the emission of the trees is stopped so the shooting range can be spawned. Once the player is at the line, the shooting part of the game begins [12].

As the player approaches the line indicating the shooting part of the game, the box with moving circle is displayed above the target. The circle is then moving back and forth in the box at speed that is calculated from the meditation level. To hit the target, the player has to press the "Space key" to shoot when the circle is in the green area. When the key is pressed, the current circle position is compared to the green interval and then either "HIT" or "MISS" text is displayed in the middle of the target. After the successful shot is made, the number of attempts needed to pass the shooting range is stored in the game and the player proceeds [12].

3.5   User Interface

The purpose of the in-game user interface is to provide feedback to the player on how well is performing during the game (Fig. 3). In the top left corner of the screen, information about the distance and the time of the run is provided. The distance tells the player how far is located from the shooting range (or the finish). A green bar is present in the top center of the screen. This bar represents current attention or meditation level of the player. Its purpose is to provide a concise way how the player can check his/her current performance rather than relying on his feeling of how fast the archer runs or the circle in the shooting bar moves.

Fig. 3. User interface of the game [12] (Color figure online)

A label above the input bar states if the current input is attention or medi-tation. In the top right corner, there is an icon indicating the connection to the NeuroSky MindWave headset. If the icon is green, the connection is established. Yellow icon indicates that there is a problem with the connection and red means that the headset is not connected. This icon is connected to the main camera object so it can be visible on every screen of the game.

The main game menu has three purposes. The first one is to provide different options to the player (i.e. start or resume the game, restart the game if needed, check the leader-board and quit the game). There is also a tutorial stating the following: "How to play: Press Space to start the game, and once you are at the shooting range, press space to shoot! Movement speed is adjusted by your attention level, speed of the shooting slider is adjusted by your meditation level. Have fun!".

Fig. 4. Leader-board and scores [12] (Color figure online)

Additionally, there are two buttons in the bottom left corner of the menu. Those are the buttons for reconnecting or disconnecting the headset. Moreover, the leader-board contains all the runs ordered by time descending (Fig. 4). This allows the player to check the attempts of other players. Information that can be seen on the leader-board consists of player's position, name, time and attempts needed at each shooting range. When the player finishes the game, a final screen is displayed with scores. The player is asked to enter his/her name. After that, a new entry in the leader-board is created as well as log file.

4   Experiment

4.1   Participants and Procedure

The testing group consisted of 15 males and 15 females ($n = 30$) and all of them had no previous experience with BCIs. Each participant was given a consent form to fill before the experiment started. Next, the BCI was attached to the participant's head and it was made sure that the connection between the device and the game is stable (Fig. 5). A basic explanation what is expected was given.

This consisted of explaining the game, introducing the headset and how the game is controlled.

Next, participants had an opportunity to see the leader-board to obtain a better understanding of time required to win the game. They were not allowed to do a training run, as the experiment was designed to observe how quickly can the player adapt to a new controlling paradigm. After giving the instructions, participants played the game. During this phase, the interaction between the test subject and the observer was reduced to minimum so the player was not distracted. The observer's role was primarily to check the connection status of the device.

Fig. 5. Female participant during the experiment [12]

4.2 Data Collection

A number of different questionnaires were used in this study. In particular, the NASA Task Load Index (TLX) questionnaire was used [9] in conjunction with an experience questionnaire and two open questions. Additionally, logs generated by the game were also used for the analysis. The main focus of the analysis was to examine gender differences in terms of user-experience, cognitive workload and performance.

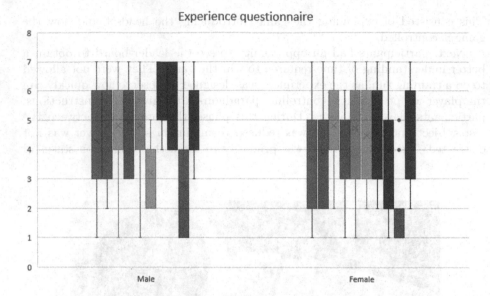

Fig. 6. Results of the user experience according to gender [12]

5   Results

5.1   User Experience

The experience questionnaire consisted of 10 questions (scale between 1 to 7). The questions are shown with the results of the questionnaire on Fig. 6. In terms of how easy participants found to control their attention or meditation levels during the game, male participants tend to rate them better than females. Similarly, for their feeling of having control of the archer. For performing a sport or an activity including active movement, both testing groups had the same results. All participants were aware of the sport of biathlon, so the game mechanics were easy to grasp. Males also stated that the mechanism which controlled movement and shooting was more natural to them.

In terms of how involved the participants were with the experience, both testing groups stated that they were rather engrossed to the experience then not involved at all. Females experienced rather longer delay between their thoughts and the expected outcome. The majority of the males stated that the adjustment to the experience took less than a minute, while for the females it took longer to adapt. Males also were more proficient in moving and interacting with the application at the end of the experiment. As for the visual display quality and the possible distraction from performing the task, females were less distracted as opposed to males. Males also rated them better when evaluating how well could they concentrate on actually playing the game rather than on controlling their attention and meditation level, but females rated themselves rather good in this aspect.

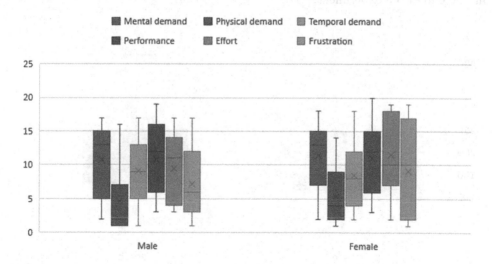

Fig. 7. Cognitive workload according to gender [12]

5.2 Cognitive Load

In terms of the cognitive load (NASA TLX) results indicate that there was not much overload for all players. Moreover, we wanted to check is there are gender differences as shown in Fig. 7. Results show that there is not significant difference between the genders. Mental demand is almost the same for both males and females. Females felt that the physical demand was a little bit higher, opposed to temporal demand, where the males stated that the demand was higher for them. In terms of performance, there was no significant difference. Females also felt that they had to put more effort and were more frustrated by the task.

5.3   Game Experiences

In terms of how easy did the participants find to control their attention or meditation level during the game, male participant tend to rate them better than females, as well as their feeling of having control of the archer. For performing a sport or an activity including active movement, both testing groups had the same results. All of the participants were aware of the sport of biathlon, so the game mechanics were easy to grasp. Males also stated that the mechanism which controlled movement and shooting was more natural to them.

In terms of how involved the participants were with the experience, both testing groups stated that they were rather engrossed to the experience then not involved at all. Females experienced rather longer delay between their thoughts and the expected outcome. Most of the males stated that the adjustment to the experience took less than a minute, while for the females it took longer to adapt. Males also were more proficient in moving and interacting with the application at the end of the experiment.

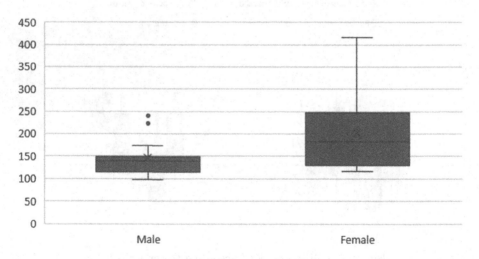

Fig. 8. Time required for finishing the game according to gender [12]

Regarding the visual display quality and the possible distraction from performing the task, females were less distracted as opposed to males. Males also rated them better when evaluating how well could they concentrate on actually playing the game rather than on controlling their attention and meditation level, but females rated themselves rather good in this aspect.

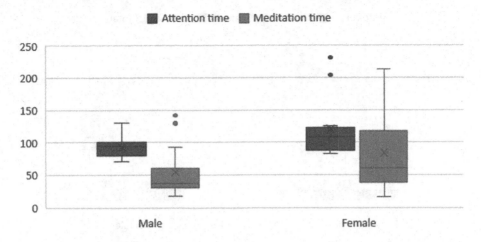

Fig. 9. Time required according to input (attention and meditation) [12]

5.4 Performance

For the purpose of the analysis of the performance, a logging application was developed. The program loads the log files from the disk and calculates the mean and the median of both attention and meditation levels of the player as well as the time spent in game using each input source. Those calculations were saved to an XML file for further processing. As Fig. 8 suggests, males overall had better results compared to females.

The same result is also noticeable when we split the time into two parts including the time spent running and the time spent shooting (Fig. 9). On average, males spent 20 s less in the running part of the game and 30 s less in the shooting part. Most of the players spent more time running, only 7 participants spent more time in the shooting part (3 males and 4 females).

Figure 10 illustrates the comparison of attempts needed on each shooting range and in total between males and females. The crucial, quite surprisingly, was the third shooting phase. Players needed more attempts to pass than on any shooting. The results reflects the times needed to finish the game – males needed less attempts then females but without significant differences. This might be linked to the playing style, females had the tendency to wait longer before taking the shot, which often resulted in decreased meditation level as they become more excited when they actually wanted to shoot. Males tend to shoot even if the circle was moving fast.

Furthermore, there are no significant differences in terms of attention and meditation between genders (Fig. 11 and Fig. 12). However, there is a trend of better performance for attention levels in males compared to females.

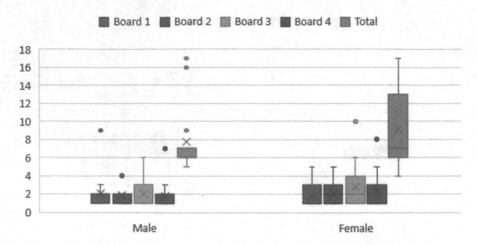

Fig. 10. Number of shooting attempts according to gender [12]

Attention

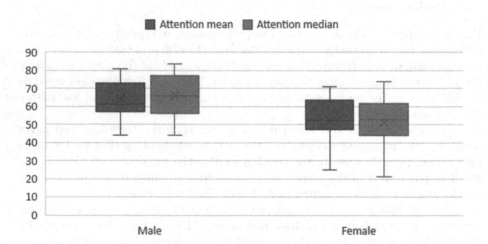

Fig. 11. Gender comparison of attention levels [12]

5.5 Qualitative Results

Participants were asked to explain what they did to control their attention and meditation level. 17 responded that they were focusing on the game screen for controlling their attention level, usually just on one exact point (the archer's legs was the dominant point of interest – 6 participants explicitly stated that they were focused on the archer's legs while running). As for controlling the meditation level, most of them tried to calm down, control their breathing and not thinking about anything specific. Watching the green area above the shooting board also helped the participants to control their meditation level. A few

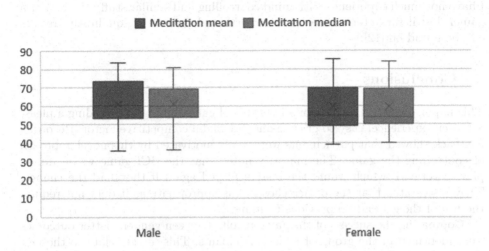

Fig. 12. Gender comparison of meditation levels [12]

participants stated that the game did not reflected their thoughts. Some of the respondent's answers are listed below [12].

"Before start I tried to control myself to calm down and focus only on the game. Then I started and I was thinking about one thing only – to beat the best time. During aiming I was trying to calm down". "At first, I was trying to control archer with my view. As I went further the control of the archer became easier when I realized it is all about focus, not about taking a look at the objects. The aiming was precisely about focus, really good experience to see how computer can reflex human brain activity". "I tried to focus on one point in the game during movement, but it was not as successful as I expected. Sometimes it seemed that the speed is set randomly. I was more successful during the shooting when I saw concrete results of my effort". "When I was running I focused on a piece of grass. When I controlled myself it got worse, more focus = worse result. As for the meditation level, I tried to focus on nothing, just breathing and it went slower. Anything on my mind = it went faster".

Participants also had the chance to express any additional thoughts and comments about the experiment. Not all respondents took this opportunity, but some valuable feedback was collected. One respondent complained about the connection indicator: "I think the connection indicator on top right part of the screen sometimes makes it hard to concentrate". Another participant was not happy with the experience as the attention and meditation levels were not reflecting her effort: "It was really frustrating. When I wanted to move it didn't work. When I wanted to calm down it really did not work". Apart from those two comments, all the other participants were excited with the experience and would like to try it again. "I liked the experience, especially the shooting part. I would like to expand the game to be longer". "Game was pretty easy to control and it was intuitive to play. Graphics looks good, controlling was weird because I have not much experience with mind controlling and similar stuff". "I am not a gamer, but it was interesting experience". More details on the qualitative results can be found on [12].

6 Conclusions

This paper presented a study of a hybrid BCI game aiming in providing a pleasant user experience, easy to grasp gameplay and a competitive factor. Recorded feedback showed that participants were really motivated by this novel approach of controlling the game. The majority noted that the BCI game was a fun to play experience which would the testers played again if they had the chance. They also stated that the device chosen was appropriate as it does not require the use of the gel and no previous training.

Comparing the success of the game results between gender, better outcomes were identified in the group of male participants. This might relate to the fact that males were more focused on the actual game result (beating the best time) rather than the way how the game was controlled as well as taking the risk in the shooting parts of the game – not waiting for the ideal speed of the moving circle. The fact that males play computer games more than females [4,21,29] could have affected the results as they could have more experience with playing games similar to the one presented in this thesis or have better grasp of what was required for finishing the game.

Acknowledgement. The authors would like to thank all participants that took place on the user evaluation study as well as Filip Škola for his guidelines.

References

1. Allison, B.Z., Brunner, C., Kaiser, V., Müller-Putz, G.R., Neuper, C., Pfurtscheller, G.: Toward a hybrid brain-computer interface based on imagined movement and visual attention. J. Neural Eng. **7**(2), 026007 (2010). https://doi.org/10.1088/1741-2560/7/2/026007
2. Bakaoukas, A.G., Coada, F., Liarokapis, F.: Examining brain activity while playing computer games. J. Multimodal User Interfaces **10**(1), 13–29 (2016). https://doi.org/10.1007/s12193-015-0205-4
3. Berger, H.: On the electroencephalogram of man. Electroencephalography and clinical neurophysiology, pp. Suppl 28:37+ (1969). http://europepmc.org/abstract/MED/4188918
4. Bonanno, P., Kommers, P.: Gender differences and styles in the use of digital games. Educ. Psychol. **25**(1), 13–41 (2005). https://doi.org/10.1080/0144341042000294877
5. Bos, D.P., et al.: Human-computer interaction for BCI games: usability and user experience. In: 2010 International Conference on Cyberworlds, pp. 277–281 (2010). https://doi.org/10.1109/CW.2010.22

6. Davidson, R.J., Schwartz, G.E., Pugash, E., Bromfield, E.: Sex differences in patterns of d asymmetry. Biological Psychology **4**(2), 119–137 (1976). https://doi.org/10.1016/0301-0511(76)90012-0
7. Ferrez, P.W., Millán, J.D.R.: Simultaneous real-time detection of motor imagery and error-related potentials for improved BCI accuracy. In: Proceedings of the 4th International Brain-Computer Interface Workshop and Training Course (2008)
8. Fiałek, S., Liarokapis, F.: Comparing two commercial brain computer interfaces for serious games and virtual environments. In: Karpouzis, K., Yannakakis, G.N. (eds.) Emotion in Games. SC, vol. 4, pp. 103–117. Springer, Cham (2016). https://doi.org/10.1007/978-3-319-41316-7_6
9. Hart, S.G., Staveland, L.E.: Development of NASA-TLX (task load index): results of empirical and theoretical research. In: Hancock, P.A., Meshkati, N. (eds.) Advances in Psychology, Human Mental Workload, vol. 52, pp. 139–183. North-Holland (Jan 1988). https://doi.org/10.1016/S0166-4115(08)62386-9. http://www.sciencedirect.com/science/article/pii/S0166411508623869
10. Kerous, B., Skola, F., Liarokapis, F.: EEG-based BCI and video games: a progress report. Virtual Reality **22**(2), 119–135 (2018). https://doi.org/10.1007/s10055-017-0328-x
11. Kober, S.E., Neuper, C.: Sex differences in human EEG theta oscillations during spatial navigation in virtual reality. Int. J. Psychophysiol. **79**(3), 347–355 (2011). https://doi.org/10.1016/j.ijpsycho.2010.12.002
12. Konečný, R.: Brain Computer Interfaces for Games. Master's thesis, Masaryk University, Faculty of Informatics, Brno, Czech Republic (2018)
13. Laaksonen, M.S., Jonsson, M., Holmberg, H.C.: The Olympic biathlon - recent advances and perspectives after Pyeongchang. Front. Physiol. **9**, 796 (2018). https://doi.org/10.3389/fphys.2018.00796
14. Leeb, R., Lancelle, M., Kaiser, V., Fellner, D.W., Pfurtscheller, G.: Thinking penguin: multimodal brain-computer interface control of a VR game. IEEE Trans. Comput. Intell. AI Games **5**(2), 117–128 (2013). https://doi.org/10.1109/TCIAIG.2013.2242072
15. Leeb, R., et al.: Walking by thinking: the brainwaves are crucial, not the muscles! Presence: Teleoperators and Virtual Environ. **15**(5), 500–514 (2006). https://doi.org/10.1162/pres.15.5.500
16. Liarokapis, F., Vourvopoulos, A., Ene, A.: Examining user experiences through a multimodal bci puzzle game. In: 2015 19th International Conference on Information Visualisation, pp. 488–493 (2015). https://doi.org/10.1109/iV.2015.87
17. Millán, J.D.R., et al.: Combining brain-computer interfaces and assistive technologies: state-of-the-art and challenges. Front. Neurosci. **4**, 161 (2010). https://doi.org/10.3389/fnins.2010.00161
18. Monori, F., Oniga, S.: Processing EEG signals acquired from a consumer grade BCI device. Carpathian J. Electron. Comput. Eng. **11**(2), 29–34 (2018). https://doi.org/10.2478/cjece-2018-0015
19. Mueller-Putz, G., et al.: Tools for brain-computer interaction: a general concept for a hybrid BCI. Front. Neuroinform. **5**, 30 (2011). https://doi.org/10.3389/fninf.2011.00030
20. Nayak, T., Ko, L., Jung, T., Huang, Y.: Target classification in a novel SSVEP-RSVP based BCI gaming system. In: 2019 IEEE International Conference on Systems, Man and Cybernetics (SMC), pp. 4194–4198 (2019). https://doi.org/10.1109/SMC.2019.8914174

21. Padilla-Walker, L., Nelson, L., Carroll, J., Jensen, A.: More than a just a game: video game and internet use during emerging adulthood. J. Youth Adolesc. **39**, 103–13 (2010). https://doi.org/10.1007/s10964-008-9390-8

22. Pfurtscheller, G., et al.: The hybrid BCI. Front. Neurosci. **4**, 3 (2010). https://doi.org/10.3389/fnpro.2010.00003

23. Plass-Oude Bos, D., et al.: Brain-Computer Interfacing and Games. In: Tan, D., Nijholt, A. (eds.) Brain-Computer Interfaces, pp. 149–178. Springer, London (2010). https://doi.org/10.1007/978-1-84996-272-8_10

24. Scherer, R., Muller, G.R., Neuper, C., Graimann, B., Pfurtscheller, G.: An asynchronously controlled EEG-based virtual keyboard: improvement of the spelling rate. IEEE Trans. Biomed. Eng. **51**(6), 979–984 (2004). https://doi.org/10.1109/TBME.2004.827062

25. Scherer, R., Pröll, M., Allison, B., Müller-Putz, G.R.: New input modalities for modern game design and virtual embodiment. In: 2012 IEEE Virtual Reality Workshops (VRW), pp. 163–164 (2012). https://doi.org/10.1109/VR.2012.6180932

26. Vidal, J.J.: Real-time detection of brain events in EEG. Proc. IEEE **65**(5), 633–641 (1977). https://doi.org/10.1109/PROC.1977.10542

27. Vourvopoulos, A., Niforatos, E., Hlinka, M., Škola, F., Liarokapis, F.: Investigating the effect of user profile during training for BCI-based games. In: 2017 9th International Conference on Virtual Worlds and Games for Serious Applications (VS-Games), pp. 117–124 (2017). https://doi.org/10.1109/VS-GAMES.2017.8056579

28. Wang, Z., Yu, Y., Xu, M., Liu, Y., Yin, E., Zhou, Z.: Towards a hybrid BCI gaming paradigm based on motor imagery and SSVEP. Int. J. Hum. Comput. Interact. **35**(3), 197–205 (2019). https://doi.org/10.1080/10447318.2018.1445068

29. Winn, J., Heeter, C.: Gaming, gender, and time: who makes time to play? Sex Roles **61**, 1–13 (2009). https://doi.org/10.1007/s11199-009-9595-7

30. Wolpaw, J.R., Birbaumer, N., McFarland, D.J., Pfurtscheller, G., Vaughan, T.M.: Brain-computer interfaces for communication and control. Clin. Neurophysiol. **113**(6), 767–791 (2002). https://doi.org/10.1016/S1388-2457(02)00057-3. http://www.sciencedirect.com/science/article/pii/S1388245702000573

Research on User Experience Optimization of Tutorial Design for Battle Royale Games Based on Grey AHP Theory

Jinghan Lin[✉], Wei Zhou, and Si-Si Yuan

User Experience Research Center, Thunder Fire Studio, NetEase,
Hangzhou, People's Republic of China
linjinghan@corp.netease.com

Abstract. In recent years, the battle royale game has become one of the main leisure activities in people's daily life. Due to diverse and endless gameplays in all kinds of battle royale games, the novice tutorial plays a significant role in helping the player master the game and quickly get involved. A good novice tutorial can help players understand and start the game very quickly which also reduces the cognition bias. The user experience of the novice tutorials has a decisive influence on players' retention and payment ratio. In the high-frequency iterative game design, evaluating user experience can help designers know about the novice tutorial's quality effectively and promptly improve the potential problems that players may encounter.

For most battle royale games, their novice tutorials not only possess the attributes of guiding players, but they also own the game attributes. Thus, it is hard to measure all the factors that affect the user experience of novice tutorials. It is a system that exterior might seem clear while the inside is vague. On account of these characteristics, this study applies grey AHP theory to construct a system evaluating the user experience of novice tutorials in battle royale games. It helps game designers evaluate the quality of the user experience objectively and obtain valuable instructions for game design. It also provides support for design iteration.

The study is as follows. Several representative emotional words related to the battle royale games were selected and novice tutorials of three battle royale games were adopted as experimental samples for perceptual evaluation experiment. Then, a system evaluating the user experience of novice tutorials in the battle royale games was established based on the experimental data. The system consisted of 3 levels and 11 level 2 indicators. The interconnect degree of comparison sequence and reference sequence were calculated using the Grey relationship analysis method. Quantitative analysis about the importance of each experience dimension was then conducted according to the interconnect degree from small to big. At last, comprehensive evaluation was performed on the obtained interconnect degree of the design plans.

The conclusions are as follows. (1) We established a model evaluating the user experience of novice tutorials in the battle royale games so that designers can evaluate the user experience quality of the design plans during the development stage. (2) We verified the possibility that the Grey AHP Theory can be applied in evaluating the user experience of novice tutorials in the battle royale games as well as other games and provide strategic guidance for game design.

© Springer Nature Switzerland AG 2021
X. Fang (Ed.): HCII 2021, LNCS 12789, pp. 75–88, 2021.
https://doi.org/10.1007/978-3-030-77277-2_6

The research conclusions of this paper are mainly as follows: (1) Created a user experience evaluation model for the novice tutorial of the battle royal games. Designers can use this model to evaluate the quality of user experience of the design plans during game development and optimize the design in a scientific way. (2) Verified the possibility of analytic hierarchy process and grey correlation analysis for experience evaluation of novice tutorials in the battle royal games, and can be extended to experience evaluation of other games and provide strategic guidance for gaming experience design.

Keywords: Gaming experience · Perceptual evaluation · The novice tutorial · The grey AHP theory

1 Introduction

User experience (UE or UX) was firstly proposed by designer Donald Norman (1997) and widely recognized in the mid-1990s. According to ISO 9241-210 (1998), user experience refers to all emotions, beliefs, preferences, feelings, physical and psychological responses, behaviors, and sense of accomplishment in the processing of how users use products and services[1]. That is, the physical and psychological feelings that users may have when interacting with a product, system or service. In recent years, user experience design has been widely used in the field of game design. Perspectives to study user gaming experience are diverse which also leads to the diversity of evaluation methods that are used. In general, there are two kinds of methods, one is the direct evaluation method, and another is to construct a user experience evaluation model at first. The direct evaluation method is usually qualitative that analyzing a series of physiological data of the player measured by an instrument as to evaluate the user experience level. Commonly used methods include eye movement and Electroencephalogram (EEG) experiments. While the method to construct an evaluation model is usually quantitative or a combination of quantitative and qualitative analyses. It mainly uses some mathematical and statistical methods, such as multiple regression analysis, to establish a model that assesses the relationship between user experience elements and ultimate goal. Since the concept of users' gaming experience is abstract and ambiguous and contains many elements, it is hard to fully reflect the real situation of user experience by a single method. Exploring the dimensions of how to evaluate users' gaming experience and making users' gaming experience specific becomes necessary. The basic idea is to divide a complex system into multiple indicators to reflect the overall situation. Bai (2019) applied theories about Kansei engineering and used the semantic differential method and Oneway ANOVA to study the differences of the player's perception influenced by each system in card games[2]. Using League of Legends as an example, Wang and Zhao (2014) studied the user's gaming experience from the perspective of senses, operation, and interaction[3]. Combined with the previous studies, it is practicable to use quantitative methods to establish the model evaluating user's gaming experience and provide scientific and reliable data to support game design.

In recent years, the battle royale games such as PUBG and APEX were very popular among players. Fast-pace and intense competitiveness are basic characteristics of such games. Therefore, whether new players can quickly understand and master basic operations of the gameplay determines the quality of the gaming experience. Hence, for the battle royale games, the novice tutorial plays a significant role in the user retention rate. For the game UX designers, it is necessary to screen out the best design plan using certain methods to evaluate and compare all the proposals during product designing. People are crucial to evaluate the game UX design. Perceptions of users about UX design obtained through some qualitative and quantitative research methods can help UX designers establish an evaluation system that gives help to guide and makes designers introspect their work. However, it is not all factors in user gaming experience can be measured. It is a complex system containing plenty of unknown factors that the exterior might seem clear while the inside is vague. In this regard, this study uses grey system related theories and the analytic hierarchy process to explore the construction of a model evaluating user experience in the battle royale games. Proposed by Prof. Deng Julong (2017) of China, grey system theory is a research method based on mathematical theory. Its main study object is usually a system with fewer samples and less information. By quantifying uncertain gray information, it solves problems that contain unknown factors[4]. The object of this study is the user experience of novice tutorials in the Battle Royale Games. It contains quantifiable and non-quantifiable information, which is a typical gray system. In such a complex system, not all factors that affect the player's experience are of equal weight.

The analytic hierarchy process (AHP) was a decision method proposed by Thomas Saaty (1980). This method treats decision making as a system and decomposes it into three layers, that is target, criterion and plan. It has good effect on solving complex decision-making problems and multi-plan optimizations. Grey AHP theory is a method combining the grey system theory and AHP absorbed the strengths and characteristics of both methods. It fits well with the object in this study.

2   Collection of Emotional Words

By emotional words, we refer to any word that conveys emotional connotations and typically is adjectives. For example, adjectives such as exquisite and smooth are emotional words we might use to describe porcelain. In the study of user experience evaluation, emotional words to describe a product are typically used to assess users' emotional dimensions about the product. Theoretically, emotional vocabulary has single adjectives as well as pairs of adjectives with opposite meanings. However, considering the similarities between adjectives, researchers usually choose pairs of adjectives with opposite meanings when constructing user experience evaluation models. For evaluation model established by grey AHP method, it is significant to select emotional vocabulary. It has a great impact on the accuracy of the evaluation results. The appropriateness of emotional vocabulary and the number of it are important factors affecting the evaluation results. Too many words may increase the burden of the participants, while too few emotional words may result in insufficient description of the evaluation object. Concerning the appropriateness, there are two types: (a) appropriateness of the evaluation object indicating whether the emotional words can accurately describe the objective evaluated, (b) appropriateness of the user referring to the frequency that users use these words as well as the familiarity with them. Therefore, researchers need to choose an appropriate number of emotional words based on their knowledge and experience. In the collection process, we need to select adjectives that can describe the cognitive characteristics of the object in every aspect. This study uses two ways for collection: (a) through websites and forums of the battle royale games, (b) from interviews with the players of the battle royale games.

In the above two approaches, the study team collected 33 pairs of emotional words in the beginning. After filtering out the less frequently used words in daily life, the remaining 30 pairs are adopted and stated in the Table 1.

Table 1. Selected emotional words

Soothing-Intense	Safe-Dangerous	Easy-Hard
Active-Serious	Independent-Dependent	Single-Multiple
Clear-Vague	Specific-General	Beautiful-Ugly
Ordinary-Unique	Enthusiastic-Indifferent	Natural-Awkward
Straightforward-Implicit	Understandable-Obscure	Interesting-Monotonous
Accomplished-Frustrated	New-Old	Flexible-Stiff
Plain-Connotative	Mutable-Unchanging	Adaptive-Rigid
Fault-tolerant-Demanding	Impassive-Responsive	Convenient-inconvenient
Smooth-Obstructive	Efficient-Inefficient	Satisfied-Disappointed
Encouraging-Withdrawing	Orderly-Disorderly	Progressive-Rapid

To screen the most representative words, we further classify and reduce the number of the above words. The study team recruited 11 participants who had a certain understanding of the Battle Royale Game. There were 9 males and 2 females, and 8 participants were design practitioners. The study team asked the participants to classify the 30 groups of emotional adjectives initially collected. The number of classifications is not limited, and the number of words in each category is controlled within 4. By counting the number of pairwise words that occurred in the same group, we got a 30 * 30 matrix. Multi-dimensional scaling was adopted to analyze the above matrix, and the dimension was set up as 2–6. Multidimensional scaling (MDS) is a method of multivariate analysis. It is commonly applied in the area of sociology, psychology, marketing, etc. The reason that the research team using multidimensional scaling analysis is to fit the research data through a lower dimension and obtain the coordinate values of each emotional word in the spatial map. This experiment measures the goodness of fitting of the spatial map according to the empirical standard proposed by Kruskal (1964) shown in the Table 2. As shown in the Table 3, the stress value indicates that the two-dimensional model fits the observed data well in this study, which is 0.071. In this way, we got the coordinate distribution of each emotional word in the two-dimensional space.

Table 2. Relationship between Kruskal stress coefficient and goodness of fit

Stress index > 0.5	Poor fits
Stress index < 0.1	Good fits
Stress index < 0.05	Very good fits
Stress index < 0.025	Great fits
Stress index = 0	Perfect fits

Table 3. Emotional vocabulary coefficient

Dimension	Stress index	RSQ explained variation
2	0.07125	0.87954
3	0.09231	0.89776
4	0.18672	0.91263
5	0.24581	0.93658
6	0.34544	0.95531

Next, a cluster analysis was performed on the two-dimensional spatial coordinates of the obtained emotional words. First, a systematic clustering analysis was conducted and a line chart was drawn with "category number" as the abscissa and "aggregation coefficient" as the ordinate, as shown in the Fig. 1 below. The broken line became slow when the category number reached 11. In this way, we can assert that there were 11 categories.

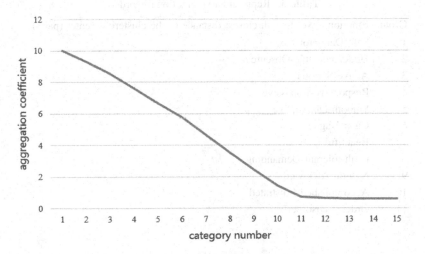

Fig. 1. Aggregation coefficient

Table 4. Categories of emotional words

Group	Emotional words in each group (pairs)
1	Soothing-Intense; Safe-Dangerous; Progressive-Rapid
2	Easy-Hard; Understandable-Obscure; Efficient-Inefficient
3	Active-Serious; Enthusiastic-Indifferent
4	Independent-Dependent; Responsive - Impassive
5	Interesting-Monotonous; Flexible-Stiff; Mutable-Unchanging; Smooth-Obstructive
6	Clear-Vague; Straightforward-Implicit; Specific-General; Plain-Connotative
7	Beautiful-Ugly; Ordinary-Unique; New-Old
8	Fault-tolerant-Demanding; Encouraging-Withdrawing
9	Natural-Awkward; Adaptive-Rigid; Convenient-inconvenient
10	Accomplished-Frustrated; Satisfied-Disappointed
11	Orderly-Disorderly; Single-Multiple

A K-means clustering analysis was then conducted on the two-dimensional coordinates of the emotional words according to the obtained aggregation coefficient, and the K value was set to 11. After calculation, the pair groups of the emotional words were sorted out and the distance of each group from the cluster center were obtained. Pairing words that were closest to the cluster center in each group turned out to be the most representative ones. The final grouping of the emotional words was shown in the Table 4. The study team renumbered the obtained 11 representative adjective pairs (E1–E9), and the results were also shown in Table 5 below.

Table 5. Representative emotional words

Group	Emotional words with closest distance to the clustering center (pairs)
1	Safe-Dangerous
2	Understandable-Obscure
3	Active-Serious
4	Responsive-Impassive
5	Smooth-Obstructive
6	Clear-Vague
7	Beautiful-Ugly
8	Fault-tolerant-Demanding
9	Natural-Awkward
10	Accomplished-Frustrated
11	Orderly-Disorderly

The interpretation of each representative emotional word is as follows.

E1 Safe: The experience of the novice tutorial makes players feel safe.

E2 Understandable: The introduction of the gameplay is easy for players to understand.

E3 Active: The teaching method of the novice tutorial is not rigid but lively.

E4 Responsive: Players are able to get feedback after finishing corresponding operation or achieving a goal.

E5 Smooth: Players will not get stuck when experiencing the novice tutorial.

E6 Clear: The interface guide of the novice tutorial is clear and straightforward.

E7 Beautiful: The interface and scene design of the novice tutorial can meet the aesthetic needs of players.

E8 Fault-tolerant: Players are allowed to misuse in the novice tutorial and the cost of mistakes is small.

E9 Natural: The interaction of the novice tutorial is natural and fit with players' interactive habits.

E10 Accomplished: Players can gain a certain sense of accomplishment after achieving the goals set in the novice tutorial.

E11 Orderly: The arrangement of the teaching modules of the novice tutorial is orderly.

3 Establish of the Evaluation Hierarchy

The analytic hierarchy process method usually consists of three layers from top to down. The uppermost layer is the target layer, which is the decision goal; the second layer is the criterion layer which mainly includes the criteria considered in the decision-making process, and there can be multiple sub-layers. The third is a plan layer, which includes several alternative plans for the decision. Combining the relative researches of user gaming experience, the target layer established in the evaluation hierarchy in this study was the user experience of novice tutorials in the battle royale games. Moreover, the study team divided the user experience into three criterion layers, that is sensory experience, behavioral experience and value experience. And the emotional words obtained above were classified into the sub-layers of the criterion layers. Since there were no design plans in this study, plan layer was not included for analysis. The schematic diagram of the final evaluation hierarchical structure is shown in the Fig. 2.

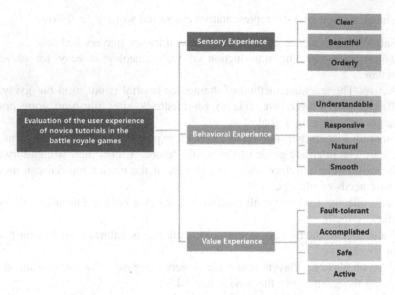

Fig. 2. Evaluation hierarchy of the user experience in novice tutorials in the Battle Royal Game

4   Perceptual Evaluation Experiment and Calculation of Subjective Weights

Before acquiring users' perceptual needs through perceptual experiment, certain samples as well as questionnaires about perceptual evaluation of the above emotional words were to collect at first. We need to understand that the purpose of this experiment was to obtain users' perceptual needs for the Battle Royale Games' novice tutorials. Thus, novice tutorials of three battle royale games were selected as samples. In order to control variables, the three games were all FPS games, called PUBG, APEX, and CODwarzone, named as D1, D2, D3. First, participants were asked to experience the novice tutorials of these three games and then filled in the semantic difference questionnaires. Participants all had a certain understanding of the battle royale games or were the target players of those games. There were 22 participants in total, of which 17 were males and 5 were females. The age range of the participants were 20–25. Questionnaires of the user's perception needs are shown in the Table 6 below.

Table 6. Perceptual questionnaires sample

Perception needs	-1	-2	-1	0	1	2	3	Perception needs
Vague								Clear
Ugly								Beautiful
Disorderly								Orderly
Obscure								Understandable
Serious								Active
Slient								Responsive
Unchanging								Mutable
Demanding								Fault-tolerant
Rigid								Adaptive
Frustrated								Accomplished
Dangerous								Safe

After calculating the average value of each sample in every emotional vocabulary group, a line chart of expected target results of users was obtained, as shown in the Fig. 3.

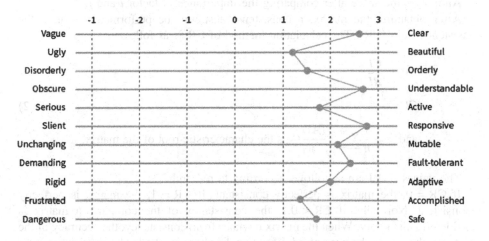

Fig. 3. Line chart of users' perceptual needs

After obtaining the users' perceptual needs for novice tutorials in the battle royale games, the study team aimed to calculate the weight of each evaluation index based on the evaluation hierarchy acquired. The study team compared the elements at the same level one by one with reference to the users' perceptual needs and produced a comparison matrix. The scaling method proposed by Professor Saaty (1980) was applied to score the comparison results[5], as shown in the Table 7.

Table 7. Scoring scale

Importance scale	Implications
1	Equally important when comparing two items
3	The former is slightly more important when comparing two items
5	The former is obviously more important when comparing two items
7	The former is strongly important when comparing two items
9	The former is extremely important when comparing two items

When comparing the indexes, we assumed that there were n criteria (i.e., $a_1, a_2 \ldots a_n$) in the next layer of the target C, it was necessary to use C as a standard to compare the importance of these criteria (i.e., $a_1, a_2 \ldots a_n$) respectively and produce the comparison matrix A. The matrix A could be expressed as follows.

$$A = \begin{bmatrix} a_{11} & a_{12} & \cdots & a_{1n} \\ a_{21} & a_{22} & \cdots & a_{2n} \\ \cdots & \cdots & \cdots & \cdots \\ a_{n1} & a_{n2} & \cdots & a_{n4} \end{bmatrix}$$

$$A = \left(a_{ij} \right)_{n \times n}, \quad i, j = 1, 2, \ldots, n \tag{1}$$

And, a_{ij} is the score after comparing the importance of factor i and j.

After obtaining the matrix, a consistency test will be performed to obtain the consistency ratio (CR). The calculation method of CR is as follows.

$$CR = \frac{CI}{RI}$$

$$CI = \frac{\lambda - n}{n - 1} \tag{2}$$

and $\lambda = \frac{1}{n} \sum_{i-1}^{n} \frac{(AW)_i}{w_i}$ is the characteristic root of the matrix.

The values of RI are as follows according to research[6].

If CR = 0, the matrix is perfectly consistent. If CR = 1, the matrix is perfectly inconsistent. Normally, if CR < 0.1, the consistency of the comparison matrix is considered satisfactory. When the matrix deviates from consistency, the accuracy of the index weights cannot be guaranteed. Based on the above methods, the consistency ratio of this experiment was calculated and CR = 0.043 < 0.1, which suggested the matrix was acceptable.

Table 8. Value of RI

n	1	2	3	4	5	6	7	8	9	10
RI	0	0	0.58	0.90	1.12	1.24	1.32	1.41	1.45	1.49

Table 9. The weight of each evaluation index

Target layer	Criterion layer	Weight	Sub-criterion layer	Weight
Experience of Novice tutorials in the Battle Royal Games	Sensory experience	0.256	Clear-Vague	0.102
			Beautiful- Ugly	0.071
			Orderly-Disorderly	0.083
	Behavioral experience	0.352	Understandable-Obscure	0.074
			Active-Serious	0.076
			Responsive - Impassive	0.113
			Safe-Dangerous	0.089
	Value experience	0.392	Mutable-Unchanging	0.105
			Fault-tolerant-Demanding	0.089
			Adaptive- Rigid	0.110
			Accomplished-Frustrated	0.088

At last, Yaahp was used to process the obtained data to calculate the weight index of each element relative to the upper layer. The player's perceptual needs can be recorded as follows.

5 Grey Relational Analysis

After obtaining the weight of each evaluation index, this paper used Grey relational analysis method to improve the hierarchical analysis model. The main purpose was to transform the data from grey to white, that is from uncertain information to definite information. As mentioned, evaluation of gaming experience is a system containing lots of fuzzy information and the cognition bias from different evaluators might also bring deviation to the experimental results. Thus, the average weight of each index obtained above is not yet an ideal result. It is necessary to combine the Grey relational analysis method to further optimize the obtained evaluation model.

(1) First, we determined the reference sequence and the comparison sequence. The reference sequence reflected the characteristics of the system referring to the best scores of each indicator about the user experience of the novice tutorial in the battle royale games here. The comparison sequence referred to data that has impact on system and needed to be sorted. Here it referred to experimental data of the novice tutorials of three the battle royale games. According to the serial number of the

plans, the comparison sequence was remarked as x_i, and i indicated the serial number, $x_i(k)$ referred to the evaluation score of the *i-th* plans within the index k.

$$x_i = (x_{1i}, x_{2i}, ..., x_{ji}), \quad i = 1, 2, ..., m \tag{3}$$

(2) Non-dimensionalization of the comparison sequences. Since dimensions impacting the evaluation indexes may be different, all indexes were made dimensionless before the comparison sequence was analyzed. All sequences were divided by the *k-th* adjustment sequence to ensure that the evaluation scores of all series fall in (0, 1). Yet the obtained matrix in the experiment was dimensionless already, non-dimensionalization was unnecessary.

$$f(x_i(k)) = \frac{x_i(k)}{A(k)}, \quad k = 1, 2, ..., n, \ i = 1, 2, ..., m \tag{4}$$

(3) Calculated the Grey relational coefficient (GRC). The GRC $\xi(x_0)$ refers to the degree of difference between the geometric shapes of the curves, that is, the difference between the curves can measure the degree of correlation. The calculation is as follows. The i refers to the serial number of the plans while k represents the index sequence.

$$\xi_i(k) = \frac{\min\limits_{i \in m} \min\limits_{k \in n} |x_0(k) - x_i(k)| + \rho \max\limits_{i \in m} \max\limits_{k \in n} |x_0(k) - x_i(k)|}{|x_0(k) - x_i(k)| + \rho \max\limits_{i \in m} \max\limits_{k \in n} |x_0(k) - x_i(k)|} \tag{5}$$

Among them, ρ is the discrimination coefficient which can improve the statistical significance between GRC. The smaller the ρ, the greater the discrimination. The general value range of ρ is (0, 1), and its general value is 0.5. According to relative research, the value of ρ is adopted as 0.5 in this study as well.

(4) Calculated the Grey interconnect degree. Since the relational coefficient is the value of the interconnect degree of the comparison and reference sequences at each time, that is, each point in the curve, it has more than one value. To prevent the information from being too scattered, all relational coefficients at each time need to become centralized as one value, that is Grey interconnect degree r_i, making it feasible for comparison as a whole. The calculation formula is as follows.

$$r_i = \sum_{k=1}^{n} w_k^G \xi_{oi}(k), \quad k = (1, 2, ..., n) \tag{6}$$

Design plans will be compared with each other for better selection according to the value of the Grey interconnect degree. If $r_i \geq r_j$, it suggests that the *plan* x_i is better than *plan* x_j. In this way, we compared three design plans in this study and selected the one with the biggest Grey interconnect degree as the best plan scores of Grey interconnect degree of three design plans were obtained, as shown in the Table 10.

Table 10. Score of the Grey interconnect degree

Design plan	Score of the Grey interconnect degree
D1	0.714
D2	0.825
D3	0.520

Combined with the weight of each evaluation index obtained, scores of weighted Grey interconnect degree of three design plans were calculated, as shown in the Table 11.

Table 11. Score of Weighted Grey interconnect degree

Design plan	Score of Weighted Grey interconnect degree
D1	0.2036
D2	0.2253
D3	0.1249

6 Conclusions and Limitations

(1) This paper discusses a method of constructing the system evaluating the user experience of novice tutorials of the battle royal games in the process of game design. This method can help designers to fully understand the satisfaction degree of users in a scientific way in the process of game development and select the most superior design plan. It also provides a certain reference for the direction of further iterations. When we were making general evaluation about the design plans, the Analytic Hierarchy Process method and Grey Relational Analysis method were applied to calculate the weighted interconnected degree of the evaluation targets and ideal plans so that the plan with higher interconnected degree was screened out. This verified the auxiliary role of the grey AHP Theory in evaluating game experience. The ideas and methods to establish the model evaluating gaming experience in this paper can be extended to experience evaluation of other game systems other than the novice tutorial and other kinds of games. It is of great significance for game design.

(2) Due to limited time and resources, only three novice tutorials of the battle royale games that were extremely popular recently were selected for evaluation in this study. In the follow-up research, this paper may adopt more samples or design plans of our own game projects for evaluation to improve the accuracy of the model. As for research methods, this study adopted online questionnaires to conduct the perceptual experiment due to physical constraints. The study team will consider applying eye-tracking equipment or other perceptual measurement methods in further research.

References

ISO 9241-11: Ergonomic requirements for office work with visual display terminals (VDTs), Part 11. Guidance on Usability. ISO (1998)

Nuan, B.: Research on Card Game Design Based on Kansei Engineer (2019)

Yan, W., Xujiang, Z.: The study on the influence of user experience in game design–an instance of "LeAgue of Legends." Design **02**, 118–119 (2014)

WeiWei, S.: Research on the Evaluation Model of APP for the Elder Based on Grey AHP (2017)

Saaty, T.L.: The Analytic Hierarchy Process. McGraw-Hill, New York (1980)

Saaty, T.L: Fundamentals of Design Making and Theory with the Analytic Hierarchy Process. Analytic Hierarchy Process (2000)

Horror Ludens: Using Fear to Construct Meaning in Video Games

Vicente Martin Mastrocola(✉)

ESPM, Rua Alvaro Alvim, 123, São Paulo, SP 04018-010, Brazil
vmastrocola@espm.br

Abstract. In this article, we discuss how fear can be a powerful element to construct meaning in some specific video games. Titles like *Phantaruk, Alan Wake, Here they lie,* and many others help us to find some answers in this scenario, but herein we intend to focus our attention on the game *Rapid Eye Movement* (PC, 2020–2021). Created by an independent Brazilian studio named Abysstrakt Games, and scheduled to be launched in late 2021, the game sets its action in a dreamlike ambient where the player has the role of a person inside a nightmare, looking for clues to set the time on different clocks, trying to wake up. As a methodological process to understand how it is possible to create meaning using fear in video games, we have employed a formal analysis of gameplay that "is based on studying a game independently of context, that is, without regarding which specific people are playing a specific instance of the game" [1]. We have observed a group of players of *Rapid Eye Movement* in order to study how moments of horror and terror create an atmosphere of fear and, consequently, the meaning of the gaming experience. In this work, we present these impressions as a qualitative research, with the objective of identifying the main points inside the fearful experience of playing *Rapid Eye Movement*, in order to comprehend how terror, horror, anxiety and despair could be used to support the game design process.

Keywords: Horror · Video game · Indie game

1 Introduction

Fear is one of the most ancient feelings orbiting the human existence. The feeling of fear, historically, has been a fertile ground for different writers, filmmakers and many other storytellers to find inspiration to create their works. Video games, legitimated as "forms of media, human expression, and cultural importance" [2], were not left out of this list; the sophistication of the latest generations of consoles elevated some fearful ludic narratives to a new frightening level.

Fear, in this essay, is understood as a creative "fuel" to develop narrative, gameplay, experience and immersion. Spinoza, in his book *Ethics* [3], set out to analyze the origin and the nature of human affections, taking as its starting point desire, joy and sadness. Spinoza postulates that human beings, by nature, are passionate and affected by external forces. The Dutch philosopher drew a deep observation about

© Springer Nature Switzerland AG 2021
X. Fang (Ed.): HCII 2021, LNCS 12789, pp. 89–98, 2021.
https://doi.org/10.1007/978-3-030-77277-2_7

feelings/passions that underlie human existence, comprising aspects of fear; this reference is fundamental in the context studied herein.

The rhetoric of fear allows the creation of games with meaning based on horror and terror. About this, Ghita [4] says that, as a refined product of fear, terror constitutes a multifocal aesthetic emotion, whose main feature is the state of anxiety, brought about by a well-balanced series of artistic elements: plot, atmosphere and characters. As an intensification of fear, horror represents a unifocal aesthetic emotion, whose main feature is the state of revulsion, brought about by the paroxysmal development of the aforementioned artistic elements.

In the context of game design, Nielsen and Schønau-Fog [5] propose three key elements for using fear/terror/horror to create meaning: (1) a deep narrative that allows the player to invest emotions into the character; (2) a deep sense of freedom to establish a connection and a deep grade of immersion; and, finally, (3) the player should feel like a victim rather than a contender. Another point to highlight in this category of games is the use of "illogical architecture to turn houses, gardens and streets into great mazes which would make no sense in the real world" [5]. In *Rapid Eye Movement*—our empirical object for this essay—we were able to identify these three elements strategically hybridized with many different aspects of terror and horror. The narrative works alternating these aspects to create a stronger immersive experience for the players.

Tajerian [6] says that anxiety is a point to highlight in terror/horror games. This author also explains that, along with fear, anxiety is perhaps the most prominent feeling experienced in video games. Unlike fear, which is a response to an imminent threat, anxiety is a response to a potential threat.

Following these initial thoughts, we will discuss in the next topic the main features of the game *Rapid Eye Movement*. It is important to highlight two points: (1) at the time this article was being written, the game in question was in development and scheduled to be launched in late 2021; (2) the author of this article is one of the professionals involved in the design and development of the game herein analyzed.

2 Rapid Eye Movement: A Horror Indie Game

Rapid Eye Movement (Abysstrakt Games, 2020–2021)—or *R.E.M.*—is an independent game created for PC, available on Steam and itch.io platforms. At the time this article was being written, the game was in the middle of its development process, so it is important to say that some images used here came from the prototype version (the release of the final version is scheduled for the end of 2021).

R.E.M. is a game about dreaming; specifically, about an agonizing nightmare. In a first-person view, the player has exactly three minutes to complete a series of puzzles structured with some clocks scattered in the scenario. Each clock has a unique color and a unique solution; the player must be fast and ingenious to decipher some hints provided by objects displayed in the rooms and then set the right time on the clocks. If the player fails to set the clocks in three minutes, they return to the initial gaming scenario and must start all over again—like in an endless nightmare. Further on we will discuss with details one of the puzzles of the game.

All the action in *R.E.M.* takes place inside a strange and distorted house; each room has walls filled with images of old distressing memories. The game design goal that best defines *R.E.M.* is to cause a feeling of estrangement in the player. Below (Fig. 1) we present a screenshot from a scenario in the prototype version.

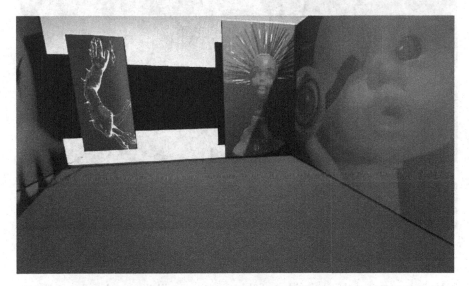

Fig. 1. Screenshot from a scenario in *Rapid Eye Movement* (prototype version).

The narrative is mysterious and subject to various interpretations. In the beginning of the game, a monotonic and depressive voice gives some hints about the gaming atmosphere and objective. Below we reproduce the full text that is the starting point for the dreamlike mood of *Rapid Eye Movement*:

> I have a recurring dream.
> In fact, it's not a dream. It's a nightmare.
> I can say it's a nightmare because I want to wake up and I can't.
> Everything always starts like this:
> I'm in my childhood home.
> I know I'm not alone.
> However, it is not a human thing that keeps me company.
> It's some kind of shadow.
> In dreams (or in nightmares) we don't question the facts, we just accept them.
> I know there are clocks around the house.
> I know I have to adjust the clocks correctly.
> I know that time is short.
> I know that if I don't succeed, everything will repeat itself. I know. I just know.

With these initial hints, the game introduces the player to the ambience, the theme, and the main plot (to adjust the clocks correctly). The name of the game—*Rapid Eye Movement*—is another hint for the dreamlike narrative: R.E.M. is a unique phase of sleep characterized by random rapid movement of the eyes, accompanied by low muscle tone throughout the body, and the propensity of the sleeper to dream vividly. In

the starting screen of the game, it is also possible to observe some neuronal connections in the background (Fig. 2).

Fig. 2. *Rapid Eye Movement* starting screen (prototype version).

Having presented the main idea of the game, we will discuss briefly, in the next topic, an important feature of game production using a popular game engine. And in topic number four we will dissert about how time pressure, anxiety, and the horror mood were created in the gaming interface.

3   A Word About Game Programming

It is not the objective of this article to discuss the coding process of the game *R.E.M.* However, we believe that talking briefly about the programming of the game may allow a deeper understanding of the game's creative process.

Rapid Eye Movement was developed using the Unity game engine. This engine can be used to craft three-dimensional, two-dimensional, virtual reality, and augmented reality games, as well as simulations and other experiences [7]. The Brazilian independent studio behind the title—Abysstrakt Games—chose this engine due to the platform's versatility, high performance rendering graphics in real time, and the online community support (it is important to highlight that Unity's community in the internet is very engaged in trying to help developers all around the word with hints, tips and ready-made codes).

After these brief technical details, we will delve into the most relevant topic in this work: how we can take advantage of components of fear and horror narratives to create an immersive experience within a game. We will also discuss how the puzzle mechanics—in this case—is a suitable choice to increase the gaming features.

4 Horror and Fear as Game Design Components

In *Rapid Eye Movement*, horror and fear are materialized in a twisted scenario filled with bizarre images, strange objects, and time pressure, accompanied by a dark ambience music theme. The involvement of the player is based on three fundamental ideas: the concept of a labyrinth, the concept of virtual presence and the concept of flow.

The idea of a labyrinth in games, as a metaphor, offers the player a chance to get lost inside the gaming world. But it's very important to present this as a challenge to be completed and not as a bad experience that leads nowhere. As Kerényi [8] wrote, the concept of a labyrinth is a cultural heritage of humanity whose origin dates back to the Stone Age, and possibly all the ludic activities result in some kind of maze.

Following this line of thought, it's important to study the concept of *presence* inside the game world. To offer the player a labyrinthine environment is easy, but the real challenge is to create the virtual presence of the player in the game (using narrative resources, coherent game mechanics, good graphics etc.) Nitsche [9] talks about forms of presence and argues that presence is understood as the mental state that causes a user to subjectively feel as if they were inside a video game space, as the result of an immersion into the content of the fictional world. It is a mental phenomenon based on a perceptual illusion. This author also says that a great number of researchers have concentrated on the idea that a state of presence should be connected to the illusion of a non-mediated experience. In this case, players do not see the interface anymore because they feel present in the world beyond the screen.

The third idea to be discussed, as proposed by Csikszentmihalyi [10], is the concept of *flow*, which should be understood as a state in which a person is fully immersed in an action and highly focused to the extent that they can experience, for example, a lack of self-consciousness and can lose track of time. A player who reaches this level of flow is clearly immersed in the game, but not necessarily *present* in the virtual space.

Besides these three ideas, we should also look into some ideas put forward by Salen and Zimmerman—both authors propose that between the player and the game there is gameplay [11], which is a formalized interaction that occurs when players follow the rules of a game and live the experience of the game system through the act of playing.

In order to strategically increase the feeling of fear and horror, our game project has been guided by the concept of "five planes" proposed by Nitsche [12]. This author theorizes that, in a video game, we have:

1. A rule-based plane defined by the mathematical rules that set, for example, physics, sounds, artificial intelligence, and game-level architecture. It is important to high-light that players do not have to understand the logic of the code to appreciate the experience in the game.
2. A mediated plane defined by the presentation, which is the space of the image plane and the use of imagery, including the cinematic form of presentation.
3. A fictional plane that lives in the player's imagination; in other words, it is the space imagined by players from their comprehension of the available images in the gaming interface.

4. A play plane (meaning space of play) which includes the player and the video game hardware.
5. A social plane defined by interaction with other people, meaning the game space of other engaged players (e.g., in a multiplayer title).

In *R.E.M.*, the rule-based plane consists of the code, the 3D modelling, and the scenario created using the Unity engine. The mediated plane is the interface filled with dark ambience; it is the interface displayed on the player's PC screen. The fictional plane is how the player understands and decrypts the mysterious narrative inside his mind (and *R.E.M.* purposefully has a very subjective narrative that invites the player to be a co-author of the story). The play plane consists of the player and their use of mouse and keyboard to solve the puzzles, move around the scenario etc. Finally, the social plane occurs through game-related interactions between players in social media platforms, or between players and their friends in person. Although the game does not have a multiplayer mode, its socialization happens as players talk about it in different platforms.

In the light of these ideas, the structure of *R.E.M.* is based on these main features: 1) time pressure created with a soundtrack that lasts three minutes and ends with a fade-out effect; this feature is used to arise the feeling of anxiety in the player, by conveying that there is no time to think too much in each room—it is necessary to explore and (sometimes) take notes of your discoveries in the gaming ambient; 2) a first-person view in a scenario filled with disturbing images, dissonant sound effects, visual distortions and strange items; these features are the most important to create estrangement in the gaming experience and subsequently arouse feelings of fear, uneasiness and horror in the players; 3) the puzzle-based mechanics [13] is the third feature to complete *R.E.M.*'s "ecosystem"; the main challenge of the game is to set the right time in five different clocks scattered around the rooms of the house. Each clock has a specific color and a hint provided by an object with the same color. Objects and clocks are in different rooms and players must be fast to decipher how the hints connect to the puzzle's resolutions.

Puzzle games, by definition, focus on logical and conceptual challenges, although occasionally the games include time pressure or other action elements. Fullerton [14] says that puzzles are also a key element in creating conflict in almost all single player games. There is an innate tension in solving the puzzle. They can contextualize the choices that players make by valuing them as moving toward or away from the solution. Next, we will present a puzzle idea and its resolution.

In this example (Fig. 3) we can see an old bible on the floor. As the player clicks on the object, he sees the bible page highlighted with the text "Corinthians 15:58. Therefore, my beloved brothers, be steadfast, immovable, always abounding in the work of the LORD, knowing that in the LORD your labor is not in vain." The snippet "Corinthians 15:58" is in blue, giving a hint to the player.

Walking around the scenario, the player will find a clock with numbers in the same color as the bible excerpt. By clicking on the clock, a panel will open, and the player can change (up and down) the numbers (Fig. 4).

The right answer for this enigma is to set the digital clock to 15:58, according to the hint provided by the bible's page.

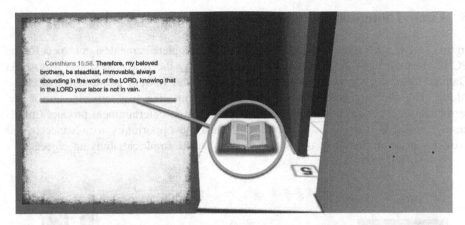

Fig. 3. Objects scattered in the gaming scenario offer a color hint (prototype version).

Fig. 4. Clock to be adjusted according to the previous hint from the bible (prototype version).

The main goal in *Rapid Eye Movement* is to set the hour on five different types of clocks, according to different hints distributed around the scenario. Narrative blends with puzzle mechanics to create a mysterious gameplay in the nightmarish ambient. In this sense, we understand that story, scenario, puzzles, hints and other elements should all be created in a way that adds to the design of the gameplay [15] and to the horror mood of the game.

Having already discussed the creative aspects of the game's environment, the use of mechanics, and a little bit of programming/production, we advance to our final considerations.

5 Final Thoughts and Conclusions

In this article, we had the opportunity to discuss a complete game design project for the PC platform; it is the second digital game created by the Brazilian studio Abysstrakt Games, following the mysterious and horror mood of its first game launched, *Mind Alone* [16]. We discussed how unpleasant sensations like fear, anxiety, horror and terror can be a central point for the development of an entertainment product (in this case, the *R.E.M.* game). In this article, we had the opportunity to advance in our previous research line [17], by using horror games as empirical studying objects.

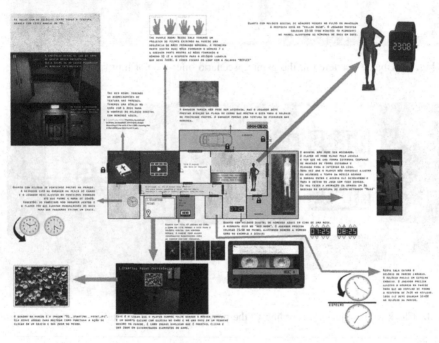

Fig. 5. Top overview of *Rapid Eye Movement*'s map and the resolution of the game's puzzles synthesized in a pre-prototype document.

Following the thoughts of Fullerton et al. [18], *R.E.M.* was created through a very synthetic game design process based on stages. The first step was the conceptual stage, when the narrative and the core gameplay were defined, based on intense research to check other similar games already published. The second step, as proposed by Fullerton, was the brainstorming stage, in which people involved in the project started the first essays about how the narrative would materialize on the gaming interface. When these ideas were established, there came a fundamental third step: the making of a prototype (or pre-prototype) of the game (Fig. 5). In this phase, it is very important to save time by creating a fast pre-visualization of the game using paper, pen and other analog components, or assembling a digital prototype for a fast beta-test play.

In *Rapid Eye Movement*, the beta-testing phase was an essential component of game development. At the time this article was being produced, the first tests with players were starting. The prototype version of the game was created with the Unity engine and was used in ten sessions with ten different players. We performed a formal analysis of gameplay by observing players' reactions during gameplay, giving them the opportunity to explore three minutes of the game as many times as they wanted. At the end of the game session, players were asked to complete a qualitative survey.

The qualitative method is one of many ways to assess the creation of meaning and relevance in the game's interface. To conduct a qualitative interview, you need a good script with clear objectives and precise questions. Cote and Raz [19] show a script guide adapted to the universe of games. 1) Create an introductory script to open the interview and recall the study goals. 2) Warm-up questions to put the participant at ease and build rapport. Some examples that the authors use are "For how long have you been playing video games?" and "What's one of your favorite gaming memories?" 3) Substantive questions to collect deeper data that answer the research questions. This part is nuclear in the interview, here you will ask for the player's feedbacks about gaming interface, mechanics and other aspects. 4) Demographic questions to gather data needed to describe participants in the final research report.

Based on these guidelines, we used the following script to assess the game sessions:

1. Today you are going to beta-test the game *Rapid Eye Movement*. In this first session, we want to investigate, as a primary objective, the gaming horror atmosphere; as a second objective, we want to evaluate mechanical issues (if the game is balanced, if the gameplay is flowing well). We ask you to give special attention to the game soundtrack, narration and sound effects.

2. Please answer: do you always play horror games? If the answer is "yes", what are your favorite horror games? If the answer is "no", please explain what you do not like about this kind of game.

3.1. Is the game frightening?

3.2. Did the game make you feel estrangement in any way?

3.3. Did you have fun with the game?

3.4. What is could be improved in mechanics, scenario or narrative?

4. Please provide us with your email address for future contact.

The careful observation of a group of ten different players yielded some interesting feedback concerning the use of fear as a meaning builder in a playful experience. Some players, at a first, felt bad about the ambience, the twisted scenario with bizarre images and the mood of the game; others felt pressure only in moments of unbridled escape. Others reported having a bad feeling about the narrator's voice in the beginning of the game [20]. Regardless of the kind of feeling, we realized that fear fueled the construction of the gaming experience from start to finish.

In the end, we were trying to answer one specific question: why do some players search for fear and other bad feelings in games? To solve this puzzle (using a suitable metaphor), we quote Suits [21], who says that playing a game "is the voluntary attempt to overcome unnecessary obstacles".

The subject addressed in this article is very broad and we hope to have enriched the discussion about game design process, narrative in games, and playful experiences.

References

1. Lankoski, P., Björk, S. (eds.): Game Research Methods: An Overview, p. 23. ETC Press, Halifax (2015)
2. Flanagan, M.: Critical Play—Radical Game Design, p. 79. MIT Press, Cambridge (2009)
3. Spinoza, B.: Ethics. Penguin Books, London (2005)
4. Ghita, C.: Discussing Romanian Gothic. In: Kattelman, B., Hodalska, M. (eds.) Frightful Witnessing: The Rhetoric and (Re)Presentation of Fear, Horror and Terror, p. 58. Inter-Disciplinary Press, Oxford (2014)
5. Nielsen, D., Schønau-Fog, H.: In the mood for horror: a game design approach on investigating absorbing player experiences in horror games. In: Huber, S., Mitgutsch, K., Rosenstigl, H., Wagner, M., Wimmer, J. (eds.) Context Matters! Proceedings of the Vienna Games Conference 2013: Exploring and Reframing Games and Play in Context, Viena, pp. 52–53. New Academic Press (2013)
6. Gamasutra. Fight or Flight: The Neuroscience of Survival Horror. https://www.gamasutra.com/view/feature/172168/fight_or_flight_the_neuroscience_.php. Accessed 10 Oct 2020
7. Unity official website. https://unity.com/. Accessed 10 Oct 2020
8. Kerényi, K.: En El laberinto, pp. 66–72. Ediciones Siruela, Madrid (2006)
9. Nitsche, M.: Video Game Spaces—Image, Play and Structure in 3D Worlds, p. 203. MIT Press, Massachusetts (2008)
10. Csiksentmihalyi, M.: Flow: The Psychology of Optimal Experience. HarperCollins, New York (1991)
11. Salen, K., Zimmerman, E.: Rules of Play: Game Design Fundamentals, p. 303. MIT Press, Massachusetts (2004)
12. Nitsche, M.: Video Game Spaces—Image, Play and Structure in 3D Worlds, pp. 15–16. MIT Press, Massachusetts (2008)
13. Adams, E.: Fundamentals of Puzzle and Casual Game Design. Pearson, San Francisco (2014)
14. Fullerton, T., Swain, C., Hoffman, S.: Game Design Workshop: A Playcentric Approach to Creating Innovative Games, p. 324. Morgan Kaufmann Publishers, Burlington (2008)
15. Ince, S.: Writing for Video Games, p. 36. A & C Black Publishers Limited, London (2006)
16. Mastrocola, V.M.: The strategic use of smartphone features to create a gaming experience of mystery: the mind alone case. In: Fang, X. (ed.) HCII 2019. LNCS, vol. 11595, pp. 180–190. Springer, Cham (2019). https://doi.org/10.1007/978-3-030-22602-2_15
17. Mastrocola, V.: Horror Ludens: medo, entretenimento e consumo em narrativas de video games. Livrus, São Paulo (2014)
18. Fullerton, T., et al.: Game Design Workshop: A Playcentric Approach to Creating Innovative Games, pp. 15–16. Morgan Kaufmann Publishers, Burlington (2008)
19. Cote, A., Raz, J.G.: In-depth interviews for game research. In: Lankoski, P., Björk, S. (eds.) Game Research Methods: An Overview, p. 104. ETC Press, Halifax (2015)
20. Rapid Eye Movement gaming intro. https://youtu.be/KBwYDUhGv10. Accessed 10 Oct 2020
21. Suits, B.: The Grasshopper: Games, Life and Utopia, p. 55. Broadview Encore Editions, Toronto (2005)

Persuasive Technology in Games: A Brief Review and Reappraisal

Umair Rehman[1]([⊠]), Muhammad Umair Shah[2], Amir Zaib Abbasi[3], Farkhund Iqbal[4], Ali Arsalan[5], and Muhammad Umair Javaid[6]

[1] User Experience Design, Wilfrid Laurier University, Brantford, ON, Canada
urehman@wlu.ca
[2] Management Sciences, University of Waterloo, Waterloo, ON, Canada
[3] Faculty of Management Sciences, Shaheed Zulfiqar Ali Bhutto Institute of Science Technology (SZABIST), Islamabad, Pakistan
[4] College of Technological Innovation, Zayed University Dubai, Dubai, United Arab Emirates
[5] Amazon Alexa Engineering, Amazon Inc., Seattle, WA, USA
[6] Department of Management Sciences, Lahore Garrison University, Lahore, Pakistan

Abstract. Persuasive technology is a new field of research that has attracted considerable attention from game designers since there is a growing interest in games promoting positive behavioral changes. Persuasive games have been exploited to tremendous effect with applications ranging from mobile healthcare, which persuade users to exercise more often and adopt a healthy lifestyle, to government programs encouraging civic engagement. Therefore, persuasive technologies have become an indispensable part of the modern game designer's toolkit, and their importance is only set to grow with time. In this paper, we begin by reviewing the existing body of work in this field while also explaining the pros and cons of emerging design models and theoretical frameworks. We then uncover major pitfalls in the current work and suggest directions for future research. Hopefully, this article will prove instructive to game designers and leave them with a better understanding of the central concepts in the field of persuasive technology.

Keywords: Persuasive technology · Persuasive games · Behavior change systems · And persuasive design models

1 Persuasion

Persuasion is a well-researched concept that evolved from the field of social psychology [1]. Different models, theories, and methods have been introduced in the past to explain this concept. Persuasion could generally be described as means to change, reinforce or shape a person's attitude or behavior [2]. Attitude and behavior are distinct psychological constructs [3] as attitude refers to one's predisposed mental outlook towards people, objects, issues, and events, generally acquired through past experiences. However, behavior refers to physical actions or noticeable emotions in response to internal or external stimuli in the environment. Persuasion was investigated in 1950 by Carl

© Springer Nature Switzerland AG 2021
X. Fang (Ed.): HCII 2021, LNCS 12789, pp. 99–109, 2021.
https://doi.org/10.1007/978-3-030-77277-2_8

Hovland as part of the Yale Communication Project [4]. The project team concluded that persuasion scenarios encompass four basic elements: an entity that conveys the persuasive message, the persuasive message itself, a target audience that receives the persuasive message, and the context of the message. The team further suggested that for the message to work effectively, the recipients must learn, accept, and retain the content of the message. Later research however affirmed that persuasion is not dependent on the content of the message but instead on how the message would influence the thought process and viewpoints of the recipients [5].

Persuasion could be classified into three main categories: interpersonal persuasion, computer-mediated persuasion, and human-computer persuasion [6]. Interpersonal persuasion is the interaction of two or more individuals without the involvement of any technology. Interpersonal persuasion can involve a personalized exchange of ideas and sentiments, adaptive personality feedback, verbal, and physical forms of communication, etc. Computer-mediated persuasion involves the use of technology as an interaction medium between persuader and persuadee. An example would be a persuadee utilizing cell phone as a medium to persuade someone to continue the daily exercise. Computer-mediated persuasion cannot be considered as persuasive technology as the technology is merely being utilized as a communication resource rather than a persuasive agent. Human-computer persuasion can be defined as stimulating behavior or attitude change with the assistance of interactive technology. In human-computer persuasion, all persuasive interactions are limited between the user and technology.

2 Persuasive Technology in Games

The term human-computer persuasion evolved into persuasive technology. Persuasive technology is officially described as "interactive computing systems designed to change people's attitudes and behaviors" [7]. BJ Fogg introduced the phenomena in his seminal work titled "Captology: the study of computers as persuasive technologies" [8]. He further advanced the field by introducing models that explained the concept in formal terms [9]. His work attracted a lot of interest from different research areas, especially human-computer interaction, as the idea of using the computer to change behavior was unique at the time and pushed researchers to think of applications outside the general use cases for computers. We see the application of persuasive technology in various domains, including video games, health, sustainability, education, economics, entertainment, safety, etc. [10].

There has been a great deal of work at the intersection of persuasive technology and games. Games are a persuasive medium and can lead to behavior change. Researchers have investigated persuasive elements embedded in video games. It's important to highlight that the difference between persuasive games and other games lies primarily in the fact that persuasive games are purposely designed with the primary objective to induce a change in behavior or attitude within the cognitive state of the player [11]. Different models have been introduced in the literature that can support the design and evaluation of persuasive games; however, most of these models aren't straightforward therefore the application of these approaches towards the design of persuasive games can be complex [12].

3 Design Models and Theoretical Frameworks

There are two major types of models that have been introduced in the persuasive technology research area. These include theoretical frameworks and design models. In this section, we review the five most prominent models from the existing literature. Fogg's Behaviour Grid [13] was omitted in favor of his newer model, The Behaviour Wizard. The Design with Intent method was not considered in this review because it is primarily a recommendation tool rather than a design model [14]. The review follows a systematic approach. We first describe the model, and then we discuss its advantages and disadvantages in the context of persuasive technology.

3.1 Functional Triad

Functional triad is a classification of the functional roles of computing technology [15]. The framework is primarily divided into three core dimensions that demonstrate that computers could be used as tools, mediums, or social actors. As tools, computing technology augments human capability and allows users to perform a variety of tasks effectively. Persuasive strategies in games such as tunneling, tailoring, reduction, etc., would fit in the broad category of tools in a functional triad. As a medium, persuasive technology in games can allow users to experience symbolic content in the form of visualizations, text, signs etc. as well as sensory content in the form of video, audio, holograms, haptics, etc. Such game experiences can be useful in motivating game players towards the desired behavior or attitude shift. As social actors, games can leverage different social influence strategies, such as social dynamics, social rewards, social sanctions, etc., to influence players to behave differently from how they would have behaved otherwise. Although there are no underlying theories behind this triadic approach, BJ Fogg does cite important work that has shown computers to effectively function, in each of the three categories, as tools [16, 17], as a medium [18–20], and as social actors [21, 22]. This classification is an important mechanism to identify the different roles of current technology; however, this work does not provide any tangible information that could assist game designers in designing persuasive systems.

3.2 Fogg's Behavior Model

Fogg's behavior model is the theory that can aid game designers to understand the psychology behind human behavior change [9]. It represents human behavior due to three core constructs that include motivation, ability, and triggers. The model postulates that these three constructs must converge concurrently for a particular behavior to occur. Undermining these construct could impact the behavior change process and make the change impractical. The first construct, motivation, is an intrinsic part of the video game experience. It can be divided into further subcomponents that include sensation, anticipation, and belonging. These subcomponents have two sides: pleasure/pain, hope/fear, and acceptance/rejection. The second construct ability could be defined as a player's capacity to undertake the desired course of action needed for a behavior change. The third construct is labeled as a trigger. Its purpose is to smoothen the behavior change process. A trigger in games are also categorized as cues, calls to action, signals prompts, etc. The theory could be utilized to break triggers in games into three main categories. A motivational trigger is applied when a player has low motivation but high ability. A facilitator trigger is applied in scenarios when a player has high motivation but low ability. Lastly, a signal trigger where both the motivation and ability are high. This model is primarily utilized as the theoretical basis for all persuasive design methods introduced by BJ Fogg, and it provides a straightforward framework for representing human behavior.

3.3 The Eight Step Design Process

The eight-step design process can be used as a guide for game designers to develop persuasive games [23]. The model comprises of eight significant steps that include: choosing a simple behavior to target, choosing a receptive audience, finding out what is preventing the audience from performing the target behavior, choosing a familiar technology channel, finding suitable examples of persuasive technology, imitating successful examples, testing and iterating quickly and lastly expanding on prior success.

The model provides indicators that make the game design process more comfortable and flexible. The model depicts how persuasive games can be developed by emphasizing a single behavior and focusing on a receptive game audience. However, the model does not provide any details related to system features, design characteristics, or persuasive techniques. Moreover, there are a set of assumptions in the model that are not theoretically grounded. For instance, the model proposes three-stage criteria for designing successful persuasive technology applications. The criteria include identifying a simple behavior, identifying a receptive audience, and imitating an existing persuasive system. It discounts critical external factors, such as the context and the user (or a game player). These factors must be considered during the design stages as they contribute to the behavior change process.

3.4 Behaviour Wizard

A behavior wizard is a tool that enables target behaviors to be mapped to solutions that can facilitate the behavior change process [24]. The behavior wizard is based on the principles stemmed from Fogg's Behaviour Model. The behavior wizard evolved from Fogg's earlier method, categorized as the behavior grid [13]. The grid comprises a two-axis matrix. On one axis of the matrix, the designers determine the type of behavior change required from the user. This includes initiating a new behavior, increasing or decreasing the intensity or frequency of existing behavior, doing a familiar behavior, or discontinuing an old behavior. On the other axis, the designer determines the frequency of the target behavior. This includes a one-time change, a change for a specific duration, or a permanent change. The grid allows the user to classify fifteen different types of target behaviors. The wizard is usually employed in a three-stage process that requires the user to identify target behavior, identify relevant triggers, and highlight the concepts and solutions related to the target behaviour on a seven-step template that acts as a resource guide. The purpose of the resource guide is to list the relevant information needed to create the persuasive experience.

A behavior wizard is a useful tool for game designers as it simplifies the mechanism of specifying player target behaviors. It can easily be assimilated in the design process of a persuasive game. Although the behavior wizard captures enough detail regarding target behavior, it doesn't provide any information regarding the player who would be performing the target behavior. As a result, few studies have utilized this framework to design persuasive games.

3.5 Persuasive Systems Design (PSD) Framework

The PSD model details a comprehensive design framework that comprises a three-stage structure [25]. In the first stage, the model emphasizes that the designer must consider the seven postulates before initiating the design process. The postulates illustrate the key issues that designers can encounter during the design process of a persuasive system. In the next phase, the designer must analyze the persuasion context. The persuasion context incorporates certain core elements that include understanding the roles of the persuader, persuadee, message content, channel, and the larger context and knowing what occurs in the information processing event. The designer can select and implement design strategies from a list of twenty-eight design principles representing the persuasive system's content and functionality in the last stage. The first step tackles the critical issues in the design process, whereas the second step improves the designer's understanding of contextual details. The third step, however, concentrates on the development of system qualities.

The PSD model is a feature-rich framework for game designers and more comprehensive than its predecessors. The framework showcases how different design elements can be modeled into system requirements and provides designers with strategies that help them consider contextual factors in the design of persuasive games. While the model's design principles are adopted from Fogg's Functional Triad, the PSD model provides a more thorough classification of the principles based on their respective persuasive function. The PSD model is theoretically well-grounded, incorporating different behavior change theories in its processes. The PSD model has also been practically applied across multiple domains supporting the design and evaluation of different persuasive technologies.

4 Behaviour Change Literature

Most of the prevailing models and methods employed in persuasive games are grounded in theoretical work derived from behavior change literature; therefore, to further explain the design development and evaluation of persuasive games, it's essential to fully understand the inner mechanisms of behavior change [12]. The behavior change literature details three overarching paradigms: behavior change techniques, behavioral interventions or behaviour change methods, behaviour change theories or theoretical models, and behavior change determinants or factors are influencing behavior change [26]. The existing literature is limited in terms of offering a conceptual and methodological connection between the three constructs. As a result, game designers often lack a systematic understanding of the fundamental mechanisms that illustrate how behavior change and behavioral interventions function. Due to a lack of operational understanding, unsuitable behavior change interventions continue to be employed in games whereas effective interventions are underutilized.

4.1 Behaviour Change Determinants

Behavior change determinants are vital factors (environmental, personal, behavioral, etc.) responsible for influencing behavior change [27]. Behavior change determinants are essentially derived from different behavior change theories. A single determinant can be used to classify multiple behavior change theories and techniques. For instance, social factors could be categorized as a behavior change determinant which caters to multiple behavior change theories that explain human behavior in term of different social concepts, such as social comparison, social learning, social influence, etc. Game designers generally recognize a single behavior change determinant as the core element of the game design process.

4.2 Behaviour Change Techniques

Behavior change techniques are essentially theory-based approaches that facilitate users to change their behavior or attitude [28]. These techniques function by influencing one or several behavioral determinants of gamers, such as habit or self-efficacy. Multiple taxonomies have been introduced in the literature that showcases different behavior change techniques [28] concerning their overall efficacy or utility in a particular domain; however, similar work relevant to persuasive games is still limited. Other than empirical experimentation, there is no predictive method of deducing whether a particular technique would effectively change a player's behavior. Some behavior change techniques influence multiple determinants and hence are better at inducing behavior change. Therefore, it's advocated to infuse a cohort of behavior change techniques during the design of persuasive games. Different techniques would target multiple determinants, thereby increasing the likelihood of inducing behavior change.

4.3 Behavior Change Theories

Behavior change theories are process-oriented conceptual representations grounded in psychological concepts that explain how behavior change functions [29]. Human behavior is incredibly complex. Many theories have been introduced in the past that explain certain aspects of behavior change; however, no theory is intended to capture the entire breadth and detail of human behavior. Details are, by choice, abstracted away to make theories applicable to different domain areas. The goal of these theories is to describe the behavior change process to be utilized for theoretical interpretation and development of behavior change techniques. Some theories originate from a particular field of research, whereas others are generic theories applicable to a wide range of domains.

5 Research Gaps and Future Direction in Persuasive Technology Research

This section focuses on research gaps that have been identified in the design of the persuasive game.

5.1 Lack of Evaluation Tools

Although different models and persuasive techniques have been introduced in the persuasive research community, the literature still lacks general frameworks or standardized tools that could help game designers evaluate the effectiveness of persuasive techniques [11, 30]. Hence, it is important to examine and shortlist a cohort of evaluation schemes that could be deemed appropriate in assessing these concepts. Only a handful of studies tackle this issue and appear to design-focused [31] or domain-specific. Also, the evaluation criteria applied in existing research is subjective, which can impact reliability standards due to the possibility of biases. Many impediments have stalled progress towards developing strict evaluation criteria for persuasive technology primarily because measuring the underlying psychological phenomena, behind persuasion, is incredibly complex. Most of the persuasive constructs are idiosyncratic and covert; therefore, there is an inherent risk of observing statistical dispersion and cognitive biases in subjective evaluations of persuasive models and techniques.

Moreover, an individual's perspectives might generally dictate idiographic assessments, but their behavior in naturalistic settings might contrast to their traditionally held beliefs. Such confounds may lead to perceptual distortion, speculation, and unreasonable interpretation of results. However, the use of standardized measures for subjective phenomena is quite common in games. Future research can present new possibilities for the development of comprehensive evaluation frameworks in this line of research. However, careful deliberation must be given towards analyzing how the issue of biases can be addressed while evaluating persuasive strategies for games. We should also consider identifying methods that could help us assess the impact of persuasive techniques in games from physiological and affective standpoints. The possibility of mapping physiological and affective data on psychometric scales representing the different persuasive constructs could greatly assist game designers by offering additional insights.

5.2 Lack of Long-Term Empirical Studies

The impact of persuasive techniques over longer durations is relatively unknown. It is difficult to determine the temporal relationship between a particular persuasive technique and its persuasive potential in games [32]. It's also complicated to infer the causation effect as only associations could be anticipated from such approaches. We can only affirm that a particular persuasive strategy is associated with behavior change. Still, we cannot be certain whether that technique led to the actual change. Therefore, such studies may contribute to exploratory analysis; however, more intricate empirical experimentations would be required for confirmatory outcomes. To reliably assess the efficacy of a persuasive game, repeated experimentation over a period of time needs to be performed on players so that series of observations and trends over time could be assessed. A longitudinal assessment approach may also help deduce which techniques are ideal for long-term, short-term, and one-time behavior change, respectively, and help conclude which techniques embedded within a game would carry a greater persuasive potential.

5.3   Limited Application of Theory to Practice

Persuasive technology literature provides insufficient information that details how theoretical models can be effectively incorporated into games. Game designers don't necessarily carry the expertise to transform persuasive theories into strategic game design elements. For instance, existing literature does provide insights into behavior change interventions. However, there is little empirically supported evidence on which specific intervention or intervention strategy would facilitate maximum persuasive effect in games. A moving question is analyzing how a game designer would determine which intervention would be robust and better suited for a specific game.

Furthermore, it's vital to determine whether an implicit intervention would work or a direct intervention. Such design questions need to be carefully addressed after analyzing contextual details and behavioral design mechanisms. Classification of similar questions would prove invaluable in the definition and ideation stages of persuasive design [33]. Currently, no cohesive framework is available to distill the different stages and activities of the persuasive game design process in a structured manner. Future studies should develop empirically grounded design guidelines that could help designers shortlist the relevant persuasive strategies based on empirical evidence.

5.4   Adaptive Persuasive Games

The performance of persuasive games in real-world conditions is still unpredictable [10]. Researchers in the past have claimed that persuasive systems are more proficient than human persuaders, substantiating their claims on study's that demonstrate humans respond to persuasive systems in similar manners as they would to human persuasion [34]. They emphasize that since computers can incessantly deliver persuasive messages with the same effect, therefore there is a higher likelihood of their success in comparison to human persuaders. However, it must be considered that those studies were conducted in controlled conditions, and the persuasive technology was tailored for those specific settings. Real-world settings, however, can be quite volatile in comparison; therefore, it's important to develop persuasive systems that can function optimally even in unpredictable situations. A possible solution to address this issue would be to design persuasive adaptive technologies. Adaptive persuasive technologies carry the capacity to tailor the content of the message, the timing of its delivery, and the persuasive strategy based on the user's context and activities [35]. However, such specifics cannot be tackled in design stages without understanding the contextual information and prior details related to the gamers. Limited work is available on adaptive persuasive games that process feedback from the players and their context and alters persuasive techniques to match the on-ground conditions. Game developers can employ player data from various channels to infer user's social setting and situational context [36]. This could help game designers deliver tailored interventions that can be more effective inducing behavior and attitude change. However, tailoring and personalization are currently geared towards the end-goal rather than adapting the persuasive techniques [35]. However, some literature addresses this subject, such as tailoring persuasive strategies in e-commerce [37]; however, mainstream research in the realm of games is still in its nascent stages as cross domain expertise, and comprehensive testing is required to gather conclusive evidence.

6 Conclusion

This paper identifies and addresses some of the most relevant questions in persuasive technology in games. The article points out a need to develop more comprehensive frameworks that game designers could utilize to evaluate persuasive technology models and concepts. The article identifies that most empirical studies related to persuasive games test variables in shorter durations; therefore, there is a need to understand if the same results would reciprocate in longer time duration studies. The article further points out that we must devise guidelines that can help game designers incorporate persuasive design concepts into their design artifacts. The article highlights the significance of adaptive persuasive systems for games and the need to develop psychologically valid data-driven models that can consider the contextual details to present the player with the most effective behavior change intervention. The article also presents a comprehensive review of major design models and theoretical frameworks and sheds light on the behavior change literature in the context of persuasive technology in games.

References

1. Petty, R.E., Cacioppo, J.T.: The elaboration likelihood model of persuasion. Adv. Exp. Soc. Psychol. **19**, 123–205 (1986)
2. O'keefe, D.J.: Persuasion: Theory and Research. Sage, Thousand Oaks (2002)
3. Wicker, A.W.: An examination of the "other variables" explanation of attitude-behavior inconsistency. J. Pers. Soc. Psychol. **19**, 18 (1971)
4. McGuire, W.J.: The Yale communication and attitude-change program in the 1950s. Am. Commun. Res. Rememb. Hist., 39–59 (1996)
5. Benoit, W.L.: Forewarning and persuasion. Persuas. Adv. Meta-Anal., 139–154 (1998)
6. Harjumaa, M., Oinas-Kukkonen, H.: Persuasion theories and IT design. In: Yvonne, K., Ijsselsteijn, W., Midden, C., Eggen, B., Fogg, B.J. (eds.) PERSUASIVE 2007. LNCS, vol. 4744, pp. 311–314. Springer, Heidelberg (2007). https://doi.org/10.1007/978-3-540-77006-0_37
7. Fogg, B.J.: Persuasive Technology. Morgan Kaufmann Publishers, Burlington (2003)
8. Fogg, B.J.: Captology: the study of computers as persuasive technologies. In: CHI 1997 Extended Abstracts on Human Factors in Computing Systems, p. 129. ACM (1997)
9. Fogg, B.J.: A behavior model for persuasive design. In: Proceedings of the 4th International Conference on Persuasive Technology, pp. 40. ACM (2009)
10. Hamari, J., Koivisto, J., Pakkanen, T.: Do persuasive technologies persuade? - a review of empirical studies. In: Spagnolli, A., Chittaro, L., Gamberini, L. (eds.) PERSUASIVE 2014. LNCS, vol. 8462, pp. 118–136. Springer, Cham (2014). https://doi.org/10.1007/978-3-319-07127-5_11
11. Wiafe, I.: A Framework for Analysing, Designing and Evaluating Persuasive Technologies, (2012)
12. Yu, K.: A new framework for the design and evaluation of persuasive technology: Persuasive experience theory and a taxonomy of persuasive experience supporting design techniques (2016)
13. Fogg, B.J.: The behavior grid: 35 ways behavior can change. In: Proceedings of the 4th international Conference on Persuasive Technology, p. 42. ACM (2009)

14. Lockton, D., Harrison, D., Stanton, N.A.: The design with intent method: a design tool for influencing user behaviour. Appl. Ergon. **41**, 382–392 (2010)
15. Fogg, B.J.: Persuasive technology: using computers to change what we think and do. Ubiquity **2002**, 5 (2002)
16. Sheridan, T.B.: Telerobotics, Automation, and Human Supervisory Control. MIT press, Cambridge (1992)
17. Shneiderman, B.: Designing the user interface: strategies for effective human-computer interaction. Pearson Education India (2010)
18. Kozma, R.B.: Learning with media. Rev. Educ. Res. **61**, 179–211 (1991)
19. Steuer, J.: Defining virtual reality: Dimensions determining telepresence. J. Commun. **42**, 73–93 (1992)
20. Turkle, S.: Who Am We? https://www.wired.com/1996/01/turkle-2/, Accessed 18 Dec 2017
21. Laurel, B., Mountford, S.J.: The Art of Human-Computer Interface Design. Addison-Wesley Longman Publishing Co., Inc., Boston (1990)
22. Reeves, B., Nass, C.: How People Treat Computers, Television, and New Media like Real People and Places. CSLI Publications and Cambridge university press, Cambridge (1996).
23. Fogg, B.J.: Creating persuasive technologies: an eight-step design process. In: Proceedings of the 4th International Conference on Persuasive Technology, p. 44. ACM (2009)
24. Fogg, B.J., Hreha, J.: Behavior wizard: a method for matching target behaviors with solutions. In: Ploug, T., Hasle, P., Oinas-Kukkonen, H. (eds.) Persuasive Technology: 5th International Conference, PERSUASIVE 2010, Copenhagen, Denmark, June 7–10, 2010. Proceedings, pp. 117–131. Springer Berlin Heidelberg, Berlin, Heidelberg (2010). https://doi.org/10.1007/978-3-642-13226-1_13
25. Oinas-Kukkonen, H., Harjumaa, M.: Persuasive systems design: key issues, process model, and system features. Commun. Assoc. Inf. Syst. **24**, 28 (2009)
26. Michie, S., Johnston, M., Francis, J., Hardeman, W., Eccles, M.: From theory to intervention: mapping theoretically derived behavioural determinants to behaviour change techniques. Appl. Psychol. **57**, 660–680 (2008)
27. Fishbein, M., Triandis, H.C., Kanfer, F.H., Becker, M., Middlestadt, S.E.: Factors influencing behavior and behavior change (2000)
28. Michie, S., Johnston, M.: Behavior change techniques. In: Encyclopedia of Behavioral Medicine, pp. 182–187. Springer, Heidelberg (2013)
29. Michie, S., Johnston, M.: Theories and Techniques of Behaviour Change: Developing a Cumulative Science of Behaviour Change. Taylor & Francis, Milton Park (2012)
30. Orji, R., Moffatt, K.: Persuasive technology for health and wellness: State-of-the-art and emerging trends. Health Inf. J. **24**(1), 66–91 (2016). https://doi.org/10.1177/1460458216650979
31. Torning, K.: A review of four persuasive design models. Int. J. Concept. Struct. Smart Appl. IJCSSA **1**, 17–27 (2013)
32. Mann, C.J.: Observational research methods. research design II: cohort, cross sectional, and case-control studies. Emerg. Med. J. **20**(1), 54–60 (2003). https://doi.org/10.1136/emj.20.1.54
33. Cash, P.J., Hartlev, C.G., Durazo, C.B.: Behavioural design: a process for integrating behaviour change and design. Des. Stud. **48**, 96–128 (2017)
34. Fogg, B.J.: Persuasive Technology: Using Computers to Change What We Think and Do (Interactive Technologies) (2002)
35. Kaptein, M., De Ruyter, B., Markopoulos, P., Aarts, E.: Adaptive persuasive systems: a study of tailored persuasive text messages to reduce snacking. ACM Trans. Interact. Intell. Syst. TiiS. **2**, 10 (2012)

36. Lazer, D., et al.: Life in the network: the coming age of computational social science. Sci. N. Y. NY. **323**, 721 (2009)
37. Kaptein, M.: Adaptive persuasive messages in an e-commerce setting: the use of persuasion profiles. In: ECIS, p. 183 (2011)

Analyzing and Prioritizing Usability Issues in Games

Umair Rehman[1]([✉]), Amir Zaib Abbasi[2], Muhammad Umair Shah[3],
Amna Idrees[4], Hassan Ilahi[5], and Helmut Hlavacs[6]

[1] User Experience Design, Wilfrid Laurier University, Brantford, ON, Canada
urehman@wlu.ca
[2] Faculty of Management Sciences, Shaheed Zulfiqar Ali Bhutto Institute
of Science and Technology (SZABIST), Islamabad, Pakistan
[3] Management Sciences, University of Waterloo, Waterloo, ON, Canada
[4] Systems Design Engineering, University of Waterloo, Waterloo, ON, Canada
[5] Department of Psychology, University of Waterloo, Waterloo, ON, Canada
[6] Research Group Entertainment Computing,
University of Vienna, Vienna, Austria

Abstract. Identifying and addressing usability issues is a vital part of improving player experiences in games. This paper delves into different methods that can be applied to shortlist usability issues in games. We specifically discuss observational studies, think-aloud protocols, questionnaires, surveys, user interviews, focus groups, and heuristic evaluations. The paper also discusses approaches to prioritize usability issues in games through severity ratings. Severity ratings allow researchers to prioritize issues in terms of their impact on player experience and other factors, including business goals, cost of redesigns, etc. We also discuss how the player's usability data can be analyzed using different approaches. Next, we discuss sources of biases in usability studies, ways of determining optimal sample size and approaches to reducing evaluator effect. Finally, we describe approaches to ideating design solutions to address usability concerns in games.

Keywords: Usability issues in games · Severity rating · Game user researchers methods

1 Usability Issues in Game User Research

Usability is defined as a system's capacity to allow a user to accomplish a task safely, effectively, and efficiently [1]. Usability related problems are termed usability issues [2]. One of the most integral parts of optimizing a User Experience (UX) is identifying and addressing usability issues. While studies related to identifying usability issues generally focus on productivity-oriented information systems (IS), usability issues are also present for hedonic forms of IS, such as digital games [3, 4].

Therefore, game user researchers commonly apply usability testing to uncover usability issues and improve player experiences. It is essential to identify usability issues in hedonic forms of IS because these issues negatively affect UX and often lead

© Springer Nature Switzerland AG 2021
X. Fang (Ed.): HCII 2021, LNCS 12789, pp. 110–118, 2021.
https://doi.org/10.1007/978-3-030-77277-2_9

to undesirable outcomes. Insights from usability tests can inform game developers and designers about aspects of the game that require improvement.

The process of identifying and addressing usability issues in games is iterative. The process generally involves identifying a usability issue, evaluating its origin or cause, and making design changes to resolve it [4]. The process may also involve classifying a product's positive aspect to ensure that such features are not lost during redesigns. To avoid confusion, results from usability tests are often referred to as usability findings. This paper will review topics associated with identifying, measuring, and prioritizing usability issues in games.

2 Methods of Capturing Usability Issues in Games

There are different methods that can be applied to capture usability issues in games. These methods generally stem from the broad fields of human-computer interaction, UX research and design, and human factors [5]. The methods we will be discussing in this section include observational studies, think-aloud protocols, questionnaires, surveys, user interviews, focus groups, and heuristic evaluations.

Observation studies can either take place in a lab or naturalistic settings [6]. Lab environments are generally easier to be controlled by the designer. However, lab studies can lead to the "Hawthorne Effect," resulting in players acting unnaturally. Naturalistic observations occur in natural environments, such as gaming cafes, e-sport events, player homes, etc. Naturalistic observation can offer more authentic details regarding player behavior, but at the same time, it can be challenging to anticipate unforeseen issues. It is crucial for researchers to remember that observations must not turn into the analysis. Observational studies should be limited to watching, recording, and reporting usability issues. It is recommended that observations occur before discussions with other researchers to avoid experimenter bias in behavioral data.

Think-aloud protocols allow researchers to infer usability concerns by capturing player narratives during gameplay [7, 8]. Two types of think-aloud protocols are applied in-game user research [9]. Concurrent think-aloud protocols simultaneously encourage users to verbalize their thoughts and feelings while they are being observed. On the other hand, in retrospective think-aloud protocols, participants are video recorded during game play. After the play session, participants are asked to verbalize their thoughts as they watch the video recording of their play session. The think-aloud protocol technique entails a certain degree of skill from players since they must respond naturally without compromising game performance. Think-aloud protocols allow researchers to gather information about what users are attempting to do, what steps they are taking to accomplish their goals, why they are taking these steps, what players expect from the game and how satisfied they are with their performance. Researchers can assess player responses to uncover usability issues that can later be addressed to augment player experiences.

Interviews are a standard process of qualitative inquiry that can provide direct insights into a player's usability-related concerns [10]. The quality of the data gathered during the interview session is often determined by the amount of information a participant discloses. Since interviews pave the way for follow-up questions, they can offer a significant amount of depth on the usability of a product. However, the process of data collection tends to take up a significant amount of time. Furthermore, uncovering patterns in data and fitting them into relevant themes can be cumbersome.

Surveys (or questionnaires) have become a standard user research method that allows researchers to collect significant amounts of self-reported data from a wide variety of players [3, 11, 12]. Usability surveys often consist of a Likert-scale or semantic differential scales that can uncover a range of usability issues. Surveys are generally administered after players have gone through a play session. Arguably, this process is less prone to bias in comparison to interviews. However, surveys-based approaches cannot capture the entire depth of player experiences. Also, surveys administered on small sample sizes can lead to confounding results. Therefore, surveys are generally applied on larger sample sizes, and its preferred that some survey participants are later interviewed to uncover additional insights.

Another standard method of qualitative inquiry is focus groups. Focus groups involve a group of players to discuss their feelings, views, and attitudes concerning usability issues in games [13, 14]. A moderator is usually present to support the discourse and steer the group towards topics of interest. A possible disadvantage of this approach is that the focus group at times gets dominated by only a few strong voices. This often prevents individual participants from providing feedback. Due to this limitation, focus groups are less frequently applied in usability studies.

The heuristic evaluation focuses on analyzing how a game design adheres to usability principles called "heuristics". Heuristic evaluation is widely considered to be a discount usability process. In this method, experts take into consideration a strict set of criteria when evaluating games. In this regard, a heuristic evaluation resembles a structured game review. Experts generally participate in gameplay and then offer feedback on whether the game adheres to the set heuristics. There are no unanimously agreed-upon criteria for game heuristics, and many authors have introduced different heuristics on different aspects of gameplay [15–19]. A significant drawback of conducting heuristics evaluation is that it can be challenging to find the relevant experts to carry out these tests.

3 Prioritizing Usability Issues in Games Through Severity Ratings

After identifying usability issues, it is necessary to prioritize them. Researchers need to understand if an issue is a mild annoyance, e.g., prolonged load time, or if it seriously affects the gamer experience, e.g., poor graphics. Researchers can determine the impact of an issue and the need to resolve it through severity ratings [20]. Using severity ratings, researchers can allocate time, attention, and resources to the most critical issues. Instead of having a long list of issues that will take considerable time and money to·fix, teams can focus on the most serious ones.

The severity of usability issues may be assessed in many different ways [21]. However mostly, there are two main ways to classify the severity of usability issues. The first focuses on only one factor, i.e., how the issue impacts the player experience. If it has a substantial impact on the player experience, it is a high severity issue.

The second focuses on a range of factors, including the business goals, the product goals, and the redesign costs.

A basic three-level severity rating can be applied in most situations – low, medium, and high severity. On occasion, there may also be a "catastrophe" level to indicate that the game is entirely unplayable.

Low severity ratings represent mild inconvenience or frustration, e.g., a player takes longer than usual to find relevant information. Medium severity ratings represent issues that cause significant distress or inconvenience; however, the player can still play the game. Such an issue will most likely impact the game experience. However, the magnitude of its impact on player satisfaction may not be substantial. Issues that are high severity impede players' ability to play at all. Such issues lead to a significant impact on the effectiveness, frustration, and enjoyment levels of the game.

Evaluators mostly uncover high-severity usability issues, whereas medium or low severity issues are often overlooked [22]. Some evaluators purposely neglect a few low severity issues due to the inconsequential effect it carries on the overall game experience. A limitation of using a three-level scale is that researchers may be reluctant to classify issues as "low severity" if they fear that the issue will be neglected during redesigns.

Some severity ratings are based on other factors, including the impact the issue has on player experience, combined with the business goals and its frequency. An example of this severity rating system was presented by Nielsen in 1993 [22]. While Nielsen's system combines only two different factors, user experience, and frequency of users experiencing the issue, additional factors can also be added depending on organizational goals and project requirements. For example, four possible factors may be combined in a severity rating system, as shown below:

- Impact on the game experience (0 = low, 1 = medium, 2 = high)
- Frequency of issue (0 = low, 1 = medium, 2 = high)
- Impact on business goals (0 = low, 1 = medium, 2 = high)
- Cost of redesign (0 = low, 1 = medium, 2 = high).

By adding each factor's scores, researchers can assess the overall impact of the issue, ranging from 0 to 8. While most severity ratings focus on one dimension, i.e., the impact on the game experience, other dimensions must also be considered in the evaluation process.

The same severity rating system can be used across multiple research studies. Multiple studies allow researchers to run comparative analysis to determine whether the design changes resulted in enhancing the player experience. This also helps the researchers make their case for redesigns to other stakeholders, e.g., senior managers. The severity levels must be clearly defined so that the categorization of issues is as accurate as possible. The researcher should also describe each level in sufficient detail with potential examples to explain each level.

While severity ratings may not be the most accurate priority measures, they are better than decisions being taken upon the discretion of individual game developers. Severity ratings at times may reflect a game user researcher biases more than variables that need to be assessed, e.g., game experience, business goal, etc. This is known as the evaluator effect [23], so it is recommended that more than one researcher assign severity ratings to ensure maximum objectivity.

4 Analyzing Usability Issues in Games

Once the researcher has identified the issue and assigned a priority level to it, the next step is to analyze these issues. The researcher may choose from a range of approaches to analyze the issue based on what they are trying to investigate.

4.1 Issues on Average Per Player

Usability issues may also be measured by how many issues each player faces on average. This allows the researcher to study the average number of issues per participant. This metric can also be combined with other metrics, e.g., frequency of unique issues or severity ratings.

4.2 Number of Players

Another approach to analyzing usability issues is calculating the number of players experiencing a specific problem. This metric is best suited to studying specific game design elements instead of the overall usability. The researcher can focus on if the frequency of players experiencing the issue changes across design variants. This metric can also be used in combination with other metrics, e.g., severity ratings. For example, the researcher may choose to focus only on high-severity issues.

4.3 Issues Per Category

The researcher may make categories with goal to uncover novel usability issues. These categories may refer to certain areas or aspects of the game, e.g., storyline, immersion, playability, and interaction. It is recommended that the researcher defines the categories as clearly as possible to make interpretation easier for stakeholders. The categories should ideally be limited to three or eight groups to avoid confusion.

4.4 Issues Present in Each Task Activity

Researchers can analyze usability by looking at which task activities are most problematic from a UX standpoint. Issues present in each task activity can be measured by calculating the number of unique issues per task activity. This will highlight the tasks that need to be reviewed and redesigned. Again, this may be done in combination with other metrics, e.g., severity ratings. For example, the researchers may identify the number of high-severity issues that occur while a user performs each task.

5 Biases in Usability Issues

It's critical to acknowledge that usability data can be biased [24]; however, understanding, acknowledging, and minimizing the bias in usability studies can improve the authenticity of the results. The primary sources of biases in usability studies could be due to the following factors: player/participants, task-related instructions and research method, functionality level, environment, and moderators.

Every player differs in terms of expertise, domain knowledge, and motivation to play the game. Also, players react differently to different aspects of the game, e.g., some game players may not be comfortable with violence in first-person shooter games, whereas others might be totally fine. These individual differences can influence the nature of the results.

Task-related instructions for a play session may be pre-defined, or these instructions may be introduced impromptu during a play session. The nature and extent of task-related instructions provided to the participants will influence the research results. Furthermore, the method chosen to evaluate a game affects the data obtained, e.g., traditional lab testing versus unmoderated testing, length of study, etc.

The level of functionality (fidelity) of a game will determine the type and quality of interaction that a user will have, e.g., fully functional versus semi-functional prototype. Therefore, games of different functionality levels will variably influence usability test results.

The player environment can also significantly impact usability test results, e.g., playtesting in-home, in a laboratory setting, or at a game cafe, etc. Other factors, including the seating, lighting, and presence of observers, can also impact the usability test results. Lastly, the moderator's level of expertise, knowledge, attitude, and presence can impact player performance and influence usability test results. Researchers' preconceived ideas can also influence the interpretations of the findings.

6 Sample Size and Evaluator Effect

There is limited research discussing the optimal number of participants in-game user research studies [25–27]. A prominent school of thought believes that having 5 participants is enough to find 80% usability issues [26]. For this reason, it is referred to as the "magic number 5." The context behind this comes from a mathematical formula that calculates the probability of a usability issue being discovered by a single user. Their research indicates that a single user will, on average, identify 30% of a product's total usability issues. This mathematical formula assumes that each usability issue has the same probability of getting discovered. Therefore, it can be inferred that one participant will identify 30% of the problems. The percentage of issues identified increases as the number of participants increases. After the fifth participant, 83% of the usability issues are generally identified.

Other than the sample size, the evaluator effect may influence test results. A critical perspective to consider is the evaluators' expertise, especially when conducting heuristic evaluations. Previous studies indicate the number and set of usability issues will vary for different evaluators [23, 28]. The evaluator effect has also been explored in the context of video games [29]. While the evaluator effect may not be eliminated, it is recommended to invite as many evaluators as possible, to maintain objectivity in usability findings.

7 Ideating

While uncovering usability issues, it's critical to think about possible solutions [30]. The ideation stage focuses on idea generation to address usability issues. These ideas are created as a result of questioning, e.g., why did the player experience this issue. The goal is to generate as many ideas as possible, refine them, and narrow down the most relevant ones. In terms of the thought process, researchers should ideally think as far and wide as possible in terms of coming up with design solutions to address game usability issues.

Design changes in games should conform to players' mental models [31]. Mental models here refer to beliefs held by the players concerning a game. Mental models are formulated by the combination of existing knowledge in memory and information perceived while interacting with elements of the interface.

Player mental models are not easy to change. For new games, the mental models of the players are not adequately structured, which impacts usability and player experience. For new games, players usually shift expectations that they have built around familiar games. This is a reason why certain game companies are hesitant in making drastic design changes to newer versions.

Understanding how mental models work can ease the ideation process. A considerable number of usability issues in games arise due to poorly formed mental models, which lead players to misperceive various game components. When developing an idea, researchers should either align with the players' pre-existing mental model or change the way the players think so that players correctly understand the new design.

It's also essential for researchers to channel creative energy and innovative thinking into the development of game design solutions. This helps expand the space for solutions, pushing the design team to think beyond the standard or obvious methods of problem-solving. This further leads to the development of more sophisticated and efficient solutions to usability issues that impact player experience.

A game designer can choose a top-down or a bottom-up approach when ideating solutions to usability issues. Top-down approach starts with the big picture first; the designer first aims to address a broad-focused usability concern, and later addresses multiple narrow-focused usability issues. Bottom-up approach requires piecing together multiple narrow-focused issues to formulate one overarching broad-focused usability concern. A designer should adopt a top-down approach if the primary usability concern is easily identifiable from the user data. If multiple smaller usability issues are available first, then bottom-up approach is more appropriate.

8 Conclusion

Identification of usability issues is a vital part of improving player experiences in games. Usability testing can help researchers assess whether the game is satisfying or frustrating to play and whether the overall experience has improved across design iterations. Severity ratings allow researchers to prioritize issues in terms of their impact on player experience and other factors, including business goals, cost of redesigns, etc. After the researcher has collected metrics for usability issues, they may analyze these ratings using different approaches, including issues on average per participant, issues per category, etc. Many factors may introduce bias into the usability test results. It is essential to consider these factors before carrying out a study to reduce the possibility of bias. For example, researchers need to maintain consistency when developing task-related instructions for participants, choosing the appropriate venue to conduct the usability study, and shortlisting the relevant usability metrics. Consistency across studies will also allow researchers to run comparative evaluations against different design variants of the game with the goal to uncover whether newer variants improve player experience. Lastly, the number of participants for a usability test depends on the specific needs of the study. There are different schools of thought that recommend five or more than five participants for each study. The optimal number of participants for a specific study may change depending on the nature and conditions of the research.

References

1. Bevana, N., Kirakowskib, J., Maissela, J.: What is usability. In: Proceedings of the 4th International Conference on HCI. Citeseer (1991)
2. Bevan, N.: Usability issues in web site design. In: HCI, no. 2. pp. 803–806 (1997)
3. Olsen, T., Procci, K., Bowers, C.: Serious games usability testing: How to ensure proper usability, playability, and effectiveness. In: Marcus, A. (ed.) DUXU 2011. LNCS, vol. 6770, pp. 625–634. Springer, Heidelberg (2011). https://doi.org/10.1007/978-3-642-21708-1_70
4. Alshamari, M., Mayhew, P.: Technical review: current issues of usability testing. IETE Tech. Rev. **26**, 402–406 (2009)
5. Dumas, J.S., Dumas, J.S., Redish, J.: A Practical Guide to Usability Testing. Intellect books, Bristol (1999)
6. Baker, L.: Observation: a complex research method. Libr. Trends. **55**, 171–189 (2006)
7. Eveland, W.P., Jr., Dunwoody, S.: Examining information processing on the World Wide Web using think aloud protocols. Media Psychol. **2**, 219–244 (2000)
8. Olmsted-Hawala, E.L., Murphy, E.D., Hawala, S., Ashenfelter, K.T.: Think-aloud protocols: a comparison of three think-aloud protocols for use in testing data-dissemination web sites for usability. In: Proceedings of the SIGCHI Conference on Human Factors in Computing Systems, pp. 2381–2390 (2010)
9. Van Den Haak, M., De Jong, M., Jan Schellens, P.: Retrospective vs. concurrent think-aloud protocols: testing the usability of an online library catalogue. Behav. Inf. Technol. **22**, 339–351 (2003)
10. Kuniavsky, M.: Observing the User Experience: A Practitioner's Guide to User Research. Elsevier, Amsterdam (2003)

11. Moizer, J., et al.: An approach to evaluating the user experience of serious games. Comput. Educ. **136**, 141–151 (2019)
12. Brühlmann, F., Mekler, E.D.: Surveys in games user research. Games User Res., 141–162 (2018).
13. Gibbs, A.: Focus groups. Soc. Res. Update **19**, 1–8 (1997)
14. Langford, J.: Focus Groups: Supporting Effective Product Development. CRC Press, Boca Raton (2002)
15. Pinelle, D., Wong, N., Stach, T.: Heuristic evaluation for games: usability principles for video game design. In: Proceedings of the SIGCHI Conference on Human Factors in Computing Systems, pp. 1453–1462 (2008)
16. Federoff, M.A.: Heuristics and usability guidelines for the creation and evaluation of fun in video games (2002)
17. Desurvire, H., Wiberg, C.: Game usability heuristics (PLAY) for evaluating and designing better games: The next iteration. In: Ant Ozok, A., Zaphiris, P. (eds.) OCSC 2009. LNCS, vol. 5621, pp. 557–566. Springer, Heidelberg (2009). https://doi.org/10.1007/978-3-642-02774-1_60
18. Korhonen, H., Koivisto, E.M.: Playability heuristics for mobile games. In: Proceedings of the 8th Conference on Human-Computer Interaction with Mobile Devices and Services, pp. 9–16 (2006)
19. Pinelle, D., Wong, N., Stach, T., Gutwin, C.: Usability heuristics for networked multiplayer games. In: Proceedings of the ACM 2009 International Conference on Supporting Group Work, pp. 169–178 (2009)
20. Hertzum, M.: Problem prioritization in usability evaluation: from severity assessments toward impact on design. Int. J. Hum.-Comput. Interact. **21**, 125–146 (2006)
21. Desurvire, H., Caplan, M., Toth, J.A.: Using heuristics to evaluate the playability of games. In: CHI'04 extended abstracts on Human Factors in Computing Systems, pp. 1509–1512 (2004)
22. Albert, W., Tullis, T.: Measuring the User Experience: Collecting, Analyzing, and Presenting Usability Metrics. Newnes (2013)
23. Jacobsen, N.E., Hertzum, M., John, B.E.: The evaluator effect in usability tests. In: CHI 98 Conference Summary on Human Factors in Computing Systems, pp. 255–256 (1998)
24. Natesan, D., Walker, M., Clark, S.: Cognitive bias in usability testing. In: Proceedings of the International Symposium on Human Factors and Ergonomics in Health Care, pp. 86–88. SAGE Publications, Los Angeles (2016.
25. Faulkner, L.: Beyond the five-user assumption: benefits of increased sample sizes in usability testing. Behav. Res. Methods Instrum. Comput. **35**, 379–383 (2003)
26. Turner, C.W., Lewis, J.R., Nielsen, J.: Determining usability test sample size. Int. Encycl. Ergon. Hum. Factors. **3**, 3084–3088 (2006)
27. Lewis, J.R.: Sample sizes for usability studies: additional considerations. Hum. Factors. **36**, 368–378 (1994)
28. Hertzum, M., Jacobsen, N.E.: The evaluator effect: a chilling fact about usability evaluation methods. Int. J. Hum.-Comput. Interact. **13**, 421–443 (2001)
29. White, G.R., Mirza-Babaei, P., McAllister, G., Good, J.: Weak inter-rater reliability in heuristic evaluation of video games. In: CHI'11 Extended Abstracts on Human Factors in Computing Systems, pp. 1441–1446 (2011)
30. Dell'Era, C., Magistretti, S., Cautela, C., Verganti, R., Zurlo, F.: Four kinds of design thinking: from ideating to making, engaging, and criticizing. Creat. Innov. Manag. **29**, 324–344 (2020)
31. Boyan, A., Sherry, J.L.: The challenge in creating games for education: aligning mental models with game models. Child Dev. Perspect. **5**, 82–87 (2011)

The Design of Buttons in MMO Mobile Game's Battle Interface

Si-Si Yuan, Jia-sheng Hu, Zun-gui Lu, Zhang-jian Wei,
and Zhi-peng Hu[✉]

NetEase Games, 599 Wangshang Road, Hangzhou 310052, China
hzyuanss@corp.netease.com

Abstract. This study investigates the relationship between both-hand input area and time delay before effective inputs, the relationship between button size and hit accuracy, as well as the influence of button size on users' perception of the ease of button touching despite the size of the touchable area. The lower-left-hand area with x coordinates between 28 mm to 36 mm is the optimal input area for left the hand and the lower-right-hand area with x coordinates between 30 mm to 40 mm is the most ideal input area for the right hand. The input area with a time delay of 400 ms on the right is slightly larger than the one on the left. When the button with a diameter of 9 mm is placed in the lower-right-hand corner with a x coordinate between 20 mm–50 mm, we can expect a hit rate of 90%. Users' perception of how easy a button is to touch is mainly related to the button size instead of the size of the touchable area. These findings provide a reference for designing buttons in landscape-orientation MMO mobile games and quantitative suggestions for the sizes of touch input area and button in landscape-orientation MMO mobile games. Based on these insights, game producers and designers can create better user experience for MMO mobile games' battle interface.

Keywords: Button design · MMO · Mobile game

1 Introduction

Since 2011, smartphones became increasingly popular around the world. Fueled by the upgrade of the cellular network, mobile games have been developing rapidly.

MMO mobile games gained their popularity after the configurations of mobile phones were brought to a higher level in 2015. According to Zhao, X [1], in the first half of 2020, the actual sales revenue of China's game market was 139.493 billion yuan, up 22.34% year-on-year, and the scale of game users was nearly 660 million people, up 1.97% year-on-year, i.e. an increase of about 12.71 million people. In 2015, mobile game *Honor of Kings* was launched, adopting the primary operation mode of double touch controls (see Fig. 1).

Along with the advancement of MMO mobile games, the double touch controls mode underwent the trial and error within the industry over the years. Nowadays, its fundamental layout has been determined and accepted. In these MMO mobile games,

X. Fang (Ed.): HCII 2021, LNCS 12789, pp. 119–132, 2021.
https://doi.org/10.1007/978-3-030-77277-2_10

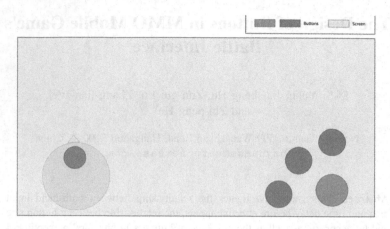

Fig. 1. Double touch controls in *Honor of Kings*

users manipulate the left virtual joystick to move in the game and touch attack/skill buttons on the right-hand side to combat with other characters.

Nevertheless, many MMO mobile games in the Chinese Top 100 Popular Chart are faced with a range of usability issues. Most of the issues center around the design of the buttons, including the way-too-small button size and inconvenient button location for touching.

Mobile devices largely reply on users' touch inputs, and thus researchers such as Im, Kim, and Jung [2] as well as Travis and Murano [3] have been paying close attention to the application of Touch User Interface (TUI). However, related research regarding mobile games remains limited, even though the design guidelines for buttons in frequently-used game interfaces are much needed in the industry. For this reason, we reckon it is urgent to conduct a deeper research into the size, location, and touchable area of buttons in MMO mobile games' battle interface, and provide a recommended area for button layout and design.

We, in the context of battle interface in landscape-orientation MMO mobile games, mainly investigated, 1) the relationship between both-hand input area and time delay before effective input; 2) the relationship between button size and accuracy of touch input; and 3) the influence of different button sizes on the perception of user' feelings despite the same touchable area size. The results of the study can provide a valuable reference for game designers and the academia.

The contribution of this study includes, 1) identification of the screen area with a relatively low time delay before effective touch input in MMO mobile games; 2) suggestion of the minimum size for the button with a 90% hit rate after calculations; and 3) evidence that users' perception towards the ease of touching a button mainly depends on the button size instead of its touchable area.

This paper is consisted of six parts. The second part briefly reviews the earlier studies and stands as a basis for our research into the button design of landscape-orientation MMO mobile games. The third part contains the first experiment regarding the relationship between touch input area and time delay before successful inputs as well as the relationship between the size of touchable area and user' accuracy of touch inputs. The fourth part explains how we investigated the influence of different button sizes on users' perceptions towards the ease of button touching despite the touchable area of the button. The fifth part proposes further suggestions based on our study. And the last part is the conclusion of our findings in this research followed by the potential contribution to the related field of study.

2 Related Work

We reviewed earlier research in two areas including button design for mobile touch-screen device and game experience design.

Some important design elements, such as button size and spacing between buttons, have been investigated by Chen and others [4]. Buttons in most of the mobile applications are square [5]. Users generally prefer buttons that can yield optimal input performance [6]. Furthermore, research related to touch accuracy has revealed that UI designers would accept the results with accuracy greater than 90% [7]. These researchers' findings are very valuable for subsequent studies, and will allow us to quickly verify the validity of our own findings.

Unlike most of the other mobile applications, games largely depend on their user experience rather than the functionality [8]. In recent years, researchers have applied various scientific methods to research on mobile games [9], and have also conducted research on experience design for games [10]. Many researchers have put forward some useful design methods and theories for games.

The types of games in nowadays' game industry are segmented, but the funda-mental interface of different games is similar and commonly used. Hence, it is worthwhile to study the size and location of the buttons that are most suitable for these interfaces.

3 First Experiment

3.1 Purpose

The first experiment was designed to determine the best areas on touchscreen to position buttons (which is indicated by the short time delay before users' effective touch inputs) in landscape-orientation MMO mobile games from the perspective of human computer interaction. Besides, we also wanted to find out the size of the touchable area for buttons that can help the users achieve the highest input accuracy in certain mobile games.

3.2 Participants

In this experiment, 20 volunteers with 20/20 vision—after or without correction—were selected as subjects. These volunteers were recruited through surveys distributed in video games. We followed the Institutional Review Board (IRB) protocols during the whole experiment to protect the rights and welfare of the participants.

To rule out the potential difference led to by gender factor, 10 subjects were male and the others were female. The age of the subjects ranged from 21 to 30, with an average age of 26.2 and their lengths of palm spanned from 154 mm to 206 mm, with an average of 179.3 mm and a standard deviation of 12.9 mm.

Besides, we looked into the gaming abilities and habits of the participants to control the variable of their proficiency in taking relevant tasks. All subjects were regular users of mobile games with an average experience of 31.5 months. They all had no difficulty in moving their hands nor musculoskeletal diseases. Therefore, there was little inherent difference in their abilities to perform tasks related to touch inputs.

3.3   Apparatus

The touchscreen device used for this experiment was a VIVO X20Plus of which the display size was 6.43 inches. Additionally, the length, width, and thickness of the device were 165.32 mm, 80.09 mm, and 7.45 mm respectively. The device had a color LCD and a display resolution of 2160 * 1080 pixels (see Fig. 2).

The interface for the experiment was developed using the C# programming language which has been widely adopted to develop mobile applications.

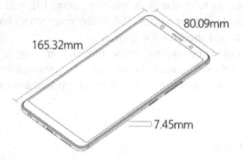

Fig. 2. Specs for experimental touchscreen device

3.4   Experimental Design

Our preliminary research focused on the button layout in landscape-orientation MMO mobile games, including the ideal button locations and sizes. We, with controllability and consistency with users' input habits as the reference, studied a number of landscape-view MMO mobile games with large user group that ranked highest in the Chinese App Store. According to the data as of January 4th, 2020, our list included more than 20 mobile games such as *Honor of Kings, Moonlight Blade, Ghost, Sword Heroes' Fate*, and *Onmyoji Arena*.

Based on the research into the mobile games mentioned above, we identified a pattern that the joystick and attack/skill buttons are usually isolated and placed on two sides, and that these buttons are generally in the shape of circles. Specifically, the size of the left joystick is between 10 mm to 15 mm, while the size of attack button and skill button ranges from 10 mm to 15 mm and 5 mm to 11mm respectively. On the basis of these findings, we defined the size of the round buttons in our experiment as integers between 5 mm to 15 mm. Buttons of various sizes appeared on the screen randomly and the whole button was touchable. Participants needed to touch the button within one second after each button showed up, or it would disappear automatically. If the participant failed to touch a specific button precisely and successfully, this attempt would be recorded as an error. There was one second between two buttons' appearance so that the participants could return their hands to the default device-holding position.

The combination of the coordinates and the size of the button is the independent variable; and the time delay before participant's effective touch input and the accuracy of the input are considered as the dependent variables in this experiment.

3.5   Task and Procedure

The primary task for the first experiment required participants' touch inputs on the screen. Each target button only appeared once and the size of it was between 5 mm to 15 mm. The position of each circular button was random and there were 500 times in total for each participate to touch a series of buttons with a one-second interval between two buttons' appearance (see Fig. 3).

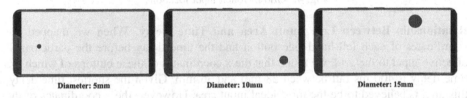

Diameter: 5mm   Diameter: 10mm   Diameter: 15mm

Fig. 3. Demonstration of the experiment interface

Before each task, we explained to the participant the purpose of the study, the task required to be performed, and relevant cautionary points during the task. Then, we asked for their consent to perform this task. Afterwards, the participant would enter the laboratory, sit in a comfortable chair, and hold the touchscreen device just as how they usually played the landscape-orientation mobile games. During the experiment, all target buttons showed up on the screen randomly as programmed. Each participant used their thumbs as the medium for touch inputs. Furthermore, each participant was given five minutes' break after every 100 touch inputs until they complete all of the 500 inputs.

3.6   Results

We collected 8,000 input data from the experiment. A grid constituted of 6 × 6 mm squares was created with the longer side of the touchscreen device as the x-axis and the shorter side as the y-axis. Each button location was depicted as a dot with a set of x coordinate and y coordinate and then mapped on the grid for us to track the relationship between the button's location and the time delay before the effective touch input (see Fig. 4). These dots concentrated on the two sides of the grid—one on the left-hand side and the other on the right—because in most of the popular MMO mobile games, joystick button is placed on the left-hand side and attack/skill buttons are positioned on the right.

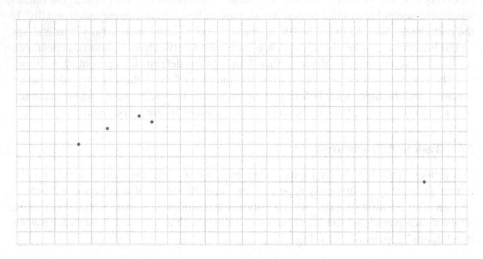

Fig. 4. Grid of touch input locations

Relationship Between Left Input Area and Time Delay. When we mapped the coordinates of each left-hand-side button and the time delay before the participants' effective input to the grid, we found that the x coordinates of these buttons of which the time delay is 400 ms fall between 28 mm and 36 mm. Given the shortest time delay, this area is believed to be the most ideal input area. However, the x coordinates of the buttons of which the time delay is greater than 500 ms fall on the left of 20 mm and on the right of 44 mm (see Fig. 5).

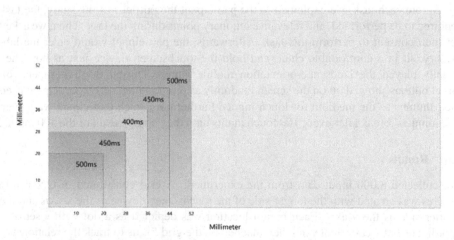

Fig. 5. Relationship between left touch input area and time delay

Relationship Between Right Input Area and Time Delay. We continued to study the relationship between right-hand-side input area and the time delay. Similarly, the x coordinates of the time delay of 400 ms fall between 30 mm and 40 mm, which is considered as the optimal input area. The secondary input area that is recommended spans from 20 mm to 30 mm on the x axis with a time delay of 450 ms. However, the area of which the x coordinates are less than 20 mm and greater than 50 mm is not recommended for frequently-used buttons because the time delay is longer than 500 ms (see Fig. 6).

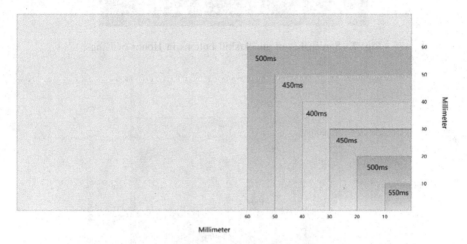

Fig. 6. Relationship between right touch input area and time delay

Comparison and Variance. After comparing these two graphs above, we noticed that the right-hand-side input area with a time delay of 400 ms is slightly larger than the one on the left, which probably can be explained by the general right-hand dexterity among the users.

Additionally, we mapped the attack/skill buttons of *Honor of Kings* (see Fig. 7) to the grid generated above. We found that the attack button is located in the x coordinate range of 20 mm to 30 mm and the skill buttons are between 20 mm and 50 mm (see Fig. 8).

In *Honor of Kings*, skill buttons are placed around the area with 400–450 ms time delay instead of completely in the optimal input area in order to avoid sheltering the in-game battle scenes.

Button Size and Input Accuracy. In this experiment, the hit rate was defined as the number of effective inputs divided by the count of all of the attempted inputs. Then, we calculated the average of accuracy based on the diameter of the buttons. Relevant research has revealed that it is desired by game UI designers when the hit rate is greater than 90% [7]. According to our experiment, when the diameter of the skill buttons is 9 mm, we can expect a hit rate of 90% (see Table 1).

Fig. 7. Screenshot of attack/skill buttons in Honor of Kings

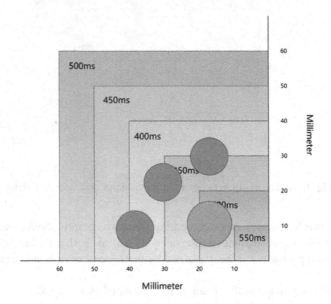

Fig. 8. Relationship of attack/skill button location and time delay in *Honor of Kings*

Table 1. Relationship between button size and accuracy of pressing skill buttons

Diameter (mm)	5	6	7	8	9	10	11	12	13	14	15
Accuracy (%)	57	73	80	85	90	90	93	94	98	99	95

As the skill button area needs to be slightly skewed to the lower right corner, attack button should be skewed to that position accordingly. Thus, it is placed in the area of 450–500 ms time delay. To neutralize the influence of longer time delay, the attack button should be reasonably enlarged. According to the study, when the diameter of the attack button reaches 10 mm, we can expect a hit rate of 90% and above (see Table 2).

Table 2. Relationship between button size and accuracy of pressing attack button

Diameter (mm)	5	6	7	8	9	10	11	12	13	14	15
Accuracy (%)	56	72	80	84	89	91	92	91	94	96	100

4 Second Experiment

4.1 Purpose

The second experiment examined users' feelings towards the situation when button sizes are different yet touchable areas remain the same. This study can give the game designers a leverage to determine the button size and touchable area in the game interface, as well as present a design guide for TUI developers and designers. The whole experiment is based on the hypothesis that most of the users perceive the touchable area of the button in mobile games as the button itself, and that when the button size decreases but the touchable area is unchanged, users still have a feeling that the button becomes harder to touch.

4.2 Participants

We recruited 7 males and 7 females as participants for this experiment. All of them had a corrected (if needed) visual acuity of 20/20 and above. The average ages for the males and females were 25.3 and 23.9 years old respectively. The length of palm ranged from 170 mm to 195 mm with an average of 182.8 mm and a standard deviation of 7.29 mm.

Furthermore, they all were regular users of mobile games with an average experience of 29.2 months.

4.3 Experimental Design

In 2020, *Ghost Mobile* redesigned the buttons in its interface. All the skill buttons were downsized from a diameter of 9.3 mm to 8.3 mm while the size of their touchable areas remained untouched. After the launch of the redesigned version, the development team received a large number of users' feedbacks mentioning that the smaller buttons led to frequent maloperations or completing missing the buttons. For example, a user told the team, "the redesigned buttons are so small that I always touched the wrong ones," and another user also complained, "it's so annoying that I frequently touched other buttons by mistake because the new buttons appear too small for my thick thumb." Although the touchable area never changed, users believed only the visible part of the button was touchable, and thus users developed a feeling that it was more difficult to touch the redesigned buttons precisely. Besides, the change of the button location also had a relatively great influence on users' habits of playing the game.

Hence, we designed two demos for the experiment: one with *Ghost Mobile*'s original button size and touchable area, and the other with the redesigned ones. The independent variables of these two demos were button size, touchable area size, and coordinates of the center of the skill button (see Table 3). The coordinates of the center of these circular buttons and their touchable area were completely the same but the only difference was the size of their button size. In Demo A, all buttons were circles with a diameter of 9.3 mm and the diameter of the touchable area was 9.3 mm, while in Demo B, the diameter of the buttons was 8.3 mm and the touchable area was the same as in Demo A. The dependent variable was related to whether the participant felt the buttons were easy to touch or not. In this experiment, we recorded the participants' subjective feelings about which demo presented buttons that were easier to touch.

Table 3. Sizes of button and touchable area in Demo A and Demo B

	Button diameter (mm)	Touchable area diameter (mm)
Demo A	9.3	9.3
Demo B	8.3	9.3

4.4 Task and Procedure

The primary task in this experiment seeks to investigate how different button sizes influence participants' perception of a definite touchable area. Figure 9 demonstrates the hit/error recognition, touch button, and touchable area defined in Demo B.

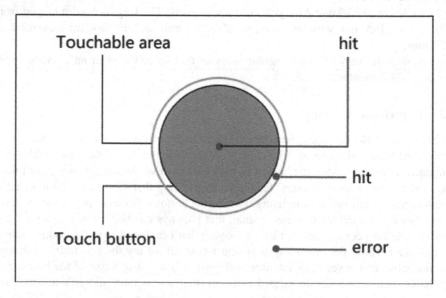

Fig. 9. Demonstration of interface in demo B

Fig. 10. Screenshot of demo A

Participants experienced two demos in the sequence of Demo A—Demo B—Demo B—Demo A, which consists with the Latin Square Design put forward by Bradley, J. V. [11].

In each round, participants were asked to touch the skill buttons on the right randomly for one minute. Figure 10 and Fig. 11 are the screenshots of the experiment interface in Demo A and Demo B respectively.

Fig. 11. Screenshot of demo B

The second experiment was carried out on a VIVO X20Plus with a 6.43-in. Super AMOLED and a resolution of 2160 × 1080 pixels (375 ppi).

Before the experiment, we informed the participants of the purpose, tasks, and other cautionary points related to this experiment. Participants' consents were obtained afterwards. Then, participants entered our laboratory, sit on a comfortable chair, and hold the experimental device as how they were used to playing landscape-orientation MMO mobile games. Throughout the experiment, the button size was fixed in each demo. Each participant used their right-hand thumb to randomly touch the target buttons. Furthermore, the inputs of each participant were consecutive.

4.5   Results

We collected 14 surveys from the second experiment. Based on this experiment, we learned that most of the participants (64.3%) found the buttons in Demo A easier to touch, while only 14.3% them chose Demo B. Additionally, 21.4 of the participants felt there was no significant difference in two demos (see Table 4).

Table 4. Survey result regarding the touchability of buttons in two demos

Choice	Count of participant	Percentage (%)
Demo A	9	64.3
Demo B	2	14.3
No significant difference	3	21.4

5   Discussion

As the mobile game industry is rapidly developing, it is worthwhile to pay more attention to the experience design of mobile games. Although many researches regarding the interaction design between human and mobile devices have been conducted, we noticed a lack of systemic design guide for the frequently-used interaction mode and the experience design of the interaction details in mobile games. We investigated the design of buttons in the battle interface of MMO mobile games and sincerely hope that there will be more research into other interfaces of mobile games. We need to outline some fundamental guidelines for the ever-evolving mobile games to ensure a good experience in these frequent-used features and interaction modes.

The second experiment stemmed from the users' feedbacks, received testification through two demos, and eventually proved the validity of our hypothesis. Thus, we encourage more game developers to pay close attention to their users' feedbacks and testify them from time to time.

6   Conclusion

This study, based on the battle interface of landscape-orientation MMO mobile games, investigated, 1) the relationship between both-hand input area and time delay; 2) the relationship between button size and accuracy of button touching; and 3) the influence of different button sizes on the perception of user' feelings despite the same touchable area size. Although not all of the experiment results matched our initial expectations, most of the findings proved the correctness of our hypotheses. These findings can provide valuable insights into the design of the interface of landscape-orientation MMO mobile games.

We drew the following conclusions from the two experiments we conducted (based on the device of VIVO X20Plus):

1. The optimal position for buttons in the lower left corner is the area with the x coordinates spanning from 28 mm to 36 mm as this will provide the highest input accuracy. If that cannot be achieved, we recommend the area with the x coordinates of 20 mm–28 mm and 36 mm–44 mm where the input accuracy is also acceptable. We discourage the placement of primary buttons in the lower-left-hand area with x coordinates less than 20 mm or above 44 mm.
2. The optimal position for buttons in the lower right corner is the area with the x coordinates spanning from 30 mm to 40 mm as this will provide the highest input accuracy. If that cannot be achieved, we recommend the area with the x coordinates of 20 mm–30 mm and 40 mm–50 mm where the input accuracy is also acceptable. We discourage the placement of primary buttons in the lower-right-hand area with x coordinates from 10 mm to 20 mm or from 50 mm to 60 mm.
3. The 400 ms time delay area for the right hand is slighter larger than that for the left hand which can probably explained by the general right-hand dexterity among the users.
4. When the button with a diameter of 9 mm is placed in the lower-right-hand corner with x coordinates from 20 mm to 50 mm, we can expect an ideal hit rate of 90% and above.
5. Given that the skill button area is usually slightly skewed to the lower right corner, attack button should be skewed to that position accordingly, leaving it in the area of 450–500 ms time delay. To neutralize the influence of longer time delay, the attack button should be reasonably enlarged. When the diameter of the attack button reaches 10 mm, we can expect a hit rate of 90% and above.
6. To avoid sheltering the battle scenes of the mobile games, the input area for skill buttons can be reasonably adjusted.
7. Users' perception towards the ease of button touching is based on the visible size of the button instead of the size of the touchable area.

This study can help the industry outline the design guidelines for landscape-orientation MMO mobile games and provide a number of quantitative evidences regarding the size of input area and button. With this in mind, game producers and designers can have a leverage in designing buttons in the MMO mobile games' battle interface with better user experience.

References

1. Zhao, X.Y.: The user scale of Chinese game market is nearly 660 million people in the first half of the year. High Technol. Ind. **291**(08), 1–9 (2020)
2. Im, Y., Kim, T., Jung, E.S.: Investigation of icon design and touchable area for effective smart phone controls. Human Fact. Ergon. Manuf. Serv. Ind. **25**(2), 251–267 (2015)
3. Travis, C., Murano, P.: A comparative study of the usability of touch-based and mouse-based interaction. Int. J. Perv. Comput. Commun. **10**(1), 115–134 (2014)
4. Chen, K.B., Savage, A.B., Chourasia, A.O., Wiegmann, D.A., Sesto, M.E.: Touch screen performance by individuals with and without motor control disabilities. Appl. Ergon. **44**(2), 297–302 (2013)
5. Chourasia, A.O., Wiegmann, D.A., Chen, K.B., Irwin, C.B., Sesto, M.E.: Effect of sitting or standing on touch screen performance and touch characteristics. Hum. Factors **55**(4), 789–802 (2013)
6. Tao, D., Yuan, J., Liu, S., Qu, X.: Effects of button design characteristics on performance and perceptions of touchscreen use. Int. J. Ind. Ergon. **64**, 59–68 (2018)
7. Park, Y.S., Han, S.H.: Touch key design for one-handed thumb interaction with a mobile phone: effects of touch key size and touch key location. Int. J. Ind. Ergon. **40**(1), 68–76 (2010). https://doi.org/10.1016/j.ergon.2009.08.002
8. Barnett, L., Harvey, C., Gatzidis, C.: First time user experiences in mobile games: an evaluation of usability. Entertain. Comput. **27**, 82–88 (2018). https://doi.org/10.1016/j.entcom.2018.04.004
9. Pappas, I., Mikalef, P., Giannakos, M., Kourouthanassis, P.: Explaining user experience in mobile gaming applications: an fsQCA approach. Internet Res. **29**(2), 293–314 (2019). https://doi.org/10.1108/IntR-12-2017-0479
10. Bostan, B. (ed.): Game User Experience And Player-Centered Design. ISCEMT, Springer, Cham (2020). https://doi.org/10.1007/978-3-030-37643-7
11. Bradley, J.V.: Complete counterbalancing of immediate sequential effects in a Latin square design. J. Am. Stat. Assoc. **53**(282), 525–528 (1958)

Research on the Quantization of User Experience of Spectator Mode in Moba Games

Zhigang Zhang, Hao Luo[(✉)], and Zi Zheng[(✉)]

NetEase Company, Hangzhou, People's Republic of China
{zhangzhigang, luohao1, zhengzi}@corp.netease.com

Abstract. In recent years, the MOBA games have been very popular all over the world, and more and more people have watched the MOBA games through the spectator mode in the game. However, compared with ordinary players participating in the game themselves, the needs of players spectating the game are inconsistent. There are usually 2 teams in a MOBA game, and everyone in the team has data such as blood volume, item volume and so on. These massive amounts of data put cognitive pressure on the players who spectate the game, which in turn affects the player's user experience. At present, the design and research of games is mainly based on personal experience and qualitative feedback of game designer. There are relatively few studies on how to quantitatively evaluate game user experience and the practical application of research results. Therefore, the quantitative experience of game user experience has high challenges and research value.

Based on the related theories of cognitive load and user experience quantification, this article takes the cognitive load generated by players spectating the game as the starting point to explore its impact on user experience. Through qualitative research and analysis, the influencing factors of the user experience of spectating the game of MOBA games are obtained. We use factor analysis to filter out the final impact factors, and construct a structural model of the user experience impact factors for MOBA game spectator mode. Next, with the help of analytic hierarchy process, the weights of each factor in the model are determined, and finally a user experience evaluation system for the MOBA game spectator mode is established, which provides valuable research ideas and methods for improving the design and optimization of the user experience in the spectating process.

Keywords: User experience · Spectator mode · MOBA games · User experience quantization

1 Introduction

With the development of the Internet technologies and the popularization of computers, the electronic game industry has developed rapidly, online games have become a popular way of leisure and entertainment. With their unique interests and playability, MOBA (Multiplayer Online Battle Arena, a subgenre of strategy games) games are gaining popularity among young people nowadays. Players control specific characters with unique abilities and are divided into two teams to compete against the other side

© Springer Nature Switzerland AG 2021
X. Fang (Ed.): HCII 2021, LNCS 12789, pp. 133–142, 2021.
https://doi.org/10.1007/978-3-030-77277-2_11

by achieving victory conditions such as destroying key buildings or eliminating enemy players. MOBA games can be traced back to the RTS games in the 1980s, and in the early 2000s, MOBA games became a separate category, gaining widespread popularity [1]. At present, "League of Legends" on PCs and "Honor of Kings" on phones are the typical representatives of MOBA games.

In addition to regular battles, in MOBA games, spectator mode is also an essential part of the gaming experience. Players can enjoy the lives or replays in their free time for entertainment or learning advanced skills, and this mode can also be seen in esports tournaments. In addition to the game scenes, the displayed content is different from regular games. While playing, the HUD mainly shows the information of our own side, especially the personal data, and the enemy's info is limited. However, in the spectator mode, all data is shown completely and fairly throughout the whole game, it can cater to the needs of various types of audiences. To maintain the legibility of the interface, some data for advanced players, such as skill cooldown time, will be hidden and can be called up manually when the player needs to know. Games have different spectator mode designs, but the main ideas of information presentation, which external performance is HUD, have some similarities. This article will take LOL's spectator mode interface as the research object, using factor analysis to explore its design method.

2   Method

Factor analysis is a branch of multivariate analysis, it is a technique that is used to reduce a large number of variables into fewer factors, and this method was developed initially by psychologists, from the theory of Spearman, Thomson, Thurstone, and Burt [2]. Exploratory and confirmatory are two types of factor analysis, both are based on the Common Factor Model, exploratory factor analysis (EFA) attempts to discover the nature of the constructs influencing a set of responses, while confirmatory factor analysis (CFA) tests whether a specified set of constructs is influencing responses in a predicted way [3]. The basic assumption of factor analysis is that for a collection of observed variables, there are a set of factors, which can explain the interrelationships among those variables.

Factor Analysis has both qualitative and quantitative research modes. The former model has been used to discuss how players see involvement with respect to how the game UI is presented between user interfaces [4], and the latter one helped to examine the dimensionality of presence and flow in the study of game immersion [5], or develop a user satisfaction measurement tool for game developers [6]. Factor Analysis is widely used in the game field and gamers: through the analysis of more than 450 games, the Game's User Experience Satisfaction Scale has been built, which can be used to evaluate user satisfaction with different types of video Games for various users [7]. And this method is also suitable to dig into one game, such as finding the relationship between game addiction and gamer motivations [8].

This study will complete two sets of experiments, using the factor analysis method, from both qualitative and quantitative perspectives, to study how game interface elements affect the player's user experience in the spectator mode [9].

3   Experiment 1

This research mainly uses two experiments to discover the weight of factors that affect the user experience during the spectator process. In the first experiment, we used the method of user interviews. The purpose is to find as much information as possible about the problems encountered by players in the process of spectating MOBA games and the factors that affect the user's spectating experience. This is a qualitative experiment. We selected 10 players who had experience in MOBA games and used the spectator mode as interview subjects.

After understanding the subjective feelings and problems encountered by players in the process of using the MOBA game spectator mode, the entire interview experiment

Table 1. Description of influencing factors of Moba game spectating experience

Num	Influencing factors
1	Whether the spectating is smooth, and there is no lag when a large number of people
2	Whether there is a recommendation for spectating the game, such as the match, etc
3	Whether to understand the progress of the game before spectating the game, such as the comparison of kills, the situation of pushing the tower
4	Whether the loading is fast when entering the match, as well as reducing the waiting time
5	Whether the spectator mode is free
6	Whether the detector is intelligent when spectating the battle process, prevent not to miss key battle
7	Whether the perspective switch freely and smoothly, such as freedom perspective, the player perspective, vision of God viewing angle
8	Whether the battle information of all parties is sufficient, such as equipment, talent allocation, economic curve
9	Whether the information of all parties is compared in the game
10	Whether there is a prediction of the trend of the match
11	Whether you can interact and communicate with other spectators during the game
12	Whether the interface can be hidden according to the player's own habits in the spectator game, so as to improve the player's efficiency
13	Whether the color style of the game in the spectator match is the same as in the normal game, so that players can easily identify
14	Whether the appearance design such as graphic controls enhance the recognition of players and facilitate users to find them quickly
15	Whether the player's cognition and operating habits are considered in the interface layout to reduce the mis-operation rate
16	Whether there is timely feedback when players make mistakes, or restrict certain operation behaviors
17	Whether players can customize the viewing interface
18	Whether there are pictures and videos for novice's guide
19	Whether the interface dynamics promptly remind players to pay attention to key information to prevent missing key messages
20	Whether the friend's delayed spectating of the game reminds the game is over in time to prevent missed teaming with friends
21	Whether there is a slow replay function for the spectator to facilitate review of the details of the last team battle

obtained a large number of materials on the factors that affect the MOBA game spectating experience, and provided for the setting of the influence factors in the quantitative experiment the basis of the research. There are 21 main factors influencing the MOBA game spectating experience summarized. The specific content is shown in the Table 1.

4   Experiment 2

There are many factors that affect user experience collected in previous qualitative experiments. The hierarchical division and mutual relationship between the influencing factors need to be further analyzed and researched through experiments. This study adopts factor analysis. Firstly, the subjective evaluation of the importance of each influencing factor by users is collected through quantitative questionnaires. The collected data is analyzed and screened, and then the factor analysis method is used to determine the primary evaluation factors and secondary evaluation factors that affect the team collaboration application experience, thereby establishing a quantitative model for team collaboration application experience evaluation.

The 21 factors that affect the user experience of team collaboration applications summarized by the previous qualitative research are designed into 21 phenotype questions. The questionnaire is assessed using the Likert scale, and the question is divided into 5 dimensions from very unimportant to very important. "5" means very important, "4" means important, "3" means fair, "2" means not important, and "1" means very important. Let the surveyed subjects score them so as to compare the importance of these factors.

5   Data Analysis

A total of 99 questionnaires were distributed in this quantitative experiment, and finally 41 (n = 41) valid questionnaires were collected. Preliminary processing of these data is carried out to calculate the mean and standard deviation. The data is shown in Table 2. A total of 99 questionnaires were distributed in this quantitative experiment, and finally 41 (n = 41) valid questionnaires were collected. Preliminary processing of these data is carried out to calculate the mean and standard deviation. The data is shown in Table 2.

From the Table 2, we can find that the mean of "Q10 Whether there is a prediction of the trend of the match" and "Q17 Whether players can customize the viewing interface" is less than 3. This shows that players believe that these two points have little impact on their experience. Therefore, these two factors are discarded, and only the remaining 19 influencing factors are retained.

After the preliminary screening has obtained 19 influencing factors, the correlation of these 19 influencing factors needs to be tested. If the correlation between the various elements is high, the validity of the scoring data for these impact data can be ensured. We use KMO and Bartlett test method to test the correlation of the scoring data of these 19 factors. The specific test results are shown in Table 3.

Table 2. Influence factor filter.

	N	Mean	Std. deviation
Q1	41	4.29	1.146
Q2	41	3.44	1.097
Q3	41	4.02	1.151
Q4	41	4.39	.919
Q5	41	4.49	.898
Q6	41	3.90	1.261
Q7	41	4.39	1.022
Q8	41	4.20	1.030
Q9	41	4.07	.985
Q10	**41**	**2.83**	**1.358**
Q11	41	3.15	1.131
Q12	41	3.95	1.244
Q13	41	3.90	1.091
Q14	41	3.98	1.012
Q15	41	3.71	1.055
Q16	41	3.46	1.120
Q17	**41**	**2.76**	**1.338**
Q18	41	3.00	1.360
Q19	41	3.56	1.050
Q20	41	3.98	1.172
Q21	41	4.00	1.013

Table 3. Test result of KMO and Bartlett.

Kaiser-Meyer-Olkin measure of sampling adequacy		.700
Bartlett's test of sphericity	Approx. Chi-Square	423.561
	Df	171
	Sig.	.000

The result proves that the value of KMO is 0.700 and The Sig of Bartlett is 0. According to the commonly used metrics, the data this time has strong correlation and is suitable for factor analysis.

Then do a factor analysis of these 19 elements, and get the following results:

As shown in the Table 4, the influencing factors of MOBA game spectating experience are arranged in order from largest to smallest. Extract the first 6 components, each value is greater than 1. These 6 components cover 74.482% cumulatively. Therefore, these 6 principal components can be used as the main factors that affect the user experience of team collaboration applications. And using normalization processing, that is equivalent to 6components all represent the overall 19 components, then the

Table 4. Total variance explained.

Component	Initial eigenvalues			Rotation sums of squared loadings		
	Total	% of Variance	Cumulative %	Total	% of Variance	Cumulative %
1	7.288	38.359	38.359	3.231	17.004	17.004
2	1.698	8.938	47.297	2.552	13.430	30.434
3	1.582	8.326	55.623	2.497	13.144	43.578
4	1.364	7.179	62.802	2.123	11.172	54.751
5	1.193	6.278	69.080	1.947	10.246	64.997
6	1.026	5.402	74.482	1.802	9.485	74.482
7	.823	4.333	78.816			
8	.798	4.201	83.017			
9	.604	3.182	86.198			
10	.519	2.732	88.930			
11	.448	2.360	91.291			
12	.397	2.092	93.382			
13	.331	1.743	95.126			
14	.265	1.392	96.518			
15	.206	1.083	97.601			
16	.196	1.032	98.632			
17	.114	.602	99.235			
18	.085	.446	99.681			
19	.061	.319	100.000			

amount of information for the first component is 17.004%/74.482% = 22.83%; the amount of information for the second component is 13.430%/74.482% = 18.03%; the amount of information for the third component is 13.144%/74.482% = 17.65%; the amount of information for the fourth component is 11.172%/74.482% = 15.00%; the amount of information for the fifth component is 10.246%/74.482% = 13.76%; the amount of information for the sixth component is 9.485%/74.482% = 12.73%.

In addition to the total variance explained above, the gravel graph can also see the effect of principal component extraction. as the Fig. 1 shows. The abscissa of the lithograph represents each corresponding component, and the ordinate is the initial characteristic value of each components. The initial eigenvalues of the first 6 components are all greater than 1. Starting from the seventh component, the initial eigenvalues are all less than 1, and the trend of the curve begins to flatten.

Similarly, from the rotated component matrix, we can see that each principal component contains several influencing factors with higher load values, so the influencing factors of higher load values in each column of principal components can be sorted from high to low. Summarize it together, remove the influencing factors with lower load values in each column, so as to determine the 6 principal components and the items contained under each principal component and the corresponding load values. The rotated component matrix is shown in Table 5.

Scree Plot

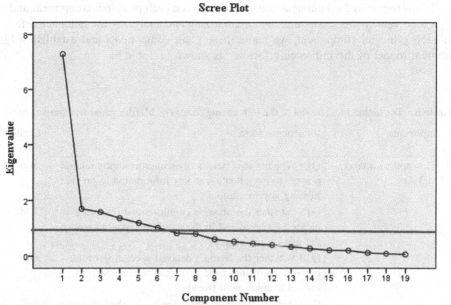

Fig. 1. Scree plot

Table 5. Rotated component matrix

	Component					
	1	2	3	4	5	6
Q19	**.806**	.196	.210	.153	.060	.068
Q15	**.778**	.233	−.042	.279	.173	.157
Q20	**.640**	.208	.112	.188	−052	.126
Q16	**.639**	.195	.392	−.038	.279	.237
Q18	**.628**	−.142	.555	−.027	.035	.194
Q5	.063	**.798**	.209	−.007	.144	.233
Q4	.203	**.780**	.311	.170	.062	−.044
Q21	.311	**.647**	−.041	.269	.109	−.015
Q14	.402	**.511**	.028	.293	.185	.267
Q6	.318	.107	**.817**	.073	.077	−.013
Q8	.039	.359	**.776**	.201	.071	.103
Q13	.194	.223	−.086	**.767**	.309	−.039
Q9	.052	.303	.286	**.719**	−.062	.362
Q12	.342	.015	.325	**.703**	.095	.170
Q1	.158	.037	−.016	.181	**.828**	.194
Q3	−.068	.223	.362	.108	**.761**	−.158
Q2	.311	.240	−.058	−.028	**.588**	.567
Q11	.225	.043	.064	.156	.023	**.834**
Q7	.151	.199	.481	.287	.175	**.532**

From the rotated component matrix, you can see each principal component and the high load value items it contains. By summarizing and analyzing the influencing factors in each principal component, we name these main components and establish a hierarchical model of the influencing factors, as shown in Table 6.

Table 6. The hierarchical model of the influencing factors of MOBA game watching experience

Components	Influencing factors	Loading plots
1. Tips and avoidance (22.83%)	Q19 Whether the interface dynamics promptly remind players to pay attention to key information to prevent missing key messages	.806
	Q15 Whether the player's cognition and operating habits are considered in the interface layout to reduce the mis operation rate	.778
	Q20 Whether the friend's delayed spectating of the game reminds the game is over in time to prevent missed teaming with friends	.640
	Q16 Whether there is timely feedback when players make mistakes, or restrict certain operation behaviors	.639
	Q18 Whether there are pictures and videos for novice's guide	.628
2. Basic functions (18.03%)	Q5 Whether the spectator mode is free	.798
	Q4 Whether the loading is fast when entering the match, as well as reducing the waiting time	.780
	Q21 Whether there is a slow replay function for the spectator to facilitate review of the details of the last team battle	.647
	Q14 Whether the appearance design such as graphic controls enhance the recognition of players and facilitate users to find them quickly	.511
3. Information validity (17.65%)	Q6 Whether the detector is intelligent when spectating the battle process, prevent not to miss key battle	.817
	Q8 Whether the battle information of all parties is sufficient, such as equipment, talent allocation, economic curve	.776
4. Vision (15%)	Q13 Whether the color style of the game in the spectator match is the same as in the normal game, so that players can easily identify	.767
	Q9 Whether the information of all parties is compared in the game	.719
	Q12 Whether the interface can be hidden according to the player's own habits in the spectator game, so as to improve the player's efficiency	.703

(continued)

Table 6. (*continued*)

Components	Influencing factors	Loading plots
5. Information pre-acquisition (13.76%)	Q1 Whether the spectating is smooth, and there is no lag when a large number of people	.828
	Q3 Whether to understand the progress of the game before spectating the game, such as the comparison of kills, the situation of pushing the tower	.761
	Q2 Whether there is a recommendation for spectating the game, such as the match, etc	.588
6. Social and other (12.73%)	Q11 Whether you can interact and communicate with other spectators during the game	.834
	Q7 Whether the perspective switch freely and smoothly, such as freedom perspective, the player perspective, vision of God viewing angle	.532

6   Result and Conclusion

As an important functional support of MOBA games, the spectator mode is an indispensable part of game competition. However, in the spectator mode, due to different usage scenarios, players have different requirements for functions. This test uses qualitative interviews and quantitative experiments to discover and cluster the factors that affect the MOBA game viewing experience. And to find out the importance weights between different types of impact factors, and establish a quantitative evaluation system for the spectating experience of MOBA games.

However, the overall design of the experiment still has certain limitations:

1. The influencing factors discovered by qualitative experiments cannot fully cover all the factors that affect the watching experience.
2. Some test players did not accurately understand the description of the questions in the quantitative experiment.
3. The summary and naming of clustering factors are affected by the subjective experience of the experiment designer.

In future research, a more detailed method should be considered to separate the influencing factors of MOBA game spectating experience. And conduct pre-experiments to reduce the impact of text descriptions on players' understanding of the meaning of questionnaire questions. And discuss the naming of clustering factors by means of expert review, in order to improve the quantitative evaluation system of MOBA game watching experience.

References

1. Mora-Cantallops, M., Sicilia, M.Á.: MOBA games: a literature review. Entertain. Comput. **26**, 128–138 (2018)
2. Lawley, D.N., Maxwell, A.E.: Factor analysis as a statistical method. J. Roy. Stat. Soc. Series D (Stat.) **12**(3), 209–229 (1962)
3. DeCoster, J.: Overview of factor analysis (1998)
4. An, G.Y., Sean, P.: Tutorials in quantitative methods for psychology **9**(2), 79–94 (2013)
5. Weibel, D., Wissmath, B.: Immersion in computer games: the role of spatial presence and flow. Int. J. Comput. Games Technol. **2011**, 1–14 (2011)
6. Yijun, M.: The Development of Game User Experience Measurement Tool: A Factor Analysis and Item Response Theory Approach. Tianjin Normal University, MA thesis (2019)
7. Phan, M.H., Keebler, J.R., Chaparro, B.S.: The development and validation of the game user experience satisfaction scale (GUESS). Human Fact. J. Human Fact. Ergon. Soc. **58**(8), 1217–1247 (2016)
8. Zanetta Dauriat, F., et al.: Motivations to play specifically predict excessive involvement in massively multiplayer online role-playing games: evidence from an online survey. Eur. Addict. Res. **17**(4), 185–189 (2011)
9. Wu, Q.: Research on the Quantization of User Experience of Application for Collaboration Based on Cognitive Load Theory (2017)

User Engagement and Game Impact

Computer-Aided Games-Based Learning for Children with Autism

Christine Dahl[1]([⊠]) [iD], Henrik Skaug Sætra[2] [iD],
and Anders Nordahl-Hansen[3] [iD]

[1] Kapellveien Centre for Neurohabilitation, N-0487 Oslo, Norway
christine.dahl@kapellveien.no
[2] Faculty of Business, Languages, and Social Science,
Østfold University College, N-1757 Halden, Norway
[3] Faculty of Education, Østfold University College, N-1757 Halden, Norway

Abstract. Autism Spectrum disorder is a neurodevelopmental disorder characterized by early onset difficulties in social communication, and unusually restricted, repetitive behaviors and interests. Children with autism are often not naturally as motivated as others by social interaction and situations involving dyadic play, and this is considered to be problematic as both are essential arenas for young children's development. In this article we explore how computer-based interventions in various guises show some promise in engaging and motivating children with autism to engage in play. This has led to the development of a range of computer-based interventions aimed at fostering learning, and these range from the use of VR to regular computer games to the use of social robots with artificial intelligence. We evaluate the evidence gathered on the use of various forms of computer-based play and also discuss the potential ethical implications of such interventions.

1 Introduction

Autism Spectrum disorder (autism from hereon) is a neurodevelopmental disorder characterized by early onset difficulties in social communication, and unusually restricted, repetitive behaviors and interests (APA 2013). Play and social engagement is a critical factor in young children's development, due to the skills acquired through interactive peer play and observation of the environment. These skills include social competence, theory of mind, communication, imitation, and cooperation (Jung and Sainato 2013). The difficulties central to the autism diagnosis often leads these children to experience low levels of social, cognitive and behavioral engagement, which in turn affect their possibility to learn crucial developmental skills in a natural way. This can have serious consequences for their development, and much research has been focused on methods that can increase engagement and learning in children with autism, as a key aspect of successful learning is engagement and motivation (Kaale et al. 2018; Rudovic et al. 2017; Keen 2009; Prensky 2003). In this article, we focus on computer-aided methods of encouraging the development of communication, social skills and behavioral flexibility through play and games.

© Springer Nature Switzerland AG 2021
X. Fang (Ed.): HCII 2021, LNCS 12789, pp. 145–158, 2021.
https://doi.org/10.1007/978-3-030-77277-2_12

As early social communication is a key challenge for children with autism, it is also a central target for early intervention. The most common intervention procedures that show promise of effects are Applied Behaviour Analysis (ABA), Naturalistic Developmental Behavioural Interventions (NDBI) and developmental science informed interventions (Sandbank et al. 2020). There is growing evidence that the use of robots and stimuli delivered by screen can contribute to higher levels of engagement in children with autism (Kumazaki et al. 2018), due to the simple, predictable and non-invasive aspects of robots as compared to interaction with humans (Mineo et al. 2009).

Since engagement, which involves initiation, response and maintenance of social interactions, also plays a pivotal part in learning, the use of computer-based intervention in learning situations has great potential. In this article we focus on various forms of computer-aided and games-based learning, including the use of robots, VR, and more conventional computer games.

The use of robots in autism intervention is typically aimed at motivating and engaging children. Social robots help create a context where social and problem-solving skills meet, which is remarkably positive for children with neurodevelopmental disorders, including children with autism (Dautenhahn and Werry 2004; Wainer et al. 2014; Fosch-Villaronga and Albo-Canals 2019). Moreover, robots can create interesting, appealing, and meaningful interplay situations that compel children to interact with them, and some even argue that robots surpass human trainers in certain situations (Cabibihan 2013). Robots also have the advantage that, unlike a human trainer, they will not tire as they can offer endless repetitions and encouragement during training (Huijnen et al. 2017).

Although the empirical evidence is scarce (Nordahl-Hansen et al. 2020), the use of virtual reality (VR) interventions for children with autism has also showed promising results, with studies indicating improved adaptive living skills and social skills (Bellani et al. 2011, Parsons and Cobb 2011). Further, a review of the VR-interventions for children with autism reported broad acceptability and less than 1% negative sentiment towards VR-devices (Dechsling et al. 2020). VR has the advantage that it can offer a wide variety of different environments for training social skills, such as how to behave in a library, a café or at the theatre. VR further do not necessitate face-to-face communication which can be stressful for individuals with autism (Parson and Cobb 2011). Individuals with autism often struggle with sustained attention, being easily distracted by stimuli in the environment. The use of a more constrained viewing area – and a virtual environment that is less cluttered and noisy than real life – can therefore be beneficial in helping the individual to focus their attention on relevant stimuli (Dechsling et al. 2021; Mineo et al. 2009). Computer training has also been shown to be successful for teaching emotional skills to children with autism. For example, the computer-based intervention program Let's Face It! (LFI!) addresses the specific face processing difficulties children with autism can have (Tanaka et al. 2010). It is also argued that the use of computer-based games has the advantage, beyond raising engagement, that the intervention can be administered in several environments, such as home, school or clinical settings (Tanaka et al. 2010).

Focusing on children with autism, we show the potential for computer-based intervention (robots, VR, computer games) to help foster engagement and motivate individuals with autism in learning situations. We evaluate the evidence gathered on the use of various forms of computer-based play and end our article by highlighting some key areas where the field of human-computer interaction (HCI) may contribute to improving such interventions for children with autism.

2 Motivation, Engagement and Learning

Motivation is a key prerequisite for learning (Deci et al. 1991). Without motivation – or a will to learn – it is hard to image effective learning taking place. In essence, motivation is a driver that energizes, directs and selects behavior toward anticipated goal states (Locke and Schattke 2019). Motivation is also a key factor for engagement in terms of time spent on an activity or task as well as the intensity of the engagement (Martin 2009).

While motivation is an internal emotive state, it is also affected by a range of external factors, such as peers, teachers, the physical location, etc. (Ormrod 2014). Various forms of rewards as forms of motivation are also often referred to as "motivation". This highlights the need to distinguish between internal, or intrinsic, and external motivation. An intrinsically motivated learner has a desire to learn for the sake of learning, while an extrinsically motivated learner might only take part in learning processes in order to receive a reward not necessarily related to what is learnt, such as prize money, being praised, or perhaps gaining a form of required certification, etc. (Deci et al. 1991, s. 328). For the extrinsically motivated learner, learning is related to means-ends for achieving something in the future (Locke and Schattke 2019), near or far.

The sort of motivation we discuss in this article is mainly external, as we focus on attempts to overcome lower levels of intrinsic motivation in certain activities in many children with autism. Extrinsic motivation can be divided into four different types: external, introjected, identified, and integrated forms of regulation (Deci and Ryan 1985). These can be argued to form a continuum in which the first type is furthest from intrinsic motivation, while the latter is rather close to it. External regulation entail being motivated by a desire to receive an award or to avoid some form of punishment. Introjected regulation relates to efforts to avoid feeling guilty, for example when someone expects a person to learn or know something, while identified regulation results from internalization of such expectations and then acting in ways that, for example, makes one feel good after doing something one perceives to be good, or right. Introjected regulation is when the good or bad feeling is mainly based on the expectations of others, while identified regulation relates to expectancies we have towards ourself. Integrated regulation is quite similar to identified regulation, and entail more fully integrating the *various* roles and conflicting expectations one might have (Deci et al. 1991). The latter is superficially similar to intrinsic motivation, but it still relates to being motivated by achieving or avoiding something not integral to the object of learning, as is thus extrinsic (Deci et al. 1991).

Another important aspect of motivation is the role feelings of achievement play in fostering it. In this context, autonomy plays a key role for allowing the learners to feel that learning is a result of what *they* have done, which is important for feeling achievement (Ormrod 2014). A central characteristic of *play* is that it involves a certain degree of freedom, which might help explain some of the motivational benefits of using play in learning situations. Research shows that in order to most effectively foster motivation through autonomy, the following factors should be limited: limited choices, threats and deadlines *(control),* external rewards, surveillance or monitoring, and evaluation (Ormrod 2014).

The term *gamification* is used to describe efforts to mix elements from games and game design with educational content (Garris et al. 2002; Sailer et al. 2013). This can entail a range of different game elements, such as point systems, awards for "achievements", high score lists, systems for measuring and showing progress, tasks and goals, storytelling, and characters (potentially with character development (Sailer et al. 2013, s. 30–31).

Gamification is heavily based on principles from behaviorism and emphasis is thus placed on actions and behavior more so than cognitive processes, meta-cognition, etc. Positive and negative reinforcement is key for fostering specific behavior, and operant conditioning involves the use of *reinforcers* to either increase or decrease particular behaviors (Skinner 1958). Modern smart phones and games such as Candy Crush and Angry Birds are often portrayed as case studies of how both children and adults' behavior are easily shaped by the desire to achieve or avoid seemingly nonsensical phenomena such as *streaks, stars,* and various *achievements* in these games. These game mechanisms trigger human reward mechanisms, and some argue that a certain type of "addiction" for such games and the associated rewards can be fostered – also for learning games such as the language learning game-app *Duolingo,* etc. (Garris et al. 2002, s. 445, 451; Sailer et al. 2013, s. 28).

Games of this kind are firmly planted on the more extrinsic side of the motivation spectrum, and research shows that these form of games based external motivation *is* important for learning (Ricci et al. 1996; Garris et al. 2002). Simultaneously, being introduced to various subjects through external motivation might trigger interest in the subject matter and intrinsic motivation. Hence, dividing extrinsic and intrinsic motivation is clearer in theory than in practice.

Play and games involves active learning rather than passive such as listening, and an active learning component is important for fostering a sense of accomplishment and a feeling of autonomy – both of which are conducive to learning (Garris et al. 2002). Best effects are, however, achieved when the students don't feel that they are controlled, evaluated, or under surveillance, and the introduction of external rewards might hinder the internalization of motivation (Deci et al. 1991, s. 335).

Deci et al. (1991) point out that autonomy is conducive to intrinsic motivation, as it fosters an interest for and valuation of learning while the learner builds trust in their own skills. We argue that while intrinsic motivation might justifiably be portrayed as the best, or most "noble" form of motivation, and that the most extrinsic forms of motivation are "bad", fostering intrinsic motivation *directly* is exceedingly hard, and building motivation by starting at extrinsic motivation and various forms of rewards, for example, might in certain circumstances be the best, or only, option available.

3   General Reward Dysfunction in Children with Autism

According to Charman et al. (2011) there is increasing evidence that multiple aetiologies may converge to disrupt the development and function of several brain areas that are implicated in the impairments seen in individuals with autism. Research has previously focused on theories such as Theory of Mind deficits or executive dysfunction as possible explanations of impairments in autism. However, the idea that social motivation deficits play an essential role in these impairments has garnered increased interest over the last years (Charman et al. 2011). The social motivation theory suggests that social deficits in individuals with autism are due to abnormal reward processing of social stimuli (Bottini 2018).

Research has shown that individuals with autism may exhibit an overall decrease in the attentional weight assigned to social information (Bottini 2018). Chevallier et al. (2012) proposes that a possible explanation for these social deficits may have their origin in a biological disruption of the orbitofrontal-striatal-amygdala circuitry as well as dysregulation of certain neuropeptides and neurotransmitters. Especially disrupted oxytocin regulation may play a crucial role in social reward dysfunction (Dichter et al. 2012; Dichter and Adolphs 2012; Chevallier et al. 2012). There is a lot of controversy related to neuroimaging findings, partially because studies often have been limited to small sample sizes (Lord et al. 2020), but it is suggested that the abovementioned regions are functionally atypical in some individuals with autism (Behrmann and Humphreys 2006). The findings suggest that the abovementioned disruptions and dysregulations in social reward processing can reduce attention to social information, including decreased orienting, attention and preferences for people, faces and speech sounds as well as discomfort in social interaction over a longer period of time and increased attention to non-social objects (Bottini 2018; Dichter et al. 2012; Dichter and Adolphs 2012; Chevallier et al. 2012). The social motivation deficits hypothesis has, however, been debated, and Jaswal and Akhtar (2019) argue that individuals with autism do not lack social motivation per se and they focus instead on the interaction between the individual with autism and their peers. They propose that their behavior (poor eye-contact, stereotyped behavior) largely accounts for the way they are perceived, and that these perceptions can lead to the social exclusion of individuals with autism by others (Jaswal and Akthar 2019). Other studies have suggested a more general reward processing dysfunction in individuals with autism, and that this is not only limited to social stimuli (Bottini 2018).

On the basis of the proposed brain-differences in individuals with autism compared to others there has been a growing interest in investigating the cognitive phenotype of individuals with autism, especially when it comes to which interventions are best suited for this group. Knowledge about the specific phenotype in individuals with autism can enable more targeted interventions focused on enhancing learning opportunities, motivation and engagement as well as targeting specific strengths and weaknesses (Charman et al. 2011). Such an approach paves the way for a more tailored intervention on the basis of the individual child's needs.

Individuals with autism also often show an uneven cognitive profile, where non-verbal abilities (Performance IQ) are typically higher than Verbal IQ, indicating a preference for visual stimuli. Sensory overload is also a well-known condition in individuals with autism. This is often caused by a heightened sensitivity for sounds, smell or touch, often leading to anxiety and discomfort (Crane et al. 2009). This has implications for how to create situations conducive to learning, and, for example, more emphasis on visual learning material, as we shortly return to.

Several decades of research have also generated robust evidence of difficulties in executive functioning as a part in the cognitive phenotype in individuals with autism (Joseph et al. 2005; Lord et al. 2020). The hypothesis regarding difficulties in executive functioning proposes that structural differences in frontal cortex and decreases in functional connectivity between the frontal lobes and other brain systems can be associated with core symptoms in autism spectrum disorder (Hill 2004, Charman et al. 2011). Executive dysfunction involves difficulties with initiation, planning and execution of behavior. It also involves problems with sustained and divided attention, mental flexibility, inhibition and working memory (Joseph et al. 2005). Executive functioning is key to success in traditional education and as such, many children with autism struggle to meet expectations within this system. Planning involves constantly monitoring your own actions, re-evaluating and changing your own behavior. It is a complex and dynamic operation. Several studies have documented that children, adolescents and individuals with autism's performance of neuropsychological tasks such as the Tower Test are impaired compared to both neurotypical test-groups, but also compared to test-groups including individuals with ADHD, dyslexia and Tourette Syndrome (Hill 2004).

Mental flexibility involves the ability to shift to a different action or thought in a given situation. Difficulties with mental flexibility often involves difficulties with social interaction, due to the inability or difficulties with following shifting rules in play with other children. It can also create difficulties in a learning environment, such as a classroom filled with distractions and noise (Hill 2004).

Executive dysfunction can make learning more inefficient since it can make accessing, organizing and coordinating multiple mental activities more challenging (Meltzer and Krishnan 2007). Learning involves information being stored and retrieved from the long-term memory. A critical aspect in this process is that the learner needs to organize and repeat the information so that storing can take place (Shifrin and Atkinson 1969). Individuals with attentional problems often struggle during this process, due to difficulties sorting, and prioritizing relevant information (Meltzer and Krishnan 2007). There is a high degree of heterogeneity within the autism population, also regarding executive functioning. Educators working with children with autism must take into account both these differences and understand the child's executive function difficulties in order to provide the child with the best opportunities to learn.

3.1   Learning in Naturalistic Settings

Play in naturalistic settings is a critical factor in young children's development, due to the skills and knowledge acquired through interactive play activities. These skills include social, communication, imitation, and cooperation skills (Jung and Sainato 2013). The key difficulties individuals with autism face can in turn affect and impair their opportunities to learn and develop crucial social skills in a natural way.

When it comes to learning and academic skills, the combination of executive and social impairments, in addition to heightened sensory perception, can make ordinary participation in a classroom challenging. This relates both to the social environment and to how information is conveyed. Open-ended tasks presented by a teacher or a trainer for instance can be challenging, due to the fact that it can be difficult to understand implicit expectations and what is required, and the tasks are often unstructured or open-ended (Landsiedel and Williams 2019). A classroom environment can also be challenging when it comes to sustained attention and it can be overwhelming for individuals with autism due to the risk of sensory overload and stress. Computer-based interventions have the advantage of lessening these demands, offering a less stressful environment which can increase task engagement (Ramdoss et al. 2012). Knowing that individuals with autism have on average a cognitive phenotype which can make learning in naturalistic settings such as through play or in a classroom challenging, there has been a growing interest in alternative forms of education such as computer-based interventions (Sharmin et al. 2018).

There is growing evidence that individuals with autism show an increased interest and engagement in stimuli delivered by screen, especially media delivered through electronic screens (Mineo et al. 2009). This is in line with the idea that individuals with autism trend towards a particular cognitive phenotype. Others argue that the game itself offers more motivating opportunities due to increased reward-feedback. It is also argued that screen or non-human interaction can be less challenging since the human social aspect is removed (Cabibihan 2013).

Research suggests that children with neurodevelopmental disorders often benefit from external rewards, (Mineo et al. 2009). As discussed, the concept of extrinsic rewards has been used extensively in digital technology, especially in computer games where players are rewarded for achieving various tasks throughout the game. Computer-based learning also has the advantage of being able to remove distracting stimuli, which can be beneficial since attention deficit is key problem area for children with autism. Thus, digital technology games for children with autism can be a good fit. Technology can also be helpful in tracking progress, even minor progress not easily detected by other methods, which can be motivational and useful for the individual with ASD and for professionals working with them and caregivers (Sharmin et al. 2018).

4 Discussion: Computer-Based Interventions (CBI) and Autism Spectrum Disorder

4.1 Learning Social and Emotional Skills Through CBI

Difficulties with social interaction, reciprocal communication and emotion recognition are well known impaired functions in children with autism. Without intervention these deficits can affect their overall quality of life (Ramdoss et al. 2012). Numerous studies have investigated which interventions are most beneficial, including intensive training, psychoeducation and participation in social skills training groups. Interventions targeted at increasing social communication and skills are, however, time consuming, both for the individual and their network (Ramdoss et al. 2012). When it comes to electronic interventions, various applications of robots, VR and screen devices have been examined.

Boyd et al. (2015) investigated whether a collaborative iPad game can be beneficial in teaching children with autism social skills. The focus in this study was to see whether a game can act as a support or a mediator in managing social relationships between children with autism and neurotypical children. The results indicated that playing an iPad-based game together, compared to playing with a Lego set together, increased engagement, physical proximity, turn-taking and empathy. They also found that the rewards for winning a game were powerful incentives for continuing playing together with another child, which is in line with the extrinsic reward hypotheses (Boyd et al. 2015). The results are supported by Kuo et al.'s (2013) research, as they found that interaction through computer-games were one of the most frequent activities that adolescents with autism engaged in with friends (Kuo et al. 2013).

Other studies have focused less on the collaborative aspect, and more on how technology can be directly used to teach individuals with autism social skills. Computer-based interventions have for instance been used to improve emotion and face recognition skills, language and social skills. Some of the interventions used are robots, encouraging children in group activities, and visual and haptic feedback encouraging appropriate social behavior (Sharmin et al. 2018). Robots such as Kaspar and NEO have also shown promising results when it comes to imitation games, increase in collaborative turn-taking, and in social initiatives (Karakosta 2019; Wainer et al. 2014; Salvadoor et al. 2015; Shamsuddin et al. 2012).

A systematic review by Ramdoss et al. (2012) found positive results in all 10 studies that assessed the effect on CBI and social and emotional skills (recognition of faces, social competence, social interaction) They conclude that CBI-based interventions can be as effective as face-to-face instruction.

4.2 Language Comprehension and CBI

Acquisition of language among children with autism is often severely delayed (Khowaja et al. 2019), and their vocabulary tend on average to be more restricted compared to other children.

Therapists working with children and students with autism often report a lack of cooperation and motivation, especially when it comes to language training. CBI is emerging as a useful method for teaching children with autism language (Khowaja et al. 2019). CBI has the advantage that the material presented can multimodal and consist of a combination of text, sound, movies, and images. As previously mentioned, the combination of visual stimuli and the absence of social demands can be beneficial for children with autism. A review conducted by Ramdoss (2011) evaluated effect of CBI-based interventions to teach communication skills to children with autism. The majority of the examined studies used regular desktop computers for their intervention programmes, and the software was specifically designed for the purpose of language training in children with autism. All of the 10 studies reported improvement in receptive language, increased frequency in spoken words, and imitation of sentences, and social and conversation initiations (Ramdoss et al. 2011).

4.3 Ethical Considerations

The abovementioned impairments that often characterize autism, such as executive functioning difficulties, sensory overload and difficulties with social interaction stresses the need for interventions that are carefully designed for individuals with autism. Individuals with autism are however a very heterogenous group that calls for a carefully tailored and flexible intervention design, that can be both engaging and facilitate learning.. A review by Ramdoss et al. (2011) emphasizes the importance of correct feedback techniques (prompting, positive reinforcement etc.) when it comes to using CBI-based interventions for improving language skills. Sharmin et al. (2018) also found through their trials that the use of cartoons instead of real images has shown to be beneficial, eliciting less stress (Sharmin et al. 2018).

Several studies have also raised concern regarding whether skills acquired through these types of interventions can be generalized into skills in everyday life. Studies have raised concerns that CBI-based interventions have shown little evidence of learning generalization (Whyte et al. 2015). Others have raised concern whether the use of CBI can reduce the amount of interaction between teacher, caregivers or peers, hence increasing social isolation and reducing real life opportunities to practice social interactions (Ramdoss et al. 2011). Although the use of CBI can reduce interaction with others outside of the game at the time of interacting with the game, CBI is not to be used as a substitute for traditional training and education but rather as a supplement. Here, it is important to note that, to the authors' knowledge, there are no studies that investigate the possible add-on effects a combination of CBI and traditional training might or might not have.

Individuals with autism, and children in particular, is a vulnerable group, and particular care must be taken when choosing methods of intervention. First of all, some might object to an approach that basically reduces these individuals to something akin to Pavlov's dogs – as objects that can be conditioned and manipulated into behaving according to ideals they themselves do not identify with. The trade-off between societal benefits, the needs of the children's surroundings (family, school, etc.) and the children's right to be treated as autonomous individuals with dignity and respect is excruciatingly difficult. While no easy answers exist.

The use of digital technologies is of great interest for autism research, as the combination of increasingly detailed personal information and the technology enabled means of delivering stimuli tailored to each individual might increase the effectiveness of interventions, and this is by some linked to behaviorist approaches to learning in the form of conditioning (Sætra 2019b; Zuboff 2019). In contemporary AI or computer ethics, these challenges are often discussed as forms of manipulation and increasingly effective *nudging* (Sætra 2019c; Yeung 2017).

Increasingly effective tools that foster motivation and engagement also entail risks of creating forms of addiction or creating situations in which the individuals with autism find the tools employed so attractive that they grow to prefer robots, for example, to human interaction (Turkle 2017). Some have also argued that social robots entail a form of deception, as people have varying capacities for distinguishing between real and living entities and life-like and sophisticated social robots (Sætra 2020a; Sharkey and Sharkey 2020).

Finally, issues related to cybersecurity, privacy, and surveillance arise as soon as computer-aided tools are introduced in interventions. Various forms of games, VR systems, and robots have a wide variety of data gathering capabilities, sensors, and cameras, and it is essential that these systems are secure. For example, the systems must not be vulnerable to hacker attacks, as such breaches would greatly imperil both the safety and privacy of those using the tools. In addition to this, great care must be taken to ensure that data gathering is based on a real need for the data, strict adherence to, for example, GDPR protocols for storage, handling, and deletion. Privacy is an important aspect of human autonomy and dignity (Sætra 2019a; 2020b), and while trading privacy for more effective intervention will at times be both legitimate and necessary, mapping and evaluating the consequences and legitimacy of such tradeoffs will be required.

5 Conclusion

In this article, we have explored how computer- and games- based interventions for individuals with autism can be a viable option in fostering learning. This is due to how this combination can be effective for creating engaging and motivating situations. Children with autism are often not naturally as motivated as others by social interaction and situations involving dyadic play, and this is considered to be problematic as both are essential arenas for young children's development.

Computer-based interventions in various guises shows some promise in engaging and motivating children with autism to engage in play. This has led to the development of a range of computer-based interventions aimed at fostering learning, and these range from the use of VR to regular computer games to the use of social robots with artificial intelligence.

Some of the key benefits of computer-based interventions are the reduced stress resulting from being able to limit social interaction in and various distractions form the learning situations and the predictable nature of computers. The visual and auditory potential of computers and robots are also beneficial for individuals with autism. When this is combined with elements of *gamification* – the introduction of various forms of games-based elements such as rewards, challenged, etc. in learning situations – engagement and motivation are further increased.

In the final section, we have stressed the need for careful considerations of the ethical implications of computer-aided games-based intervention. A range of ethical challenges arise alongside the use of computers and devices with the ability to sense, store, and manipulate data. There is also the question of whether or not social robots, for example, are deceptive, and that using extrinsic motivation and such robots with children with autism involves some sort of illegitimate trickery or manipulation. Finally, however, we wish to stress the need for a research- and evidence-based knowledge of autism and the associated challenges for individuals with autism in any team of developers of therapists that use computers-aided interventions. While technology holds great potential, it must be applied in a considered and appropriate manner, and we also encourage stakeholder involvement, including researchers, clinicians, educationalists, and last but not least parents and individuals with autism (Nordahl-Hansen et al. 2018), in decisions to use computer-aided interventions in new areas.

References

American Psychiatric Association. Diagnostic and statistical manual of mental disorders (DSM-5). American Psychiatric Publishing (2013)

Behrmann, M., Thomas, C., Humphreys, K.: Seeing it differently: visual processing in autism. Trends Cogn. Sci. **10**(6), 258–264 (2006)

Bellani, M., Fornasari, L., Chittaro, L., Brambilla, P.: Virtual reality in autism: state of the art. Epidemiol. Psychiatric Sci. **20**(3), 235–238 (2011)

Bottini, S.: Social reward processing in individuals with autism spectrum disorder: a systematic review of the social motivation hypothesis. Res. Autism Spectr. Disord. **45**, 9–26 (2018)

Bosseler, A., Massaro, D.W.: Development and evaluation of a computer-animated tutor for vocabulary and language learning in children with autism. J. Autism Dev. Disord. **33**(6), 653–672 (2003)

Boyd, L.E., Ringland, K.E., Haimson, O.L., Fernandez, H., Bistarkey, M., Hayes, G.R.: Evaluating a collaborative iPad game's impact on social relationships for children with autism spectrum disorder. ACM Trans. Access. Comput. (TACCESS) **7**(1), 1–18 (2015)

Cabibihan, J.J., Javed, H., Ang, M., Aljunied, S.M.: Why robots? A survey on the roles and benefits of social robots in the therapy of children with autism. Inter. J. Soc. Robot. **5**(4), 593–618 (2013)

Charman, T., Jones, C.R., Pickles, A., Simonoff, E., Baird, G., Happé, F.: Defining the cognitive phenotype of autism. Brain Res. **1380**, 10–21 (2011)

Chevallier, C., Kohls, G., Troiani, V., Brodkin, E.S., Schultz, R.T.: The social motivation theory of autism. Trends Cogn. Sci. **16**(4), 231–239 (2012)

Crane, L., Goddard, L., Pring, L.: Sensory processing in adults with autism spectrum disorders. Autism **13**(3), 215–228 (2009)

Dautenhahn, K., Werry, I.: Towards interactive robots in autism therapy: Background, motivation and challenges. Pragmat. Cogn. **12**(1), 1–35 (2004)

Dechsling, A., et al.: Virtual reality and naturalistic developmental behavioral interventions for children with autism spectrum disorder. Res. Dev. Disabil. **111** (2021). https://doi.org/10.1016/j.ridd.2021.103885

Dechsling, A., Sütterlin, S., Nordahl-Hansen, A.: Acceptability and normative considerations in research on autism spectrum disorders and virtual reality. In: Schmorrow, D.D., Fidopiastis, C.M. (eds.) HCII 2020. LNCS (LNAI), vol. 12197, pp. 161–170. Springer, Cham (2020). https://doi.org/10.1007/978-3-030-50439-7_11

Deci, E.L., Ryan, R.M.: Intrinsic Motivation and Self-Determination in Human Behavior. Plenum, New York (1985)

Deci, E.L., Vallerand, R.J., Pelletier, L.G., Ryan, R.M.: Motivation and education: the self-determination perspective. Educ. Psychol. **26**(3–4), 325–346 (1991)

Dichter, G., Adolphs, R.: Reward processing in autism: a thematic series (2012)

Dichter, G.S., Felder, J.N., Green, S.R., Rittenberg, A.M., Sasson, N.J., Bodfish, J.W.: Reward circuitry function in autism spectrum disorders. Social Cogn. Affect. Neurosci. **7**(2), 160–172 (2012)

Fosch-Villaronga, E., Albo-Canals, J.: 'I'll take care of you', said the robot: reflecting upon the legal and ethical aspects of the use and development of social robots for therapy. Paladyn J. Behav. Robot. **10**(1), 77–93 (2019)

Garris, R., Ahlers, R., Driskell, J.E.: Games, motivation, and learning: a research and practice model. Simul. Gaming **33**(4), 441–467 (2002)

Hill, E.L.: Executive dysfunction in autism. Trends Cogn. Sci. **8**(1), 26–32 (2004)

Huijnen, C.A.G.J., Lexis, M.A.S., de Witte, L.P.: Robots as new tools in therapy and education for children with autism. Int. J. Neurorehabil. **4**(4), 1–4 (2017)

Jaswal, V.K., Akhtar, N.: Being versus appearing socially uninterested: challenging assumptions about social motivation in autism. Behav. Brain Sci. **42** (2019)

Joseph, R.M., McGrath, L.M., Tager-Flusberg, H.: Executive dysfunction and its relation to language ability in verbal school-age children with autism. Dev. Neuropsychol. **27**(3), 361–378 (2005)

Jung, S., Sainato, D.M.: Teaching play skills to young children with autism. J. Intellect. Dev. Disabil. **38**(1), 74–90 (2013)

Kaale, A., Smith, L., Nordahl-Hansen, A., Fagerland, M.W., Kasari, C.: Early interaction in autism spectrum disorder: Mothers' and children's behaviours during joint engagement. Child Care Health Dev. **44**(2), 312–318 (2018)

Karakosta, E., Dautenhahn, K., Syrdal, D.S., Wood, L.J., Robins, B.: Using the humanoid robot Kaspar in a Greek school environment to support children with autism spectrum condition. Paladyn J. Behav. Robot. **10**(1), 298–317 (2019)

Keen, D.: Engagement of children with autism in learning. Aust. J. Spec. Educ. **33**(2), 130–140 (2009)

Khowaja, K., Salim, S.: Serious game for children with autism to learn vocabulary: an experimental evaluation. Int. J. Human–Comput. Interact. **35**(1), 1–26 (2019)

Kumazaki, H., et al.: The impact of robotic intervention on joint attention in children with autism spectrum disorders. Molec. Autism **9**(1), 1–10 (2018)

Kuo, M.H., Ormond, G.I., Cohn, E.S., Coster, W.J.: Friendship characteristics and activity patterns of adolescents with an autism spectrum disorder. Autism **17**(4), 481–500 (2013)

Landsiedel, J., Williams, D.M.: Increasing extrinsic motivation improves time-based prospective memory in adults with autism: relations with executive functioning and mentalizing. J. Autism Dev. Disord. **50**(4), 1133–1146 (2019). https://doi.org/10.1007/s10803-019-04340-2

Locke, E.A., Schattke, K.: Intrinsic and extrinsic motivation: Time for expansion and clarification. Motivation Science **5**(4), 277 (2019)

Lord, C., et al.: Autism spectrum disorder. Nat. Rev. Dis. Primers. **6**(1), 1–23 (2020)

Martin, A.J.: Motivation and engagement across the academic life span: a developmental construct validity study of elementary school, high school, and university/college students. Educ. Psychol. Measur. **69**(5), 794–824 (2009)

Lynn, M., Kalyani, K.: Executive function difficulties and learning disabilities. In: Executive Function in Education: From Theory to Practice, pp. 77–105 (2007)

Mineo, B.A., Ziegler, W., Gill, S., Salkin, D.: Engagement with electronic screen media among students with autism spectrum disorders. J. Autism Dev. Disord. **39**(1), 172–187 (2009)

Nordahl-Hansen, A., Dechsling, A., Sütterlin, S., Børtveit, L., Zhang, D., Øien, R., Marschik, P.: An overview of virtual reality interventions for two neurodevelopmental disorders: intellectual disabilities and autism. In: Schmorrow, D.D., Fidopiastis, C.M. (eds.) Augmented Cognition. Human Cognition and Behavior: 14th International Conference, AC 2020, Held as Part of the 22nd HCI International Conference, HCII 2020, Copenhagen, Denmark, July 19–24, 2020, Proceedings, Part II, pp. 257–267. Springer International Publishing, Cham (2020). https://doi.org/10.1007/978-3-030-50439-7_17

Nordahl-Hansen, A., Hart, L., Øien, R.: The scientific study of parents and caregivers of children with ASD: a flourishing field but still work to be done. J. Autism Dev. Disord. **48**(4), 976–979 (2018). https://doi.org/10.1007/s10803-018-3526-9

Ormrod, J.E.: Human Learning. Pearson Education International, London (2014)

Parsons, S., Cobb, S.: State-of-the-art of virtual reality technologies for children on the autism spectrum. Eur. J. Spec. Needs Educ. **26**(3), 355–366 (2011)

Prensky, M.: Digital game-based learning. Comput. Entertain. (CIE) **1**(1), 21 (2003)

Ramdoss, S., Lang, R., Mulloy, A., Franco, J., O'Reilly, M., Didden, R., Lancioni, G.: Use of computer-based interventions to teach communication skills to children with autism spectrum disorders: a systematic review. J. Behav. Educ. **20**(1), 55–76 (2011)

Ramdoss, S., et al.: Use of computer-based interventions to teach communication skills to children with autism spectrum disorders: a systematic review. J. Behav. Educ. **20**(1), 55–76 (2011)

Ramdoss, S., Machalicek, W., Rispoli, M., Mulloy, A., Lang, R., O'Reilly, M.: Computer-based interventions to improve social and emotional skills in individuals with autism spectrum disorders: a systematic review. Dev. Neurorehabil. **15**(2), 119–135 (2012)

Ricci, K.E., Salas, E., Cannon-Bowers, J.A.: Do computer-based games facilitate knowledge acquisition and retention? Mil. Psychol. **8**(4), 295 (1996)

Rudovic, O., Lee, J., Mascarell-Maricic, L., Schuller, B.W., Picard, R.W.: Measuring engagement in robot-assisted autism therapy: a cross-cultural study. Front. Rob. AI **4**, 36 (2017)

Sailer, M., Hense, J., Mandl, H., Klevers, M.: Psychological perspectives on motivation through gamification. IxD&A **19**, 28–37 (2013)

Salvador, M.J., Silver, S., Mahoor, M.H.: An emotion recognition comparative study of autistic and typically-developing children using the zeno robot. In: 2015 IEEE International Conference on Robotics and Automation (ICRA), pp. 6128–6133. IEEE (2015)

Sandbank, M., et al.: Project AIM: autism intervention meta-analysis for studies of young children. Psychol. Bull. **146**(1), 1–29 (2020). https://doi.org/10.1037/bul0000215

Sharkey, A., Sharkey, N.: We need to talk about deception in social robotics! Ethics Inf. Technol. (2020). https://doi.org/10.1007/s10676-020-09573-9

Shamsuddin, S., Yussof, H., Ismail, L.I., Mohamed, S., Hanapiah, F.A., Zahari, N.I.: Humanoid robot NAO interacting with autistic children of moderately impaired intelligence to augment communication skills. Procedia Eng. **41**, 1533–1538 (2012)

Sharmin, M., Hossain, M.M., Saha, A., Das, M., Maxwell, M., Ahmed, S.: From research to practice: Informing the design of autism support smart technology. In: Proceedings of the 2018 CHI Conference on Human Factors in Computing Systems, pp. 1–16 (2018)

Shiffrin, R.M., Atkinson, R.C.: Storage and retrieval processes in long-term memory. Psychol. Rev. **76**(2), 179 (1969)

Skinner, B.F.: Reinforcement today. Am. Psychol. **13**(3), 94 (1958)

Sætra, H.S.: Freedom under the gaze of big brother: preparing the grounds for a liberal defence of privacy in the era of big data. Technol. Soc. **58**, 101160 (2019a)

Sætra, H.S.: The ghost in the machine. Human Arenas **2**(1), 60–78 (2019b). https://doi.org/10.1007/s42087-018-0039-1

Sætra, H.S.: When nudge comes to shove: liberty and nudging in the era of big data. Technol. Soc. **59**, 101130 (2019c)

Sætra, H.S.: The foundations of a policy for the use of social robots in care. Technol. Soc. **63**, 101383 (2020a)

Sætra, H.S.: Privacy as an aggregate public good. Technol. Soc. **63**, 101422 (2020b)

Tanaka, J.W., et al.: Using computerized games to teach face recognition skills to children with autism spectrum disorder: the Let's Face It! program. J. Child Psychol. Psychiatry **51**(8), 944–952 (2010)

Turkle, S. (2017). *Alone together: Why we expect more from technology and less from each other*. Hachette UK.

Wainer, J., Robins, B., Amirabdollahian, F., Dautenhahn, K.: Using the humanoid robot KASPAR to autonomously play triadic games and facilitate collaborative play among children with autism. IEEE Trans. Auton. Ment. Dev. **6**(3), 183–199 (2014)

Whyte, E.M., Smyth, J.M., Scherf, K.S.: Designing serious game interventions for individuals with autism. J. Autism Dev. Disord. **45**(12), 3820–3831 (2015)

Yeung, K.: 'Hypernudge': big data as a mode of regulation by design. Inf. Commun. Soc. **20**(1), 118–136 (2017)

Zuboff, S.: The Age of Surveillance Capitalism: The Fight for a Human Future at the New Frontier of Power: Barack Obama's Books of 2019. PublicAffairs, New York (2019)

Analysis of the Competitiveness of Asymmetric Games in the Market

Jiawei Dai[✉] and Xinrong Li[✉]

University of Leeds, Leeds, UK
{ml192jd, ml19xl19}@leeds.ac.uk

Abstract. Traditional types of industries undoubtedly occupy a large market in a long time, with convenient and direct benefits. Nowadays, with the advancement of technology and the improvement of people's living standards, virtual products as new consumption hotspots appeared in the public. People began to pay attention to the service of the product and the emotional experience given by products, which also means that many people are willing to pay for the virtual data. A good example is the online gaming industry has sprung up in recent years. People only need to use their daily media such as mobile phones or computers to release emotional pressure in a short time of gaming. In addition, after the gaming industry gathers a large part of the consumer groups, it needs to constantly innovate to avoid the loss of customers.

The paper is aimed to analyze the situation and profitability of online games in marketing and conduct in depth exploration of a type of innovation called asymmetric games. Whether this emerging game type has the ability to compete with the traditional symmetrical game model will be analyzed by using the review of literature and questionnaire interviews.

Keywords: Online gaming market · Asymmetric game · Symmetric game

1 Introduction

The wide application of the Internet and the arrival of the era of big data have provided new sales hotspots for the market and led to the development of a series of related industries. It is necessary for people engaged in related industries to understand the trend of the market in order to face the opportunities and challenges. Marketing is a huge broad concept, "exchange is a central concept in marketing, and it may well serve as the foundation for that elusive 'general theory of marketing' [1]." The early market first went through a period of barter, and then the invention of equivalent exchange laid the foundation for the emergence of coins. It can be simply said that the traditional handicraft industry, resource-based industries and offline stores are all around the characteristics of equivalent exchange. These traditional types of industries undoubtedly occupy a large market in a long time, with convenient and direct benefits.

X. Fang (Ed.): HCII 2021, LNCS 12789, pp. 159–167, 2021.
https://doi.org/10.1007/978-3-030-77277-2_13

However, with the advancement of technology and the improvement of people's living standards, virtual products as new consumption hotspots appeared in the public. People began to pay attention to the service of the product and the emotional experience given by products, which also means that many people are willing to pay for the virtual data. A good example is the online gaming industry and virtual reality technologies have sprung up in recent years. People only need to use their daily media such as mobile phones or computers to release emotional pressure in a short time of gaming. This article will focus on the online gaming industry and related marketing analysis. The first section will introduce the marketing value and profitability of the online gaming industry to give readers a preliminary impression. After the gaming industry gathers a large part of the consumer groups, it needs to constantly innovate to avoid the loss of customers. The second body section will analyze the strengths and weaknesses of traditional symmetric gaming and innovative asymmetric gaming. The final section of the body part will demonstrate the asymmetric gaming have the ability to compete with traditional symmetric gaming through a concrete example.

2   Related Work

Primary research and secondary research are the investigative methodology in this article. The secondary research is based on papers published by experts in related fields and comments made by related amateurs on the Internet. A questionnaire has been compiled for primary research through these resources and literature reviews. The primary research method in this article is interviews related to the topic. The conclusions obtained through a large number of interviews make the article authentic and universal.

2.1   The Trend of Marketing

The trend of marketing is gradually developing from a single traditional industry to a diversified direction. Including handicrafts, traditional manufacturing and resource industries are widely regarded as traditional industries. Traditional industries often have complete industrial chain, and the division of labor between producers and sellers is clear. The efficient cooperation of each department can quickly realize a complete process from production to consumption. However, Grönroos [2] had advanced that "because the classical marketing axioms were based on the exchange of physical goods, which could not provide a sufficient understanding on services". They undoubtedly created huge wealth profits in the early days, but as people's living standards improved, traditional industries had a clear disadvantage in providing services and emotions. The market and design are gradually evolving towards a service-oriented and integrated direction, which are revolves around the concept of human-centered thinking.

In addition to shortening the delivery time, the demand for product reliability and operators' response speed and processing time has also shown varying degrees of growth [3]. People are paying more and more attention to better quality and service, and overall solutions to their individual problems are gradually appearing in the market

[4]. Market trends to be globalized and diversified, which means that traditional industries face multiple challenges from competition and internal adjustment. At the same time, this is an opportunity for the emerging high-tech industry. Increasing the agility of supply chains and services is the key to the sustainable development of all industries.

2.2 Online Gaming in Marketing

The development of technology has promoted the birth and prosperity of new technology industry industries, such as artificial intelligence, virtual reality and gaming industry gradually appear in front of the public. In addition to bringing convenience to people, the popularization of the Internet has also created new sales hotspots for merchants. People are starting to pay for virtual numbers, which breaks the concept of equivalent exchange in traditional industries.

According to Avedon [5] who is an expert of game studies described game as an "exercise of voluntary control systems in which there is an opposition between forces, confined by a procedure and rules in order to produce a disequilibria outcome." (Avedon 1981) This outlines the concept of the game in terms of how the game is constructed and how people participate in the experience.

Compared with the physical exchange of traditional industries, the online gaming industry is more to position its goods in the service. The reason is that games can greatly give users a sense of participation and satisfaction. Players gain experience and discover problems in the process of the game, which are fed back to the developer to promote the iterative update of the game. Users are no longer just passively accepting input from the market; they are allowed as co-creators to immerse and participate in the architecture of the game system and game world. According to Huorari [6], "Games are always regarded as systems that require an active involvement by the player. Games are thus co-produced by the game developer and the player(s)." This means that customers in the gaming industry are not just consumers, but also common producers. In the course of game, players face uncertain factors and make different reflection, which can be regarded as the customer's unique production process. The player also determines the ultimate value, which gives the player a great deal of free space. These unknown and variable characteristics allow the player to maintain a sense of freshness while also giving the motivation of continues playing and exploring it.

From another point of view, the original intention of many people to play the game is an emotional sustenance. People use games to release pressure or get the honor in the gaming world and they through this way to make up for the shortcomings of real life. Nevertheless, the gaming industry is also facing negative factors by short life cycle, fluctuating demand and timeliness.

2.3   Ways for Online Gaming Companies to Earn Profits

One obvious phenomenon is the number of people who choose to spend their leisure time with games have increased quickly, which also means that more people have the urge to spend for online gaming. Figure 1 presents the number of mobile phone gamers in the United States from 2011 to 2015 as well as a forecast until 2020. The annual rise of data in mobile game reflects that the growing popularity of the online gaming. After experiencing a period of substantial increase, the latter showed a steady growth trend.

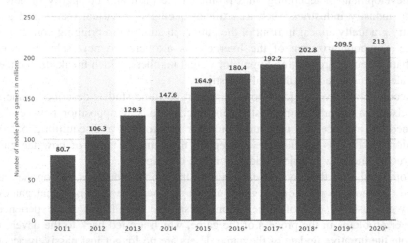

Fig. 1. The number of mobile phone gamers in the United States from 2011 to 2015 as well as a forecast until 2020. Available from Statista: https://www.statista.com/statistics/234635/number-of-mobile-gamers-forecast/

A profit channel for gaming companies come from the game's copyright downloads and other is the players' consumption of game-specific scenes. According to Alha and other experts [7, 8] said, 'Virtual goods and other forms of in-game content have rapidly become one of the biggest forms of online consumption for gamers and de facto revenue model for game publishers.'

The use of high-tech production of a complete game system and exquisite graphics are the major advantages of the gaming industry. Game companies launch some attractive virtual productions based on different game positioning, generally reflected in more exquisite apparel, rare equipment and higher quality effects. For senior players, the joy of getting rare equipment even goes beyond the reality of buying the desired clothes. In addition, some game companies are adept at hunger marketing, which means commodity provider intends to reduce production to maintain product brand image and higher price. Game companies have seized on people's consumer psychology and they occasional launches limited virtual productions, which is a temptation for many players.

3   Definition and Competitive Analysis of Different Categories of Games

3.1   Definition of Traditional Symmetric Gaming

As a rapidly developing industry, the online gaming begins to occupy the leisure time of people's lives and its classification gradually diversified. This section will focus on the type of confrontation game, which is current popular and respectively explain the definition of traditional symmetric gaming and asymmetrical gaming.

From the early simple man-machine confrontation to the emergence of asymmetric gaming, people are constantly moving in the direction of exploration and innovation. When it comes to traditional symmetric games, experts point out that 'every player is identical with respect to the game rules.' [9]. This means that the setting of this type of game is based on the principle of balance and the two sides of the game battle are limited by the same rules. This type of game requires an equal number of members on both sides of the battle, and there will not be a big gap between the original strength of the two sides of the battle. Players need to use strategies to enhance the numerical attributes of their characters. Such representative games include League of Legends, Dota, etc.

3.2   Definition of Asymmetric Gaming and Disputes Faced

As an emerging form, asymmetric games are a bold attempt and a new challenge in the game of confrontation. According to Burgun [10] who is game designer says, 'a definition- "asymmetry", refers to the player of players having different abilities from the start of a match.' It breaks with the traditional balanced pattern of confrontation, which most intuitively reflected in the number and initial strength of the two sides. In addition to the above-mentioned obvious differences, the judgment of the victory conditions of the competing teams is also not consistent.

It is obvious that innovation in the industry not only brings attention and exposure, but also generates disputes of varying degrees. The biggest controversy of asymmetric game is whether it can achieve the fairness of the opposing sides under the initial unbalanced setting conditions. For players, the opposing side of the confrontation is too strong or weak will greatly influence the experience of the game. Compared with the symmetric gaming, the asymmetric gaming is harder to grasp the balance. How to handle and coordinate the relationship between opposing parties is a huge challenge for game developers.

3.3   Reasons for the Competitiveness of the Asymmetric Gaming

This aspect will show the reasons why asymmetric gaming has the ability to compete with the traditional symmetric gaming. Traditional symmetric gaming with the balance for the principle of rules to maintain the stability of the game, this is its advantage, and also its shortcomings. Some players have accumulated a certain amount of experience after a long gaming time and they will form a general cognition of the limited changes of the game, which leads to produce fatigue and the solidification of thinking.

In contrast, asymmetric games are more innovative and more varied. Players can choose the lineup that suits them according to their own preferences. Different lineups have completely different game ideas and game modes. This versatile game experience is more likely to stimulate people's interesting in games. Besides, the unequal number of people and the initial power setting add more unknown elements to the asymmetric gaming. This unknown situation can produce many unpredictable. Players need to maintain high quality concentration all the time, which avoids the fixed thinking to some extent. The following will specifically analyze a successful asymmetric game to prove the view of the claim.

4   Case Analysis

4.1   The Example of Asymmetric Gaming: Identity V

This part will analyze a popular online gaming, which named Identity V to prove the asymmetric gaming will compete the traditional symmetric gaming.

The developer of Identity V is Chinese NetEase, which is an Internet technology company. It was released in April of 18 and its specific positioning in the big category of asymmetric games is the survival horror game. Official data shows that the number of appointments before the game officially went online exceeded six million. On the first day of the launch, it has ranked first in the free App Store game list, the first in the App Store and the iPad in the total.

Chinese gamers enthusiastically sought it after as soon as it went public. Due to its widespread popularity, we selected mainstream people in the 18–30 age group as the research subjects and conducted a series of questionnaires and in-deep interviews to collect data and analyze the reasons. According to the results of 80 questionnaires, people with or without gaming experience are attracted to a certain degree of difference. In one-to-one in-depth interviews, some interviewees stated that they did not understand the specific types of games at first but were attracted by the Gothic style of games. The graphic style of the game usually gives people the most intuitive first impression, and the characteristic art style is gradually enlarged in the public's field of vision as a key factor. Such interviewees said that in many cases, they would decide whether to get a preliminary understanding or give up directly based on the artistic style of the game and the exquisite production. Game enthusiasts and some experienced game players said that they pay more attention to the core point of the game, which is an asymmetric confrontation of 1versus 4. They are keen to experience game concepts and any technological innovations. There were also a small number of players said because the game was free to download. The combination of these factors has contributed to the success of this game in the market. It is not difficult to find that because of the rapid growth of the online game market, developers need to consider all aspects of users in continuous innovation to maintain competitiveness.

4.2   Details of Identity V

The background of the game is that the player plays a detective and receives a mysterious letter of entrustment. The player enters the notorious estate to investigate a disappearance based on the information of the letter. In the course of the investigation, the player can choose to act as a regulator or a survivor to launch a fierce confrontation. As the game continues to update, players will gradually get closer to the truth in game.

The rule of the game is that there are five players simultaneously in one scene map and four of survivors need to fight against with one regulator. Both the survivor lineup and supervisor lineup have multiple different roles that can be used for selection. Different roles have different positioning and functions, and players can choose the lineup and roles. The game's producers will continue to launch new roles and new maps to maintain the freshness of players.

Asymmetry is fully reflected in the internal confrontation. The resources owned by the two sides are functionally misplaced; the interaction and final goals are completely different. Regulator has a stronger physical and initial strength, but the number is inferior. The purpose of the regulator is to capture four survivors within the map and win by catching at least three survivors and ending them. In contrast, the initial strength of the survivor is weak but with the number of advantages. The purpose of the survivor is to escape the chase of the regulator and win the victory by at least three players successfully fleeing the map.

In addition, another attraction of this game is the dark gothic game style, which can be seen in Fig. 2.

Fig. 2. Identity V-The dark gothic game style Available from: http://kongbakpao.com/identity-v-neteases-escape-survival-game-release/

The most striking feature undoubtedly is the setting of the puppet, and the rich Tim Borton style. From the perspective of artistic techniques, the gorgeous and decadent Gothic elements, with exaggerated colors, strange characters, Victorian costumes, touched the audience again and again. The hair of the roles in the game refers to the elements of the sewing puppet and their eyes are drawn from the common buttons, which can be seen in Fig. 3. The limbs of them are spread over the clear seams. The dark and weird style of painting aptly reveals whimsical and distinctive features, which can give audiences a visual impact. Its qualifications are short, but its complete game system and interesting game style is the key to success.

Fig. 3. The elements of the sewing puppet and their eyes are drawn from the common buttons
Available from: https://www.touchtapplay.com/identity-v-cheats-tips-strategy-guide/

5 Conclusion

Nowadays, it is a fiercely competitive society, especially in the Internet era where technology is rapidly upgraded, and services are gradually becoming integrated and experienced. Only continuous innovation and maintaining the agility of reflection cannot be eliminated by the market. The increase in people's consumption level has promoted the continuous transformation of the industry, and the continuous updating of the industry has given people new consumption hotspots. It is undeniable that every industrial innovation will always bring about various disputes. Good innovations can stand the test of time and create huge profits for enterprises.

At present, asymmetric games are a bold and successful industrial innovation in the online game industry. Although there are still some defects, they have the ability to compete with traditional symmetric games. Traditional symmetric games have a more stable and balanced system and a longer experience, but they also limit its variability. Compared to traditional symmetric gaming, asymmetric games have less qualifications and triggers lots of fairness controversy but wins with more selectivity and unknown variability.

Many experienced game players admit that asymmetric games will be broader and more random in choice and strategy, so it is very difficult to find a set of regular winning routines in asymmetric games. If people want to win the game, in addition to the need for technical operations and high concentration of attention, good luck is also indispensable. In contrast, when the symmetric game is mastered over a period of time, it is related easy to form a set of winning regular gameplay in players' mind and its stability limits the possibility of more changes.

If innovative online games are accurately positioned and have a complete game system and attractive game style, they can have the potential to compete with established traditional games. In general, both symmetrical games and asymmetrical games have their advantages and disadvantages, which both need to continuously upgrade and improve themselves in feedback to improve competitiveness and avoid the loss of players.

References

1. Bagozzi, R.P.: Marketing as exchange. J. Mark. **39**, 32–39 (1975)
2. Grönroos, C.: Service Management and Marketing: A Customer Management in Service Competition, 3rd edn. Wiley, Hoboken (2007)
3. Mentzer, J.T.: Supply Chain Management. Sage Publications, Inc., London (2001)
4. Gold, S.L., Nagel, R.N., Preiss, K.: Agile Competitors and Virtual Organizations: Strategies for Enriching the Customer, Van Nostrand Reinhold Book, New York (1995)
5. Avedon, E.M., Sutton-Smith, B.: The Study of Games. Wiley, New York (1981)
6. Huotari, K., Hamari, J.: A definition for gamification: anchoring gamification in the service marketing literature. Electron. Mark. **27**(1), 21–31 (2016). https://doi.org/10.1007/s12525-015-0212-z
7. Alha, K., Koskinen, E., Paavilainen, J., Hamari, J.: Critical acclaim and commercial success in mobile free-to-play games. In: Proceedings of DiGRA FDG conference, Dundee, Scotland, 1–6 August 2016 (2016)
8. Lehdonvirta, V.: Virtual item sales as a revenue model: identifying attributes that drive purchase decisions. Electron. Commerce Res. **9**(1e2), 97e113 (2009)
9. Daniel, M., Michael, P.: Notes on Equilibria in Symmetric Games. Institutional Knowledge at Singapore Management University (2004). https://ink.library.smu.edu.sg/sis_research/1213/
10. Burun, K.: Asymmetry in Games (2015). http://keithburgun.net/asymmetry-in-games/

A Systematic Review of the Effect of Gamification on Adherence Across Disciplines

Robin De Croon[✉], Jonas Geuens, Katrien Verbert, and Vero Vanden Abeele

Department of Computer Science, KU Leuven, Celestijnenlaan 200a, Leuven, Belgium
robin.decroon@kuleuven.be

Abstract. Systematic reviews of gamification research often focus on effects on motivation and engagement. Fewer studies systematically investigate the effect of gamification on 'adherence', the extent to which individuals use a gamified service and experience its content, as envisioned by the creators, to derive a certain benefit. To this end, this paper presents a systematic review of the effect of gamification on adherence across disciplines, including only studies with experimental designs and empirical measurements of adherence. The results lend support to the hypothesis that gamification has a positive effect on adherence: 19 out of 27 studies report a significantly positive effect or trend. However, we also demonstrate that further debate is necessary on how to conceptualize and measure adherence across disciplines, and suggest that studies on gamification on adherence not only measure the usage behavior of individuals, but equally provide an a priori operationalization of intended use along with a justification.

Keywords: Gamification · Adherence · Retention rate · Attrition · Drop out · Intended usage

1 Introduction

Gamification, *"the intentional use of game elements for a gameful experience of non-game tasks and context,"* [1] is an interdisciplinary research area; a combination of game design, user experience design, behavioral economics and motivational psychology [2]. Gamification is most often a means to an end, i.e., many gamified services aim to increase motivation and engagement with the ultimate aspiration of promoting a certain behavior. To date, review studies that systematically investigate the effect of gamification mostly focus on a combination of psychological outcomes (e.g., intrinsic motivation, engagement), and/or behavioral outcomes at large (i.e., usage, retention) [3].

As the gamification field matures [4,5], there is a call for a stronger effort in defining precise research questions on the basis of existing theorizations, and to further refine the understanding of the kind and size of the effects gamification

© Springer Nature Switzerland AG 2021
X. Fang (Ed.): HCII 2021, LNCS 12789, pp. 168–184, 2021.
https://doi.org/10.1007/978-3-030-77277-2_14

has on individuals [5]. Hence, to further the field, it is needed to more clearly articulate the type of psychological and behavioral outcomes expected.

In this study, we focus specifically on one behavioral outcome of gamification, *adherence*, i.e., the extent to which individuals use a gamified service or system and experience its content, as defined or implied by its creators, in order derive a certain benefit [6–8]. Thus far, only few gamification studies focus on *adherence* itself, and the studies that do typically limit themselves to one specific product and application domain, such as health apps [9,10], online learning software [11,12], or programming [13]. To date, there has been no study that systematically investigates the effect of gamification on adherent behavior across diverse implementations and disciplines.

The contributions of the paper are twofold. The first contribution is empirical in nature, as we report on the impact of gamification on adherence across disciplines, from 27 academic papers. The results of our systematic review lend support to the hypothesis that gamification has a positive effect on adherence. The second contribution is theoretical in nature, as we further the understanding of adherence in gamification studies and promote both a more refined conceptualization as well as a set of standard elements to be present in any gamification study on adherence.

2   Background

We first discuss the concept of adherence and define it as one specific behavioral outcome, that is pertinent for much gamification research yet different from engagement. We end this section with the research objectives of the paper.

2.1   The Concept of Adherence

Although the term adherence is perhaps most established in the health domain [14], the concept itself has long been used in other domains as well. The Oxford dictionary defines adherence in layperson terms as "*attachment or commitment to a person, cause, or belief,*". From this definition, we learn that adherence is not about short lived, single-point-in-time behavior, attachment and commitment imply *sustained behavior*. The Cambridge dictionary defines adherence as: "*the fact of someone behaving exactly according to rules, beliefs, etc.*" This definition highlights the existence of rules and beliefs, in other words, there is an envisioned *intended behavior*. Hence, from these two definitions, the reader can understand that adherence implies both a temporal aspect (behavior as it unfolds over a longer period) and an intended usage aspect (behavior as according to rules, beliefs).

More targeted definitions that elaborate on these temporal and behavioral aspects can be found in the health domain. For example, the World Health Organization (WHO) defines adherence as "*the extent to which a person's behaviour - taking medication, following a diet, and/or executing lifestyle changes, corresponds with agreed recommendations from a health care provider.*" [14] With respect to eHealth, as a form of interactive technology close to the realm of gamified technology, Christensen et al. [15] put forward the following definition of adherence: "*the extent to which individuals experience the content of the Internet intervention.*" Again, these definitions encompass a temporal aspect (experiencing a certain 'dosage' of content) and intended usage (following agreed recommendations). To this end, Kelders et al. [6] promote a definition of adherence for interactive systems and services in eHealth that encapsulates both aspects, as "*the extent to which individuals experience the content to derive maximum benefit from the intervention, as defined or implied by its creators.*" Interestingly, the aforementioned definition of adherence lends itself well to the domain of gamification, as "*the extent to which individuals use a gamified service or system and experience its content, as defined or implied by its creators, in order to derive a certain benefit,*" and can also apply to situations beyond eHealth, such as e-learning and customer loyalty.

Basing themselves on Kelders' definition of adherence, Sieverink et al. [7] suggest three elements to be present in any adherence studies:

1. The ability to measure the usage behavior of individuals.
2. An operationalization of intended use.
3. An empirical, theoretical, or rational justification of the intended use.

In combination, these three elements not only ensure empirical measurement of the behavioral outcome, but also that this outcome is compared to a pre-specified value or threshold (~intended use) and that authors need to be able to justify this value or threshold.

2.2   Adherence Versus Engagement

At the heart of gamification lie the interrelated concepts of engagement and behavior change [1]. Therefore, gamification scholars may consider adherent behavior simply as an outcome of increased engagement. While related, adherence and engagement are different concepts. For example, people can be engaged to lose weight, but still not adhere to their weight plan. As aforementioned, adherence starts from the notion of usage behavior that is sustained and as intended, whereas engagement on the other hand, foreground the affective, psychological experience. For example, Brown and Cairns [16], Brockmyer et al. [17], and Denisova et al. [18] conceptualize engagement as a multi-dimensional construct encompassing a user's *absorption, flow, presence,* and *immersion.* Hence, it is possible for a gamified intervention to have engaged users who do not fully experience the content of the services as intended by its creators or prescribers (and are thus not adherent). Vice versa, users may show adherence to the recommended gamified plan, yet show a lack of engagement. To date, as the lines are blurry, the elusive concept of 'engagement' is frequently measured through behavioral variables such as 'returning visits' or 'regular use' [19]. Also the opposite exists, where a less strict understanding of the concept of adherence equates it to measures of engagement. For example, [20] and [21] measure non-adherence as a *"lack of participant engagement,"* i.e., they are using engagement as a proxy for adherence. Yet as the field of gamification matures, it is beneficial to more clearly delineate and separate these theoretical concepts, to refine our understanding and measurement of the impact of specific gamification strategies.

2.3 Studies on Gamification and Adherence

There are multiple review studies on the effect of gamification on psychological (e.g., engagement, motivation), behavioral outcomes (e.g., retention, increased usage) outcomes, e.g., [1, 22–25]. However, only the systematic review study of Brown et al. [26] on Web-Based Mental-Health Interventions explicitly studies adherence. The authors reported that web-based health interventions incorporating gamification features had a higher mean adherence rate. Yet, they also found both adherence and usage data were inconsistent or underreported.

In sum, the aforementioned study [26] suggests that gamification has a positive impact on adherence. However, it is limited to the mental health domain. To this end, this study sets out to broaden this scope and systematically investigate the effect of gamification on adherent behavior, across applications and/or disciplines. We set out to explore to what extent current studies conceptualize adherence according to the definition put forward by Kelders et al. [6] and adhere to standards recommended by Sieverink et al. [7], i.e., measuring usage behavior, operationalization of intended use, and a justification of intended use. Additionally, we aim to broaden our understanding of which gamification techniques are most popular and have the strongest impact, and which disciplines perform most studies on gamification and adherent behavior.

3 Materials and Methods

3.1 Search String

The protocol that was used to find and review the studies was developed according to the PRISMA guidelines [27]. In this systematic review we solely focus on gamification techniques hence the truncated keyword '*gamif**'. We used Brown et al. [26]'s synonyms for adherence. However, we modified 'retention rate' to 'retention' to also include studies that, for example, report on customer and employee retention. Finally, 'compliance' and 'concordance' were added to include papers that use a less authoritative approach to describe adherence [28]. We therefore built on their work and extended the search string:

> *gamif * AND (adherence OR attrition OR dropout OR drop-out OR non-completers OR non-completers OR "lost to follow up" OR withdrawal OR nonresponse OR non-response OR "completion rate" OR "did not complete" OR retention OR loss OR compliance OR concordance).*

3.2 Data Collection

To find gamification studies across disciplines, a comprehensive search of seven electronic databases was conducted and produced a set of 1122 papers: Scopus (life sciences, social sciences, physical sciences and health sciences, n = 300), PubMed (life sciences and biomedical, n = 86), ACM Digital Library (all computing and information technology domains, n = 222), IEEExplore (computer science, electrical engineering and electronics, n = 56), Web-of-Science (multidisciplinary, n = 193), ScienceDirect (physical sciences and engineering, life sciences, health sciences, and social sciences and humanities, n = 12), and ProQuest (multidisciplinary, n = 253).

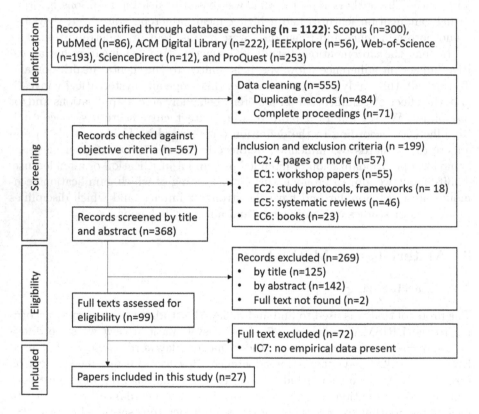

Fig. 1. Flow diagram according to the PRISMA guidelines.

3.3 Inclusion Criteria

Our review focused on high-quality research reporting original work on the effect of gamification on adherence. From this perspective, we developed the following inclusion criteria:

1. Peer-reviewed conference or journal papers.
2. Full papers (minimum length of four pages).
3. Explained research methods.
4. Researched effect of gamification on adherence as main research subject.
5. Reported how gamification was applied.
6. Reported the effect of gamification on adherence.
7. Reported behavioral or attitudinal measurements.

Criteria 1–2 were chosen to maximize the inclusion of high-quality and original research. Criteria 3–4 were included to enable an assessment of the quality of the work. Criteria 5 ensured that the included papers report on gamification, and not on serious games or persuasive technology. Finally, criteria 6–7 were chosen to ensure the included papers research the effect of gamification on adherence in a user study, and not only provide a conceptual discussion.

3.4 Exclusion Criteria

The exclusion criteria were designed to exclude duplicate reporting of earlier versions of studies fully reported later. We excluded papers with the following characteristics:

1. Extended abstracts, work-in-progress, workshops.
2. Study protocols or conceptual designs.
3. Studies that only cover serious games.
4. Studies that do not report an effect.
5. Systematic reviews.
6. Non-scholarly books.
7. Papers not written in English.

Criteria 1–2 exclude early and incomplete versions of studies. Criteria 3 excludes studies that mislabel serious games as gamification. Criteria 4 makes sure that the effect on adherence can be compared. Criteria 5 excludes studies that did not focus on one particular study. Criteria 6 excludes books that do not have a scholarly focus. Finally, we only included original research written in English.

3.5 Classification

Effect: Studies were classified as 'significantly positive' when they explicitly mention a significant positive effect. When they only mention a trend, they are classified as 'positive trend'. Studies reporting no effect are classified as 'no effect'. Studies that report a negative effect are classified as 'negative'.

Adherence: To research how adherence is defined and measured in the gamification domain, we built on [26]'s findings to classify the papers: attrition, dropout, noncompleters, lost to follow-up, participant withdrawal, nonresponse, completion rate, did not complete, retention, loss, and compliance. Effectiveness was also added as a classification term as two papers explicitly used the term effectiveness. Additionally, drawing on Sieverink et al. [7], we developed an Adherence Rationale Index (ARI), to classify studies as follows:

A study specifies intended use and provides a theoretical justification,
B study specifies intended use but lacks a theoretical justification,
C study neither specifies intended use nor theoretical justification.

Gamification techniques: In this systematic review, we used the classification proposed by Hamari et al. [3] to classify gamification techniques as shown in Table 2. The following list was used: points, leaderboards, achievements/badges, levels, story/theme, clear goals, feedback, rewards, progress, and challenge. However, as multiple studies included social motivational affordances into their gamification research, we augmented Hamari's set with 'social affordances' which grouped guilds/teams, social network, social status, opponents, and direct communication. Finally, although serious game studies are excluded by the exclusion criteria, 'serious game' was added to the coding table as four studies [10, 29–31] each apply three conditions in their study design: the control condition, a gamified intervention, and a serious game as a third condition.

Study design and criteria: Each paper was classified as either a randomized control study (RCT) or as a baseline study. Studies were classified as an RCT when they had a randomized control group in parallel with the intervention group. Studies were classified as a baseline study when they could compare their results to a baseline value. Additionally, the sample size, demographics, and duration of each study were listed.

Scientific fields: A scoping review by O'Donnel et al. [32] shows that gamification became a multidisciplinary research topic, applied and used in several domains. To remain consistent, we used O'Donnel et al. [32]'s ten categories to classify the primary scientific fields of the papers: (1) Sciences; (2) Information & Computing Science & Technology; (3) Medical & Health Sciences; (4) Education; (5) Economics, Commerce, Management, Tourism & Services; (6) Psychology & Cognitive Sciences; (7) Law & Legal Studies; (8) Engineering, Built Environment & Design; (9) Arts, Humanities, & Social Sciences; and (10) Games, Digital Entertainment Media. This is a condensed format of the 22 top-level divisions of the Australian and New Zealand Standard Research Classification.

3.6 Intercoder Reliability

All studies were coded and calculated by two independent coders (RDC and JG). Intercoder reliability was calculated using Cohen's kappa statistic. The mean value was 0.78 ($\pm$ 0.13) and all values were significant $P < 0.001$. Overall, all intercoder reliability values were at an acceptable level, i.e., > 0.60 [33, 34].

All the adherence terms, rationales (Table 1), as well as the scientific fields were consistently coded with a kappa agreement of 0.82 ($P < 0.001$), 1.0, and 0.80 ($P < 0.001$) respectively. The gamification techniques were also reliably coded and values were found to be between 0.62 and 1.0 kappa agreement depending on the technique. The lowest rated principle in terms of intercoder reliability was 'story/theme' (kappa agreement: 0.62). The lower agreement is due to the blurry line between graphic additions and a theme. For example, is the addition of a penguin [35] a graphical asset, a story, or even an avatar?

4   Results

As shown in Fig. 1, a total of 1122 papers were retrieved from the database searches by using the search terms described in Sect. 3.1. After removing duplicates and filtering papers based on the inclusion and exclusion criteria, 99 papers were evaluated by considering their full texts. Twenty-seven papers focusing on both gamification and adherence met the criteria and were thus included in this systematic review.

4.1   Effect of Gamification on Adherence

The results as reported by the authors are summarized in Tables 1, 2, and 3: of the 27 studies, 33% reported a scientifically significant positive effect of gamification techniques on adherence. Additionally, 37% reported positive trends, but could not provide significant effects. Finally, 30% reported no effects at all, while no studies reported a negative effect. However, a decrease in adherence over time was reported by 26% [29, 30, 36–40], either to the intervention or to the gamification techniques themselves. For example, Bodduluri et al. [29]'s results suggest *"that the motivating effects of gamification 'wear-off' and become boring as participants continue in a session that is lengthy, unless there is greater variety or progression of challenge in the task."* This is similar to Dugas et al. [36] who also state that their participants' motivation diminished as the study continued, which resulted in decreasing adherence over time. Fotaris et al. [30] noticed the demotivating aspect of leaderboards as *"students [...] began to lose interest once they trailed behind in the leaderboard."*

4.2   Adherence Measurement Variables

As illustrated in Table 1, not adherence (15%) but retention (26%) was the term used most frequently. Other terms were compliance (19%), completion rate (15%), attrition (11%), effectiveness (7%), and dropout (4%). Scrutinizing the ARI, the majority of studies (70%) neither specified intended use, nor provided a theoretical justification. Instead, they followed a *"the more, the better"* approach. Just 19% specified intended use but lacked theoretical foundation. Only three studies both specified predefined use and provided *some* theoretical foundations. Cafazzo et al. [43] assess treatment adherence at baseline and post-intervention using the validated 14-item Self-Care Inventory [55]. A participant is adherent when they have three or more measurements, as *"frequent self-monitoring of blood glucose (≥ times daily) is associated with better glycemic control among patients with type 1 diabetes."* Gremaud et al. [37] selected a 1250 steps per day threshold as a conservative estimate based on previous research that found adding 1385 steps per day resulted in significant reductions in multiple cardiometabolic risk factors. Finally, Leinonen et al. [10] followed the Finnish national recommendations for those in the age group of 13 to 18 years as at least 1.5 h of daily physical activity [56]. In the end, most studies simply calculated

Table 1. Overview of the terms used: ARI *(A. studies specify intended use and provide a theoretical justification, B: studies specify intended use but do not provide a theoretical justification, C: studies neither specify intended use nor provide a theoretical justification)*, measurement variables, study design, sample size, duration, and reported outcome (++ significantly positive, + positive trend, = no effect).

Study	Term	ARI	Measurement variable	Design	Sample	Days	Effect
[41]	Completion rate	B	Average percentage of students that submitted a solution to an assignment	RCT	37	28	++
[29]	Completion rate	C	Absolute completion rate between three interventions	Baseline	144	1	=
[42]	Adherence	C	Number of self-reported sessions	RCT	78	30	=
[43]	Adherence	A	Average value of daily average frequency of blood glucose	Baseline	20	84	++
[44]	Compliance	C	One inspection per day by a project manager whether work tools are returned and employees are compliant with safety regulations	Baseline	28	31	+
[45]	Completion rate	C	Class attendance & Attitudinal survey	RCT	371	365	=
[36]	Adherence	C	Points for achieving daily goals related to reporting and reaching target levels of glucose, exercise, nutrition, and medication adherence	Baseline	27	91	++
[30]	Completion rate	C	Average class attendance and exercise completion rate	Baseline	106	84	+
[37]	Compliance	A	Average daily steps and active minutes	RCT	146	60	+
[46]	Retention rate	C	Total number of students in class (anonymous) and number of students who registered and participated at the final exam	Baseline	1375	70	++
[47]	Effectiveness	C	Time spent, the number of exercises completed, and the number of words used	RCT	94	84	=
[48]	Retention rate	C	Completed at least one quiz per week	Baseline	1763	56	+
[11]	Retention rate	C	Number of videos watched	RCT	206	28	++
[49]	Dropout	C	Time spent in application	Baseline	?	93	++
[10]	Compliance	A	Number of times the user logged into the application, physical activity level based on wearable measurements	RCT	498	186	=
[50]	Attrition	B	Mean number of sessions completed per participant and percentage of users that completed at least X sessions	RCT	482	6	=
[51]	Attrition	C	Completed questions and number of players that keeps on playing each day	Baseline	92	97	++
[52]	Dropout	C	Number of participants that did not complete the study	RCT	41	20	=
[12]	Retention rate	C	Percentage of students retained	Baseline	394	84	+
[53]	Retention rate	C	The extent to which children retain their willingness in completing skill-builder modules between sessions	Baseline	30	8	=
[13]	Compliance	B	Coding convention compliance as assessed by automatic Checkstyle script	RCT	17	47	+
[38]	Compliance	B	Number of participants who continued to log steps at least once per week and compliance to step goal (10,000)	RCT	110	50	+
[31]	Adherence	B	Number of application sessions logged	Baseline	24	17	+
[40]	Retention rate	C	User retention curve as defined by the proportion of users who revisited the tool and the frequency and duration of their sessions	RCT	206	60	+
[35]	Attrition	C	Number of usable trials, i.e., correctly labeling the target image	RCT	16	1	++
[39]	Retention rate	C	Completed workout sessions	RCT	30	70	++
[54]	Effectiveness	C	Daily number of times the application was accessed and daily walking time	RCT	99	14	++

adherent behavior by measuring and comparing a quantitative, behavioral measure. This ranges from the daily average frequency of blood glucose measurements [43], the number of exercises completed [47], to the number of app sessions [40]. Even studies that conceptualized engagement as (part of) adherence still relied on behavioral measurements exclusively. For example, Stanculescu et al. [40] claim that *"The average session length falls into the online behavior metrics and is a good indicative of user engagement."* Finally, some studies, such as the one from Dugas et al. [36] use a combination of variables to calculate adherence: *"points were used to assess treatment adherence during the intervention. Points were allocated for achieving daily goals related to reporting and reaching target levels of glucose, exercise, nutrition, and medication adherence."*

4.3 Gamification Techniques

A multitude of gamification techniques were being integrated to improve adherence as shown in Table 2. All studies used at least three different gamification techniques with on average 5.7 (± 1.8) techniques. The majority of the studies implemented points (85%) and feedback (67%). These points were often simple numerical values for an action or a combination of actions and were used in distinct forms. For example, Ryan et al. [38] use the step count as points, while Dugas et al. [36] use traditional points. Points are typically displayed on a leaderboard (63%) or used to calculate badges/achievements (52%). All four studies [31,45,47,48] that did not use points focused on progress in a certain theme/story.

Feedback was also implemented in a great variety, either immediate feedback with pop-up messages, e.g., [54], or in the form of reports, e.g., [13]. Additionally, information visualizations [43], summary screens [11], or the ability to monitor results [50] were classified as feedback. Rewards were implemented with a similar variety, such as virtual rewards [31,38,54], candy [30], iTunes music [43], actual money [13,50], physical trophies [51] or grades [13].

Another highly popular technique was the addition of social affordances (56%). Scase et al. [31] reported that the bonding aspect between partici-

Table 2. Frequency of the gamification techniques used in the included studies grouped by reported outcome. Note that all studies use at least three different gamification techniques.

Gamification Techn.	Significantly positive study	Positive trend study	No effect study	Total
Points	[11,35,36,39,41,43,46,49,51,54]	[12,13,30,37,38,40,44]	[10,29,42,50,52,53]	85%
Feedback	[11,35,39,41,43,51,54]	[13,30,38,40,44,48]	[10,29,42,50,52]	67%
Leaderboards	[11,39,41,46,49,51,54]	[12,13,30,37,38,40,44]	[10,45,52]	63%
Social affordances	[11,36,39,43,46,51,54]	[13,30,31,37,38,40]	[10,45]	56%
Progress	[11,36,39,41,51,54]	[44]	[31,38,42,45,47,48,50,53]	56%
Achievements/badges	[11,39,41,43,49,51]	[12,30,38,40,44]	[45,47,53]	52%
Rewards	[41,43,51,54]	[13,30,31,38,40,44]	[45,50,53]	48%
Story/theme	[35,39]	[30,37]	[10,31,42,47,48,50,52]	41%
Clear goals	[35,36,43,54]	[13,38,40]	[42,50]	33%
Levels	[39,51]		[29,42,45,47,50,53]	30%
Challenge	[11,39,46]	[30,37]	[45,52,53]	30%
Serious game		[30]	[29,31,53]	15%

pants helped encourage their participants to adhere. Like all other gamification techniques, social affordances were implemented differently: social networking [10,31,39,43,46,54], teams [13,30,38,51] opponents [11], social status [30], and communication features [36].

Challenges (30%) and levels (30%) were found to be the least commonly used gamification technique in the selected studies.

4.4 Study Design Criteria

An RCT approach was used by 56% of the studies to study the effect of gamification on adherence, while 44% of the studies compared the gamified version to some baseline (see Table 1). A difference was most noticeable in the papers that reported no effect of gamification on adherence: six RCTs reported no effect, while only two baseline studies reported no effect.

Sample sizes varied greatly, ranging from 16 [35] to 1763 (284 versus 1479 control) [48]. The median sample size is 97 participants, while the lower and upper quartile lie between 30 and 200 participants. The duration also varied ranging from one day [35] (adherence measured as more usable trials) to one year [45] as shown in Table 1.

4.5 Scientific Fields and Gamification Studies on Adherence

As shown in Table 3, the Education, Medical & Health Sciences, and Psychology & Cognitive Sciences fields are well represented in the selected studies with ten, nine, and four studies respectively. Humanities & Social Sciences, Economics, Engineering, and ICT were also represented with one study each.

Table 3. The representative scientific fields of study of the included studies grouped by reported outcome.

Field	Sign. positive (33%)	Pos. trend (37%)	No effect (30%)	Total
Education	6 [11,35,41,46,49,51]	3 [12,30,48]	1 [45]	10 (37%)
Medical & health sciences	3 [39,43,54]	4 [31,36–38]	2 [10,29]	9 (33%)
Psychology & cognitive sciences	0	0	4 [42,47,50,53]	4 (15%)
Arts, humanities, & social sciences	0	0	1 [52]	1 (4%)
Economics; commerce, management, tourism & services	0	1 [40]	0	1 (4%)
Engineering, built environment & design	0	1 [44]	0	1 (4%)
Information & computing science & technology	0	1 [13]	0	1 (4%)

5   Discussion

We first discuss the results obtained with respect to the impact of gamification on adherence across disciplines. Next, we reflect on the extent to which the recommendations by Sieverink et al. [7] were found. We end the discussion section with a reflection on the specific gamification strategies used.

5.1   Impact of Gamification on Adherence

The results of our systematic review lend support to the hypothesis that gamification has a positive effect on adherence. Nineteen out of 27 studies report a significantly positive effect or a positive trend. We emphasize that we applied strict standards with respect to scientific quality, and only included peer-reviewed conference or journal papers, and limited ourselves to studies that (1) conducted an experimental design and (2) studied adherence as a research goal and not as a consequence of the methodology used. Moreover, sample sizes and intervention duration were high among studies, suggesting that research studies have been conducted in a scientifically adequate manner.

Nevertheless, we must remain cautious. Although none of the papers reported a negative effect, 26% mentioned some form of a decrease in adherence over time. This is in line with the work of Koivisto et al. [57] who found that the perceived usefulness of gamification declines with use. This novelty effect should be considered when evaluating gamified systems and services as it can skew the results [58] with respect to adherence studies. This also highlights the importance of specifying how adherence is measured.

5.2   Pre-specifying and Justifying Adherence Measurements

Our study also foregrounds that further debate is necessary on how to conceptualize and measure adherent behavior in gamification studies. As shown in Table 1, all authors used distinct terms and distinct measurement variables. This is of course a natural consequence of the different disciplines and research objectives. Yet, transcending the different disciplines, we found both intended use and empirical, theoretical, or rational justifications of intended use were mostly lacking. Only five studies did specify intended use [13,31,38,41,50], and only three [10,37,43] did provide a additional justification of the intended use [7].

Unfortunately, the lack in specifying intended use a priori, and the lack of providing an accompanying justification might introduce researcher bias, as a researcher is currently completely unconstrained in defining what and how to measure. Moreover, it is hard to compare effects of gamification on adherence when measurements variables and thresholds differ between studies. The lack of a pre-specified intended use and the lack of justification in the current studies urges us to remain cautious in making bold claims about the impact of gamification on adherence.

5.3 Gamification Techniques

We found that all papers used a combination of minimum three distinct gamification techniques, with on average 5.7 ($\pm$ 1.8) techniques. At first sight, this
large average number may indicate the maturity of the implementations. On
the other hand, the frequent occurrence of points and leaderboards might also
suggest that the included studies focus largely on the PBL (points, badges,
leaderboards) triad [59]. Limiting gamification to the PBL triad may result in
failing to capture what makes games engaging, which in its turn leads to ineffec-
tive systems, and this is fundamental criticism of the field [60]. Due to the large
distribution of gamification techniques and the large variety in their implementation (and perhaps the quality), no conclusions can be made about adherence
and its relation to specific gamification techniques used in the study.

6   Limitations

This study has a number of limitations that affect the contribution. First, the
terms used in the search string might have impacted the results, as we did
not include domain-specific constructs of adherence, such as customer loyalty
and learner conversion. Such studies may in fact implicitly report adherence
measurements when they report impact. In these studies, however, improving
adherence is often not the main goal, and therefore were excluded from this
study. Moreover, we based ourselves for our search string on the findings of
Brown et al. [26]. We acknowledge that these terms could have induce a bias
towards papers in the health domain. However, 37% of the studies were from
the education domain, 33% of the health domain, and 15% from psychology
and cognitive sciences. This suggest that we were able to include studies across
disciplines.

Second, we did not score for 'quality' of the implemented gamification techniques or the gamified application. Gamification designers often critique the
approach of using individual gamification techniques without acknowledging the
quality of the implementation [61]. Moreover, gamified applications are perceived
as 'gestalts' by their users, they are perceived as one whole, rather than a mere
atomistic addition of gamification elements [60]. Hence, future research may
attempt to include measures of quality of implemented gamification techniques
as perceived by end-users.

7   Conclusions and Future Work

This paper first explored the concept of adherence and presented a tailored
definition for the gamification domain as "*the extent to which individuals use
a gamified service or system and experience its content, as defined or implied
by its creators, in order to derive a certain benefit.*" Next, it reports on a systematic literature review summarizing the published research on the effect of
gamification on adherence, across disciplines. Twenty-seven papers focusing on

both gamification and adherence, and including empirical measurements, met the criteria. The results of our systematic review lend support to the hypothesis that gamification has a positive effect on adherence. However, our results also suggest the need for a more refined conceptualization, as well as a set of standard elements to be present in any gamification study on adherence: (1) the ability to measure the usage behavior of individuals, (2) an operationalization of intended use, (3) an empirical, theoretical, or rational justification of the intended use.

Acknowledgments. This work is part of the research projects PANACEA Gaming Platform with project number HBC.2016.0177, and Personal Health Empowerment with project number HBC.2018.2012, which are financed by Flanders Innovation & Entrepreneurship.

References

1. Seaborn, K., Fels, D.I.: Gamification in theory and action: a survey. Int. J. Hum. Comput. Stud. **74**, 14–31 (2015)
2. Chou, Y.-K.: Actionable Gamification: Beyond Points, Badges, and Leaderboards. Octalysis Group, Fremont (2016)
3. Hamari, J., Koivisto, J., Sarsa, H.: Does gamification work? - a literature review of empirical studies on gamification. In: 2014 47th Hawaii International Conference on System Sciences, (Hawai, USA), pp. 3025–3034. IEEE (2014)
4. Nacke, L.E., Deterding, S.: The maturing of gamification research. Comput. Hum.Behav. **71**, 450–454 (2017)
5. Rapp, A., Hopfgartner, F., Hamari, J., Linehan, C., Cena, F.: Strengthening gamification studies: current trends and future opportunities of gamification research. Int. J. Hum. Comput. Studi. **127**, 1–6 (2019)
6. Kelders, S.M., Kok, R.N., Ossebaard, H.C., Van Gemert-Pijnen, J.E.W.C.: Persuasive system design does matter: a systematic review of adherence to web-based interventions. J. Med. Internet Res. **14**(6), e152 (2012)
7. Sieverink, F., Kelders, S.M., van Gemert-Pijnen, J.E.: Clarifying the concept of adherence to eHealth technology: systematic review on when usage becomes adherence. J. Med. Internet Res. **19**(12), e152 (2017)
8. Christensen, H., Griffiths, K.M., Korten, A.E., Brittliffe, K., Groves, C.: A comparison of changes in anxiety and depression symptoms of spontaneous users and trial participants of a cognitive behavior therapy website. J. Med. Internet Res. **6**, e46 (2004)
9. De Croon, R., et al.: Motivational design techniques to increase adherence to a telemonitoring therapy a study with adolescent pectus patients. In: 2019 IEEE International Conference on Healthcare Informatics (ICHI), pp. 1–12 (2019)
10. Leinonen, A.-M., Pyky, R., Ahola, R., et al.: Feasibility of gamified mobile service aimed at physical activation in young men: population-based randomized controlled study (MOPO). JMIR mHealth uHealth **5**(10), e146 (2017)
11. Krause, M., Mogalle, M., Pohl, H., Williams, J.J.: A playful game changer: fostering student retention in online education with social gamification. In: Proceedings of the Second (2015) ACM Conference on Learning @ Scale, L@S 2015, New York, NY, USA, pp. 95–102. ACM (2015)

12. Pechenkina, E., Laurence, D., Oates, G., Eldridge, D., Hunter, D.: Using a gamified mobile app to increase student engagement, retention and academic achievement. Int. J. Educ. Technol. High. Educ. **14**(1), 1–12 (2017)
13. Prause, C.R., Jarke, M.: Gamification for enforcing coding conventions. In: Proceedings of the 2015 10th Joint Meeting on Foundations of Software Engineering, New York, NY, USA, pp. 649–660. ACM (2015)
14. Sabaté, E.: Adherence to long-term therapies. Technical report, World Health Organization (2013)
15. Christensen, H., Griffiths, K.M., Farrer, L.: Adherence in internet interventions for anxiety and depression. J. Med. Internet Res. **11**, e13 (2009)
16. Brown, E., Cairns, P.: A grounded investigation of game immersion. In: CHI 2004 Extended Abstracts on Human Factors in Computing Systems, CHI EA 2004, New York, NY, USA, p. 1297–1300. Association for Computing Machinery (2004)
17. Brockmyer, J.H., Fox, C.M., Curtiss, K.A., McBroom, E., Burkhart, K.M., Pidruzny, J.N.: The development of the game engagement questionnaire: a measure of engagement in video game-playing. J. Exp. Soc. Psychol. **45**(4), 624–634 (2009)
18. Denisova, A., Nordin, A.I., Cairns, P.: The convergence of player experience questionnaires. In: Proceedings of the 2016 Annual Symposium on Computer-Human Interaction in Play, CHI PLAY 2016, New York, NY, USA, pp. 33–37. ACM (2016)
19. Sardi, L., Idri, A., Fernández-Alemán, J.L.: A systematic review of gamification in e-health. J. Biomed. Inform. **71**, 31–48 (2017)
20. Guertler, D., Vandelanotte, C., Kirwan, M., Duncan, M.J.: Engagement and nonusage attrition with a free physical activity promotion program: the case of 10,000 steps Australia. J. Med. Internet Res. **17**, e176 (2015)
21. Saul, J.E., Amato, M.S., Cha, S., Graham, A.L.: Engagement and attrition in internet smoking cessation interventions: insights from a cross-sectional survey of "one-hit-wonders." Internet Interventions **5**, 23–29 (2016)
22. Hassan, L., Hamari, J.: Gameful civic engagement: a review of the literature on gamification of e-participation. Gov. Inf. Q. **37**, 101461 (2020)
23. Koivisto, J., Hamari, J.: The rise of motivational information systems: a review of gamification research. Int. J. Inf. Manag. **45**, 191–210 (2019)
24. Koivisto, J., Malik, A.: Gamification for Older Adults: A Systematic Literature Review. The Gerontologist (2020)
25. Looyestyn, J., Kernot, J., Boshoff, K., Ryan, J., Edney, S., Maher, C.: Does gamification increase engagement with online programs? a systematic review. PLoS One **12**(3), e0173403 (2017)
26. Brown, M., O'Neill, N., van Woerden, H., Eslambolchilar, P., Jones, M., John, A.: Gamification and adherence to web-based mental health interventions: a systematic review. JMIR Ment. Health **3**, e39 (2016)
27. Moher, D., Liberati, A., Tetzlaff, J., Altman, D.G., Prisma Group: Preferred reporting items for systematic reviews and meta-analyses: the PRISMA statement. PLoS Med. **6**(7), e1000097 (2009)
28. Grönvall, E., Verdezoto, N., Bagalkot, N., Sokoler, T.: Concordance: a critical participatory alternative in healthcare IT. In: Aarhus Series on Human Centered Computing, vol. 1, p. 4 (Oct 2015)
29. Bodduluri, L., Boon, M.Y., Ryan, M., Dain, S.J.: Impact of gamification of vision tests on the UX. Games Health J. **6**(4), 229–236 (2017)
30. Fotaris, P., Mastoras, T., Leinfellner, R., Rosunally, Y.: From hiscore to high marks: empirical study of teaching programming through gamification. In: Proceedings of the European Conference on Games-based Learning, Bristol, UK, pp. 186–194. UWE Bristol (2015)

31. Scase, M., Marandure, B., Hancox, J., Kreiner, K., Hanke, S., Kropf, J.: Development of and adherence to a computer-based gamified environment designed to promote health and wellbeing in older people with mild cognitive impairment. Stud. Health Tech. Inf. **236**, 348–355 (2017)

32. O'Donnell, N., Kappen, D.L., Fitz-Walter, Z., Deterding, S., Nacke, L.E., Johnson, D.: How multidisciplinary is gamification research? results from a scoping review. In: Extended Abstracts Publication of the Annual Symposium on Computer-Human Interaction in Play, CHI PLAY 2017 Extended Abstracts, New York, NY, USA, pp. 445–452. ACM (2017)

33. Landis, R.J., Koch, G.G.: The measurement of observer agreement for categorical data. Biometrics **33**, 159–174 (1977)

34. Lombard, M., Snyder-Duch, J., Bracken, C.C.: Content analysis in mass communication: assessment and reporting of intercoder reliability. Hum. Commun. Res. **28**(4), 587–604 (2002)

35. Zamuner, T.S., Kilbertus, L., Weinhold, M.: Game-influenced methodology: addressing child data attrition in language development research. Int. J. Child-Comput. Interact. **14**, 15–22 (2017)

36. Dugas, M., et al.: Individual differences in regulatory mode moderate the effectiveness of a pilot mHealth trial for diabetes management among older veterans. PLoS One **13**(3), e0192807 (2018)

37. Gremaud, A.L., et al.: Gamifying accelerometer use increases physical activity levels of sedentary office workers. J. Am. Heart Assoc. **7**(13), 1–12 (2018)

38. Ryan, J., Edney, S., Maher, C.: Engagement, compliance and retention with a gamified online social networking physical activity intervention. Transl. Behav. Med. **7**(4), 702–708 (2017)

39. Zhao, Z., Arya, A., Whitehead, A., Chan, G., Etemad, S.A.: Keeping users engaged through feature updates: a long-term study of using wearable-based exergames. In: Proceedings of the 2017 CHI Conference on Human Factors in Computing Systems, New York, NY, USA, pp. 1053–1064. Association for Computing Machinery (2017)

40. Stanculescu, L.C., Bozzon, A., Sips, R.-J., Houben, G.-J.: Work and play: an experiment in enterprise gamification. In: Proceedings of the 19th CSCW, New York, NY, USA, pp. 346–358. ACM (2016)

41. Anderson, P.E., Nash, T., McCauley, R.: Facilitating programming success in data science courses through gamified scaffolding and learn2mine. In: Proceedings of the 2015 ACM Conference on Innovation and Technology in Computer Science Education, New York, NY, USA, pp. 99–104. ACM (2015)

42. Boot, W.R., Souders, D., Charness, N., Blocker, K., Roque, N., Vitale, T.: The gamification of cognitive training: older adults' perceptions of and attitudes toward digital game-based interventions. In: Zhou, J., Salvendy, G. (eds.) ITAP 2016, Part I. LNCS, vol. 9754, pp. 290–300. Springer, Cham (2016). https://doi.org/10.1007/978-3-319-39943-0_28

43. Cafazzo, J.A., Casselman, M., Hamming, N., Katzman, D.K., Palmert, M.R.: Design of an mHealth app for the self-management of adolescent type 1 diabetes: a pilot study. J. Med. Internet Res. **14**(3), E70 (2012)

44. Cunha Leite, R.M., Bastos Costa, D., Meijon Morêda Neto, H., Araújo Durão, F.: Gamification technique for supporting transparency on construction sites: a case study. Eng. Constr. Archit. Manag. **23**(6), 801–822 (2016)

45. De-Marcos, L., Domínguez, A., Saenz-de Navarrete, J., Pagés, C.: An empirical study comparing gamification and social networking on e-learning. Comput. Educ. **75**, 82–91 (2014)

46. Harrington, B., Chaudhry, A.: TrAcademic: improving participation and engagement in cs1/cs2 with gamified practicals. In: Proceedings of the 2017 ACM Conference on Innovation and Technology in Computer Science Education, ITiCSE 2017, New York, NY, USA, pp. 347–352. Association for Computing Machinery (2017)
47. Kelders, S.M., Sommers-Spijkerman, M., Goldberg, J.: Investigating the direct impact of a gamified versus nongamified well-being intervention: an exploratory experiment. J. Med. Internet Res. **20**(7), e247 (2018)
48. Khalil, M., Ebner, M., Admiraal, W.: How can gamification improve MOOC student engagement? In: Proceedings of the European Conference on Game Based Learning, Sonning Common, UK, pp. 819–828. ACPI (2017)
49. Lehtonen, T., Aho, T., Isohanni, E., Mikkonen, T.: On the role of gamification and localization in an open online learning environment: Javala experiences. In: Proceedings of the 15th Koli Calling Conference on Computing Education Research, Koli Calling 2015, New York, NY, USA, pp. 50–59. Association for Computing Machinery (2015)
50. Lumsden, J., Skinner, A., Coyle, D., Lawrence, N., Munafo, M.: Attrition from web-based cognitive testing: a repeated measures comparison of gamification techniques. J. Med. Internet Res. **19**(11), 1–18 (2017)
51. Nevin, C.R., et al.: Gamification as a tool for enhancing graduate medical education. Postgrad. Med. J. **90**(1070), 685–693 (2014)
52. Palacin-Silva, M.V., Knutas, A., Ferrario, M.A., Porras, J., Ikonen, J., Chea, C.: The role of gamification in participatory environmental sensing: a study in the wild. In: Proceedings of the 2018 CHI Conference on Human Factors in Computing Systems, CHI 2018, New York, NY, USA, pp. 1–13. Association for Computing Machinery (2018)
53. Pramana, G., Parmanto, B., Lomas, J., Lindhiem, O., Kendall, P.C., Silk, J.: Using mobile health gamification to facilitate cognitive behavioral therapy skills practice in child anxiety treatment: open clinical trial. JMIR Serious Games **6**(2), 1–15 (2018)
54. Zuckerman, O., Gal-Oz, A.: Deconstructing gamification: evaluating the effectiveness of continuous measurement, virtual rewards, and social comparison for promoting physical activity. Pers. Ubiquit. Comput. **18**(7), 1705–1719 (2014)
55. Lewin, A.B., et al.: Validity and reliability of an adolescent and parent rating scale of type 1 diabetes adherence behaviors: the self-care inventory (SCI). J. Pediatr. Psychol. **34**(9), 999–1007 (2009)
56. ukkinstituutti.fi. Helsinki: Ministry of Education and Culture & Nuori Suomi ry. Recommendation for the physical activity of school-aged children (2018)
57. Koivisto, J., Hamari, J.: Demographic differences in perceived benefits from gamification. Comput. Hum. Behav. **35**, 179–188 (2014)
58. Clark, K.R.: The effects of the flipped model of instruction on student engagement and performance in the secondary mathematics classroom. J. Educ. Online **12**(1), 91–115 (2015)
59. Werbach, K., Hunter, D.: For the Win: How Game Thinking Can Revolutionize Your Business. Wharton Digital Press, Philadelphia (2012)
60. Deterding, S.: Eudaimonic design, or: Six invitations to rethink gamification. In: Rethinking Gamification, pp. 305–331, Lüneburg, Germany. Meson Press, Lüneburg (June 2014)
61. Bogost, I.: Why gamification is bullshit. Gameful World Approach. Issues Appl. **65**, 65–79 (2015)

An Exploration of the Fear of Attack Strategy in Chess and Its Influence on Class-A Players of Different Chess Personalities: An Exploration Using Virtual Humans

Khaldoon Dhou[✉]

College of Business Administration, Texas A&M University-Central Texas,
Killeen, Texas, USA
kdhou@tamuct.edu

Abstract. The topic of virtual humans is increasingly important in the field of Artificial Intelligence. A virtual human can be defined as a computer simulation that mimics an actual human. Virtual humans are widely used in gaming, business, and many other domains. This paper presents an experiment that utilizes virtual chess players that simulate real players to examine the chess personalities of four chess players: a grandmaster and three class-A players. The selected grandmaster is Chigorin who is characterized by his fear of attack strategy. On the other hand, the class-A players represent three chess personalities: negligence of the center and capturing more than usual pieces, employment of traps in the opening phase, and solid openings and control of the center. To this end, the experiment represents simulations of games between Chigorin and each of the three class-A players. The errors of Chigorin and class-A players were utilized as dependent variables to measure the performance of the players. The findings reveal that although the class-A players have almost similar chess ratings, they performed differently during the simulations. Likewise, the outcomes showed that Chigorin played differently while competing against each of the class-A opponents. The results indicate that chess personalities play a significant role in predicting game outcomes between different players and it should be used as a factor along with the chess ratings.

Keywords: Virtual humans · Chess · Grandmaster · Fear of attack · Mikhail Chigorin · Games

1 Introduction

Recent trends in Artificial Intelligence have led to a proliferation of studies that explore the role of virtual humans in many fields including games. A virtual human can be thought of as a computer simulation that has features of an actual

© Springer Nature Switzerland AG 2021
X. Fang (Ed.): HCII 2021, LNCS 12789, pp. 185–195, 2021.
https://doi.org/10.1007/978-3-030-77277-2_15

human [23]. In chess, virtual humans are computer opponents that simulate real chess players of various skills such as Kasparov [8–10]. Virtual chess players made it possible to explore a wide range of chess players, even the ones who existed a long time ago. Additionally, virtual humans allow investigating the psychology of competition between players who existed in different time eras. For example, Dhou [8] employed virtual humans to explore the chess personalities of Anderssen (1818–1879) and Leko (1979-Now), and how they are influenced by the personalities of a set of less-skilled chess players.

The advantage of employing virtual players in designing experiments is that they offer much flexibility in choosing opponents depending on the parameters to be explored. In other words, a researcher can match players of different personalities and allow them to match for data collection. Additionally, exploring grandmasters from the past is possible with the utilization of virtual chess players that allow simulating their chess personalities. For example, the Chessmaster software offered by Ubisoft allows competing with a virtual player that simulates Bobby Fischer and many other players [21]. While it is not possible to play with chess players who existed in the past, it is also impractical to design experiments with certain parameters that include existing grandmasters and other less-skilled players. Fortunately, virtual chess players made it possible to design these types of experiments, and they can play at the same strengths as human players.

Each virtual chess player is characterized by two attributes: rating and chess personality. A chess rating is numeric that measures the strength of a chess player against other players that exist in the chess community [12,13]. Chess ratings are offered by many organizations such as the World Chess and the United States Chess Federations. On the other hand, chess personality describes the style of a chess player while competing against other players. Examples of chess personalities are attack, defense, and controlling the center. For example, Judit Polgar is an aggressive player whose endeavor is to gain initiative from the beginning of the game. Unlike Polgar, Leko is inclined towards certain defensive opening styles. While chess rating is widely used as a factor to classify chess players into various categories, chess personality seems to be a neglected factor and there is a dearth of studies that examined chess personalities. The extensive search reveals that only three studies explored the personalities of virtual chess players and how they perform against other virtual opponents [8–10].

This paper takes an interdisciplinary approach by investigating the personalities of four virtual players: a grandmaster and three class-A players that have distinct chess personalities. The selected grandmaster is Chigorin who is described by his feared attacking style and sometimes considers an Evans Gambit as a line of play. The chess personalities of the three other class-A players include many aspects including controlling and neglecting the center, capture a substantial number of pieces, solid opening knowledge, and using traps in the opening phase. The Chessmaster Grandmaster Edition was used to generate the games between Chigorin and other class-A players and was also utilized in analyzing the games. Two measurements were used as dependent variables: the Chessmaster agreement percentage on the moves by class-A players, and the Chessmaster agreement percentage on the moves made by Chigorin.

This paper is structured as follows: Sect. 2 provides an overview of existing research in the field of chess psychology, virtual humans, and personalities; Sect. 3 presents the method utilized in the paper including participants, materials, and procedure; Sect. 4 reports the results of the experiment; Sect. 5 provides a general discussion of the outcomes based on existing research studies; Sect. 6 concludes the paper.

2 Related Work

This section reviews existing research in the field of virtual humans that led to further understanding of the contest between chess players of different personalities. Additionally, it reviews related literature in chess psychology and personalities related to the current topic.

2.1 Virtual Chess Players

Virtual humans are computational characters that are created to act like actual humans. Existing research has shown that virtual humans are able to simulate many social aspects that exist in the actual interplay between real humans such as playing games and medical simulations [7,9]. One of the main applications of virtual humans is their utilization as chess players that mimic real chess players. Similar to real human players, virtual chess players have ratings that classify them into different chess categories such as grandmasters and class-A players. Additionally, each chess player has a personality and follows certain strategies while competing against other chess players. The extensive search reveals that the literature on virtual chess players has highlighted few attempts that explore the personalities of chess players via the utilization of virtual humans.

The first detailed study of virtual chess players examined two grandmaster chess personalities and how they were influenced by three class-B chess personalities [8]. The study explored the personalities of the grandmasters Anderssen and Leko. While Anderssen was an attacker grandmaster who begins to attack at an early stage of the game, Leko was a solid defensive player. The two grandmasters competed with class-B players that vary in their endgame and opening skills: a player who is strong at the opening phase, a player who gets stronger when approaching an endgame, and a balanced player. The study considers measuring the errors made by the players in the study, along with the number of the moves. The findings showed that Anderssen had fewer errors than Leko, and Anderssen's opponents also made fewer errors as opposed to Leko's opponents. Additionally, the games against Anderssen were longer than the games against Leko, and that indicates further resistance from the side of the opponents of Anderssen.

Similar to the experiment in [8], Dhou [11] utilized Leko and Anderssen in the competition against three class-A players that vary in the involvement of knights and bishops. The findings showed that the class-A players performed better when they competed against Andressen as opposed to when they competed against

Leko. Likewise, the investigation showed that Anderssen had fewer mistakes than Leko while competing against the other class-A players in the experiment. Additionally, the outcomes showed that the games played against Anderssen were longer than the games against Leko. All these findings have strong correlation with the outcomes from the experiment in [8]. The author showed a connection between the findings in this study and existing research on the behavior of cats that vary in their ability to kill rats [1].

To further examine the issue of virtual chess players, Dhou [9] conducted a follow-up study that considers the investigation of the personality of Kasparov. In his study, he utilizes a virtual chess player that simulates Kasparov while competing against three other class-A players. The chess personality of Kasparov that was investigated was able to calculate quickly and identify creative patterns that can be advantageous. The class-A players in his experiment represent three chess personalities: a chess player who values material, a balanced player, and a player who controls the center. The study utilized five dependent variables that include the errors of Kasparov and class-A players, the number of moves, and the Chessmaster's agreement percentages on the moves made by Kasparov and the three class-A players. The study found that on average, the games against a player who controls the center were the longest in the simulation. Additionally, the Chessmaster had the highest agreement percentages on the moves made by the same player who controls the center. His research study also showed opening variations and how they influenced the outcomes of the games between Kasparov and his opponent that controls the center of the board.

An investigation of virtual chess players also includes the exploration the examination of attack strategies in chess and how they could help in analyzing the performance of a fearless attacker against other class-A players. To this end, Dhou [10] designed an experiment that involved the virtual grandmaster Josh Waitzkin along with three other class-A players. While Waitzkin symbolizes a fearless attacker, the three other class-A players represent a set of chess personality characters including controlling and neglecting the center, capturing more than usual pieces, and considering opening traps. The findings show that the player who controls the center well had the best performance among the three other class-A players. Likewise, Waitzkin performed the best while competing against the same player compared to other opponents.

2.2   The Psychology of Chess

The early investigations in the psychology of chess players date back to 1965 when de Groot [6] performed a chess experiment on masters and beginners. In his experiment, he allowed both types of players to view meaningful chess positions for a period of time and asked them to build them from memory after that. He found that masters outperformed beginners. The same experiment was repeated with random chess positions over the board and the performance of the players from the two categories was equal [4]. A follow-up study was conducted by Chase and Simon [5] who found that chess experts are able to recognize a chess position and encode it as chunks that are made up of recognizable patterns along with relationships between them. The skill of a chess player has two main parts: the capacity of a chess player to search for the best moves to be chosen, and his capability to judge chess positions to identify the best choices [14].

The studies in [4–6] established a solid foundation for more research studies in chess psychology. Many researchers followed suit by developing new studies to further understand chess players and the choice of their movements. For example, Vollstädt-Klein et al. [22] investigated the personality of competitive chess players and how it affects their chess skills. They found that female players had further positive personality attributes than the common females in society. On the other hand, their study indicated that the personalities of male chess experts did not differ much from other normal males. In similar, Iqbal [15] explored male and female chess players the purpose of which is to determine if they differ in aesthetics. Their research was able to identify that on average, games between males were more beautiful than those among females for one of the datasets he used for testing.

The extensive research in chess led to more explorations in chess pieces and how they can be utilized in various chess purposes such as attack and defense. For example, Botvinnik [3] investigated attack and defense and how they are utilized in working out chess problems and estimated a function for an attacking route. Additionally, attack and defense were among the aspects that have been heavily investigated in the literature of chess, psychology, and many other domains such as marketing. One example from the field of chess is the experiment of Saariluoma [18] who investigated the response of players from different skills to identify an attack pattern and found that experts had a faster detection. Furthermore, attack strategies are prevalent in the marketing domain and they are used in competitions between different companies and brands (i.e. [2,16,19,20]).

While these previous studies and many others provided great insights on game patterns and the personality of chess players, there is a need for more studies on virtual humans and how they can help us explore many chess personalities. Additionally, there is a dearth of studies that involve virtual chess players and how they can be used to investigate the contest between players of different categories. This study adds to the literature body in virtual chess players and understanding the chess psychology of feared attack.

3   Method

3.1   Participants

The author selected four virtual players: three class-A players and one grandmaster from the Chessmaster offered by Ubisoft, a video game company. The class-A players have been previously investigated in the context of chess and virtual humans [10]. Additionally, Chigorin's playing style has been explored in chess literature [17]. It is essential to mention that all the investigated players in this study simulate real players that exist in real-life. Below are the personalities of four players chosen in this study, as Ubisoft describes them [21]:

- Chigorin: an eminent chess grandmaster who is known for his feared attacking and defensive styles. Additionally, he considers a positional playing manner.
- Buck: a class-A player that considers openings with substantial captured pieces. On the other hand, Buck neglects to control the center of the chessboard. He is rated at 2355 USCF.
- J.T.: a class-A chess player who chooses openings that are meant to get his opponents into designed traps. He is rated at 2330 USCF.
- Lili: a class-A player with a solid opening background, however, she chooses lines of play that can put her in minimal disadvantageous situations. Additionally, as opposed to Buck, she maintains well control of the center of the board. She is rated at 2394 USCF.

3.2 Materials

All the game experiments were conducted using the Chessmaster Grandmaster Edition [21]. The present design involves the manipulation of two independent variables:

- IV1: The color of the pieces of Chigorin. The experiment was designed in a way that Chigorin plays half of the games using white pieces and the other half with the black pieces.
- IV2: The personality class-A players employed in the experiment. This includes three levels: (a) the personality of Buck; (b) the personality of J.T.; and (c) the personality of Lili.

All the games were analyzed using the Chessmaster, which is a highly reputable software in the chess community and it can play at a grandmaster's level. Therefore, the author considers these measurements generated by the Chessmaster reliable. The author uses two measurements that were provided by the Chessmaster as dependent variables: the Chessmaster's agreement percentages on the moves made by Chigorin and each of the class-A players employed in the experiment. A two-way ANOVA was conducted that examined the effect of the color of Chigorin and the personality of class-A players involved on each of the dependent variables.

3.3 Procedure

For the sake of the experiment, Chigorin played 78 games against each of the class-A players: Buck, J.T, and Lili. Half of the games Chigorin played against each of the class-A players were with the white pieces, and the rest were with the black pieces. Each player had 3 min per game to complete all his moves.

4   Results

Since the design involves two dependent variables, the data was analyzed using two two-way ANOVA tests. There was a significant main effect of the personality of class-A players on the Chessmaster's agreement percentages on the moves made by Chigorin, $F(2, 228) = 5.006$, $p = 0.007$. Pairwise comparisons show that the Chessmaster significantly agrees more on the moves made by Chigorin when playing against Lili ($M = 97.821$) than the moves made by Chigorin while playing against J.T. (96.449). Additionally, there was a significant main effect of the color of the grandmaster on the Chessmaster's agreement percentages on the moves played by Chigorin, $F(1, 228) = 6.134$, $p = 0.014$. That is to say, the Chessmaster agrees more on the moves played by Chigorin when he plays with the white pieces ($M = 97.538$) than when he plays with the black pieces ($M = 96.658$). Concerning the Chessmaster's agreement percentages on the moves made by class-A players, the two-way ANOVA test reveals that there was a significant main effect of the personality of class-A players, $F(2, 228) = 3.140$, $p = 0.045$. Pairwise comparisons show that the Chessmaster agrees more on the moves made by Lili ($M = 94.551$) than the moves made by J.T. ($M = 92.795$). The visualization in Fig. 1 shows the Chessmaster agreement percentages on the moves made by Chigorin and class-A players.

5   General Discussion

The present study was designed to investigate the competition between Chigorin, a chess grandmaster who is characterized by his feared attack style, and three class-A players that have different chess personalities. The investigation employed the Chessmaster Grandmaster Edition offered by Ubisoft to generate the game simulations between four virtual players: Chigorin and three class-A players. The simulations of the games represent the contest between Chigorin and three chess personalities related to class-A players: a player who prefers to have lots of captures and neglects the center of the chessboard, a player who considers traps, and a player who has solid control of the center, but might choose lines that would get her into slightly disadvantageous situations. Although the four players in the experiment were virtual, they simulate chess personalities that exist among real chess players.

The current study found that there is a strong correlation between the personality of the four virtual players and the errors they make. Another important finding was that the personality of a chess player can also influence the errors made by his opponent. For example, Fig. 1 shows that on average, the highest Chessmaster's agreement percentages are on the games between Chigorin and Lili. Likewise, the Chessmaster's agreement percentages were higher on the moves made by Lili as opposed to the moves made by J.T. and Buck. These patterns are similar to the findings of a previous study that utilized an attacker and defensive grandmaster personalities against three class-B players [8]. The outcomes from the study in [8] reveal that class-B players tend to make mistakes that are correlated with the mistakes made by their grandmaster opponents. In other words, an attacker grandmaster in [8] performed better than a defensive grandmaster while competing against three class-B players. Similarly, the same less skilled players in the study had fewer mistakes while competing against an attacker grandmaster.

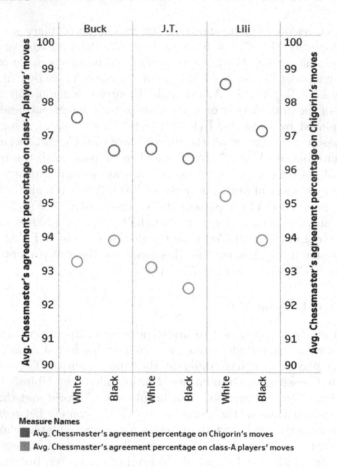

Fig. 1. The Chessmaster average agreement percentages on the moves made by class-A players and Chigorin

Previous studies also confirmed that the personality of a chess player can influence his performance while competing against other players [8–10]. These players include virtual grandmasters such as Kasparov and Waitzkin. For instance, Dhou [9] explored the personality of Kasparov while competing against class-B players and found that Kasparov performed differently depending on the chess personalities of his opponents. The same study showed that class-B players had different errors while competing against Kasparov although their ratings were almost the same. Similarly, the study in [10] showed that the Chessmaster's agreement percentages on Waitzkin's moves varied depending on his class-A opponents. Additionally, the class-A players have had different Chessmaster's agreement percentages while competing against Waitzkin although they belong to the same chess class and have almost identical USCF ratings.

Another finding from this study is that controlling the center is a powerful aspect. This was evidenced by the outcomes from the games of Lili who has solid control of the chessboard. Among the three class-A players, the Chessmaster agrees more on the moves of Lili as opposed to the moves made by Buck and J.T. A comparison of these findings with those of another study confirms that controlling the center leads to fewer errors compared with other chess attitudes such as playing tricks in the opening phase and center negligence [10].

6 Conclusion

In this investigation, the aim was to assess the utilization of virtual chess players to explore the competition between a grandmaster personality and three class-A personalities. The four virtual players in the experiment have different chess personalities. The grandmaster's personality was represented by Chigorin, who is characterized by his fear of attack style. The investigation of the chess personalities of the three class-A players focused on the tendency of capturing a lot of chess pieces, controlling and neglecting the center, solid openings, and offering traps during the opening phases. While the investigated players in this research study are virtual, their chess personalities resemble actual chess personalities of real players.

The findings from this study clearly indicate that chess players of different classes (i.e. grandmasters, class-A players) can perform differently depending on their chess personalities and the chess personalities of their opponents regardless of the ratings. In other words, two chess players of the same rating and different chess personalities might perform differently when they meet a particular chess player. This main finding was also confirmed by other studies that involve virtual humans designing experiments that explore various chess personalities such as the ones in [8,9].

These findings have significant implications for the understanding of how players of certain personalities can influence the outcomes of chess games. In other words, the findings can probably help in answering particular questions about the results of chess games and how players can perform depending on the personalities of their chess opponents. While these findings are considered interesting from an academic perspective, further research is needed to explore their practicality in other domains that involve strategies such as marketing.

References

1. Adamec, R.: The behavioral bases of prolonged suppression of predatory attack in cats. Aggressive Behav. 1(4), 297–314 (1975), https://onlinelibrary.wiley.com/doi/abs/10.1002/1098-2337%281975%291%3A4%3C297%3A%3AAID-AB2480010404%3E3.0.CO%3B2-U
2. Ausness, R.C.: Will more aggressive marketing practices lead to greater tort liability for prescription drug manufacturers. Wake Forest L. Rev. 37, 97 (2002)

3. Botvinnik, M.: A mathematical representation of chess. In: Computers, Chess and Long-Range Planning, pp. 11–25. Springer (1970). https://doi.org/10.1007/978-1-4684-6245-6
4. Chase, W.G., Simon, H.A.: The mind's eye in chess. In: Visual Information Processing, pp. 215–281. Elsevier (1973)
5. Chase, W.G., Simon, H.A.: Perception in chess. Cogn. Psychol. **4**(1), 55–81 (1973)
6. De Groot, A.: Thought and choice in chess (1965)
7. DeVault, D., et al.: SimSensei kiosk: a virtual human interviewer for healthcare decision support. In: Proceedings of the 2014 International Conference on Autonomous Agents and Multi-Agent Systems, pp. 1061–1068 (2014)
8. Dhou, K.: Towards a better understanding of chess players' personalities: a study using virtual chess players. In: Kurosu, M. (ed.) HCI 2018. LNCS, vol. 10903, pp. 435–446. Springer, Cham (2018). https://doi.org/10.1007/978-3-319-91250-9_34
9. Dhou, K.: An innovative employment of virtual humans to explore the chess personalities of Garry Kasparov and other class-A players. In: Stephanidis, C. (ed.) HCI International 2019 - Late Breaking Papers, pp. 306–319. Springer International Publishing, Cham (2019). https://doi.org/10.1007/978-3-030-30033-3_24
10. Dhou, K.: A novel investigation of attack strategies via the involvement of virtual humans: A user study of Josh Waitzkin, a virtual chess grandmaster. In: Stephanidis, C., et al (eds.) HCI International 2020 - Late Breaking Papers: Cognition, Learning and Games, pp. 658–668. Springer International Publishing, Cham (2020). https://doi.org/10.1007/978-3-030-60128-7_48
11. Dhou, K.: An exploration of chess personalities in grandmasters and class-a players using virtual humans. Int. J. Entertainment Technol. Manage. (2021). (in Press)
12. Elo, A.E.: The rating of chessplayers, past and present. Arco Pub. (1978)
13. Glickman, M.E., Jones, A.C.: Rating the chess rating system. CHANCE-BERLIN THEN NEW YORK- **12**, 21–28 (1999)
14. Gobet, F., Simon, H.A.: Templates in chess memory: a mechanism for recalling several boards. Cogn. Psychol. **31**(1), 1–40 (1996). https://www.sciencedirect.com/science/article/pii/S0010028596900110
15. Iqbal, A.: Which gender plays more beautiful chess? In: Social Sciences and Interdisciplinary Behavior: The 4th International Congress on Interdisciplinary Behavior and Social Science (ICIBSoS 2015), Kazan Federal University, Kazan, Russia, 22–23 October 2015 & Arya Duta hotel, Jakarta, Indonesia, 07–08 November 2015, p. 375. CRC Press (2016)
16. Kurt, D., Hulland, J.: Aggressive marketing strategy following equity offerings and firm value: the role of relative strategic flexibility. J. Mark. **77**(5), 57–74 (2013). https://doi.org/10.1509/jm.12.0078
17. Linder, I., Linder, V.: Wilhelm Steinitz: 1st World Chess Champion, vol. 3. SCB Distributors (2014)
18. Saariluoma, P.: Chess players' intake of task-relevant cues. Mem. Cognit. **13**(5), 385–391 (1985)
19. Šramová, B.: Aggressive marketing, consumer kids and stereotyping of media contents. Procedia. Soc. Behav. Sci. **140**, 255–259 (2014)
20. Stošić-Mihajlović, L., Trajković, S.: Aggressive vs. discrete marketing. J. Process Manage. New Technol. **7**(2), 7–12 (2019)
21. Ubisoft: Chessmaster grandmaster edition. http://chessmaster.uk.ubi.com/xi/index.php

22. Vollstädt-Klein, S., Grimm, O., Kirsch, P., Bilalić, M.: Personality of elite male and female chess players and its relation to chess skill. Learn. Individ. Differ. **20**(5), 517–521 (2010). http://www.sciencedirect.com/science/article/pii/S1041608010000403
23. Yuan, Y., Qi, L., Luo, S.: The reconstruction and application of virtual Chinese human female. Comput. Meth. Programs Biomed. **92**(3), 249–256 (2008). https://www.sciencedirect.com/science/article/pii/S0169260708001260, medical Imaging and Medical Informatics (MIMI)

The Factorial Structure and Underlying Contributors of Parents' Behavioral Involvement in Children's Video Game Use

Heqing Huang⬤, You Zhou, Xiaolin Qi, Fangbing Qu⬤, and Xiaocen Liu(✉)⬤

Capital Normal University, Beijing, People's Republic of China
cindyliu@cnu.edu.cn

Abstract. Nowadays, parents are increasing engaged in their children's video game use. However, it is still unclear how and why parents are involved and how they interact with their children. The present study aims to explore the structure and underlying factors of parents' involvement in their children's video game use. The sample for the present study included 1,495 parents of preschoolers who completed a questionnaire on their involvement in their children's video game use, their worries about their children's video game use, and their evaluation of the available video games. The result found the factorial structure underlying parents' involvement in their children's use of video games consisted of five dimensions: parents using video games as a parenting tool, parents exercising control over children's video game use, parents use video games with their parents, and parents use video game themselves, and parents providing video game equipment or software. The results also indicated that parents' video game worries and quality evaluations predict parents' video game involvement both independently and interactively.

Keywords: Video game use · Parent behavioral involvement · Worries · Quality evaluation

1 Introduction

In recent decades, various video games have taken over children's lives. From an increasingly earlier age, children are usually immersed in media-rich homes and are frequently allowed to use different technologies and play video games [1, 2]. The video game invasion has challenged families and parents. Consequently, intense and complex changes have taken place in the interaction between parents and children. However, up to now, it is still not clear how and why parents are involved in and interact with their young children's video gaming activities. The present study aims to explore the structure and underlying factors of parents' involvement in their children's video game use.

© Springer Nature Switzerland AG 2021
X. Fang (Ed.): HCII 2021, LNCS 12789, pp. 196–209, 2021.
https://doi.org/10.1007/978-3-030-77277-2_16

1.1 Parents' Behavioral Involvement in Children' Video Game Use

Parents have no choice but to be involved in their children's video game use. With the increasing invasion of various video games, parents are more and more engaged in children's video game playing [3]. Whether and how parents are involved in children's video game use plays an important role not only in children's developmental outcomes but also in the parent-child relationship [4].

With the increasing trend of video game use in families, parents have to deal with video game-related problems and different interactions concerning video game use. Previous research has identified various practices parents use to deal with children's video game use.

Most research concerning parenting and children's video game use deals with how to manage and control children's video game use [5]. For example, Martins et al. have examine parental mediation of video game play and divided the parents' mediation into three the positive, negative, neutral types [6]. However it is not the only form for parents involved in children's video game use. There is also research examining parents' use of video games as parenting and educational tools. Some parents use video games to calm babies or children. Parents also accept video games as a learning tool for children [7], especially in the context of COVID-19 [8]. Some research has identified an interaction between children and parents in that the parents also play video games [9]. While there are rare studies suggesting how parents deal with children playing video games and there have been a small number of studies on video game use in general, there is an absence of a whole and systematic understanding of the phenomenon.

1.2 The Underlying Factors in Parents' Involvement in Children's Video Games

The complexity of parents' behaviors toward children's video games is at least partly driven by the complex and multiple effects of video games on children. Previous research suggested that video games may have both positive and negative roles in children's development [10]. Researchers have shown that excessive use of video games contributes to obesity in children and young people. It can also be harmful to the eyesight of individuals [11, 12]. Meanwhile, some active video games have proved to be a useful way to address inactivity and obesity in children. Researchers found that video games involve risk factors for children's social and emotional development [13]. Meanwhile, an increasing number of games have been developed to improve children's social and emotional development [14–16]. Although research has identified a link between academic problems and video game use [17, 18], some specially designed video games are increasingly being used to improve children's learning and their intellectual training [19]. Whether and how parents' engage in behavioral involvement in children's video game use is related to many factors. The two most common factors are parents' emotional and cognitive reactions. The former relates to how the parents feel about their children's video game use, and the latter means how parents evaluate the video games. The complex effects of video games inevitably cause complicated cognitive and emotional responses in parents. The emotional and cognitive factors are highly complex. Therefore, to investigate the underlying mechanism of parents' multi-dimensional involvement, it is necessary to examine the underlying emotional and cognitive factors. Based on previous studies and our early pilot research, we focus on the emotional factor, parents' worries about children's video game use, and the cognitive factor, parents' evaluation of video game use.

Parents' Worries About Children's Video Game Use. Worry is one of the most typical emotional reactions of parents to their children's video games. In our modern society, parents experience different kinds and levels of worries about their children's video game use. Some research indicated that parents worry that video gaming might be addictive and harmful for their children [20]. Moreover, researchers have suggested that children have very different beliefs to those of their parents concerning video games [21]. These differences can negatively affect parent–child relationships in some families [22]. However, the nature and the degree of parents' worries about children's video game use were not clearly identified up to now.

Parents' Quality Evaluation About Children's Video Game Use. Parents' behavior involvement is also related with how they recognize and evaluate the video game. When determine how to respond to children's video game, parents try to get more information to evaluate the video game, and consequently make better decisions. According to the Entertainment Software Association (ESA, 2014) [23], 95% of the parents surveyed claimed that, "they pay attention to thecontent of the games their children play" (p 8).

If the parents evaluate the game is well designed and of good quality, he will be more willing to let children use games and reduce the restrictive requirements. While if they evaluate that the quality of the game is not good, their supportive behavior may decrease and restrictive behavior may increase. In the present research, we will investigate how parents' quality evaluation of video games related to their behavioral involvement in children's video game use.

Other Background Factors. Previous research also suggested that, how parents perceive video games, cognitively or emotionally, is also affected by the demographic variables, such as children's age and gender, whether he or she the only child in the family, parents' socioeconomic status, and so on [24, 25]. Accordingly, there demographic variable will be controlled in the present study.

1.3 The Present Study

Arising from gaps identified in previous research, the present study aimed to examine the factor structure of parents' involvement in their children's video game use. We also aimed to investigate the potential emotional and cognitive factors underlying parents' involvement and the role of SES in this relationship.

2 Method

2.1 Respondents

The respondents come from the north and west provinces of China. The original sample consisted of 1,496 parents of young children. We did not include 78(5.2%) respondents in the analyses because of incomplete information. There were 193(12.9%) respondents whose children had never played video games and were, therefore, deleted from the analyses. The final sample consisted of 1,225 parents of young children. There were 53.7% boys and 46.3%. The age range of the participant' children was 2.10 to 5.06 years, with a mean age of 3.77 years (SD = 0.74). 73.4% of the children were the only children, 26.6% were non-only children, and 1.1%. We used a formula to compose an integrated index of participants' social economic status (SES): Mses = 0.032, SDses = 1.01, Rangeses = −5.05 to 2.60.

2.2 Procedure and Materials

The data were collected from 2018 to 2020, and this research was a part of a larger cross-sectional study examining Chinese children's video game use and their parenting factors. All of the questionnaires consisted of 150 questions and required approximately 30 min to complete. The questionnaires were published and delivered to the respondents through their children's preschool. The experimenter explained the items to the respondents who had difficulties in reading and writing and help them to complete the questionnaire.

The present study used approximately 80 of the questions in the questionnaires, covering four aspects of the information.

Questions about Background Information. Background information on the children (e. g., date of birth, gender, urban or rural, only child status) and their parents (e.g., age, occupation, education, annual household income) was collected.

Questions about how Parents are Involved in Children's Video Game Use. We collected 27 items through literature and parents interview which reflected parents' behavioral involvement in their children's video game use. After an expert's evaluation, five items were deleted due to their repetitive or inappropriate nature.

Questions about Parents' Worries about their Children's Video Game Use. We collected 35 items also through literature and parents interview which reflected parents' worries about their children's video game use. The rating expert's suggested deleting seven repetitive items. Therefore, 28 items were included in the following analysis.

Questions about the Parents' Evaluation of the video Games. There were two items concerning parents' evaluation of the contents and the picture quality.

3 Results

Three sets of analyses were conducted. First, using exploratory factor analysis (EFA), the structure of parents' behavioral involvement in children's video game use was examined. Second, the structure of parents' worries about children's video game use was examined using EFA. Third, we carried out correlation and regression analyses to investigate the role of emotional factors (parents' worries about children's video game use) and the cognitive factors (parents' evaluation of video game quality) in parents' involvement in children's video games use.

3.1 Parents' Behavioral Involvement in Their Children's Video-Game Use

An EFA was used to identify the structure and the dimensions of the parents' behavioral involvement in their children's video game use. A principal components analysis with an Oblimin rotation was performed on these 22 items. The scree test suggested five or six factors. As our criterion for tenable factors was at least two variables with loadings greater than or equal to 0.30 [26], the inappropriate items were deleted one by one. The EFA led to the exclusion of two items, leaving a final questionnaire comprising 20 items organized in five sub-scales. Subscale loadings from the pattern matrices and the cumulative percentages for the remaining factor solutions are presented in Table 1.

In the EFA solution, the first factor contained six items that reflected *parents' use of video games as a parenting tool*, accounting for approximately 38.27% of the variance. The second factor in the five-factor solution contained five items concerning parents' control over children's video game use (13.97%). The other three factors contained three items, respectively. According to their meaning, they were described as follows: *Parents' co-play with children, parents use video games themselves,* and *parents provide video game equipment or software*.

These factors accounted for 6.73%, 6.00%, and 5.02% of the variance, respectively. The alphas for the five factors were 0.82, 0.83, 0.84, 0.81 and 0.70, respectively.

3.2 Structure of Parents' Worries About Their Children's Video-Game Use

We also used an EFA to explore the structure of the parents' worries about their children's video game use. Based on the 28 items, a principal components analysis with an oblimin rotation was performed. The EFA procedure and criterion for tenable factors were the same as in the EFA for the parents' behavioral involvement. The scree test suggested four or five factors, and the parallel analysis suggested three to five factors. After deleting one by one, the items were organized into five sub-scales. Subscale loadings from the pattern matrices and the cumulative percentages for the remaining factor solutions are presented in Table 2.

Table 1. Structure matrix of parents' behavioral involvements in children's videogame use

Items	Factor 1	Factor 2	Factor 3	Factor 4	Factor 5
You often use video games as a tool to keep your child quiet	.78				
You often use video games as a reward for good performance	.76				
If you have no time to accompany your child, you'll let them play video games	.74				
You usually use video games as an educational tool for your children	.69				
You often discuss video games with your child about the videogame's contents, strategies, information, and so on	.65				
You usually readily agree when the child asks to play the game	.52				
You usually readily agree when the child asks to play the game		-.89			
You will control the time and frequency of children playing games		.86			
You think you can effectively control your child's playing video games		.79			
When children play video games, you will accompany and guide them		.74			
Children who do not follow the rules of playing video games will be punished		.73			
You believe video game use facilitates the parents-children communication			.85		
When you are playing video-games, your children often require video game use too			.80		
You have invited your child to play video games with you			.75		
You likes play video-game too				.86	
You play video games when your kids are present				.81	
You are keen on collecting various electronics				.73	
You often pay for video game software for your kids					.84
You often pay for video game equipment for your kids					.81
Your kids likes the game you like					.42

In the EFA solution, the first factor contained 14 items that reflected parents' worries about the effects of video games on the social and mental health of their children. This accounted for approximately 37.63% of the variance. The second factor in the three-factor solution contained eight items concerning children's cognition and the development of their intelligence. This factor accounted for 16.47% of the variance. The third factor, which accounted for 12.11% of the variance, contained four items, reflecting the parents' worries about the negative effect of video games on children's physical health. The alphas for the three factors were 0.86, 0.84, and 0.80, respectively.

Table 2. Structure matrix of parents' worries about their children's video game use

Items of parents' worries	Factor 1 Worry of Social & emotional development	Factor 2 Worry of cognition & attention	Factor 3 Worry of physical health
Good living habits	.75		
Cherish life	.72		
Emotion regulation	.71		
Social understanding	.70		
Helping behaviors	.70		
Emotion understanding	.69		
Self management	.68		
Control of violet behavior	.65		
Learning interest	.63		
Parent-child relationship	.63		
Distinguish imagination from reality	.62		
Aesthetic	.61	.43	
Cooperation	.60		
Peer relationship	.59		
Response capacity		.82	
Sensory coordination		.82	
Fine movement		.68	
Spatial Perception		.67	
Imagination	.43	.65	
Attention		.65	
Intelligence	.52	.62	
Time perception		.54	
Eye sight			.72
Overall physical fitness			.69
Somatic movement			.68
Hearing ability			.66

3.3   Roles of Worry and Quality Evaluation in Parents' Behavioral Involvement in Children's Video Game Use

The descriptive and correlative analyses of parents' involvement in children's video game use, their worries about their children's video game use, and their quality evaluation are shown in Table 3.

The correlation analysis suggested multiple relationships between the variables. A hierarchical regression was performed with the five parents' behavioral involvement dimensions as dependent variables to further explore the factors underlying the parents' involvement in their children's video game use. The demographic variables (age, gender, single child, SES) were entered at Step 1. Next, the parents' three kinds of worry and the parents' quality evaluation were entered at Step 2. Finally, we examined the interaction effects between each of the parents' video game worries and quality evaluation by entering an interaction between the cognitive factors and age at Step 3. The results are presented in Table 4.

The regression analysis indicated that parents' behavioral involvement in children's video games is not only predicted by their video game worries and video game quality evaluation independently but also by the interaction between the two variables.

First, parents' behavior involvement was found to be negatively predicted by their worries about children's social and cognitive development, suggesting that the more parents worry that video games will harm their children's social and cognitive development, the less likely they will be to use video games as parenting and educating tools. The results also indicate that parents' quality evaluation independently predicted their use of video games as parenting tools. Second, concerning parents' control over children's video game use, there are significant interactive effects between parents' quality evaluation and worries about children's cognitive development. A simple-slopes analysis was used to examine this interaction effect. We divided the whole sample into three groups, low, middle, and high-quality evaluation. The results showed that, after controlling for the demographic variables, it is in the low and middle-quality evaluation groups that worry can significantly predict parents' control over video game use.

Third, the results indicate that parents' co-play video game with their children was significantly negatively predicted by their worry about children's cognitive development while it was positively predicted by their quality evaluation of video games. Fourth, parents' using video game by themselves was negatively predicted by all three kinds of video game worries and it was positively predicted by their game quality evaluation. Finally, parents' material providence were negatively predicted by parents' worries about theirs children' social and physical development, while it was positively predicted by parents' worries about their children's cognitive development.

Table 3. Correlative statistics for behavior involvement and the underlying worries and quality evaluations of their children's video game use

Variables	M	SD	2	3	4	5	6	7	8	9	10	11	12	13
1 Children's age	4.64	1.09	−0.04	.05*	0.06	−.07*	−0.03	−.07*	0.05	.07**	−0.03	0.04	0.00	0.02
2 Children's gender	1.46	0.50		−0.02	−0.01	0.03	0.05	0.05	0.03	−0.04	0.03	−0.03	−0.03	0.00
3 Only child or not	1.25	0.44			−.15**	−0.04	−0.05	−0.05	−.05*	−.05*	−0.02	−0.02	−.10**	−.08**
4 SES	0.06	0.85				−0.01	−0.02	0.01	.10**	−0.04	0.03	−.12**	−0.05	0.02
5 Worry of social	3.52	0.78					.74**	.69**	−.33**	−.38**	−.30**	−.18**	−.33**	−.30**
6 Worry of cognition	3.07	0.84						.61**	−.32**	−.37**	−.40**	−.17**	−.32**	−.23**
7 Worry of physical	3.83	0.75							−.23**	−.35**	−.19**	−.21**	−.30**	−.28**
8 Quality evaluation	2.81	0.91								.28**	.23**	.08*	.18**	.17**
9 Parenting Tool	2.48	0.88									.36**	.57**	.50**	.56**
10 Video-game control	3.31	0.98										.18**	.24**	.28**
11 Co-use with children	2.19	0.94											.43**	.43**
12 Use by themselves	2.49	1.02												.48**
13 Material providence	2.17	0.93												1.00

Table 4. Hierarchical regressions predicting the five dimension of parents' behavioral involvement in children's video games

	Parenting Tool			Video-game control			Co-use with children			Use by themselves			Material providence		
	B	β	t	B	β	t	B	β	t	B	β	t	B	β	t
Model 1	F(4, 938) = 1.24, p > 0.05, R² = .05			F(4, 936) = 0.618, p > 0.05, R² = .003			F(4, 935) = 2.53, p = .04, R² = 0.011			F(4, 937) = 3.67, p = 0.006, R² = 0.02			F(4, 934) = 0.61, p < .05, R² = .003		
Children's age	.02	.03	.92	.03	.04	1.15	.013	.014	.44	-.00	-.003	-.11	-.02	-.02	-.65
Children's gender	-.09	-.05	-1.52	.02	.01	.36	-.07	-.04	-1.19	-.12	-.06	-1.83*	-.03	-.02	-.58
Only child or not	-.12	-.04	-1.25	-.04	-.02	-.51	.02	.01	.20	-.25	-.10	-3.10**	-.07	-.03	-.89
SES	.01	-.03	.81	.03	.03	.79	-.11	-.09	-2.86	-.07	-.06	-1.85*	.03	.03	.84
Model 2	F(8, 930) = 13.01, p < .001, R² = .101, ΔR² = .093			F(6, 934) = 14.70, p < .001, R² = .112, ΔR² = .105			F(6, 933) = 3.08, p = .002, R² = 0.026, ΔR² = .017			F(8, 933) = 12.53, p < .001, R² = .10, ΔR² = .089			F(8, 930) = 6.42, p < .001, R² = 0.052, ΔR² = .044		
Children's age	.02	.02	.65	.01	.02	.54	.01	-.01	-.43	-.01	-.01	-.33	-.02	-.02	-.72
Children's gender	-.10	-.06	-2.06*	.02	.01	.38	-.09	-.07	-2.21	-.14	-.01	-.43	-.06	-.03	-.95
Only child or not	-.05	-.02	-.74	-.04	-.02	-.61	.04	-.09	-2.78	-.22	-.07	-2.21*	-.04	-.02	-.55
SES	-.04	-.04	-1.33	-.00	-.00	-.03	-.11	-.07	-2.14*	-.08	-.09	-2.78**	.04	.03	.97
Worry_social	-.10	-.09	-1.73*	.04	.04	.76	-.08	-.11	-2.12	-.15	-.07	-2.14*	-.21	-.16	-3.25**
Worry_cognition	-.06	-.06	-1.25	-.38	-.34	-7.73**	.09	-.08	-1.90	-.11	-.10	-2.12*	.12	.10	2.13*
Worry_physical	-.12	-.11	-2.64**	.17	.15	3.65**	-.13	-.10	-2.54*	-.14	-.08	-1.90*	-.16	-.13	-3.09**
Quality Evaluation	.14	.17	5.27**	.12	.15	4.50**	.04	.09	2.58*	.08	-.10	-2.54*	.04	.04	1.24
Model 3	F(11, 927) = 9.46, p < .001, R² = 0.101, ΔR² = .09			F(11, 925) = 11.34, p < .001, R² = .119, ΔR² = .108			F(7, 932) = 2.78, p < .01, R² = .03, ΔR² = .02			F(11, 930) = 8.47, p < .001, R² = 0.10, ΔR² = .00			F(11, 927) = 4.80, p < .001, R² = 0.05, ΔR² = .043		
Children's age	.02	.02	.67	.01	.02	.54	.01	.01	.41	-.02	-.02	-.56	-.02	-.02	-.63
Children's gender	-.10	-.06	-2.05*	.02	.01	.31	-.09	-.05	-1.53	-.14	-.07	-2.17	-.06	-.03	-.98
Only child or not	-.05	-.02	-.73	-.04	-.02	-.55	.04	.02	.47	-.22	-.09	-2.83**	-.04	-.02	-.49
SES	-.04	-.04	-1.35	.00	.00	.02	-.11	-.09	-2.84**	-.08	-.07	-2.10**	.03	.03	.97
Worry_social	-.09	-.08	-1.65	.03	.02	.44	-.09	-.07	-1.39	-.15	-.11	-2.18*	-.21	-.16	-3.20**
Worry_cognition	-.06	-.06	-1.30	-.37	-.33	-7.39**	.11	.09	1.87*	-.10	-.08	-1.75*	.11	.09	2.04
Worry_physical	-.12	-.11	-2.63**	.17	.15	3.58**	-.13	-.10	-2.36*	-.14	-.10	-2.44*	-.17	-.13	-3.15**
Quality Evaluation	.14	.18	5.26**	.12	.14	4.35**	.04	.04	1.28	.09	.09	2.61*	.04	.04	1.18
QE ×Wor soc	.01	.01	.23	-.01	-.01	-.18	-.11	-.12	-2.25*	-.01	-.01	-.16	.01	.01	.21
QE ×Wor cog	-.02	-.02	-.51	.08	.09	2.04*	.07	.08	1.68*	.03	.04	.76	-.01	-.01	-.13
QE ×Wor phy	.01	.01	.23	-.01	-.01	-.30	.05	.06	1.28	-.07	-.07	-1.54	.03	.03	.75

4 Discussion

The present study examined parents' behavioral involvement in their children's video game use and its underlying emotional and cognitive factors. The present research also examined how and to what extent the two factors predict parents' behavioral involvement in children's video games use. The present study broadens our knowledge and understanding of parents' interaction with children on video game use by examining the following two aspects.

4.1 Structure and Levels of Parents' Behavioral Involvement

To the best of our knowledge, this is the first attempt to systematically examine the factorial structure underlying parents' behavioral involvement in children's video game use. Although previous research examined parents' involvement in children's video game use, however the emphases has been put on how to manage the manage the control children's video game use.

Our research indicated that parents' involvement in children's video game use is an multiple dimension and complex structure, and thy parents involve in children's video game with multiple strategies, including five basic ways: parents use video games as a parenting tool, parents exercise control over children's video game use, parents use video game with their children, parents use video games themselves, and parents provide video game equipment or software.

4.2 Factors Underlying Parents' Involvement in Children's Video Game Use

The complexity of parents' behaviors toward children's video game use was partly driven by the complex and multiple effects of video games on children. As previous research suggested, video game use may have both positive and negative roles in children's various developmental areas. The complex effects of video game use cause the parents' complicated cognitional and emotional reactions. Therefore, to investigate the underlying mechanism of parents' multiple dimension involvement, it is necessary to examine the underlying emotional and cognitive factors. The present research examines the typical emotional factor, parents' worries about children's video game use, and the typical cognitive factor, parents' evaluation of the quality of the video games.

The present research reveals that most of the parents' worries contributed to the more strict management of children's video game use. As an anxious feeling and emotion, worry plays a fundamental role in parents' behavioral involvement in children's video game use. It alerts parents to children's misuse or overuse of video games, helping to avoid the negative effects of video games [5]. This research also indicate that parents' worries also help themselves regulating their involvements, for example, reducing their co-use video game with their children and using video games by themselves. However, the results also show that parents' worries about children's cognitive development positively predicted their material providence. The results may indicate that parents feel confused and uncertain about whether video game use will benefit or harm their children's cognitive development.

The results indicate that the cognitive quality evaluation of the video games plays an important role in the parents' involvement in children's video game use. The quality evaluation predicted parents' involvement in children's video game use not only in direct but also in interactive ways. However, many researchers have suggested that parents have difficulties in fully understanding video game use. Although in some countries and areas, the video game rating provided by professional institute is available [27], however the people still feel confused with dealing with their children's video game use: On the one hand, parents usually over- or underestimate the role of video games in children's development [5, 6]. On the other hand, parents lack detailed knowledge about some aspects of video game use [28]. The survey by Nikken et al. suggested that the majority of parents thought it important to access to have ratings of the video games in case of possible negative game effects arising from warnings such as "realistic," "gory," or "gross" regarding alcohol/drugs, fantasy violence, foul language and, nudity [29]. Our research further suggests that a more comprehensive rating system concerning the positive and negative effects of the video games is needed to guide the parents.

This study was an attempt to integrate the potential factors of parents' reactions to children's video game use. The results provide valuable insight into how emotional and the rational aspect (the parents' quality evaluation of the available video game) to parents' behavioral involvement into their children's video game use. However, several limitations of this study must be mentioned. First, as parents' involvement in children's video games is a complicated issue involving many factors, some important aspects were not examined in this research, for example, parenting styles. Second, the parents' involvement and the underlying factors were all based on self-reports. Therefore societal stereotypes could bias self-report evaluation. Future studies should include more related factors and employ various methods, especially behavioral indexes, to identify the potential mechanism (s) underlying parents' responses to their children's video game use.

Acknowledgments. This study was funded by the National Social Science Fund of China (18BSH130) and Capacity Building for Sci-Tech Innovation–Fundamental Scientific Research Funds (20530290062). Moreover, we appreciate the support from the Infant and Child Development Laboratory and all the individuals who provided assistance or participated in our study.

References

1. Chaudron, S., Beutel, M., Navarrete, V.D., Dreier, M.: Young children (0–8) and digital technology: a qualitative exploratory study across seven countries. Institute for the Protection and Security of the Citizen (Joint Research Centre) (2015). https://doi.org/10.2788/00749

2. Maldonado, N.S.: How much technology knowledge does the average preschooler bring to the classroom?. Childhood Edu. **86**, 124–126 (2010). https://doi.org/10.1080/00094056.2010.10523130

3. Huang, H., Zhou, Y., Qu, F., et al.: The role of parenting styles and parents' involvement in young children's videogames use. HCI in Games (2020) https://doi.org/10.1007/978-3-030-50164-8_20

4. Ofcom: Children and parents: Media use and attitudes report (2015). http://stakeholders.ofcom.org.uk/market-data-research/other/research-publications/childrens/children-parents-nov-15/

5. Sekarasih, L.: Restricting, distracting, and reasoning: parental mediation of young children's use of mobile communication technology in indonesia. In: Lim, S.S. (ed.) Mobile Communication and the Family, pp. 129–146. Springer Netherlands, Dordrecht (2016). https://doi.org/10.1007/978-94-017-7441-3_8

6. Martins, N., Matthews, N.L., Ratan, R.A.: Playing by the rules: parental mediation of video game play. J. Family Issues 38(9), 1–24 (2015) https://doi.org/10.1177/0192513X15613822

7. Bourgonjon, J., Valcke, M., Soetaert, R., et al.: Parental acceptance of digital game-based learning. Comput. Educ. 57(1), 1434–1444 (2011) https://doi.org/10.1016/j.compedu.2010.12.012

8. Ritonga, M., Sartika, F., Kustati, M.: Madrasah al-Ula for children: an effective learning management in the family during Covid-19 pandemic. lkretim Online 20(1), 968–976 (2021). https://doi.org/10.17051/ilkonline.2021.01.97

9. Yang, L., Chen, X., Wang, Y., et al.: Factors related to the preference of urban primary school students in Grade 4 and Grade 6 indulge in computer games. Mod. Prev. Med 22, 115–116 (2008) (In Chinese)

10. Ray, M., Jat, K.R.: Effect of electronic media on children. Indian Pediatr. 47(7), 561–568 (2010). https://doi.org/10.1007/s13312-010-0128-9

11. Chastin S.F.M., et al.: The SOS-framework (Systems of Sedentary behaviours): An international transdisciplinary consensus framework for the study of determinants, research priorities and policy on sedentary behaviour across the life course: a DEDIPAC-study. Int. J. Behav. Nutr. Phys. Act 13(1), 1–13 (2016) https://doi.org/10.1186/s12966-016-0409-3

12. Arundell, L., Parker, K., Timperio, A., Salmon, J., Veitch, J.: Home-based screen time behaviors amongst youth and their parents: familial typologies and their modifiable correlates. BMC Public Health 20, 1492 (2020). https://doi.org/10.1186/s12889-020-09581-w

13. Shao, R., Wang, Y.: The relation of violent video games to adolescent aggression: an examination of moderated mediation effect. Front. Psychol. 10, 384 (2019). https://doi.org/10.3389/fpsyg.2019.00384

14. Svjetlana, K., Sanja, S., Martinac, D., et al.: Evaluation of serious game for changing students' behaviour in bullying situation. J. Comput. Assist. Learn. 36(4), 1–12 (2019). https://doi.org/10.1111/jcal.12402

15. Baldassarri, S., Passerino, L., Ramis, S., et al.: Toward emotional interactive videogames for children with autism spectrum disorder. Universal Access in the Information Society 1, 2020 https://doi.org/10.1007/s10209-020-00725-8

16. Wong, R.S.M., Yu, E.Y.T., Wong, T.W., et al.: Development and pilot evaluation of a mobile app on parent-child exercises to improve physical activity and psychosocial outcomes of Hong Kong Chinese children. BMC Public Health 20, 1544 (2020). https://doi.org/10.1186/s12889-020-09655-9

17. Qu, F., Gu, C., Huang, H., Zhang, A., Sun, M., Liu, X.: Relationship between young children's problematic behaviors, video gaming status, and parenting styles. In: Fang, X. (ed.) HCII 2020. LNCS, vol. 12211, pp. 318–329. Springer, Cham (2020). https://doi.org/10.1007/978-3-030-50164-8_23

18. Forrest, C.J., King, D.L., Delfabbro, P.H.: The measurement of maladaptive cognitions underlying problematic video-game playing among adults. Comput. Hum. Behav. 55, 399–405 (2016). https://doi.org/10.1016/j.chb.2015.09.017

19. Liu, X., Liao, M., Dou, D.: Video Game Playing Enhances Young Children's Inhibitory Control. HCI in Games. Capital Normal University (2019)
20. Nielsen, R.K.L., Kardefelt-Winther, D.: Helping parents make sense of video game addiction. In: Ferguson, C.J. (ed.) Video game influences on aggression, cognition, and attention, pp. 59–69. Springer, Cham (2018). https://doi.org/10.1007/978-3-319-95495-0_5
21. Kutner, L.A., Olson, C.K., Warner, D.E., et al.: Parents' and Sons' perspectives on video game play: a qualitative study. J Adol Res 23(1), 409–413 (2008)
22. Hughes, T., Brooks, D.: Grasping gaming: Parent management training for excessive videogame use in children. J Ame Academy of Child & Adole Psychi 59(7), 794–796 (2020).https://doi.org/10.1016/j.jaac.2020.01.009
23. Entertainment Software Association. Essential facts about the computer and video game industry. Washington, DC: ESA (2014)
24. Wegener, D.T., Fabrigar, L.R.: Analysis and design for nonexperimental data: Addressing causal and noncausal hypotheses. In: Reis, H.T., Judd, C.M. (eds.), Handbook of research methods in social and personality psychology, pp. 412–450. Cambridge University Press, New York (2000)
25. Pratibha, B., Neeraj, S.: A Study of the Socio-Economic Status of Women via Self-help Groups in the Rural Areas of Karnal District in Haryana. World Rev Entrep Manag & Sus Dev (2020)
26. Wegener, D.T., Fabrigar, L.R.: Analysis and design for nonexperimental data: addressing causal and noncausal hypotheses. In: Reis, H.T., Judd, C.M. (eds.) Handbook of research methods in social and personality psychology. Cambridge University Press, New York, pp. 412–450 (2000)
27. Wilson, T.D.: Revisitinguserstudies and information needs. J. Docum 62(6), 680–684 (2006)
28. Harrelson, D.D.: Rated M for monkey: An ethnographic study of parental information behavior when assessing video game content for their children. Dissertation for Ph.D degree, University of North Texas (2016)
29. Nikken, P., Jansz, J., Schiouwstra, S.: Parents' interest in videogame ratings and content descriptors in relation to game mediation. Eur. J. Commun. 22(3), 315–336 (2007). https://doi.org/10.1177/0267323107079684.

In-Game Virtual Consumption and Online Video Game Addiction: A Conceptual Model

Ali Hussain[1(✉)], Ding Hooi Ting[1], Helmut Hlavacs[2],
and Amir Zaib Abbasi[3]

[1] Department of Management and Humanities, Universiti Teknologi
PETRONAS, 32610 Seri Iskandar, Perak, Malaysia
ting.dinghooi@utp.edu.my
[2] Research Group Entertainment Computing, University of Vienna,
Vienna, Austria
helmut.hlavacs@univie.ac.at
[3] Faculty of Management Sciences, Shaheed Zulfikar Ali Bhutto Institute
of Science and Technology (SZABIST), Islamabad, Pakistan

Abstract. Research from the various domain of life intensely focused on the understanding of the role of different psychological factors related to online video game addiction. The current study intends to propose a conceptual model to examines the relationship of in-game virtual consumption with online video game addiction. Different in-game virtual products enable the players to overcome the deficiencies they are facing in the gaming world like lack of power, control, beauty, and even sexual relations. Currently, how these in-game virtual content consumption may develop and maintain problematic game addictive behavior in the players is vague. Therefore, this conceptual paper seeks to investigate this important issue and provide a better understanding of video game addiction. We try to provide a behavioral link between in-game virtual consumption with online video game addiction.

Keywords: Video game addiction · In-game content · Virtual consumption · And conceptual model

1 Introduction

According to [1], over the last few years, adolescents interact with different media such as video games, computer networks, the virtual world, websites, and handheld devices, and these interactive behavior have exponentially increased. Among all these media, we will focus on the video game (which have created some behavioral issues that interest both academics and practitioners). Video games have emerged as a preferred pastime activity for many people, especially the adolescent [2, 3]. The video game is defined as games that are played through any electronic format such as computer, console or digital phone [4]. The first home-based video game was introduced to the market in 1972 and have seen an upward surge in its popularity. It has become the mainstream entertainment activity that can be enjoyed on several different platforms [5]. To illustrate, it is

© Springer Nature Switzerland AG 2021
X. Fang (Ed.): HCII 2021, LNCS 12789, pp. 210–218, 2021.
https://doi.org/10.1007/978-3-030-77277-2_17

anticipated that consumer global video game-related spending has escalated from $137.7b in 2018 to $180.1b in 2021 [6].

An important element in the surging growth of the gaming industry is mainly due to a new shift in the business model where video games not only are treated as an activity or product, but also as services. This new shift is the free-to-play (F2P) or freemium business model, where the basic features of the games are available free of charge (and can be upgraded with a fee or through premium feature available against subscription fee or by selling in-game virtual products) just like many other online services [7]. In-game purchases are the most important source of revenue generation for many online video game publisher and developers. Virtual goods and any other related contents like purchasing avatars of favorite characters, weapons and ammunition, sexual relationships, coins, extra lives, outfits and skipping stages are frequent forms of virtual consumption for gamers [8]. Prior studies suggest that the top 300 games on Apple's App store fall under this business model where core game is available free of charge just to engage the user and if players want to enjoy advanced features, they have to pay for in-game contents [9].

Most of the F2P game developers create demand for this in-game virtual consumption by creating specific caveats and obstacles which are difficult to cross without some additional power or support which is available in the form of virtual content consumption [10]. Additionally, game publishers also foster players to consume functionals goods within the gaming environment which help them to speed-up their progress and to be more competitive in the game as compare to other players [11]. In fact, prior studies suggest that this in-games content act to balance the level of attraction by making the game as enjoyable as possible. Players who are using these in-game products, their powers can be enhanced, and they can achieve even more difficult goals and complete missions of an aggressive nature. This amusing, interactive and entertaining nature of video games makes this activity more attractive application on the internet and these are the primary reasons many adolescents spend hours playing these video games on daily basis [12].

2 Self-determination Theory

Self-determination theory (SDT) is a widely employed framework in the video game context which postulates that satisfaction of three basic needs autonomy, competence and relatedness during the activity engagement will enhance pleasurable experiences and increase repetitive and potentially addictive behavior [13, 14]. Prior studies also illustrated that inherently humans have a psychological need for autonomy, competence and relatedness and once these needs available the activity becomes more enjoyable and enhance the engagement in the activity [15, 16]. The first need described in SDT is autonomy, which refers to the condition in which a human wants to satisfy his/her desire for self-fulfillment by acting under their own inner volition [17]. Competency refers to the feeling of more effective and skilled as compare to others, while relatedness describes a sense of connection and feel socially integrated [18].

Jimenez, San-Martin [19] speculated that different people motivated toward this gaming world for a variety of reasons which may include socialization, competing, enjoyment, seeking recognition and other reasons. Based on this, SDT primarily focused on the intrinsic and extrinsic motivational factors which compel some individuals to develop and maintain high involvement with the activity [20]. Prior studies have employed SDT in the explanation of greater human engagement in a number of contexts like education, sports, work and social networking sites [21]. Finding of Chantal, Vallerand [22] was the first to explore the video game addictive behavior by using SDT perspective and illustrate that players having intrinsic motives of enjoyment and fun, development of skills and curiosity, pastime and interest will play a significant role in intensifying player engagement in the gaming world.

3   Related Work

3.1   Consumption of In-Game Virtual Content

Virtual content consumption has become the most common form of consumption in the online digital gaming world. These in-game virtual products refer to the digital goods such as avatars, weapons, vehicles, gifts, currencies, powerful tools and properties which player can use solely within the gaming environment [10, 23]. With the continuous development in technology, video games are not only viewed as entertainment or activity but also as services, where the basic feature of the games available freely but you have to pay to unlock the advance or premium features of the games [24]. Many free-to-play model games compel the player to purchase these in-game virtual products or features to become more competitive and progressive as compared to other players [25]. The video game industry is considered as one of the immense and advance industry, therefore different in-game virtual products are offered, depending on the type and genre of the game.

The video game allows players to acquire different functional features by purchasing in-game virtual content. For example, in the shooter or battle war games, by purchasing powerful guns and weapons, you can perform better and make more competitive and dominant moves or actions in the gaming world as compared to other players which may also fulfil their desire for competency as illustrated in SDT [26]. Likewise, relatedness is also an important motive of video game players. Based on this, different game publishers offer the players to purchase various in-game virtual gifts in the form of special emoticons, properties, extra coins, and cosmetic items to enhance physical attractiveness which helps to develop interactions and relations with other players and streamers [27]. Furthermore, in the gaming environment, a player chooses their favourite avatars which are often called the digital or graphical representation of the player, these avatars provide players with a separate identity and abled them to enjoy their virtual world life according to their own ideal selves [28].

3.2   Adolescents Online Game Addictive Behavior

By the start of the 1990s, usage of home computers increased, and the era of new entrainment industry start which is called video game industry and from last many years researcher claimed that video game addiction emerged most addictive activities notably in the adolescents [29]. Historically, before the advancement in the video game industry, most video games had simplistic and fixed features [30]. Contrary to this, the modern gaming environment is height interactive and realistic with many features that enable the player to develop a unique virtual identity, alter personal traits, skills and appearances [31]. Therefore, these features in video games seem to be more relevant to overall video game addictive behavior. Online video games are rapidly gaining worldwide popularity, many past studies suggested that excessive usage of this activity could be related to addictive behaviors [32, 33]. According to [34], due to the rapid advancement in technology and changes in the environment of the virtual gaming world, online game addiction has been recognized as the fastest emerging societal problem in the world. American Physical Association (APA) explained that as game addictive, where gamers who play online games compulsively and this recurrent activity consequently develop psychological impairment. Due to lake of consensus on the conceptual validity of video game addiction, different terms were used by scholars to explore this notion, for example, gaming disorder, obsessive use of video game, video game dependency and problematic usage of video gaming.

Despite some scholars emphasize on educational function of online games and the strategic importance of online game on positive youth development, there are great concerns present over the kind of activities and the content being enabled within this virtual gaming world. When adolescents spend an extensive amount of time in this virtual gaming world, it contributes to adverse consequences in their psychological health which may include aggression, conflict, and delinquent behavior [35]. Though numerous past studies on game addiction have been done and identify different elements such as family environment [36], parenting style [37], and lack of attention [38] play important role in the formation of this addictive behavior in adolescents.

The common thing we have witnessed in the prior research is, these studies try to explore the video game addictive behavior in adolescents because of the influence of external environment elements but less attention has been paid to the internal video game environment, which makes this activity more fantasies and attractive. To address this issue, the present study is interested to explore the video game addiction behavior in adolescents due to the availability of in-game virtual content which makes this gaming world attractive and fantasized for the teenagers which compel them to stay longer within the activity [39]. Thus, we have proposed a conceptual model (as shown in Fig. 1), based on the SDT which stated that activities that help to fulfil the desire of the autonomy, relatedness and competency provide more pleasurable experience and enhance engagement, physiological arousal which motive to stay longer in the activity [16]. On this basis, we have proposed the hypotheses, that adolescents in-game virtual consumption will positively influence online video game addiction.

H1: In-game virtual consumption has a significant positive influence on online video game addiction.

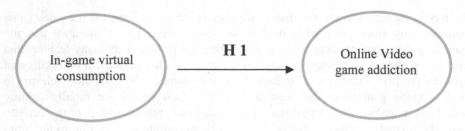

Fig. 1. The study conceptual model

4 Discussion

Considering the enormous increase in video game users and the popularity of its addictive characteristics especially in adolescents, online video game addiction has emerged as a critical topic of research for academia and practitioners. In the field of marketing and video games, a sustainable amount of literature focused on the purchase of in-game virtual content and how this consumption effect player game enjoyment level [40]. However, there is a limited number of research studies available which explored video game addictive behaviour from the perspective of in-game virtual consumption [41]. Recently a systematic review study Green, Delfabbro [14] revealed the significant relationship between the virtual avatars or digital characters available in the gaming world and online game addiction. The study also proposed to further explore the role of these in-game virtual characters and features on the general phenomenon of excessive game playing. [42] further added that this in-game virtual content helps the players to gain different competencies and skills depending on the genre of game and need of the player as mentioned in SDT, like in fighting games players can purchase virtual avatars which are more powerful, those players who want to be more socializer in the gaming world can purchase virtual gifts for other players and can also purchase virtual island who enjoy exploring virtual gaming environment. As a result of this in-game virtual content consumption, players engagement within the video games enhanced and in turn, make players desire to keep playing for longer hours. Nevertheless, only a small number of research studies have explored the notion of in-game virtual consumption on video game addictive behavior. Thus, the present study examined the role of in-game virtual products on adolescent's video game addiction, that is while playing online games these in-game virtual resources greatly affected player behavior by making the gaming world more pleasurable, attractive, and competitive as compared to other activities. The proposed conceptual model proposed that this in-game virtual content consumption not only allow the players to enjoy the theme of the game but can also enjoy other activities like virtual interactive events, gift sharing, get married with different avatars, develop their own virtual community just like in the real world. Within the self-determination theory, in F2P games players acquire these in-game virtual products to fulfil their conspicuous consumption necessities as well as to satisfy their need for autonomy, competence and relatedness during the activity. Likewise, video games from different genres (e.g., shooter, racing, fighting, strategy) introduced these in-game virtual content and therefore this virtual content consumption becoming more relevant to the video game addictive behavior in adolescents.

5 Contribution and Future Researches

This study contributes to expanding the existing limited knowledge on the relationship of in-game virtual consumption and video game addictive behavior in the following ways: Firstly, we utilized popular self-determination theory, to conceptualization how these in-game virtual content helps the player to satisfy their goal of autonomy, relatedness, and competency. Notably, with the rise of F2P game model where players can only enjoy the basic features of the video games, these in-game virtual products help the players to broaden their thinking and freedom (e.g., virtual products used to perform the favorite activity) and thus playing offers rich opportunities for satisfying the three needs described in SDT. Secondly, in the context of the video game addition, current research significantly contributes to explore the addictive nature of video games from the perspective of an in-game environment. From a psychological perspective, many past studies have extensively discussed different social elements which directly or indirectly influence game addictive behavior, but the present study is arguably the prior research to relate the consumption of in-game virtual content with the video game addictive behavior in the players. This research is also important for psychology perspective and will help future studies to further understand this additive game behavior in the players. Therefore, this conceptual model has the potential to provide insight into how different in-game virtual products enhance the player's engagement in the games and consequent develops game addiction behavior. The current study is conceptual in nature therefore empirical study which validates this conceptual model will be welcomed.

6 Conclusion

In summary, the current research study provides a first look to understand the role of in-game consumption of virtual products on video game addictive behavior. Especially after the rise of the free-to-play business model these in-game virtual items mainly used to enhance the offensive and defensive power of the character, socialization, beauty, and other motives which help the players to enjoy unlimited freedom in a simulated gaming world. Owing to this, game developers and publishers now pay more attention to the elements that evoke players motives to stay longer, engage, and complete every game level. Additionally, the introduction of some new features and element in the gaming world notably in-game virtual products (Avatars, weapons/tools, unlimited ammunition, racing cars, extra lives etc.) makes outcomes more tangible by gaining more skills and expertise by purchasing and using these virtual in-game resources. Like when they are playing the game with the outfit of their favorite characters (Commander Shepard, Mario, Master chief etc.) their motivation of relatedness and satisfaction secondly most of the video games based on challenges which increased with the improvement of the levels and with help of these in-game variables this come very easy for the player to compete with other and finish the level quickly as compare to other peers which again aroused their emotion as defined in this theory. Therefore, using the self-determination theory perspective, we have developed a conceptual model that with the consumption of in-game virtual content, players have more opportunities to comply with the basic psychological need or undermine motives include competence, autonomy and relatedness that is connected to game addictive behavior.

Acknowledgement. Ali Hussain is a PhD student at Universiti Teknologi PETRONAS under the Graduate Research Assistantship scheme, Fundamental Research Grant Scheme (FRGS), Ministry of Higher Education, Malaysia, grant FRGS/1/2019/SS06/UTP/02/1.

References

1. Al-Ali, N.M., et al.: Parents' knowledge and beliefs about the impact of exposure to media violence on children's aggression. Issues Ment. Health Nurs. **39**(7), 592–599 (2018)
2. Drummond, A., Sauer, J.D.: Timesplitters: playing video games before (but not after) school on weekdays is associated with poorer adolescent academic performance. A test of competing theoretical accounts. Comput. Educ. **144**, 103704 (2020)
3. Abbasi, A.Z., Hussain, A., Hlavacs, H., Shah, M.U., Ting, D.H., Rehman, U.: Customer inspiration via advertising value of pop-up ads in online games. In: Fang, X. (ed.) HCII 2020. LNCS, vol. 12211, pp. 251–259. Springer, Cham (2020). https://doi.org/10.1007/978-3-030-50164-8_17
4. Ferguson, C.J., et al.: Digital poison? Three studies examining the influence of violent video games on youth. Comput. Hum. Behav. **50**, 399–410 (2015)
5. Schilling, M.A.: Technological leapfrogging: Lessons from the US video game console industry. Calif. Manag. Rev. **45**(3), 6–32 (2003)
6. Abbasi, A.Z., et al., The effects of consumer esports videogame engagement on consumption behaviors. J. Prod. Brand Manag. (2020, forthcoming)
7. Teece, D.J.: Business models, business strategy and innovation. Long Range Plan. **43**(2–3), 172–194 (2010)
8. Balakrishnan, J., Griffiths, M.D.: Loyalty towards online games, gaming addiction, and purchase intention towards online mobile in-game features. Comput. Hum. Behav. **87**, 238–246 (2018)
9. Brockmann, T., Stieglitz, S., Cvetkovic, A.: Prevalent business models for the Apple app store. In: Wirtschaftsinformatik (2015)
10. Hamari, J., Lehdonvirta, V.: Game design as marketing: how game mechanics create demand for virtual goods. Int. J. Bus. Sci. Appl. Manag. **5**(1), 14–29 (2010)
11. Jin, W., et al.: Why users purchase virtual products in MMORPG? An integrative perspective of social presence and user engagement. Internet Res. **27**(2), 408–427 (2017)
12. Kim, E.J., et al.: The relationship between online game addiction and aggression, self-control and narcissistic personality traits. Eur. Psychiatry **23**(3), 212–218 (2008)
13. Mills, D.J., Allen, J.J.: Self-determination theory, internet gaming disorder, and the mediating role of self-control. Comput. Hum. Behav. **105**, 106209 (2020)
14. Green, R., Delfabbro, P.H., King, D.L.: Avatar-and self-related processes and problematic gaming: a systematic review. Addict. Behav. **108**, 106461 (2020)

15. Cruz, C., Hanus, M.D., Fox, J.: The need to achieve: players' perceptions and uses of extrinsic meta-game reward systems for video game consoles. Comput. Hum. Behav. **71**, 516–524 (2017)
16. Wu, A.M., Lei, L.L., Ku, L.: Psychological needs, purpose in life, and problem video game playing among Chinese young adults. Int. J. Psychol. **48**(4), 583–590 (2013)
17. Ryan, R.M., Rigby, C.S., Przybylski, A.: The motivational pull of video games: a self-determination theory approach. Motiv. Emot. **30**(4), 344–360 (2006). https://doi.org/10.1007/s11031-006-9051-8
18. Peng, W., et al.: Need satisfaction supportive game features as motivational determinants: an experimental study of a self-determination theory guided exergame. Media Psychol. **15**(2), 175–196 (2012)
19. Jimenez, N., et al.: What kind of video gamer are you? J. Consum. Mark. **36**(1), 218–227 (2019)
20. Przybylski, A.K., et al.: Having to versus wanting to play: background and consequences of harmonious versus obsessive engagement in video games. Cyberpsychol. Behav. **12**(5), 485–492 (2009)
21. King, D., Delfabbro, P.: Motivational differences in problem video game play. J. Cyberther. Rehabil. **2**(2), 139–149 (2009)
22. Chantal, Y., Vallerand, R.J., Vallieres, E.F.: Motivation and gambling involvement. J. Soc. Psychol. **135**(6), 755–763 (1995)
23. Mäntymäki, M., Salo, J.: Why do teens spend real money in virtual worlds? A consumption values and developmental psychology perspective on virtual consumption. Int. J. Inf. Manag. **35**(1), 124–134 (2015)
24. Wang, L., et al.: From freemium to premium: the roles of consumption values and game affordance. Inf. Technol. People **34**(1), 297–317 (2020)
25. Hamari, J., Keronen, L.: Why do people buy virtual goods: a meta-analysis. Comput. Hum. Behav. **71**, 59–69 (2017)
26. Shi, S.W., Xia, M., Huang, Y.: From minnows to whales: an empirical study of purchase behavior in freemium social games. Int. J. Electron. Commer. **20**(2), 177–207 (2015)
27. Wohn, D.Y., Freeman, G.: Live streaming, playing, and money spending behaviors in eSports. Games Cult. **15**(1), 73–88 (2020)
28. Lee, H.: Self-awareness for virtuality and self-concept of adolescence—based on the user and avatar characters in the cyberspace. J. Korea Des. Knowl. **15**, 469–479 (2007)
29. Toker, S., Baturay, M.H.: Antecedents and consequences of game addiction. Comput. Hum. Behav. **55**, 668–679 (2016)
30. Burleigh, T.L., Stavropoulos, V., Liew, L.W.L., Adams, B.L.M., Griffiths, M.D.: Depression, internet gaming disorder, and the moderating effect of the gamer-avatar relationship: an exploratory longitudinal study. Int. J. Ment. Health Addict. **16**(1), 102–124 (2017). https://doi.org/10.1007/s11469-017-9806-3
31. Przybylski, A.K., et al.: The ideal self at play: the appeal of video games that let you be all you can be. Psychol. Sci. **23**(1), 69–76 (2012)
32. King, D.L., Delfabbro, P.H.: Video game addiction. In: Adolescent Addiction, pp. 185–213. Elsevier (2020)
33. Griffiths, M.D., Kuss, D.J., King, D.L.: Video game addiction: past, present and future. Curr. Psychiatry Rev. **8**(4), 308–318 (2012)
34. Seok, H.J., et al.: Understanding internet gaming addiction among South Korean adolescents through photovoice. Child. Youth Serv. Rev. **94**, 35–42 (2018)
35. Li, H., Wang, S.: The role of cognitive distortion in online game addiction among Chinese adolescents. Child. Youth Serv. Rev. **35**(9), 1468–1475 (2013)

36. Choi, C., Hums, M.A., Bum, C.-H.: Impact of the family environment on juvenile mental health: eSports online game addiction and delinquency. Int. J. Environ. Res. Public Health **15**(12), 2850 (2018)
37. Özgür, H.: Online game addiction among Turkish adolescents: the effect of internet parenting style. Malays. Online J. Educ. Technol. **7**(1), 47–68 (2019)
38. Abedini, Y., et al.: Impacts of mothers' occupation status and parenting styles on levels of self-control, addiction to computer games, and educational progress of adolescents. Addict. Health **4**(3–4), 102 (2012)
39. Hao, L., et al.: Avatar identification mediates the relationship between peer phubbing and mobile game addiction. Soc. Behav. Pers. Int. J. **48**(10), 1–15 (2020)
40. Molesworth, M.: The pleasures and practices of virtualised consumption in digital spaces (2005)
41. You, S., Kim, E., Lee, D.: Virtually real: exploring avatar identification in game addiction among massively multiplayer online role-playing games (MMORPG) players. Games Cult. **12**(1), 56–71 (2017)
42. Zhong, Z.-J., Yao, M.Z.: Gaming motivations, avatar-self identification and symptoms of online game addiction. Asian J. Commun. **23**(5), 555–573 (2013)

Player Types and Game Element Preferences: Investigating the Relationship with the Gamification User Types HEXAD Scale

Jeanine Krath[✉] and Harald F. O. von Korflesch

University of Koblenz-Landau, Universitaetsstrasse 1, 56070 Koblenz, Germany
{jkrath, harald.vonkorflesch}@uni-koblenz.de

Abstract. Gamification has gained scientific attention as a motivational tool for behavior change in various contexts. When designing gamification, several scholars emphasize the importance of tailoring content to the needs of different users, e.g. by using the gamification user types HEXAD typology. From a theoretical point of view, researchers suggest correlations between HEXAD types and certain game elements, but empirical validation of these assumptions is still lacking. Previous studies show limitations either in terms of sample size or comprehensiveness of analysis. Therefore, this study aims to empirically identify game element preferences of different HEXAD types and to validate both the English and a corresponding German version of the HEXAD scale in a quantitative study design with 1,073 participants. The validation shows that the HEXAD scale is a valuable tool for identifying HEXAD types, with some improvements needed for a better model fit. Correlation analysis shows highly significant correlations between HEXAD types and specific game elements. While Philanthropists are motivated by gifting, administrative roles, and knowledge sharing, Free Spirits prefer creativity tools, exploratory tasks, and learning. Both Achievers and Players like challenges, leaderboards, levels, and competition, but Players are additionally attracted by extrinsic elements such as achievements, points, and rewards. Socializers like social elements, i.e., teams, social discovery, and social networks. Finally, Disruptors like anarchic game-play and innovation platforms. In general, the results suggest that the HEXAD typology provides helpful and validated guidance for tailored gamification, and our findings should successfully drive future gamification design to maximize the desired behavioral outcome.

Keywords: Gamification · HEXAD · Player types · User types · Gamification design · Game elements · Tailored gamification

1 Introduction

Gamification – the use of game design elements in a non-game context [1] – has gained scientific attention as a motivational tool for behavioral change in various application contexts [2–6]. While results of gamification are predominantly positive [2, 5–9], some mixed results have also been reported in terms of motivation, engagement, and learning

© Springer Nature Switzerland AG 2021
X. Fang (Ed.): HCII 2021, LNCS 12789, pp. 219–238, 2021.
https://doi.org/10.1007/978-3-030-77277-2_18

outcomes [10–12]. Thus, gamification does not appear to be effective per se [13]. Instead, several scientists emphasize the importance of tailoring content to the needs and motivations of different users [14–18] to achieve the desired results. In this context, player typologies from gaming research, such as Bartle's player types [19] and Yee's five motivations to play MMORPGs [20], have been used to identify different types of users and their game element preferences and thus to enable tailoring gamification to their specific needs [21]. However, they exhibit difficulties to be applied in the non-game context of gamification [22–24]. To address this issue, the gamification user types HEXAD typology [25] has been developed explicitly for gamification and is now one of the most widely used personalization typologies [21, 26].

Nevertheless, providing a typology alone is not sufficient for successful gamification design in terms of personalization. To best achieve the intended behavioral outcome of gamification, researchers and practitioners need reliable recommendations on *how* to personalize their intervention for different user types [27], i.e. which game elements to select for meeting the needs of a specific user type. From a theoretical perspective, scientists [21, 25] hypothesize relationships between HEXAD types and preference for specific game elements, but empirical validation of these assumptions is still lacking. Previous studies provide valuable starting points, but show limitations either in terms of sample size [24, 28] or comprehensiveness of the analysis since only a limited set of game elements [29] or more general persuasive strategies [30] are investigated.

Therefore, a comprehensive validation and extension of these preliminary results with larger and more diverse samples are essential to derive reliable suggestions for tailored gamification design [23]. To fill this gap, this study aims to identify the game element preferences of different HEXAD types with a large sample to assist in tailored gamification design emphasized by many scholars. Moreover, we attempt to validate both the English version [23] and a corresponding German version of the HEXAD scale. Our results confirm that the HEXAD scale [23] is a valuable tool for the identification of HEXAD types, with some improvements needed for a better model fit. Moreover, we identify highly significant correlations between HEXAD types and preference for specific game elements.

2   Related Work

In the following section, we introduce the concept of gamification and discuss previous research on tailored gamification design. Furthermore, we describe the gamification user types HEXAD scale and existing studies on the relationship between HEXAD types and game element preferences as a basis for our work.

2.1   Gamification

While a game refers to structured play with rules and goals for entertainment [31], gamification is characterized by a serious purpose. *Gamification* can be defined as *the use of game elements in non-game contexts* [1]. A particular emphasis is placed on game *elements*, which include e.g. levels, points, badges, or leaderboards [24, 32], and distinguish gamification from *serious games*. While both share a serious purpose, serious games are full-fledged games with a virtual environment [1] and thus closer to the concept of a game than gamification.

Since the emergence of the research field in the 2010s [1, 3], gamification has been used to transfer the positive effects of games, such as motivation and engagement [33], to various contexts, e.g. education [7, 32, 34], healthcare [35, 36], business [37–39] or sustainability [40, 41]. However, even though the majority of empirical studies report positive effects of gamification [2, 5–9], the results are not unanimously positive [2, 11]. For example, some works report no effects on intrinsic motivation [10, 12], behavioral learning outcomes [11], or engagement with the system [42], which indicates that gamification may not be effective per se [13]. For instance, the success of gamification particularly depends on the design elements and principles selected [42]. In this context, an important principle emphasized by many scholars [14–18, 43–45] is to personalize the content and mechanics of the gamified system to the individual needs and motivations of the user – also referred to as tailored gamification design [21].

2.2 Tailored Gamification Design

Tailored gamification design corresponds to concepts such as personalization and adaption [21] and describes the alteration of aspects of the gamified system with the most appropriate solution to fulfill the specific needs of the user [46]. Since users' needs, personalities, and motivations influence the expected benefits [47, 48] and actual performance [49] in gamified systems, gamification designers in both academia and practice need to be supported with knowledge on *how* to design tailored gamification [27].

In this regard, a variety of typologies have been proposed that classify players based on their needs, characteristics, and motivations [21, 50, 51]. Although they differ in their labels and number of types, several typologies share common concepts of various strengths expressed in different player types, such as achievement, exploration, sociability, domination, and immersion [50]. Among those, Bartle's player types [19], the BrainHex archetypes [52], and Yee's five motivations to play MMORPGs [20] are most commonly used to design tailored gamification [21, 26].

However, the application of player typologies from game research in the serious context of gamification has been criticized [22, 23], as users might experience game elements embedded in applications differently in a non-game context than in games [24]. To address this criticism, the gamification user types HEXAD typology [25] has been developed explicitly for the context of gamification. Based on *four drives theory* [53] and especially *self-determination theory* [54], which is the most widely used motivation theory in gamification research [3], Marczewski distinguishes between six user types: *Philanthropists, Disruptors, Free Spirits, Achievers, Players,* and *Socializers* [25]. *Philanthropists* are motivated by purpose and are considered altruistic, while *Socializers* are motivated by relatedness and primarily want to interact with others [23]. *Achievers* and *Players* are both strive to improve themselves, but Achievers are primarily motivated by competence, while Players seek extrinsic rewards [23]. *Free Spirits* usually prefer autonomy and freedom to create and explore [23]. Finally, *Disruptors* are motivated by change and tend to test the boundaries of the system [23].

In gamification research, the gamification user types HEXAD have gained popularity as a basis to design tailored gamification [21, 26], e.g. for personalizing energy-saving recommendations [55], deciding on features in a game-based learning system [56], or selecting game design patterns and mechanics for a rehabilitation game [57].

2.3   The Gamification User Types HEXAD Scale

To identify and measure the gamification user types HEXAD, the research group around Marczewski, in particular, Gustavo Tondello [23, 28, 58], systematically constructed and refined an appropriate questionnaire for the six HEXAD types. The final scale was validated in English and Spanish and consists of four items for each of the six HEXAD types [23].

From a theoretical point of view, both Marczewski himself [25] and other scholars [21] hypothesize relationships between HEXAD types and preference for certain game elements. Initial studies have attempted to empirically investigate the suspected relations. Tondello et al. surveyed 133 students at the University of Waterloo, Canada about their HEXAD types and game element preferences and found significant correlations for all HEXAD types except Philanthropist [28], e.g., Socializers preferred teams, social networks, and social competition, while Achievers were attracted by challenges, certificates, badges, and levels. Broadening the focus, they used a similar study design with a sample of 188 respondents through an online survey and aggregated the individual game elements into components [24], similar to those proposed by Hamari and Tuunanen [50], identifying significant correlations between HEXAD types and game element components, e.g. socialization elements were preferred by Socializers, risk/reward elements were mostly related to Achievers and Players and altruism elements were strongly preferred by Philanthropists. In addition, a larger study by the same research group examined the relationships between HEXAD types and six selected game elements (leaderboards, teams, challenges, voting, gifting, and exploration) with a sample of 925 participants [29] and confirmed suspected correlations between teams and the Socializer type, exploration, and the Free Spirit type, and challenges and the Achiever type, but similar to [28], failed to identify a significant relationship between gifting and the Philanthropist type. Also, the research group investigated the correlation between HEXAD types and ten persuasive strategies with a sample of 543 respondents [30] and found that e.g. Socializers were attracted to all persuasive strategies, while Players mostly liked competition and reward.

However, except for the first study, these previous studies did not explore the relationship between HEXAD types and the wide variety of individual game elements. Aggregating the game elements into components and persuasive strategies or considering only a limited set of six game elements, prevents researchers and practitioners from directly and efficiently determining which game elements to select for each user type in order to design successful tailored gamification. Although the first study provides valuable insights in this regard, its sample size of 133 students is insufficient to derive reliable recommendations for tailored gamification design. The research group around Tondello et al. therefore explicitly calls for a comprehensive validation and extension of these preliminary results with larger and more diverse samples, which are imperative to derive reliable suggestions for tailored gamification design [23].

3 Method

Addressing this gap, this work aims to *validate both the English version* [23] *and a corresponding German version of the HEXAD scale* and *to identify the game element preferences of different HEXAD types*. To meet these research objectives, we employ a quantitative study design based on the questionnaires used in prior studies [23, 28]. For scale validation, we use a scale reliability analysis, an exploratory factor analysis with oblique rotation for correlating factors [59], since a partial overlap of HEXAD types is expected, and a confirmatory factor analysis. To identify the game element preferences of the different HEXAD types, we use bivariate correlation analysis.

3.1 Questionnaire and Procedure

To ensure comparability with the validation study conducted by Tondello et al. [23], we used the final validated English scale from [23]. During the original development of the HEXAD scale, a German version was also constructed [28], which was made publicly available on the Gamified UK website [60]. However, the German version of the HEXAD scale was not included in the second and third validation steps [23], so that some items of the validated scale were not yet translated into German. Furthermore, as native German speakers, we perceived the wording of some other German items as complicated and in need of grammatical improvement. Therefore, the English items of the validated English scale [23] were independently translated and back-translated [61] by three native German speakers with at least C1 English proficiency and then refined in a committee format [61] into the final, decentered scale used for this study, as documented in Table 5 (in the Appendix).

The questionnaire was designed as an online survey consisting of two parts. The first part contained the 24 items of the HEXAD scale, and the second part asked participants to rate 35 game elements, adapted from the literature analysis by Tondello et al. [24], each on a seven-point Likert scale. At the end of the survey, participants were invited to voluntarily provide demographic data, such as age, gender, and nationality. Participants were free to choose English or German in the questionnaire, depending on their language proficiency. In addition to the distribution in our network, we promoted the survey on Facebook to reach a diverse sample of participants from different continents. The survey took place in October 2020 and the participants received no compensation other than the calculation of their HEXAD type at the end of the survey.

3.2 Participants

In total, 1.075 participants answered the study, of which two were excluded during data anomaly checking. The final sample consists of 1.073 participants from 59 different countries, of which Germany (n = 380), Portugal (n = 84), Canada (n = 72), the United States (n = 43) and Italy (n = 40) account for the largest shares. The total distribution is illustrated in Table 1.

Table 1. Distribution of nationalities in the final sample.

Country	No. of participants	Percentage	Country	No. of participants	Percentage
Germany	380	35,4%	Turkey	33	3,1%
Portugal	84	7,8%	Greece	31	2,9%
Canada	72	6,7%	Belgium	21	2,0%
United States	43	4,0%	United Kingdom	17	1,6%
Italy	40	3,7%	New Zealand	14	1,3%
Spain	39	3,6%	France	13	1,2%
Australia	34	3,2%	Philippines	13	1,2%
Other (Estonia, Bangladesh, Netherlands, Poland, Norway, Bulgaria, Indonesia, Ireland, Romania, Sweden, Austria, Pakistan, Egypt, India, Myanmar, Serbia, Switzerland, Vietnam, Algeria, Bosnia and Herzegovina, Croatia, Finland, Hungary, Malaysia, Namibia, Slovakia, South Africa, Albania, Andorra, Bahrain, Bhutan, Brazil, China, Denmark, Djibouti, Ethiopia, South Korea, Libya, Malta, Mauritius, Mexico, Papua New Guinea, Russian Federation, Syria, Tunisia)	125	11,6%			
Not provided	114	10,6%			

The mean age is $M = 27,51$, $SD = 7,335$. 13,2% of the participants are 20 years old or younger, 59,5% are between 21 and 30 years old, 22,3% are between 31 and 40 years old, 4,2% are between 41 and 50 years old and 1% are 51 years old or older. 540 of the 1.073 participants are male, 340 are female, 23 identify as another gender, and 170 participants did not indicate their gender. Regarding the language chosen, 67,9% of the participants answered the survey in English, 32,1% in German.

4 Results

In the following, we first report on the analysis of the HEXAD scale in English and German, using a scale reliability analysis, an exploratory factor analysis, and a confirmatory factor analysis to ensure comparability with the validation study by Tondello et al. [23]. Second, we analyze the relationship between HEXAD types and preference for specific game elements with correlation analysis.

4.1 Validation of the HEXAD Scale in English and German

First, we checked whether the partial overlap, i.e. intercorrelation, of HEXAD types [23, 28] also applies to our analysis, which determines whether factor analysis is performed with oblique rotation or with orthogonal rotation [59]. For the correlation analysis, we used Kendall's τ_b due to the non-parametric Likert scales of the HEXAD scale.

Table 2. Bivariate correlation coefficients between the HEXAD types (** $p < .01$).

User type	Philanthropist	Socializer	Free spirit	Achiever	Player
Socializer	.365**				
Free spirit	.155**	.042			
Achiever	.213**	.158**	.310**		
Player	.062**	.126**	.127**	.259**	
Disruptor	−.02	.024	.295**	.148**	.067**

As shown in Table 2, we find partial overlap between the user types, which is overall consistent with the findings of Tondello et al. [23, 28]. Only the correlation between Socializer and Free Spirit reported in the former studies cannot be confirmed.

In general, Achiever *(M = 24,05, SD = 3,328)* and Philanthropist *(M = 23,96, SD = 3,304)* are the most dominant HEXAD types in our sample, followed by Free Spirit *(M = 22,92, SD = 3,405)*, Player *(M = 21,5, SD = 4,216)* and Socializer *(M = 21,1, SD = 5,092)*. In accordance with the results of Tondello et al. [23], Disruptor showed the lowest mean score *(M = 15,84, SD = 4,912)*.

The results of the internal scale reliability analysis (Cronbach's α) overall and for each subscale per survey language are presented in Table 3. While the Socializer, Achiever, and Philanthropist scales can be considered as reliable in English (α > 0.7), issues arise with the Free Spirit scale, in concordance with Tondello et al. [23]. Furthermore, the Player and Disruptor scales in both languages and the Philanthropist scale in German show values below the acceptable threshold.

Table 3. Internal reliability scores for each HEXAD user type (overall and per language).

User type	α (overall)	α (English)	α (German)
Philanthropist	0,72	0,729	0,605
Socializer	0,846	0,841	0,785
Free spirit	0,659	0,652	0,678
Achiever	0,741	0,749	0,724
Player	0,650	0,638	0,682
Disruptor	0,571	0,528	0,670

Exploratory factor analysis reveals that certain items have low factor loadings and should therefore be further improved to enhance the overall reliability of the scales. To ensure comparability with previous studies [23, 28], we used the Unweighted Least Squares method for factor extraction, combined with an oblique Promax rotation due to partial overlap of factors [59] in IBM SPSS statistics 26, forcing extraction of six factors. The Kaiser-Meyer-Olkin test (KMO = .817 for the English sample and KMO = .775 for the German sample) and Bartlett's Test of Sphericity (χ^2 = 5013.35, p < .01 for the English sample and $\chi^2 = 2229,8$ p < .01 for the German sample) support the suitability of the data for factor analysis [62]. Table 6 (English) and Table 7 (German), located in the Appendix, show the factor loadings for each of the HEXAD survey items.

The analysis of the HEXAD scales indicates that the items F2 and P3 (both languages), F4, D1 and A1 (English), and D2 (German) cause difficulties in factor extraction and should therefore be further improved for better reliability of the scale. R3 (German) and F1 (English) also have comparatively low factor loadings, which requires refinement. However, the vast majority of the items load well on distinguishable factors, which is supportive of a general validity of the HEXAD scales.

To evaluate the fit of the HEXAD scales with the theoretical model, we conducted a confirmatory factor analysis using structural equation modeling with a maximum likelihood method in IBM SPSS Amos 26, following the method of Tondello et al. [23]. We modeled the six HEXAD types as latent variables and added the survey items as observed variables.

Overall, the Chi-Square Test ($\chi^2 = 1620.1$, p < .01 for the English sample and $\chi^2 = 796.72$, p < .01 for the German sample), the calculated RMSEA (.086 for the English sample and .079 for the German sample) and the calculated CFI (.715 for the English sample and .729 for the German sample) do not support evidence for a good model fit [63], in line with the results of Tondello et al. [23]. Table 8 (in the Appendix) shows the standardized (β) and unstandardized (B) regression weights and standard errors (SE) for both the English and German samples. Similar to the results of Tondello et al. [23], items F2 and R3 have low weights on their subscales in the English sample. Also, confirming the observations from the exploratory factor analysis, items F4 and D1 need further adjustment for a better model fit. On the German scale, F2 and R3 are similarly problematic, and additionally, P3 should be enhanced to improve the goodness of fit. In general, the majority of the items load highly on the respective subscales.

Conclusively, the validation shows that the HEXAD scale in English [23] and German is a valuable instrument for adequate identification of HEXAD types, but some improvements in both languages are needed to increase the reliability of the subscales and to achieve a better model fit.

4.2 HEXAD Types and Game Element Preferences

To assess the relationship between HEXAD types and preference for specific game elements, we perform a correlation analysis. Due to the non-parametric nature of the 7-point Likert HEXAD and game element rating scales, we used Kendall's τ_b for the analysis. Table 4 presents the correlations of HEXAD types with game elements according to suggestions in the scientific literature [21, 25], both in aggregate form and for each game element. For readability, we only show correlations with a coefficient value of at least .125. Correlations with a coefficient greater than .20 are marked in bold.

Table 4. Correlations of the HEXAD types with game elements ($\tau_b \geq .125$, ** $p < .01$).

User type	Suggested Items [21, 25]	Philanthropist	Socializer	Player	Achiever	Free spirit	Disruptor
Philanthropist	Philanthropist elements	.222**	.174**	.173**	.160**		
	Collection			.131**			
	Gifting	.194**	.165**	.162**			
	Knowledge sharing	.174**	.148**		.154**	.142**	
	Administrative roles	.176**	.129**				
Socializer	Socializer elements		.299**	.253**	.199**		
	Guilds or teams	.177**	.377**	.143**	.157**		
	Social networks		.231**	.164**			
	Social comparison		.191**	.223**	.190**		
	Social competition		.291**	.285**	.287**		.126**
	Social discovery		.200**	.167**	.128**		
	Tips		.131**	.139**			
	Social status		.159**	.227**	.144**		
Player	Player elements			.367**	.172**		
	Points			.281**	.180**	.146**	
	Rewards or prizes			.366**	.161**		
	Leaderboards		.166**	.296**	.211**		
	Achievements			.267**			
	Virtual economy			.190**			
	Chance						
Achiever	Achiever elements	.125**	.139**	.281**	.297**	.201**	
	Learning	.155**			.234**	.191**	
	Levels			.212**	.184**		
	Progression			.225**	.196**		
	Challenges	.130**	.134**	.209**	.418**	.196**	
	Certificates		.137**	.252**	.176**		
	Quests			.160**	.141**	.159**	
Free spirit	Free spirit elements				.129**	.214**	
	Unlockable content			.187**	.127**		
	Exploratory tasks					.186**	
	Nonlinear gameplay					.151**	
	Easter eggs						
	Creativity tools					.225**	
	Narrative or story						
	Customization			.140**		.134**	
Disruptor	Disruptor elements			.125**	.163**	.191**	.172**
	Voting			.131**	.125**		
	Innovation platforms			.128**	.194**	.168**	.132**
	Development tools			.127**			
	Anonymity						
	Anarchic gameplay						.207**

The correlation analysis reveals highly significant correlations between HEXAD types and certain game elements and largely supports the findings of both previous studies [24, 28, 29] and suggestions from the literature [21, 25], as the aggregated game elements show significant correlations with the assumed HEXAD types. Deepening the analysis to individual game elements, Socializers prefer social game elements, such as teams, social networks, competition (and related, leaderboards), and social discovery. Free Spirits are the users who like exploratory tasks, nonlinear gameplay, and creativity tools. Notably, Players show high correlations with a variety of game elements, similar to previous results [28]. Achievers are particularly motivated by challenges, learning, competition, and leaderboards. In contrast to the study by Tondello et al. [28], we find significant correlations only between Disruptors and anarchic gameplay, innovation platforms, and social competition, but not with development tools, anonymity, and voting mechanisms. In total, three other game elements besides anonymity, namely narratives, easter eggs, and chance, show no relevant significant correlation with HEXAD types ($\tau_b \leq .125$). However, we identify significant, although weak correlations between Philanthropists and proposed game elements such as gifting, knowledge sharing, and administrative roles that previous studies were unable to identify [28, 29].

In general, it can be stated that the HEXAD typology provides valuable guidance for tailoring gamification design and the selection of specific game elements for different users. However, since user types partially overlap, there are also relevant and significant correlations between HEXAD types and game elements not directly suspected in the scientific literature [21, 25]. In particular, Players seem to like a variety of game elements in addition to extrinsic rewards, such as social comparison and competition, levels and progression, challenges, and certificates, supporting the findings of previous studies [28].

5   Discussion and Implications

This study aimed to validate the English version, previously validated by Tondello et al. [23], and a corresponding German version of the gamification user types HEXAD scale to assess the value of the HEXAD scale for identifying different user types in gamified systems. Furthermore, our goal was to evaluate the relationships between HEXAD types and game element preferences with a large and diverse sample to confirm and extend the suggestions of scientific literature [21, 25] and previous studies [24, 28, 29].

Our results support the overall validity of the HEXAD scale in both English and German. However, the scale reliability analysis shows that the Free Spirit, Player, Disruptor (both languages) and Philanthropist (German) scales need further improvement to reach the acceptable threshold. In particular, the exploratory and confirmatory factor analysis reveals that certain items cause problems that lead to lower scale reliability. Items F2 and P3 and R3 require refinement in both languages, indicating that the items in their current form may not be appropriate to measure the corresponding HEXAD type, an observation consistent with the results of the previous validation study [23]. For example, the curiosity that Free Spirits exhibit when exploring a system may not imply that Free Spirits are curious in the sense of a trait, as item F2 suggests ("I often let curiosity guide me"). Also, the concept of return of investment (R3: "Return of investment is important to me") may be too broad and not suitable to express the expectation of rewards for performing actions within the gamified system. Since items D1 and F4 present problems only in the English version of the HEXAD scale, which contradicts the findings of Tondello et al. [23], it can be assumed that the cause might be a lack of language proficiency to understand the concepts of self-presentation and provocation since two-thirds of the participants from over 50 countries answered the English version of the HEXAD scale, but only about 15% were from English-speaking countries (Canada, U.S., Australia, Great Britain, and New Zealand). It is possible that cultural differences in these concepts related to the open display of self-consciousness also play a role. Besides this need for further refinements, we consider the HEXAD scales in English and German as valuable instruments for further research and practice to identify HEXAD user types and use them as a basis for tailored gamification design.

Second, our results confirm the suggestions of scientific literature [21, 25] and findings from previous studies [24, 28, 29] on the relationships between HEXAD types and preference for certain game elements. We addressed the limited sample size of Tondello et al. [28] by increasing the sample to over 1.000 participants from 59 countries, and we included the wide variety of individual game elements that have previously only been considered in aggregated form [24, 30] to derive reliable recommendations for researchers and practitioners in efficiently selecting appropriate game elements for each user type. Supporting the validity of the HEXAD types and the suggested game element preferences [25], Socializers prefer social elements such as guilds or teams, social networks, social competition, and social discovery, while Achievers like social competition and leaderboards, but also learning, levels and progression, and challenges. Philanthropists especially favor gifting, knowledge sharing, and administrative roles, but are also attracted to teams and learning. Free Spirits, in turn, mostly like creativity tools, exploratory tasks, nonlinear gameplay, and customization, but are also motivated by learning and challenges.

Extending the theoretical propositions, our results show that Players are motivated by a variety of game elements. In addition to the extrinsic rewards stated in theory, such as prizes, points and, achievements, they also enjoy levels and progression, challenges, certificates, social comparison, social status, and social competition – which may be explainable by the observation that social approval is an even more powerful motivational reward than tangible prizes [64].

Another interesting finding is that Disruptors prefer anarchic gameplay and show weak relationships with innovation platforms and social competition, but in general, it seems difficult to design tailored gamification systems in a way that Disruptors appreciate the selected game elements. Considering that Disruptors are significantly less present than any other HEXAD type, the results should not alienate gamification designers, but rather Disruptors should be proactively involved in co-designing and improving the gamified system so that their drive to explore the boundaries of the system is used to improve quality instead of making them adversaries of the system [25].

Comprehensively revealing the individual game element preferences of different HEXAD types, our findings provide valuable guidance for researchers and practitioners in designing scientifically grounded, tailored gamification that takes into account the needs and motivations of different users.

6   Limitations and Future Work

As with any other scientific work, this study is not without limitations. Even though we consider our study design, which replicated previous studies on the validation of the HEXAD scale [23] and the relationships between HEXAD types and game element preferences [28], to be appropriate, our sample included a large number of participants with native languages other than English, which may have affected the validation of this scale. We invite further research to broaden our focus with more native English speakers to obtain more reliable results. Moreover, validating the HEXAD scale in other languages, such as Mandarin, Indian, or Japanese, would open up opportunities to use the HEXAD typology for tailored gamification design in many more countries and cultures than just focusing on Western culture.

Second, we identified specific items in the HEXAD scales that have low factor loadings and negatively affect internal scale reliability. We invite further research to build on our explanations of why these items may cause problems in order to improve the HEXAD scales and increase their validity.

In addition, we identify the Disruptor type as particularly challenging for tailored gamification design, as only single game elements showed significant correlations with the Disruptor type. Even though we suggest co-design as an alternative for onboarding Disruptors early in the design process, further research should investigate whether other game elements or game design processes not explored in this study can improve successful tailored gamification design for Disruptors.

7   Conclusion

Considering the needs and motivations of different user types is critical to designing gamification in such a way that it achieves the desired results. In this study, we validated an instrument for identifying different user types, the gamification user types HEXAD scale, in English and German. Although some items of the scale still need improvement, we consider the HEXAD scale a valuable tool for tailored gamification design in research and practice. In addition, we found significant correlations between HEXAD types and preference for specific game elements, highlighting the usefulness of the HEXAD typology for selecting game elements in tailored gamification design, as suggested by the scientific literature and previous studies. While Philanthropists are motivated by gifting, administrative roles, and knowledge sharing, Free Spirits mostly like creativity tools, exploratory tasks, and learning. Both Achievers and Players prefer challenges, leaderboards, levels, and competition, and Players are additionally attracted by extrinsic elements such as achievements, points, and rewards. Socializers enjoy social elements, such as teams, competition, social discovery, and social networks.

Finally, Disruptors can be motivated by anarchic gameplay and innovation platforms. Our findings contribute to refining the HEXAD scale as an instrument for identifying different user types and should successfully guide future gamification design in research and practice that is tailored to the needs and motivations of different user types to maximize the desired outcomes.

Appendix

Table 5. English and German user types HEXAD scales used in the study.

User types	Final validated English scale [23]	According German item from [60], based on the original scale from [28]	Used German item after committee selection
Philanthropist	P1: It makes me happy if I am able to help others	Es bereitet mir Freude, wenn ich anderen helfen kann	Es macht mich glücklich anderen zu helfen
	P2: I like helping others to orient themselves in new situations	Ich helfe anderen gerne dabei, sich in neuen Situationen zurecht zu finden	Ich mag es, anderen dabei zu helfen, sich in neuen Situationen zurecht zu finden
	P3: I like sharing my knowledge	Ich teile mein Wissen gerne mit anderen	Ich teile gerne mein Wissen
	P4: The well-being of others is important to me	Mir liegt das Wohl anderer am Herzen	Das Wohlergehen anderer ist mir wichtig
Socializer	S1: Interacting with others is important to me	Mir ist Interaktion mit anderen wichtig	Die Interaktion mit anderen ist mir wichtig
	S2: I like being part of a team	Ich bin gerne Teil eines Teams	Ich bin gerne Teil eines Teams
	S3: It is important to me to feel like I am part of a community	Es ist mir wichtig, mich als Teil einer Gemeinschaft zu fühlen	Es ist mir wichtig, mich als Teil einer Gemeinschaft zu fühlen
	S4: I enjoy group activities	Ich mag Gruppenaktivitäten	Gruppenaktivitäten machen mir Spaß
Free Spirit	F1: It is important to me to follow my own path	Es ist mir wichtig, meinen eigenen Weg zu gehen	Es ist mir wichtig, meinen eigenen Weg zu gehen
	F2: I often let curiosity guide me	Ich lasse mich oft von meiner Neugier leiten	Ich lasse mich oft durch Neugier leiten
	F3: Being independent is important to me	Mir ist meine Unabhängigkeit wichtig	Unabhängigkeit ist mir wichtig
	F4: Opportunities for self-expression are important to me	–	Gelegenheiten zur Selbstentfaltung sind wichtig für mich

(continued)

Table 5. (*continued*)

User types	Final validated English scale [23]	According German item from [60], based on the original scale from [28]	Used German item after committee selection
Achiever	A1: I like overcoming obstacles	–	Ich mag es, Hindernisse zu überwinden
	A2: I like mastering difficult tasks	Ich mag es, schwierige Aufgaben zu meistern	Ich mag es, schwierige Aufgaben zu meistern
	A3: It is important to me to continuously improve my skills	–	Es ist mir wichtig, meine Fähigkeiten ständig weiter zu entwickeln
	A4: I enjoy emerging victorious out of difficult circumstances	–	Ich mag es, aus schwierigen Umständen siegreich hervorzugehen
Player	R1: I like competitions where a prize can be won	Ich mag Wettbewerbe, bei denen ich einen Preis gewinnen kann	Ich mag Wettbewerbe, bei denen man Preise gewinnen kann
	R2: Rewards are a great way to motivate me	Belohnungen sind eine tolle Möglichkeit, mich zu motivieren	Belohnungen sind ein tolles Mittel, um mich zu motivieren
	R3: Return of investment is important to me	Es ist wichtig für mich, dass ich einen Nutzen von meinem Aufwand habe	Das Kosten-Nutzen Verhältnis ist mir wichtig
	R4: If the reward is sufficient, I will put in the effort	Wenn der Lohn stimmt, strenge ich mich gerne an	Bei angemessener Belohnung strenge ich mich gerne entsprechend an
Disruptor	D1: I like to provoke	Ich provoziere gerne	Ich provoziere gerne
	D2: I like to question the status quo	Ich mag es, den Status Quo in Frage zu stellen	Ich stelle den Status Quo gerne in Frage
	D3: I see myself as a rebel	Ich sehe mich als Rebell	Ich würde mich als rebellisch bezeichnen
	D4: I dislike following rules	Ich halte mich nicht gerne an Regeln	Ich halte mich nicht gerne an Regeln

Table 6. Rotated factor loadings for the HEXAD survey items in English (factor loads ≥ 0.25).

User type	Items	Factor 1 (S)	Factor 2 (P)	Factor 3 (D, F)	Factor 4 (A)	Factor 5 (R)	Factor 6
Socializer	S4	.811					
	S2	.798					
	S1	.687					
	S3	.434	.364				
Philanthropist	P4		.736				
	P2		.570				
	P1		.564				
	P3		**.407**				**.270**

(*continued*)

Table 6. (*continued*)

User type	Items	Factor 1 (S)	Factor 2 (P)	Factor 3 (D, F)	Factor 4 (A)	Factor 5 (R)	Factor 6
Disruptor	D3			.753			
	D4			.583			
	D2			.525			
	D1	**.337**		**.368**			
Free spirit	F3			.410			
	F4		**.320**	**.398**			
	F1			**.365**			
Achiever	A2				.942		
	A4				.619		
	A1				**.483**		**.393**
	A3				.399		
Player	R4					.740	
	R2					.734	
	R3					.448	
	R1					.400	
Free spirit	**F2**						**.431**

Table 7. Rotated factor loadings for the HEXAD survey items in German (factor loads ≥ 0.25).

User type	Items	Factor 1 (S)	Factor 2 (A)	Factor 3 (D)	Factor 4 (R)	Factor 5 (F)	Factor 6 (P)
Socializer	S1	.787					
	S3	.674					
	S4	.650					
	S2	.613					
Achiever	A2		.812				
	A1		.614				
	A3		.550				
	A4		.507				
Free spirit	**F2**		**.251**				
Philanthropist	**P3**		**.294**				**.256**
Disruptor	D3			.703			
	D4			.529			
	D1			.529			
	D2	**.337**		**.483**			
Player	R4				.836		
	R2				.728		
	R1				.461		
	R3				**.369**		

(*continued*)

Table 7. (*continued*)

User type	Items	Factor 1 (S)	Factor 2 (A)	Factor 3 (D)	Factor 4 (R)	Factor 5 (F)	Factor 6 (P)
Free spirit	F3					.670	
	F1					.569	
	F4					.407	
Philanthropist	P1						.605
	P4						.577
	P2						.545

Table 8. Regression weights for survey items of the HEXAD scales in English and German.

User type	Items	β (EN)	B (EN)	SE (EN)	β (D)	B (D)	SE (D)
Philanthropist	P1	,657	1,000		,622	1,000	
	P2	,713	1,385	,107	,540	1,149	,179
	P3	,573	1,026	,088	**,284**	**,508**	,127
	P4	,621	1,285	,105	,675	1,423	,222
Socializer	S1	,777	1,000		,755	1,000	
	S2	,849	1,115	,051	,687	,825	,078
	S3	,632	,846	,051	,641	,868	,086
	S4	,772	1,027	,050	,688	,872	,082
Player	R1	,483	1,000		,539	1,000	
	R2	,733	1,096	,113	,692	1,016	,123
	R3	**,431**	**,709**	,089	**,346**	**,491**	,095
	R4	,674	1,111	,113	,828	1,261	,158
Achiever	A1	,609	1,000		,526	1,000	
	A2	,825	1,551	,114	,898	1,571	,192
	A3	,548	,913	,079	,492	,805	,115
	A4	,638	,938	,073	,622	1,096	,134
Free Spirit	F1	,623	1,000		,669	1,000	
	F2	**,298**	**,463**	,085	**,347**	**,475**	,092
	F3	,625	1,087	,165	,730	1,120	,142
	F4	**,342**	**,664**	,110	,569	,816	,107
Disruptor	D1	**,402**	**1,000**		,525	1,000	
	D2	,506	,925	,118	,580	,885	,128
	D3	,794	1,867	,230	,768	1,373	,192
	D4	,560	1,231	,150	,512	,925	,143

References

1. Deterding, S., Dixon, D., Khaled, R., Nacke, L.: From game design elements to gamefulness: defining "gamification." In: Proceedings of the 15th International Academic MindTrek Conference: Envisioning Future Media Environments, Tampere, pp. 9–15 (2011). https://doi.org/10.1145/2181037.2181040
2. Hamari, J., Koivisto, J., Sarsa, H.: Does gamification work? - a literature review of empirical studies on gamification. In: 47th Hawaii International Conference on System Sciences, pp. 3025–3034 (2014). https://doi.org/10.1109/HICSS.2014.377
3. Seaborn, K., Fels, D.I.: Gamification in theory and action: a survey. Int. J. Hum. Comput. Stud. **74**, 14–31 (2015). https://doi.org/10.1016/j.ijhcs.2014.09.006
4. Kasurinen, J., Knutas, A.: Publication trends in gamification: a systematic mapping study. Comput. Sci. Rev. **27**, 33–44 (2018). https://doi.org/10.1016/j.cosrev.2017.10.003
5. Albertazzi, D., Ferreira, M.G.G., Forcellini, F.A.: A wide view on gamification. Technol. Knowl. Learn. **24**(2), 191–202 (2018). https://doi.org/10.1007/s10758-018-9374-z
6. Koivisto, J., Hamari, J.: The rise of motivational information systems: a review of gamification research. Int. J. Inf. Manage. **45**, 191–210 (2019). https://doi.org/10.1016/j.ijinfomgt.2018.10.013
7. Barata, G., Gama, S., Jorge, J., Gonçalves, D.: Studying student differentiation in gamified education: a long-term study. Comput. Human Behav. **71**, 550–585 (2017). https://doi.org/10.1016/j.chb.2016.08.049
8. Huang, B., Hew, K.F., Lo, C.K.: Investigating the effects of gamification-enhanced flipped learning on undergraduate students' behavioral and cognitive engagement. Interact. Learn. Environ. **27**(8), 1106–1126 (2019). https://doi.org/10.1080/10494820.2018.1495653
9. Putz, L.-M., Hofbauer, F., Treiblmaier, H.: Can gamification help to improve education? findings from a longitudinal study. Comput. Human Behav. **110**, 106392 (2020). https://doi.org/10.1016/j.chb.2020.106392
10. Mekler, E.D., Brühlmann, F., Tuch, A.N., Opwis, K.: Towards understanding the effects of individual gamification elements on intrinsic motivation and performance. Comput. Human Behav. **71**, 525–534 (2017). https://doi.org/10.1016/j.chb.2015.08.048
11. Sailer, M., Homner, L.: The gamification of learning: a meta-analysis. Educ. Psychol. Rev. **32**(1), 77–112 (2019). https://doi.org/10.1007/s10648-019-09498-w
12. Facey-Shaw, L., Specht, M., van Rosmalen, P., Bartley-Bryan, J.: Do badges affect intrinsic motivation in introductory programming students? Simul. Gaming. **51**(1), 33–54 (2020). https://doi.org/10.1177/1046878119884996
13. Sailer, M., Hense, J.U., Mayr, S.K., Mandl, H.: How gamification motivates: an experimental study of the effects of specific game design elements on psychological need satisfaction. Comput. Human Behav. **69**, 371–380 (2017). https://doi.org/10.1016/j.chb.2016.12.033
14. Sezgin, S., Yüzer, T.V.: Analysing adaptive gamification design principles for online courses. Behav. Inf. Technol. (2020). https://doi.org/10.1080/0144929X.2020.1817559
15. Laine, T.H., Lindberg, R.S.N.: Designing engaging games for education: a systematic literature review on game motivators and design principles. IEEE Trans. Learn. Technol. **13**(4), 804–821 (2020). https://doi.org/10.1109/TLT.2020.3018503
16. Morschheuser, B., Hassan, L., Werder, K., Hamari, J.: How to design gamification? a method for engineering gamified software. Inf. Softw. Technol. **95**, 219–237 (2018). https://doi.org/10.1016/j.infsof.2017.10.015

17. Chen, Y.: Exploring design guidelines of using user-centered design in gamification development: a delphi study. Int. J. Hum. Comput. Interact. **35**(13), 1170–1181 (2019). https://doi.org/10.1080/10447318.2018.1514823

18. Liu, D., Santhanam, R., Webster, J.: Toward meaningful engagement: a framework for design and research of gamified information systems. MIS Q. **41**(4), 1011–1034 (2017)

19. Bartle, R.: Hearts, clubs, diamonds, spades: players who suit MUDs. J. MUD Res. **1**(1), 19 (1996)

20. Yee, N.: The demographics, motivations, and derived experiences of users of massively multi-user online graphical environments. Presence Teleoperators and Virtual Environ. **15**, 309–329 (2006). https://doi.org/10.1162/pres.15.3.309

21. Klock, A.C.T., Gasparini, I., Pimenta, M.S., Hamari, J.: Tailored gamification: a review of literature. Int. J. Hum. Comput. Stud. **144**, 102495 (2020). https://doi.org/10.1016/j.ijhcs.2020.102495

22. Bartle, R.: Player Type Theory: Uses and Abuses. Causal Connect (2012). https://www.youtube.com/watch?v=ZIzLbE-93nc, Accessed 29 Jan 2021

23. Tondello, G.F., Mora, A., Marczewski, A., Nacke, L.E.: Empirical validation of the gamification user types hexad scale in English and Spanish. Int. J. Hum. Comput. Stud. **127**, 95–111 (2019). https://doi.org/10.1016/j.ijhcs.2018.10.002

24. Tondello, G.F., Mora, A., Nacke, L.E.: Elements of gameful design emerging from user preferences. In: CHI Play 2017 – Proceedings of Annual Symposium Computer Interaction Play, New York, pp. 129–140 (2017). https://doi.org/10.1145/3116595.3116627

25. Marczewski, A.: User types. In: Even Ninja Monkeys Like to Play, pp. 65–80. CreateSpace Independent Publishing Platform (2015)

26. Mora, A., Riera, D., González, C., Arnedo-Moreno, J.: Gamification: a systematic review of design frameworks. J. Comput. High. Educ. **29**(3), 516–548 (2017). https://doi.org/10.1007/s12528-017-9150-4

27. Böckle, M., Novak, J., Bick, M.: Exploring gamified persuasive system design for energy saving. J. Enterp. Inf. Manag. **33**(6), 1337–1356 (2020). https://doi.org/10.1108/JEIM-02-2019-0032

28. Tondello, G.F., Wehbe, R.R., Diamond, L., Busch, M., Marczewski, A., Nacke, L.E.: The gamification user types Hexad scale. In: CHI Play 2016 – Proceedings of 2016 Annual Symposium Computer Interaction Play, New York, pp. 229–243 (2016). https://doi.org/10.1145/2967934.2968082

29. Mora, A., Tondello, G.F., Calvet, L., González, C., Arnedo-Moreno, J., Nacke, L.E.: The quest for a better tailoring of gameful design: an analysis of player type preferences. In: Proceedings of XX International Conference on Human Computer Interaction, New York, pp. 1–8 (2019). https://doi.org/10.1145/3335595.3335625

30. Orji, R., Tondello, G.F., Nacke, L.E.: Personalizing persuasive strategies in gameful systems to gamification user types. In: Proceedings of the 2018 CHI Conference on Human Factors in Computing Systems, pp. 1–14. ACM, New York (2018). https://doi.org/10.1145/3173574.3174009

31. Cheng, M.-T., Chen, J.-H., Chu, S.-J., Chen, S.-Y.: The use of serious games in science education: a review of selected empirical research from 2002 to 2013. J. Comput. Educ. **2**(3), 353–375 (2015). https://doi.org/10.1007/s40692-015-0039-9

32. Zainuddin, Z., Chu, S., Shujahat, M., Perera, C.: The impact of gamification on learning and instruction: a systematic review of empirical evidence. Educ. Res. Rev. **30**, 100326 (2020). https://doi.org/10.1016/j.edurev.2020.100326

33. Bozkurt, A., Durak, G.: A systematic review of gamification research: in pursuit of homo ludens. Int. J. Game-Based Learn. **8**(3), 15–33 (2018). https://doi.org/10.4018/IJGBL.2018070102

34. Hew, K.F., Huang, B., Chu, K.W.S., Chiu, D.K.W.: Engaging Asian students through game mechanics: findings from two experiment studies. Comput. Educ. **92–93**, 221–236 (2016). https://doi.org/10.1016/j.compedu.2015.10.010

35. Orji, R., Moffatt, K.: Persuasive technology for health and wellness: state-of-the-art and emerging trends. Health Inf. J. **24**(1), 66–91 (2018). https://doi.org/10.1177/1460458216650979

36. Sardi, L., Idri, A., Fernández-Alemán, J.L.: A systematic review of gamification in e-Health. J. Biomed. Inform. **71**, 31–48 (2017). https://doi.org/10.1016/j.jbi.2017.05.011

37. Landers, R.N., Bauer, K.N., Callan, R.C.: Gamification of task performance with leaderboards: a goal setting experiment. Comput. Human Behav. **71**, 508–515 (2017). https://doi.org/10.1016/j.chb.2015.08.008

38. Tobon, S., Ruiz-Alba, J.L., García-Madariaga, J.: Gamification and online consumer decisions: is the game over? Decis. Support Syst. **128**, 113167 (2020). https://doi.org/10.1016/j.dss.2019.113167

39. Wanick, V., Bui, H.: Gamification in management: a systematic review and research directions. Int. J. Serious Games. **6**(2), 57–74 (2019). https://doi.org/10.17083/ijsg.v6i2.282

40. AlSkaif, T., Lampropoulos, I., van den Broek, M., van Sark, W.: Gamification-based framework for engagement of residential customers in energy applications. Energy Res. Soc. Sci. **44**, 187–195 (2018). https://doi.org/10.1016/j.erss.2018.04.043

41. Oppong-Tawiah, D., Webster, J., Staples, S., Cameron, A.-F., Ortiz, A., de Guinea, T., Hung: Developing a gamified mobile application to encourage sustainable energy use in the office. J. Bus. Res. **106**, 388–405 (2020). https://doi.org/10.1016/j.jbusres.2018.10.051

42. Alexandrova, A., Rapanotti, L.: Requirements analysis gamification in legacy system replacement projects. Req. Eng. **25**(2), 131–151 (2019). https://doi.org/10.1007/s00766-019-00311-2

43. Gooch, D., Vasalou, A., Benton, L.: Exploring the use of a gamification platform to support students with dyslexia. In: 2015 6th International Conference on Information, Intelligence, Systems and Applications (IISA), pp. 1–6. IEEE, Corfu (2015). https://doi.org/10.1109/IISA.2015.7388001

44. Hsieh, H.C.L., Yang, H.H.: Incorporating gamification into website design to facilitate effective communication. Theor. Issues Ergon. Sci. **21**(1), 89–111 (2020). https://doi.org/10.1080/1463922X.2019.1645920

45. Israel, M., Marino, M.T., Basham, J.D., Spivak, W.: Fifth graders as app designers: how diverse learners conceptualize educational apps. J. Res. Technol. Educ. **46**(1), 53–80 (2013). https://doi.org/10.1080/15391523.2013.10782613

46. García-Barrios, V.M., Mödritscher, F., Gütl, C.: Personalisation versus Adaptation? A User-centred Model Approach and its Application. In: Proceedings of the International Conference on Knowledge Management (I-KNOW). pp. 120–127. Graz (2005).

47. Nasirzadeh, E., Fathian, M.: Investigating the effect of gamification elements on bank customers to personalize gamified systems. Int. J. Human-Comput. Stud. **143**, 102469 (2020). https://doi.org/10.1016/j.ijhcs.2020.102469

48. Uskov, A., Sekar, B.: Smart gamification and smart serious games. In: Sharma, D., Favorskaya, M., Jain, L., and Howlett, R. (eds.) Fusion of Smart, Multimedia and Computer Gaming Technologies, pp. 7–36. Springer Cham (2015). https://doi.org/10.1007/978-3-319-14645-4_2

49. Lopez, C.E., Tucker, C.S.: The effects of player type on performance: a gamification case study. Comput. Human Behav. **91**, 333–345 (2019). https://doi.org/10.1016/j.chb.2018.10.005

50. Hamari, J., Tuunanen, J.: Player types: a meta-synthesis. Trans. Digit. Games Res. Assoc. **1**(2), 29–53 (2014). https://doi.org/10.26503/todigra.v1i2.13

51. de Vette, F., Tabak, M., Dekker van Weering, M., Vollenbroek-Hutten, M.: Engaging elderly people in telemedicine through gamification. JMIR Serious Games 3(2), e9 (2015). https://doi.org/10.2196/games.4561

52. Nacke, L.E., Bateman, C., Mandryk, R.L.: BrainHex: a neurobiological gamer typology survey. Entertain. Comput. 5(1), 55–62 (2014). https://doi.org/10.1016/j.entcom.2013.06. 002

53. Pink, D.H.: Drive: The Surprising Truth About What Motivates Us. Canongate Books, New York (2009)

54. Ryan, R.M., Deci, E.L.: Self-determination theory and the facilitation of intrinsic motivation, social development, and well-being. Am. Psychol. 55(1), 68–78 (2000). https://doi.org/10. 1037/0003-066X.55.1.68

55. Kotsopoulos, D., Bardaki, C., Lounis, S., Pramatari, K.: Employee profiles and preferences towards IoT-enabled gamification for energy conservation. Int. J. Serious Games. 5(2), 65–85 (2018). https://doi.org/10.17083/ijsg.v5i2.225

56. Herbert, B., Charles, D., Moore, A., Charles, T.: An investigation of gamification typologies for enhancing learner motivation. In: Proceedings - 2014 International Conference Interacting Technol. Games, iTAG 2014, pp. 71–78. IEEE, Nottingham (2014). https:// doi.org/10.1109/iTAG.2014.17

57. Holmes, D., Charles, D., Morrow, P., McClean, S., McDonough, S.: Rehabilitation game model for personalised exercise. In: 2015 International Conference on Interactive Technologies and Games, pp. 41–48. IEEE, Nottingham (2015). https://doi.org/10.1109/ iTAG.2015.11

58. Diamond, L., Tondello, G.F., Marczewski, A., Nacke, L.E., Tscheligi, M.: The HEXAD gamification user types questionnaire : background and development process. In: Workshop on Personalization in Serious and Persuasive Games and Gamified Interactions (2015)

59. Everitt, B.S., Dunn, G.: Exploratory factor analysis. In: Applied Multivariate Data Analysis, pp. 271–290. John Wiley & Sons, Ltd., West Sussex, UK (2001). https://doi.org/10.1002/ 9781118887486.ch12

60. Gamified   UK: Gamification   User   Type   Test   German, https://gamified.uk/UserTypeTest2016/user-type-test.php?q=l&lang=de#.YBFwsuhKiUk, Accessed 29 Jan 2021

61. Brislin, R.W.: Comparative research methodology: cross-cultural studies. Int. J. Psychol. 11 (3), 215–229 (1976). https://doi.org/10.1080/00207597608247359

62. Shrestha, N.: Factor analysis as a tool for survey analysis. Am. J. Appl. Math. Stat. 9(1), 4–11 (2021). https://doi.org/10.12691/ajams-9-1-2

63. Fabrigar, L.R., Wegener, D.T., MacCallum, R.C., Strahan, E.J.: Evaluating the use of exploratory factor analysis in psychological research. Psychol. Methods. 4(3), 272–299 (1999). https://doi.org/10.1037/1082-989X.4.3.272

64. Deci, E.L.: Effects of externally mediated rewards on intrinsic motivation. J. Pers. Soc. Psychol. 18(1), 105–115 (1971). https://doi.org/10.1037/h0030644

The Foundations and Frontiers of Research on the Effect of Video Games on Child Development

A Scientometrics and Knowledge-Mapping Analysis Based on CiteSpace

Xiaocen Liu[1]([✉]) [iD], Heqing Huang[1] [iD], Fangbing Qu[1] [iD], and Donghui Dou[2]

[1] Capital Normal University, Beijing, People's Republic of China
cindyliu@cnu.edu.cn
[2] Central University of Finance and Economics, Beijing, People's Republic of China

Abstract. In this media-rich world, video games have become almost ubiquitous in children's lives. Therefore, researchers have shown increased interest in the relationship between video gaming and child development (VGCD). Despite the considerable amount of publications in this area, there have been few attempts to take a macro- and multi-disciplinary approach to synthesizing this literature. To understand the evolution of and trends in VGCD research, we conducted a scientometrics and knowledge-mapping analysis with the aid of CiteSpace. The analysis was based on 3,541 publications retrieved from the Web of Science database. The results showed that: (1) The past 37 years have witnessed dramatic progress in VGCD research, with the number of annual publications and citations following cubic accelerating curves; (2) The United States is at the center of the global research network; (3) Psychology plays a pivotal role among all the disciplines; (4) Reference co-citation analysis yielded 10 large clusters that can be grouped into three categories: video games and psychological development, video games and physical health, and video games and education; (5) Nowadays, the most active research themes in VGCD studies are *serious games*, *autism spectrum disorder*, *virtual reality*, *internet gaming disorder*, and *effect sizes*. The results of this study indicate that VGCD has received greater attention across a number of disciplines in recent years. The existing research recognizes that video games are a double-edged sword with respect to child development. At present, experiments, interventions, and educational research that draw on the benefits of video games have become the mainstream of research.

Keywords: Video games · Electronic games · Child development · CiteSpace · Scientometrics · Knowledge mapping

X. Fang (Ed.): HCII 2021, LNCS 12789, pp. 239–257, 2021.
https://doi.org/10.1007/978-3-030-77277-2_19

1 Introduction

1.1 Video Games and Child Development

The term *electronic games* refers to all interactive games that run on electronic devices. Because *video games* are currently the most widespread form of electronic games, this term has become the most common way to refer to *electronic games* in English [1]. Video games were originally displayed on raster video equipment such as televisions [2]. However, because of the prevalence of the term *video games*, it now stands for any type of electronic game. In addition to *video games*, terms related to *electronic games* also include *computer games*, *serious games*, *digital games*, *online games*, and *simulation games* [3].

Numerous studies have shown that video game players are increasingly younger and that child gamers are now commonplace [4]. With frequent reports of psychological and social problems associated with problematic gaming behaviors among children, children's exposure to video games and their effects have received attention from researchers in many disciplines. In the field of psychology, a great number of studies consistently point to the mental health risks that violent games and gaming addiction pose for children [5]. Consistent with the *Diagnostic and Statistical Manual of Mental Disorders* (DSM-5®) [6], the *World Health Organization* has defined "gaming disorder" as a new mental health disorder based on concerns about the dangers of violent games and gaming addiction [7]. However, other psychologists de-emphasize these concerns and point to the potential benefits of playing video games [8]. Similar debates regarding the detriments and benefits of gaming for children prevail in other disciplines, such as health sciences, pediatrics, nutrition, and education. Thus, an interdisciplinary and macro-level analysis is essential for a deep understanding of the relationship between video gaming and child development (VGCD).

1.2 Scientometrics Analysis, Knowledge Mapping, and Citespace

With the rise of interdisciplinary research and the explosion of frontier knowledge, the knowledge structure of and hotspot areas in VGCD are undergoing rapid transformation. Given the enormous amount of research literature, scholars face serious challenges in thoroughly exploring the information and impartially conducting multidisciplinary analysis so as to trace the historical evolution and grasp the frontier trends in the field of VGCD accurately. Fortunately, scientometrics analysis and knowledge-mapping techniques provide us with a key to unlock the massive bibliometric data. These techniques are uniquely suited to probing the relationship between video gaming and child development. Scientometrics is the quantitative study of science, technology, and innovation [9], and knowledge mapping refers to the use of visualization tools or processes to portray knowledge structures. The two techniques are well integrated into CiteSpace.

CiteSpace is a Java application for visualizing and analyzing the research literature in a knowledge domain. By analyzing bibliographic information (especially citation information from databases like the Web of Science), CiteSpace allows users to outline the blueprints of and new developments in a research domain rapidly and develop a good understanding of the scientific publications efficiently. Figure 1 displays the conceptual model of CiteSpace. In a co-citation network (co-citation means two publications are cited together by the same studies), the intellectual base is shaped by the most cited references, whereas the research front is formed by the most citing studies [10]. In other words, through the use of scientometrics analysis and knowledge-mapping techniques, CiteSpace can reveal not only the knowledge base and historical evolution of VGCD but also the emerging trends and new developments in this research domain.

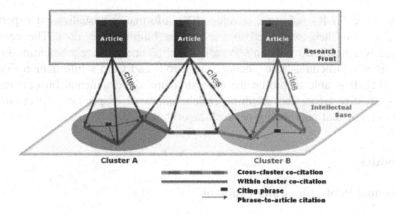

Fig. 1. Illustration of the CiteSpace conceptual model [10].

1.3 The Present Study

This study set out to give a holistic, systematic, and objective portrait of VGCD research, elicited from the scientometrics analysis and knowledge-mapping technique provided by CiteSpace. The bibliometric data were retrieved from the most widely used multidisciplinary bibliographic database, the Web of Science (WoS). The following issues will be addressed in this paper: (1) The growth patterns of annual publications and citations in VGCD studies; (2) Scholarly cooperation among authors, institutions, and countries; (3) Disciplines and source journals involved in this field; (4) Historical evolution of hot research areas and topics; and (5) Emerging trends and new developments in the knowledge domain.

2 Method

2.1 Data Collection

The input bibliometric data for CiteSpace were extracted from four databases in the Web of Science Core Collection, namely Science Citation Index Expanded (SCIE), Social Science Citation Index (SSCI), Arts & Humanities Citation Index (A&HCI), and Emerging Sources Citation Index (ESCI), based on a topic search for papers published between 1900 and 2020 on VGCD. The search was limited to articles and reviews in

English only. The search formula was set as TS = ("video game*" OR "electronic game*" OR "digital game*" OR "computer game*" OR "serious game*" OR "online game*" OR "simulation game*" OR "internet game*" OR "MMORPG") AND TS = ("child*" OR "infant*" OR "toddler*" OR "kid*" OR "preschooler*" OR "kindergartener*" OR "pupil*"). Through data cleansing, 3,541 documents were finally retrieved for the period 1983–2020. The data were downloaded on December 31, 2020, and the database had been updated on December 30, 2020.

2.2   Research Tools

The CiteSpace 5.7.R4 software, developed by information visualization expert Professor Chaomei Chen, was used to analyze the bibliographic data. The design of CiteSpace was inspired by Kuhn's Paradigm-Shift Theory, Price's Scientific Frontier Theory, Burt's Structural-Hole Theory, and Pirolli and Card's Information Foraging Theory [11]. It is able to profile the core structure, developmental history, research hotspots, frontier areas, and scientific collaborations of a specific field through co-citation analysis and pathfinding network algorithms.

3   Results

3.1   Annual Publications and Citations

By the end of 2020, the number of published articles on the relationship between video games and child development was 3,541, with 103,556 citations (Fig. 2). The h-index was 141, and the average citations of each article was 29.28. The growth patterns of annual publications and citations conform to cubic function distributions, $y_{\text{publications}} = -5.534 + 3.85x - 0.429x^2 + 0.016x^3$, $R^2 = 0.992$; $y_{\text{citations}} = -70.295 + 77.491x - 12.924x^2 + 0.537x^3$, $R^2 = 0.995$ (x represents the ordinal number of the published year).

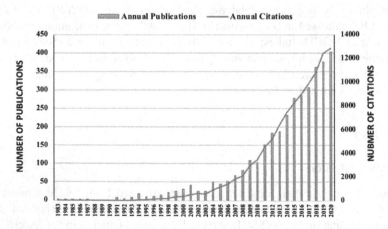

Fig. 2. Number of annual publications and citations over the period from 1983 to 2020.

3.2   Research Cooperation

Regional Partnerships. The ten top-ranked countries (by citation counts) in this field are mainly scattered in Europe and North America (Fig. 3), namely the United States (1,345), the United Kingdom (353), Australia (255), Canada (251), the Netherlands (191), Spain (186), China (134), Germany (128), Italy (122), and Brazil (111). Among them, the United States, with the largest number of publications and the earliest origin of research (year 1983), is most outstanding and is situated at the center of the global research network.

In terms of research institutions, six of the US universities are among the top 10 (1-Iowa State Univ, 2-Harvard Univ, 3-Michigan State Univ, 6-Univ Michigan, 8-Univ Minnesota), whereas the other four leading institutions are in the Netherlands (5-Univ Amsterdam, 9-Radboud Univ Nijmegen), Australia (4-Deakin Univ), Canada (7-Univ Ottawa), and New Zealand (10-Univ Auckland).

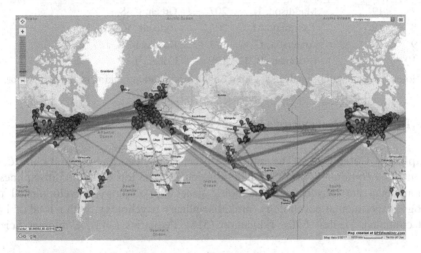

Fig. 3. Visualization map of regional partnerships. Because geographic data analysis is not available in CiteSpace 5.7.R4, this map is derived from data obtained on February 6, 2018, and from results analyzed via CiteSpace 5.2.R2.

Influential Authors. The intellectual output of highly prolific and frequently cited authors is often a good indicator of the overall state of an academic field (Table 1). Psychologists Anderson, Gentile, and Bushman have a close academic collaboration, and they share with Bandura and Ferguson a particular interest in the effects of violent play and media on aggressive behavior by children. Among them, Anderson and Bushman have proposed the General Aggression Model (GAM); Bandura is known for his Social Learning Theory; and Gentile and Ferguson have devoted their attention to the positive effects of video games. Griffiths is an expert on game addiction, whereas Green focuses on the effects of action video games on brain plasticity, learning, and vision. As for the psychiatrists, the American Psychiatric Association proposed the criteria for diagnosing internet gaming disorders. Overall, the leading psychologists and psychiatrists in the field are interested in the impacts of violent games and gaming addiction on children and the positive effects of video games. In contrast, experts on health, nutrition, and pediatrics such as Baranowski, Gao, Chaput, Maddison, and Tremblay focus on the use of video games to help children with respect to, for example, obesity, physical activity, sedentary behavior, and dietary intake.

Table 1. Top 10 most productive and cited authors.

Rank	Highly prolific authors		Most cited authors	
	Publications	Name	Citations	Name
1	36	Gentile, D. A.	458	Anderson, C. A.
2	32	Ferguson, C. J.	380	Gentile, D. A.
3	28	Gao, Z..	285	Baranowski, T.
4	24	Baranowski, T.	273	Ferguson, C. J.
5	19	Chaput, J. P.	269	Bandura, A.
6	19	Griffiths, M. D.	264	American Psychiatric Association
7	19	Maddison, R.	207	Green, C. S.
8	19	Tremblay, M. S.	206	Rideout, V. J.
9	18	Anderson, C. A.	197	Bushman, B. J.
10	17	Bushman, B. J.	195	Cohen, J.

Note: The cited author analysis is based on the local citation ranking of the first author.

3.3   Disciplinary Categories and Source Journals

Disciplinary Categories. "The relationship between video gaming and child development" is a common concern of many disciplines. The top 10 ranked disciplines by citation count are: Psychology (including general psychology, developmental psychology, experimental psychology, multidisciplinary psychology, with a total of 1,823 local citations), Health (650), Education (516), Pediatrics (343), Computer Science

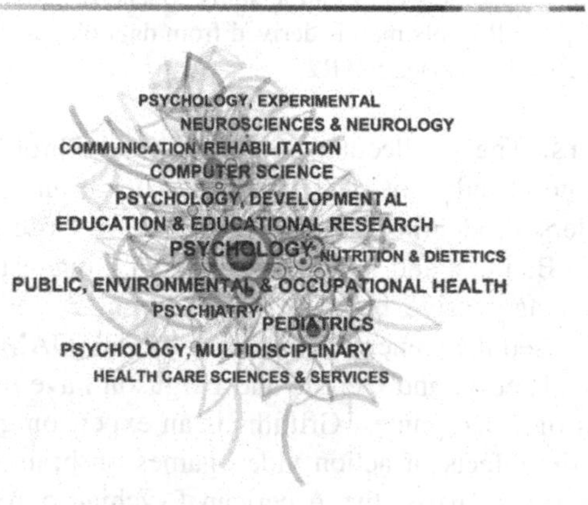

PSYCHOLOGY, EXPERIMENTAL
NEUROSCIENCES & NEUROLOGY
COMMUNICATION REHABILITATION
COMPUTER SCIENCE
PSYCHOLOGY, DEVELOPMENTAL
EDUCATION & EDUCATIONAL RESEARCH
PSYCHOLOGY NUTRITION & DIETETICS
PUBLIC, ENVIRONMENTAL & OCCUPATIONAL HEALTH
PSYCHIATRY
PEDIATRICS
PSYCHOLOGY, MULTIDISCIPLINARY
HEALTH CARE SCIENCES & SERVICES

Fig. 4. Disciplines involved in VGCD research. The size of a node positively correlates to the local citation counts in the corresponding discipline.

(264), Rehabilitation (140), Psychiatry (199), Neuroscience (195), Communication (162), and Dietetics (158). As can be seen from Fig. 4, Psychology plays a pivotal role among all the disciplines in this field.

Source Journals. Analysis of cited journals provides access to the intellectual base of the research field, whereas analysis of the citing journals is useful in obtaining information about the distribution of cutting-edge knowledge [12]. As shown in Table 2, more than half of the top ten citing and cited journals are related to psychology, indicating that psychological research constitutes both the intellectual base and the research front in the field.

Table 2. Top 10 citing and cited journals.

Rank	Citing Journals		Cited Journals	
	Publications	Name of Journal	Citations	Name of Journal
1	79	COMPUT HUM BEHAV*	1423	PEDIATRICS*
2	72	GAMES HEALTH J*	824	ARCH PEDIAT ADOL MED
3	61	BMC PUBLIC HEALTH	678	COMPUT HUM BEHAV*
4	60	PLOS ONE*	669	PLOS ONE*
5	58	COMPUT EDUC	638	PSYCHOL BULL*
6	48	PEDIATRICS*	589	PSYCHOL SCI*
7	43	INT J ENV RES PUB HE	578	DEV PSYCHOL*
8	38	INT J BEHAV NUTR PHY	573	COMPUT EDUC
9	38	JMIR SERIOUS GAMES*	571	JAMA-J AM MED ASSOC*
10	33	FRONT PSYCHOL*	566	CHILD DEV*

Note: Journals marked with "*" accept articles in psychology.

Dual-Map Overlays of journals can show journal citation routes [13]. As shown in Fig. 5, the left part is the citing journal area, and the right part is the cited journal area. Similar disciplines are marked with the same color, and the connecting lines represent the citation routes of the journals (the thickness of the lines representing the closeness between disciplines). This analysis once again demonstrates that research on VGCD has not only tended to originate early in psychology but also that this field has been at the forefront of disciplines working on this topic.

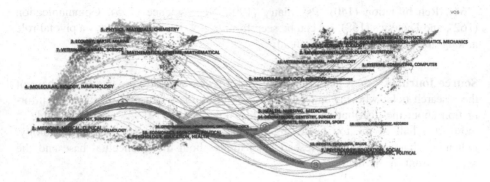

Fig. 5. A dual-map overlay of journals publishing research on VGCD, showing three main citation routes (citing journals on the left – cited journals on the right): ① Medicine, medical, clinical – health, nursing, medicine; ② Psychology, education, health – health, nursing, medicine; ③ Psychology, education, health – psychology, education, social.

3.4   Evolution of Research Hotspots

Hot Areas. On the basis of Kuhn's Paradigm-Shift Theory, literature co-citation analysis can reflect shifts in the research paradigm [14]. To be specific, the higher the frequency of a certain two documents being cited by other literature, the closer the relationship and the more similar the disciplinary background.

The literature co-citation and clustering analysis was carried out with a time slice of 1 year. Key articles were generated using g-index, yielding 1,590 nodes, 6,557 links, and 10 major clusters (Fig. 6). The cluster labels were extracted from citing articles' titles using the LLR algorithm. Chen [15] suggested that the quality of clustering can be evaluated by the network modularity index – silhouette score (S). When S > 0.7, this indicates that the overall clarity of the configuration is high. In this study, the silhouette values for each cluster were all greater than 0.86.

In the timeline diagram of the major clusters (Fig. 6), the horizontal axis represents the time of publication. The time legend is located at the top of the view; the increasing warmness of the shade as one approaches the right indicates nearness to the present time. The nodes on the horizontal line represent the representative references in the cluster, and the node radius corresponds to the number of citations in the literature. The connecting lines between clusters indicate co-citation relationships, with their thickness signifying the intensity of co-citation. The text behind the horizontal line is the cluster label. The color of the cluster labels indicates when the clusters were formed; the time span of the literature in the clusters can reflect the rise and fall of the research field.

In ascending order of time, the historical evolution of the hotspot areas is as follows (see Fig. 6 and Table 3): #0 media violence (affiliated to the Developmental Psychology discipline) – #8 body fatness (Endocrinology & Metabolism) – #1 sedentary behavior (Health) – #7 video game play (Multidisciplinary Psychology) – #2 active video games (Rehabilitation) – #6 physical activity (Physiology) – #3 violent video games (Multidisciplinary Psychology) – #9 cerebral palsy (Rehabilitation) – #4 serious

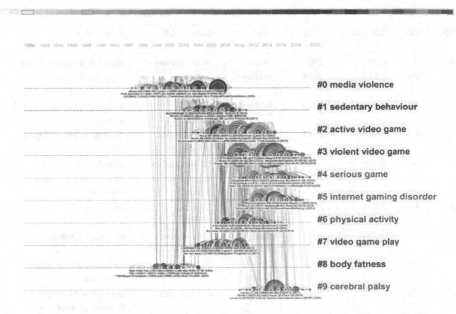

Fig. 6. A timeline view of the 10 largest clusters. Each node represents a landmark article, and the size of the node is proportional to the number of citations in the dataset.

games (Education) – #5 internet gaming disorder (Psychiatry). The areas that have remained popular in recent years are consistent with the most cited clusters and are focused on the influence of violent games and gaming addiction (#3 & #5) and the positive outcomes of video games (such as exergames and serious games, #9 & #4).

Owing to their revolutionary impacts, the most cited references are regularly considered as the landmark literature, and the articles with the highest citation coverage are commonly regarded as the frontier literature [16]. Combining the analysis of the representative works (Table 4 and Table 5) and the co-citation lines between clusters (Fig. 6), the ten major clusters can be classified into three prominent categories according to their disciplines:

1. *Video Games and Psychological Development.* Researchers in this category are mainly psychologists and psychiatrists. This category covers clusters #0 media violence, #7 video game play, #3 violent video games, and #5 internet gaming disorder. Research in this category first focused on the effects of children's exposure to media violence on their cognitive and social development [17]. Then, scholars shifted their focus to the impacts of video game playing on aggressive behavior by children and on intervention strategies [18]. Nowadays, psychologists are not only aware of the negative effects of violent games and internet gaming disorder [19] but also of the possible positive effects of video games on, for example, brain plasticity, prosocial behavior, and visuospatial cognition [20, 21].

Table 3. 10 major clusters of co-cited references.

ID	Size	Silhouette	Year Ave.	Label (LSI)	Label (LLR)	Label (MI)
#0	144	0.864	2000	effects	media violence	aggression-related norm
#1	109	0.879	2005	children	sedentary behavior	body mass
#2	109	0.91	2010	children	active video games	health-enhancing physical activity
#3	108	0.92	2013	children	violent video games	short-term psychological effect
#4	107	0.896	2014	children	serious games	educational video games
#5	100	0.894	2015	children	internet gaming disorder	adolescent psychological adjustment
#6	97	0.862	2010	physical activity	physical activity	obesity needs
#7	81	0.904	2007	video games	video game play	computer game development
#8	77	0.956	2000	physical activity	body fatness	musculoskeletal pain syndrome
#9	74	0.914	2014	children	cerebral palsy	interactive video game technology exercise

2. *Video Games and Physical Health.* This category comprises cluster #8 body fatness, #1 sedentary behavior, #2 active video games, #6 physical activity, and #9 cerebral palsy. Researchers in this field are mainly from health, pediatrics, rehabilitation, physiology, metabolism, and other related disciplines. Such studies initially examined the relationships between media use, obesity, and sedentary behavior in children [22]. Later, scholars emphasized reducing screen time to help children control their diet and prevent obesity [23]. Today, researchers are focusing more on the use of active video games and exergames to enhance children's physical activity [24], especially employing such video games to help non-typically developing children [25].

3. *Video Games and Educational Learning.* This category is composed of, for example, cluster #4 serious games, #7 video game play, #2 active video games, and #9 cerebral palsy. The experts largely consist of educators, psychologists, and neuro-scientists. Such research is based on the knowledge that video games alter cognitive development and brain plasticity [26], and emphasizes how serious games can be used as a tool to improve students' motivation and academic achievement [27].

Table 4. Landmark references by local citation counts.

ID	Cluster label (LLR)	Citations	Top 2 most cited references in each cluster	
			Author (Year)	Title
#0	media violence	40	Anderson, C. A. (2007)	Violent video game effects on children and adolescents
		31	Gentile, D. A. (2004)	The effects of violent video game habits on adolescent hostility, aggressive behaviors, and school performance
#1	sedentary behavior	30	Marshall, S. J. (2004)	Relationships between media use, body fatness and physical activity in children and youth: a meta-analysis
		29	Rey-Lopez, J. P. (2008)	Sedentary behaviour and obesity development in children and adolescents
#2	active video games	91	Rideout, V. J. (2010)	Generation M^2: Media in the lives of 8- to 18-year-olds
		71	Biddiss, E. (2010)	Active video games to promote physical activity in children and youth: a systematic review
#3	violent video games	89	Granic, I. (2014)	The benefits of playing video games
		87	Anderson, C. A. (2010)	Violent video game effects on aggression, empathy, and prosocial behavior in eastern and western countries: a meta-analytic review
#4	serious games	32	Boyle, E. A. (2016)	An update to the systematic literature review of empirical evidence of the impacts and outcomes of computer games and serious games
		28	Primack, B. A. (2012)	Role of video games in improving health-related outcomes: a systematic review
#5	internet gaming disorder	65	American Psychiatric Association. (2013)	Diagnostic and statistical manual of mental disorders (DSM-5®)
		35	Hale, L. (2015)	Screen time and sleep among school-aged children and adolescents: a systematic literature review
#6	physical activity	64	Tremblay, M. S. (2011)	Systematic review of sedentary behaviour and health indicators in school-aged children and youth
		25	Pearson, N. (2011)	Sedentary behavior and dietary intake in children, adolescents, and adults: a systematic review
#7	video game play	32	Olson, C. K. (2010)	Children's motivations for video game play in the context of normal development
		25	Ferguson, C. J. (2010)	Much ado about nothing: the misestimation and overinterpretation of violent video game effects in Eastern and Western nations: comment on Anderson et al. (2010)
#8	body fatness	17	Andersen, R. E. (1998)	Relationship of physical activity and television watching with body weight and level of fatness among children: results from the Third National Health and Nutrition Examination Survey
		15	Robinson, T. N. (1999)	Reducing children's television viewing to prevent obesity: a randomized controlled trial
#9	cerebral palsy	44	Gao, Z. (2015)	A meta-analysis of active video games on health outcomes among children and adolescents
		20	Gao, Z. (2014)	Are field-based exergames useful in preventing childhood obesity? A systematic review

Table 5. Frontier literature in the 10 largest clusters.

ID	Cluster label (LLR)	Coverage	Top 2 citing references with the highest citation coverage in each cluster	
			Author (Year)	Title
#0	media violence	17	Anderson, C. A. (2003)	The influence of media violence on youth
		16	Browne, K. D. (2005)	The influence of violent media on children and adolescents: a public-health approach
#1	sedentary behavior	19	Mulligan, D. A. (2010)	Policy statement—children, and adolescents, obesity, and the media
		15	Rey-Lopez, J. P. (2008)	Sedentary behavior and obesity development in children and adolescents
#2	active video games	26	LeBlanc, A. G. (2013)	Active video games and health indicators in children and youth: a systematic review
		25	O'Loughlin, E. K. (2012)	Prevalence and correlates of exergaming in youth
#3	violent video games	24	Ferguson, C. J. (2015)	Do angry birds make for angry children? A meta-analysis of video game influences on children's and adolescents' aggression, mental health, prosocial behavior, and academic performance
		14	Ferguson, C. J. (2013)	Not worth the fuss after all? Cross-sectional and prospective data on violent video game influences on aggression, visuospatial cognition, and mathematics ability in a sample of youth
#4	serious games	10	Penuelas-Calvo, I. (2020)	Video games for the assessment and treatment of attention-deficit/hyperactivity disorder: A systematic review
		9	Edrerin Espinosa-Curiel, I. (2020)	Relationship between children's enjoyment, user experience satisfaction, and learning in a serious video game for nutrition education: Empirical pilot study
#5	internet gaming disorder	14	Straker, L. (2016)	Australia and other nations are failing to meet sedentary behavior guidelines for children: Implications and a way forward
		13	Paulus, F. W. (2018)	Internet gaming disorder in children and adolescents: a systematic review
#6	physical activity	17	Carson, V. (2016)	Systematic review of sedentary behaviour and health indicators in school-aged children and youth: an update
		17	Saunders, T. J. (2014)	Sedentary behaviour as an emerging risk factor for cardiometabolic diseases in children and youth
#7	video game play	26	Ferguson, C. J. (2010)	Blazing angels or resident evil? Can violent video games be a force for good?
		18	Prot, S. (2012)	Video games: good, bad, or other?
#8	body fatness	13	Marshall, S. J. (2004)	Relationships between media use, body fatness and physical activity in children and youth: a meta-analysis
		12	Kautiainen, S. (2005)	Use of Information and Communication Technology and prevalence of overweight and obesity among adolescents
#9	cerebral palsy	16	Page, Z. E. (2017)	Do active video games benefit the motor skill development of non-typically developing children and adolescents: a systematic review
		14	Benzing, V. (2018)	Exergaming for children and adolescents: strengths, weaknesses, opportunities and threats

Hot Topics. The evolution of hot topics can be illustrated by the timezone diagram of the representative terms. In CiteSpace, the terms are extracted from articles' titles, abstracts, keywords, and extended keywords, so the use of terms provides more insight into the text content and reflects more comprehensive information than keyword analysis. In timezone diagrams, nodes are placed in coordinate time zones according to the time when the term is first cited (Fig. 7). The size of the nodes is positively correlated with the frequency of the occurrence of the terms, and the connecting lines between the nodes reflect the inherited relationships between the hot topics.

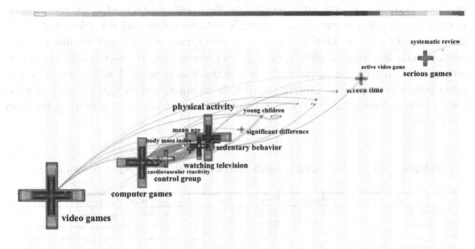

Fig. 7. A timezone view of the evolution of hot topics in the field of VGCD.

As can be seen from Fig. 7, the most commonly examined term related to *electronic games* is *video games*, followed by *computer games*, whereas there has been relatively less research on *electronic games*, *digital games*, *simulation games*, or *online games*. However, driven by the wave of gamification, research on *serious games* has also begun to emerge. In terms of the impact of video games on physical development, early research largely focused on the effects of video games on, for example, *cardiovascular reactivity*, *body mass index*, *sedentary behavior*, and *physical activity*, whereas current research focuses on using *action video games* to help children enhance their *physical activity* and reduce *sedentary behavior*. As far as the participants are concerned, *young children* and *mean age* occupy a place in the historical evolution map of hot topics, indicating that researchers in this field value the impacts of video games on young children and on children of different ages. Moreover, the appearance of the terms *control group*, *serious games*, *active video games*, *screen time*, and *significant difference* implies that intervention research has become a booming research paradigm. In addition, the figure also indicates that early researchers tended to explore video gaming and *television viewing* together, but now researchers are conducting *systematic reviews* and research on video games in particular.

3.5   Emerging Trends

A citation burst is the detection of a burst event that can be utilized as an indicator of an extremely vigorous research domain [28]. Similarly, burst detection and visualization of terms can show us the fast-growing themes [29]. Therefore, we used burst detection of terms to identify the emerging trends and new developments in VGCD study.

Table 6 shows ten emerging terms that have gained considerable attention in recent years, including *virtual reality, effect sizes, serious games, autism spectrum disorder, internet gaming disorder, online games, mental health, sedentary time, sedentary behavior,* and *body mass index.* According to the evolutionary trajectory of the burst terms, early researchers primarily focused on the negative effects of video games, such as the effects of *online games* on children's *sedentary time and behavior, body mass index, mental health,* and *internet gaming disorder.* However, the still popular research themes (such as *virtual reality, serious games, autism spectrum disorder*) reveal scientists' concern with the positive effects of video games as well as the application of video games in improving children's lives. In addition, researchers are now increasingly concerned with the reliability and validity of research, as evidenced by the term *effect sizes.*

Table 6. Top 10 most recent research-front terms with the strongest citation bursts.

Terms	Burst	Begin	End	Range (1983–2020)
virtual reality	9.02	2018	2020	
effect sizes	6.57	2018	2020	
serious games	25.98	2017	2020	
autism spectrum disorder	9.5	2017	2020	
internet gaming disorder	8.34	2016	2020	
online games	6.95	2016	2018	
mental health	9.58	2016	2017	
sedentary time	7.89	2012	2016	
sedentary behavior	8.39	2010	2016	
body mass index	6.59	2007	2013	

4   Discussion

4.1   Advantages and Applications of CiteSpace Analysis

Advantages of CiteSpace Analysis. Compared to the traditional literature analysis method, the use of CiteSpace to conduct scientometrics and knowledge-mapping analysis on VGCD research has unique advantages: (1) CiteSpace can process a large amount of data in a short time, which can save time and effort in getting a glimpse of the entire knowledge domain. For example, by analyzing more than 100,000 cited references, it speedily assisted us in locating the "most studied terms related to video games." (2) By interpreting the results with objective indicators and scientific algorithms, it helps researchers to adopt an unbiased approach to analyzing the research literature. For instance, different scholars may have their own opinions on the transitions of research hotspots, but if they use the same CiteSpace parameters to analyze the same batch of research literature, they will reach a consensus. Again, it can break down disciplinary barriers and help with interdisciplinary research. As *Child Development* consists of multidisciplinary fields of knowledge, such as psychology, pediatrics, health, nutrition, education, and others, CiteSpace analysis of VGCD will be conducive to the exchange of knowledge among experts in various disciplines. (3) The visualization outcomes generated by CiteSpace are intuitive and show the wisdom of the saying that "a picture is worth a thousand words" [30]. To give an example, by comparing the size and order of the nodes in a timezone diagram, one can easily learn the importance of the hot topics and the order of their first appearance in history.

Applications of CiteSpace Analysis. When applying CiteSpace, the following matters should be noted: (1) The selection of search terms is directly related to the reliability of the research results. Therefore, when choosing search terms, we need to refer to existing studies, make a trade-off between the search rate and accuracy rate, and perform data cleansing. As an illustration, some articles with the term "simulation games" published before 1983 are not related to video games; they need to be deleted manually. (2) The initial results cannot be interpreted literally on their own; one needs to go deeper into the text for secondary interpretation. Although CiteSpace analysis has the effect of "seeing both the trees and the forest," it still requires researchers to have a certain understanding of the domain they are analyzing. Take the term "building rule," for example: it does not refer to "making rules" for children's screen time but is actually a computer science term for "constructing rules."

4.2   Trends in the Development of Research Hotspots

Based upon the dual-map overlay, co-citations network, burst detection analysis, and so on, the changing trends in VGCD research hotspots can be summarized as follows:

1. Research in this area has shifted from having a marginal status to being part of the mainstream core, and the research topics have been affected by the times. In the research field of "video games and psychological development," it is obvious that the theme of scientific research has altered from "media violence" to "violent video games," reflecting the increasing importance of video games in people's lives. In addition, a condensed history of the technological development of video games can be seen in the change of terms from "simulation games, computer games, and video games" to "online games, exergames, and serious games."

2. The viewpoints of research have shifted from being passive to inclusive, and the potential benefits of video games have gradually been recognized. Expressions about the negative effects of video games have emerged in the co-citation network during the period of the last century, such as "media violence, aggressive behavior, cardiovascular reactivity, body mass index, sedentary behavior, etc." However, at the beginning of this century, many scholars put forward the view that video games may be beneficial to psychological development. As a result, "visual-spatial cognition, brain plasticity, prosocial behavior, etc." began to appear in influential publications.

3. The orientation of research has shifted from being theoretical to practical, and interventional and educational studies have proliferated. Whereas early theoretical conceptions (such as the Ecological Techno-Microsystem Theory and the General Aggression Model) were originally proposed to provide mechanistic explanations of phenomena [31, 32], the recent rise of serious game research in education has been both theoretical and practical. A case in point is that many educators designed computer games based on innovative educational models to improve students' learning [27]. At present, video games are also quite useful in the fields of psychotherapy, physical training, and skills enhancement, so terms such as "autism spectrum disorder" have come to the forefront. The rise of applied research may be related to both the refinement of video game experiences and the spread of computer science education.

4. Research methods have shifted from investigations and physiological measurements to experiments, interventions, and systematic reviews, focusing on the generalizability and application of the results. In early studies, psychologists relied more on self-reported or retrospective questionnaire measurements, and health scientists placed extra emphasis on examining indicators such as "heart rate and blood pressure." Nowadays, the terms "control group, effect sizes, and systematic review" appear among the frontier terms, indicating that experimental, interventional, and meta-analytic research is receiving unprecedented attention. At the same time, experimental research in all disciplines now places great emphasis on the ecological validity and generalizability of results and tends to conduct field experiments in the context of children's lives.

4.3   Limitations of This Study

With regard to research methods, a number of limitations of the present study need to be acknowledged. First, the bibliometric data retrieved from the database were mainly determined by the terms used for search. However, there is no standard method for choosing the search terms. Although the terms we used were borrowed from several studies [3, 33], there may still be omissions. Second, the input data used in this study were only extracted from the Web of Science Core Collection. Although WoS is one of the most comprehensive interdisciplinary citation resources, the retrieval results may not reflect the full picture of the research field. Therefore, if we could integrate bibliometric data from a variety of distinguished databases (including conference databases), the results would be more convincing. Third, this study proposed a holistic view of VGCD research; thus, it only outlines the major research areas. However, bibliometric indicators are useful but not perfect, so we should not use them as the only approach for assessment [34]. Hence, for a deeper understanding of the VGCD field, further synthesis of other research methods is needed.

5 Conclusion

The following conclusions can be drawn from the present study: (1) Over the past 37 years, there has been a dramatic increase in research on "video gaming and child development." The growth patterns of annual publications and citations conform to cubic accelerating curves; (2) The United States is the most influential country, and experts such as Gentile, Anderson, Ferguson, and Baranowski, among others, are the most authoritative authors in this field; (3) Among many disciplines that focus on the influences of video games on child development, psychology has achieved the most results; (4) Reference co-citation analysis yielded 10 clusters that were largest, which can be grouped into three categories: "video games and psychological development, video games and physical health, and video games and education"; (5) The forefront themes appearing in recent years are "serious games, autism spectrum disorder, virtual reality, internet gaming disorder, effect sizes, online games, mental health, sedentary time, sedentary behavior, and body mass index."

Acknowledgments. This research was funded by the National Social Science Fund of China (18BSH130).

References

1. Liu, X., Huang, H., Huo, M., Dou, D.: Brief exposure to two-player video games stimulates young children's peer communication and prosocial behavior. Psychol. Sci. **41**, 364–370 (2018). (in Chinese)
2. Ueda, H., Yagi, H.: Video game system having reduced memory needs for a raster scanned display. U.S. Patent 5, 560–614 (1996)
3. Boyle, E.A., et al.: An update to the systematic literature review of empirical evidence of the impacts and outcomes of computer games and serious games. Comput. Educ. **94**, 178–192 (2016)
4. Liu, X., Liao, M., Dou, D.: Video game playing enhances young children's inhibitory control. In: Fang, X. (ed.) HCI in Games. HCII 2019, LNCS, vol. 11595, pp. 141–153. Springer, Cham (2019). https://doi.org/10.1007/978-3-030-22602-2_12
5. Anderson, C.A., et al.: Violent video game effects on aggression, empathy, and prosocial behavior in Eastern and Western countries: a meta-analytic review. Psychol. Bull. **136**(2), 151–173 (2010)
6. American Psychiatric Association: Diagnostic and Statistical Manual of Mental Disorders (DSM-5®). American Psychiatric Pub (2013)
7. WHO: 6C51 Gaming disorder. https://icd.who.int/dev11/l-m/en#/http://id.who.int/icd/entity/1448597234. Accessed 31 Dec 2020
8. Granic, I., Lobel, A., Engels, R.C.: The benefits of playing video games. Am. Psychol. **69**(1), 66–78 (2014)
9. Kim, M.C., Zhu, Y.: Scientometrics of scientometrics: mapping historical footprint and emerging technologies in scientometrics. In Jibu, M., Osabe, Y. (eds.) Scientometrics, pp. 9–28. IntechOpen (2018)
10. Chen, C.: CiteSpace II: Detecting and visualizing emerging trends and transient patterns in scientific literature. J. Am. Soc. Inf. Sci. Tech. **57**(3), 359–377 (2006)

11. Borner, K., Chen, C., Boyack, K.: Visualizing knowledge domains. Annu. Rev. Inform. Sci. **37**, 179–255 (2003)
12. Synnestvedt, M., Chen, C., Holmes, J.: CiteSpace II: visualization and knowledge discovery in bibliographic databases. In: AMIA Annual Symposium Proceedings, pp. 724–728 (2005)
13. Chen, C., Leydesdorff, L.: Patterns of connections and movements in dual-map overlays: a new method of publication portfolio analysis. J. Am. Soc. Inf. Sci. Tech. **65**(2), 334–351 (2014)
14. Chen, C.: CiteSpace: A Practical Guide for Mapping Scientific Literature. Nova Science, Hauppauge (2016)
15. Chen, C.: A glimpse of the first eight months of the COVID-19 literature on Microsoft Academic Graph: themes, citation contexts, and uncertainties. Front. Res. Metr. Anal. **5**, 24 (2020)
16. Chen, C., Hu, Z., Liu, S., Tseng, H.: Emerging trends in regenerative medicine: a scientometric analysis in CiteSpace. Expert Opin. Biol. Th. **12**(5), 593–608 (2012)
17. Cantor, J.: Media violence. J. Adolescent Health **27**(2), 30–34 (2000)
18. Anderson, C.A., et al.: The influence of media violence on youth. Psychol. Sci. Publ. Int. **4**(3), 81–110 (2003)
19. Kuss, D.J., Griffiths, M.D.: Online gaming addiction in children and adolescents: a review of empirical research. J. Behav. Addict. **1**, 3–22 (2012)
20. Ferguson, C.J.: Blazing angels or resident evil? Can violent video games be a force for good? Rev. Gen. Psychol. **14**(2), 68–81 (2010)
21. Liu, X., Huang, H., Yu, K., Dou, D.: Can video game training improve the two-dimensional mental rotation ability of young children? A randomized controlled trial. In: Fang, X. (ed.) HCI in Games. HCII 2020. LNCS, vol. 12211. pp. 305–317. Springer, Cham (2020). https://doi.org/10.1007/978-3-030-50164-8_22
22. Marshall, S.J., Biddle, S.J., Gorely, T., Cameron, N., Murdey, I.: Relationships between media use, body fatness and physical activity in children and youth: a meta-analysis. Int. J. Obesity **28**(10), 1238–1246 (2004)
23. Marsh, S., Mhurchu, C.N., Maddison, R.: The non-advertising effects of screen-based sedentary activities on acute eating behaviours in children, adolescents, and young adults: a systematic review. Appetite **71**, 259–273 (2013)
24. Gao, Z., et al.: Impact of exergaming on young children's school day energy expenditure and moderate-to-vigorous physical activity levels. J. Sport Health Sci. **6**(1), 11–16 (2017)
25. Page, Z.E., Barrington, S., Edwards, J., Barnett, L.M.: Do active video games benefit the motor skill development of non-typically developing children and adolescents: a systematic review. J. Sci. Med. Sport **20**(12), 1087–1100 (2017)
26. Green, C.S., Bavelier, D.: Action video game modifies visual selective attention. Nature **423**(6939), 534–537 (2003)
27. Hwang, G.J., Yang, L.H., Wang, S.Y.: A concept map-embedded educational computer game for improving students' learning performance in natural science courses. Comput. Educ. **69**, 121–130 (2013)
28. Chen, C., Dubin, R., Kim, M.C.: Emerging trends and new developments in regenerative medicine: a scientometric update (2000–2014). Expert Opin. Biol. Th. **14**(9), 1295–1317 (2014)
29. Chen, C.: How to use CiteSpace. https://leanpub.com/howtousecitespace. Accessed 02 Feb 2021
30. Li, J., Chen, C.M.: CiteSpace: Scientific Text Mining and Visualization. Capital University of Economics and Business Press, Beijing (2016). (in Chinese)
31. Johnson, G.: Internet use and child development: the techno-microsystem. Aust. J. Educ. Dev. Psychol. **10**, 32–43 (2010)

32. DeWall, C.N., Anderson, C.A., Bushman, B.J.: The general aggression model: theoretical extensions to violence. Psychol. Violence **1**(3), 245 (2011)

33. Pei, L.S., Shang, J.J.: The context and hotspot analysis of video game and education: based on the bibliometric results based on the hundred years literature of Web of Science (WOS). Dist. Educ. J. **2**, 104–112 (2015). (in Chinese)

34. Davis, S.: Bibliometrics: putting librarianship on a new track. Inform. Outlook **20**, 4–6 (2016)

Using Neural-Network-Driven Image Recognition Software to Detect Emotional Reactions in the Face of a Player While Playing a Horror Video Game

Hermann Prossinger[1]([✉]), Jakub Binter[2,3], Tomás Hladký[2,3], and Daniel Říha[2,3]

[1] Department of Evolutionary Biology, Faculty of Life Sciences, University of Vienna, Vienna, Austria
hermann.prossinger@univie.ac.at
[2] Faculty of Humanities, Charles University, Prague, Czech Republic
[3] Faculty of Science, Charles University, Prague, Czech Republic

Abstract. Image analysis of the webcam images of the player playing horror video games is used to infer his/her emotional state. We initially relied on the received wisdom that there are three distinguishable emotional states: joy, agitation (a combination of fear and surprise) and neutral. We applied modern image analysis techniques to extract the player's face in three sets of 50 consecutive frames by first generating 150 feature vectors and then using an auto-encoder neural network to dimension-reduce these to a mapping of 150 points on a 2D manifold. We find that these mapped points are not uniformly distributed in a plane and an overlap between neutral and each of the two affective states is highly improbable. We derive convex hulls using a k-medoids clustering algorithm; they seem to indicate a difference between the mouth region expression and that around the eyes. We use kernel density estimation and Monte Carlo methods to determine that the affective states joy and agitation have a small probability of overlap (6.6% and 10.6%, respectively), which can be interpreted as a confusion probability. Our advanced statistical analysis thus confirms that modern image analysis can indeed be used to monitor the player's emotional state while playing.

Keywords: Image analysis using neural networks · Auto-encoder · k-medoids clustering · Face alignment algorithm · Horror videos · Facial expression of emotion · Monte Carlo methods of probability estimation

1 Introduction

The facial muscles are largely under involuntary control and communicate the affective state to others. The eyes play a major role in allowing inference of one's emotional state as the *orbicularis oculi* muscles around the eyes are more difficult to control than other facial muscles [1]. The so-called "Duchenne smile," also known as the "true smile" is typically achieved by the contraction of these *orbicularis oculi* muscles, as opposed to the "fake smiles" that involve only the *zygomatic major* muscles [1].

© Springer Nature Switzerland AG 2021
X. Fang (Ed.): HCII 2021, LNCS 12789, pp. 258–265, 2021.
https://doi.org/10.1007/978-3-030-77277-2_20

Since, in this paper, we research facial communication by players of horror games, the negative counterpart to joy is an expression that superimposes weightings of fear and of surprise. These latter two emotional states are closely related and oftentimes merge [1]. The major difference in the facial expression between these two occurs in the lower half of the face [2]. Neta et al.'s study shows that jaw drop and open mouth (surprise) and lips stretched backwards (fear) are, in an ideal case, the differentiating factor. Thus, these two emotions not only mix to a high degree, especially when they temporally follow each other, but also can be impossible to distinguish due to verbal, such as narrating, and para-verbal communication, such as screams and warnings. We conclude that our AI-driven facial analysis of horror video players must deal with three expressions of emotion: joy, agitation (the intermixing of fear and surprise) and neutral.

While players are emotionally involved in a video horror game, the intensity of their participation is monitored by the image analysis of their face that is being photographed by the webcam, frame by frame, consecutively. In this paper, we investigate to what reliability image analysis can be used for such monitoring. More specifically, we statistically analyze consecutive frames from a webcam so as to confirm or refute whether the emotional states joy and agitation can indeed be monitored and distinguished from each other and from the neutral state.

2 Materials

While playing *Until Dawn* (details: see Appendix), the player presents his gaming experiences on his online channel, wherein he makes comments about them. Involuntarily, he also exhibits his emotional involvement via facial expressions, displayed in a small frame inserted in the upper right-hand corner of the screen. One co-author (TH) selected three scenes (partially relying on the comments by the player) in which the commentator exhibited the emotions joy, agitation, and neutrality. Along with the selected frame, 25 frames before the selected scene and 24 after it were stored for subsequent analyses.

3 Methods

For each frame, we extracted a rectangle that frames only the player's face. We then aligned the face (primarily via the eyes and the tip of the nose) within each rectangle with every other face in all 150 rectangles. We then applied an image analysis algorithm (supplied by MATHEMATICA® from WOLFRAM Technologies™) to characterize each image as a feature vector. These 150 feature vectors were combined in a matrix and a non-linear artificial neural network [3], specifically an auto-encoder with seven layers, was used to extract 2D coordinates for each feature vector. These were then graphed as points in a plane. For each emotion represented by the 50 dimension-reduced feature vector points, we used the k-medoid clustering algorithm for finding three clusters (enclosed by the convex hulls in Fig. 1) per emotion. We used KDE (kernel density estimation) with a Parzen window optimized by the Silvermann rule-of-thumb [4] to find three *pdf*s (probability density functions), one for each emotion. We generated contour plots of these *pdf*s in order to identify the distinctness of the regions of highest likelihood. With a Monte Carlo method, we generated 15000 random points for each *pdf* and defined a cutoff for lowest likelihood needed for subsequent analysis. We calculated the fraction of random points of one emotion that lay in the region of high likelihood of another emotion.

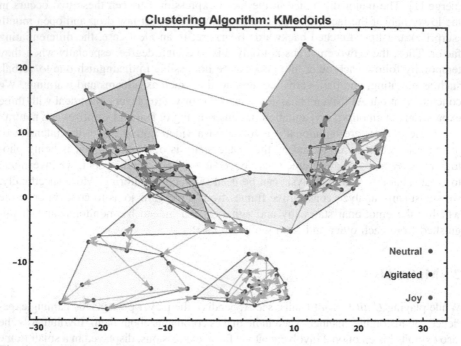

Fig. 1. The dimension-reduced feature vectors projected on a 2D manifold as points and the convex hulls determined using a *k*-medoids clustering algorithm. Points are the dimension-reduced feature vectors; the arrows show their sequence from one frame to the next. The *k*-medoids clustering algorithm is supervised; we specified 3 clusters per emotion. We observe that most of the points for each emotion are within only one of the three convex hulls of this emotion.

4   Results

The *k*-medoids clustering algorithm applied to the points for each emotion documented that the three clusters per emotion only partially overlap (Fig. 1). A display of the sequence of the points for each emotion shows that one convex hull is predominantly occupied (Fig. 1). This observation is a first indicator that the image analysis of facial expression can distinguish emotions. The contours of the KDE-derived *pdf*s confirm this (Fig. 2). Overlapping contours of the *pdf*s of the emotions are those of low like-lihood—further confirmed by the distributions of random points above the cutoff $\frac{1}{10}L_{max}$ (Fig. 3). The probabilities of observing random points above $\frac{1}{10}L_{max}$ are 79.6% (agitation), 81.7% (neutral), and 78.5% (joy). The choice of this cutoff is very rea-sonable and allows for a clear, more reliable alternative for identifying separation of facial expressions to using the *k*-medoids clustering algorithms. Furthermore, convex hulls, because of their convexity, can overlap, and probability estimates cannot be derived using them.

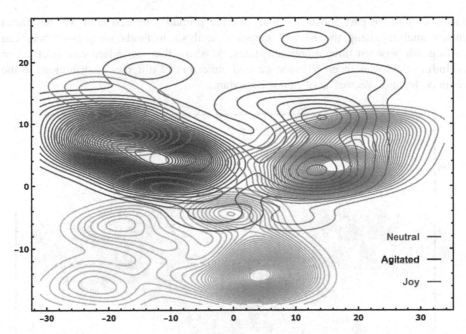

Fig. 2. The contour lines of the *pdf* (probability density function) obtained with KDE (kernel density estimation) of the points rendered in Fig. 1. The contours are equally spaced in likelihood. We observe that the contours with highest likelihood for each emotion separate very well.

We use the random points to estimate the fraction of overlap, which is interpretable as a measure of confusion probability between emotional states. The confusion probability of a joy expression being an agitation expression is 6.6%, and the converse confusion (agitation being interpreted as joy) is 10.6%. We point out that this method of determining confusion via random points and contour overlap does not include the emotion neutral. A neutral facial expression, we find, is never confused with the emotion joy nor with the emotion agitate.

5 Discussion

The images of the face included motions/deformations of the mouth, cheeks and lips due to the commentator verbally expressing his emotions. We interpret the points enclosed by the rarely visited convex hulls (Fig. 1) as those driven by facial expressions predominantly involving mouth, cheek, and lip movement. We cannot construct a control analysis for this interpretation, however, because—even though we can repeat our image analysis for the eyes and nose regions without mouth, cheeks and lips—the extraction of feature vectors and reduction onto a 2D manifold would result in a very different display. We suspect, furthermore, that the feature vectors would detect the stronger signal of muscle activity while talking, rather than the emotional state expressions. In addition, conventional supervising webcams, used to monitor the 'flow' [5] of the participant's engagement in a horror video game always involves the whole face, not just the part above the nose. We are primarily interested in whether facial image analysis using the AI and statistical analysis methods we present here can distinguish between three emotional states; we show that we indeed can, even when including the lower face. Whether we find indicators of different contributions to the reduced features vectors is of minor importance.

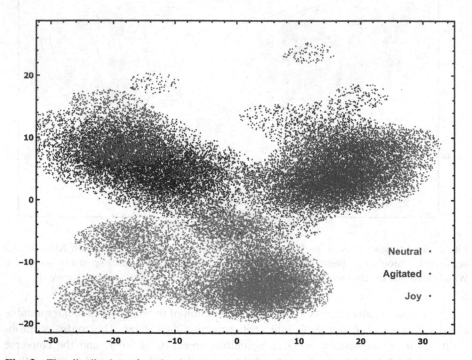

Fig. 3. The distribution of randomly generated points for each emotion *pdf* via Monte Carlo. The displayed points are those within a cutoff of $\frac{1}{10}L_{max}$ for each emotion. For joy there are 11773 points, for agitated there are 11935 points, and for neutral there are 12257 points. Although 15000 random points were generated for each *pdf*, the cutoff retains differing numbers of points for each emotion-dependent cutoff, because L_{max} differs from emotion to emotion.

In other, seminal, work, facial expressions were used to distinguish between the emotional states, and that the separate state of boredom (in our case: the equivalent to neutral) was easy to track [5]. Our analysis confirms these claims.

Joy and agitation are the two emotions on the opposite ends of spectrum of facial expressions. They are therefore pertinent to any consequences of assessment, such as when humans derive a putative emotion after looking at a photograph of a face. The general accuracy of emotional assessment was estimated to approximately 92% when one human infers another's emotion based on still images, such as photographs or drawings (Ekman [6]). Our findings extend these observations to a sequence of moving and/or changing faces. We find a confirming parallel. The overlap (Fig. 4) can be interpreted both as a confusion probability and as an unreliability test. We find the confusions to be 6.6% and 10.6%; both these derived estimators compare very favorably with Ekman's [6] findings.

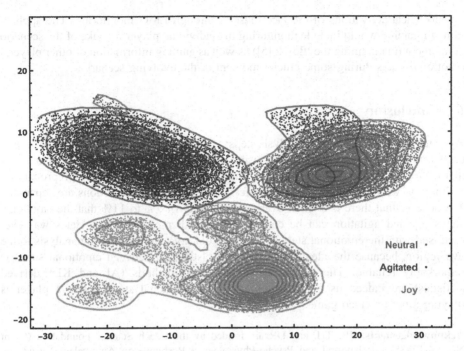

Fig. 4. Contours of the KDE-*pdf*s as well as the randomly generated points for each emotion. The cut-off for the random points is $\frac{1}{10}L_{max}$ and the contours are at likelihoods $\frac{k}{10}L_{max}$, with $k = 1 \ldots 9$. The overlap of some likelihood regions of one emotion within the likelihood region of another emotion can be used to determine confusion probabilities (see text).

The reliability of our findings has a further application when the software attempts to maintain a 'flow' [5] of the participant's attention and emotional reaction while playing a horror video game: the case when several players participate together. Then each participant's facial expressions communicates their involvement and engagement to the others. Our findings show that such communication can be interpreted reliably by the image analyses presented here and has a confusion probability of about 10%—arguably a small probability. Because the probabilities calculated in these analyses are not significances, we need not compare probability outcomes with significance levels.

This new method of analyzing facial expressions can be used to clarify the physiological relationship of facial manifestations and the expression of emotions in humans [6]. Previous studies have failed in linking specific facial expression with discrete emotions; the observed predominant link is relating the dimensions of valence and arousal separately. Further application of our new method can bring clarity to this topic. A cautionary note is keeping in mind that neural networks do not allow for a completely reproducible, external understanding of the neural network's inner working. There are ways of addressing this problem, most notably via simulations.

Furthermore, we note that the use of the webcam is highly appropriate because it is unobtrusive and does not need the employment of sensors that directly record the physiological activations of the face muscles through EMG monitoring. The applications in gaming would include monitoring the individual player for sake of the scenario adjustment (maintaining the 'flow'; [5]) as well as gaining information of other players' emotional states during some crucial moment of the evolving scenario.

6 Conclusion

By using the sequence of five analysis steps: (1) feature vector extraction of the face in each frame, (2) dimension reduction using an auto-encoder, (3) k-medoids clustering algorithms, (4) KDE-determined pdfs, and (5) Monte Carlo methods of probability estimation, we find that the facial manifestations of the three emotions are separable. We observe that there is a small overlap probability of 7% to 11% that the emotional states joy and agitation can be confused; but neither of these two states was ever confused with the emotional state neutral. We did not need to limit the analysis to the eye region, because the identification of and distinction between emotional states is remarkably reliable. The use of these advanced methods (AI and KDE-derived statistics) are indeed useful for monitoring the emotional status while a player is playing a horror video game.

Acknowledgements. JB, TH, and DR are funded by the Czech Science Foundation (Grant No. 19-12885Y "Behavioral and Psycho-Physiological Response on Ambivalent Visual and Auditory Stimuli Presentation") and DR is further funded by the Ministry of Education, Youth and Sports, Czech Republic and the Institutional Support for Long-term Development of Research Organizations, Faculty of Humanities, Charles University, Czech Republic (Grant PROGRES Q21 "Text and Image in Phenomenology and Semiotics").

Ethics Statement. This project has been conducted using only materials publicly available online and does not reveal any personal information.

Appendix

The horror video game is called *Until Dawn* (Supermassive Games/Sony Computer Entertainment, 2015). The game revolves around the story of eight characters that the player may save (or not) by their actions in a "butterfly effect" system whereby each character's decision can create a situation that intentionally scares the player.

References

1. Ekman, P.: An argument for basic emotions. Cogn. Emot. **6**(3–4), 169–200 (1992)
2. Neta, M., Tong, T.T., Rosen, M.L., Enersen, A., Kim, M.J., Dodd, M.D.: All in the first glance: first fixation predicts individual differences in valence bias. Cogn. Emot. **31**(4), 772–780 (2017)

3. Strang, G.: Linear Algebra and Learning from Data. Wellesley-Cambridge Press, Wellesley, MA, USA (2019)
4. Murphy, K.P.: Machine Learning: A Probabilistic Perspective. MIT Press, Cambridge, MA, USA (2012)
5. Burns, A., Tulip, J.: Detecting flow in games using facial expressions. In: 2017 IEEE Conference on Computational Intelligence and Games (CIG), pp. 45–52. IEEE (2017)
6. Ekman, P., Friesen, W.: Pictures of Facial Affect. Consulting Psychologists Press, Palo Alto, CA, USA (1976)

Exploratory and Confirmatory Factor Analysis of the Chinese Young Children's Video-Gaming Questionnaire

Fangbing Qu⬥, Xiao Niu⬥, Heqing Huang⬥,
and Xiaocen Liu[✉]⬥

College of Preschool Education, Capital Normal University,
Beijing, People's Republic of China
cindyliu@cnu.edu.cn

Abstract. The study aimed to validate the self-designed Chinese Young Children's Video-gaming Questionnaire (CVQ). The original CVQ consisted of 34 items. Eight hundred and nineteen (819) young children aged 3 to 6 years old from different parts of China were enrolled in this research. An exploratory factor analysis was undertaken on a random sample of half of the completed surveys, with eight items dropped afterwards. A confirmatory factor analysis was run on the other half of the original sample using structural equation modeling. Examination of the fit indices indicated that the model came close to fitting the data, with goodness-of-fit coefficients just below recommended levels. A second model was analyzed using the same four factors with 25 items and the results suggested that Model 2 fit the data well. These results led to a refined, shortened version of the CVQ. Future research is needed to see if this model would fit other samples in China and other countries.

Keywords: Confirmatory factor analysis · Exploratory factor analysis · Young children · Video game

1 Introduction

With the rapid development of technology, video games are successfully marketed to and easily obtained by young children. Research studies have indicated that video games have become a routine part of normal childhood. However, a growing number of recent studies have expressed concerns regarding the effects of video game use on children's problematic behavior and mental health (Mazurek and Engelhardt 2013; Tortolero et al. 2014; Lobel et al. 2017). In particular, excessive video game playing may lead to negative effects on players' daily functioning, resulting in a loss of control and emotional disorders (Lau et al. 2018).

To have a better measure of children's video game playing status and its relationship with problematic behaviors, a number of methods and self-designed questionnaires have been applied. For example, Gentile et al. (2012) asked participants to indicate how many hours they played video games during each of three time periods (morning, afternoon, and evening) on a typical school day and on a typical weekend.

© Springer Nature Switzerland AG 2021
X. Fang (Ed.): HCII 2021, LNCS 12789, pp. 266–278, 2021.
https://doi.org/10.1007/978-3-030-77277-2_21

The average weekly video game playing time was then calculated. Linebarger (2015) employed a 24-h time diary method to track children's video game exposure, which was operationalized as the total number of hours of video game play parents reported during the previous 24 h. Apart from a basic measurement of video game exposure, Mazurek and Engelhardt (2013) used a modified version of the Problem Video Game Playing Test (PVGT) (King et al. 2011) to examine players' problematic video game playing, which is based on the behavioral addiction model. In Mazurek and Engelhardt's modified version, they made wording adjustments to increase relevance for younger participants, and modified the format from self-report to parent-report format. The items assessed whether an individual plays games as a means of changing his or her mood, and parents demonstrated a difficulty in determining this.

The fifth edition of the Diagnostic and Statistical Manual for Mental Disorders (DSM-5) provided a description of Internet Gaming Disorder (IGD), which may provide insight into the measure of video game playing. The appendix of DSM-5 described IGD as "persistent and recurrent use of the Internet to engage in games, often with other players, leading to clinically significant impairment or distress as indicated by five (or more) of the following (criteria) in a 12-month period" (American Psychiatric Association 2013). These factors are very similar to diagnosis of substance and gambling addiction, such as a preoccupation with gaming, withdrawal symptoms when not gaming, build-up of tolerance (i.e., more time needed for game playing), loss of interest in other hobbies, use of gaming as an escape, and continued overuse of gaming, despite understanding the negative impact on day-to-day functioning (Lau et al. 2018). In the ICD-11 Beta draft, gaming disorder was proposed as a disorder, described as a "pattern of persistent or recurrent gaming behavior, which may be online or offline, that is causing significant impairment or interference with the individual. This includes loss of control over gaming, prioritizing gaming over daily activities and other activities of interests, and gaming despite occurrence and re-occurrence of negative consequences for at least 12 months" (World Health Organization 2018).

Based on the above research and proposed criteria, we proposed that video game playing problems may contain the following patterns: difficulty stopping the video game, a desire to play video games, emotional engagement in the game and loss of social interaction due to video game use. The present paper puts forward a four-factor Chinese Young Children's Video-gaming Questionnaire (CVQ) to measure young children's video game playing behavior, which is part of a larger study of the relationships between young children's problematic behaviors and video game use (Zhou 2019; Qu et al. 2020). The purpose of the present study was to validate a self-designed instrument, the Chinese Young Children's Video-gaming Questionnaire (CVQ). Exploratory and confirmatory factor analysis were conducted to validate the factor structure of this questionnaire. After the factor analysis, we produced a shortened version of the CVQ with different items and arrangement of factors.

2   Methods and Measures

2.1   Sample

We initially recruited 819 young children–parent dyads from two cities in China (Beijing and Taiyuan). All children were aged 3 to 5 years old (mean age = 4.25, SD age = 1.00). Valid responses were collected from 728 dyads, representing a final effective rate of 89%. Informed consent was obtained from all parents for both their own and their children's participation. The demographic information of the sample is reported in Table 1. As young children might not have a good awareness of their daily video game playing patterns, the CVQ was completed by their parents or teachers.

Table 1. Basic information on the young children in our sample.

Variable	Group	Beijing (%)	Taiyuan (%)	Total (%)
Sex	Male	391 (47.7)	40 (4.9)	431 (52.6)
	Female	329 (40.2)	59 (7.2)	388 (47.4)
	Total	**720 (87.9)**	**99 (12.1)**	**819**
Age	3	378 (48.3)	37 (4.7)	415 (53)
	4	211 (26.9)	38 (4.9)	249 (31.8)
	5	99 (12.6)	20 (2.6)	119 (15.2)
	Total	**688 (87.9)**	**95 (12.1)**	**783**
Kindergarten region	Urban	497 (61)	0	497 (61)
	Town	187 (22.9)	99 (12.1)	286 (35.1)
	Rural	32 (3.9)	0	32 (3.9)
	Total	**716 (87.9)**	**99 (12.1)**	**815**

Notes: Of the 819 young children initially enrolled, 20 were under 3 years old, two were over 5 years old, and 14 had parents unwilling to supply their age; this left valid age data on 783 children. Also, as four children were not enrolled in school, we collected region data on 815 children

2.2   Data Analysis

In order to determine the best factor structure to represent the CVQ, an exploratory factor analysis (EFA) and a confirmatory factor analysis (CFA) were conducted. The data from 728 young children was randomly split in half. The first half of the sample was used for the EFA while the second half was used for the CFA.

We used the EFA to investigate the factor structure of the CVQ by analyzing the relationships between items using the first half of the sample. Principal axis factoring and oblimin rotation were used. These methods were chosen because an underlying theoretical structure was hypothesized and it was assumed that the dimensions or factors describing the structure might be intercorrelated.

For factor extraction, a decision about the number of factors to retain was based initially on eigenvalues, retaining any factor with an eigenvalue of 1.0 or higher. A scree plot was also examined, looking for a change in the slope of the line connecting the eigenvalues of the factors. The next step was to rotate the factors. An oblique rotation (oblimin) was used because the factors were assumed to be related. Finally, items that loaded strongly on each factor were examined to see if the items actually fit together.

Moreover, we employed CFA to determine whether the factors and structures from the previously conducted EFA could have a good fit with the second half of the sample.

All tested models used maximum likelihood estimation. Model goodness of fit (GOF) in CFA was evaluated using the following indices: Chi-square/df ratio, Root Mean Square Error of Approximation (RMSEA), Comparative Fit Index (CFI), Tucker-Lewis Index (TLI) and the Standardized Root Mean Square Residual (SRMR). TLI and CFI values usually range from 0 to 1.0, and values of 0.90 or greater are considered to be evidence of good model fit. RMSEA values of less than 0.06 indicate good model fit. When models are fully nested, meaning that models are subsets of each other, the Chi-square difference test can be used. The difference between the Chi-square of the two models was evaluated as a Chi-square statistic using degrees of freedom that are the difference between the degrees of freedom in the two models (Johnson and Stevens 2001).

3   Results

3.1   Exploratory Factor Analysis

The purpose of the EFA was to investigate the relationship between 34 items and possible factors underlying the CVQ. Before the EFA was conducted, three items (item 32, 33, 34) were excluded from the original 34-item CVQ due to participants' misunderstanding of the meanings (Table 2).

Table 2. Items excluded from the original CVQ.

Item	Description of the item
32	Children would or probably would lose important social relationships or education chances due to video game playing
33	Children need to maintain their relationships with friends via video game playing
34	Children's eyesight was impaired due to video game exposure
8	Children like to play video games when they are excited
10	Children are excited when they play video games
14	The pleasure of video game playing comes from the game itself other than communicating with others
15	Children give up when they are confronted with difficulties in the game
22	Children try every means to continue playing when you forbid them to play

The EFA was then conducted and principal axis factoring analysis with oblimin rotation was run using SPSS 22. Four factors with eigenvalues over 1.0 were extracted, accounting for 64.6% of the variance. The scree plot indicated that the four factors had the biggest change in slope. We then examined the rotated factor loadings for each item. Those items which did not have a loading above 0.3 were eliminated, which was a commonly used cutoff for any one factor. For those items that had substantial loadings on more than one factor, we further examined whether it made sense to retain

Table 3. Item communality and final EFA results.

	Factor loading			
	Difficulty stopping	Desire to engage	Emotional engagement	Social interaction
29	.774			
27	.766			
30	.756			
28	.748			
25	.747			
26	.728			
24	.695			
31	.690			
23	.558		.407	
3		.740		
4		.740		
1		.735		
6		.712		
7		.692		
2		.680	.451	
5		.655	.445	
8	.452	.607		
18			.827	
17			.817	
20			.798	
16			.646	
19			.624	
11				.804
12				.765
21				.665
13				.544

the item in both factors. In some cases it did, and so they were retained; in other cases it made no sense, and so the item was eliminated. Five items (item 8, 10, 14, 15, 22) did not load substantially on any of the four factors and were finally eliminated from the questionnaire (see Table 3). Item 23 had substantial loadings both on Factor 1 and 2: we retained this item on Factor 1 as it had a bigger factor loading. This was also the case for item 8.

After the EFA, a four-factor model with 26 items was retained and showed better interpretation (Table 4). Of the eight items eliminated, three items were excluded due to misunderstanding of the meanings while the other five items did not load substantially on any of the four factors. Therefore, in comparison to the original 34 items, the remaining 26 items had better interpretation.

Table 4. Factors and items of CVQ after EFA.

No	Factor description	No. of items included
Factor 1	Difficulty stopping	9
Factor 2	Desire to engage	8
Factor 3	Emotional engagement	5
Factor 4	Social interaction	4

3.2 Confirmatory Factor Analysis

CFA was performed to test the four-factor model (Model 1) developed using the EFA with the first half of the sample on the cross-validation sample. Using the second half of the data set, with 364 cases, correlations among the 26 remaining CVQ items were calculated.

A structural equation model was tested using Mplus 8.3. The four latent variables of Model 1 were identified in the previous EFA. The 26 observed variables were the actual items. Parameters led to each item from the factor or factors hypothesized to represent that item. The resulting GOF indices are shown in the first column of Table 5. The Chi-square/df ratio was more than 5.0, indicating that the model did not fit the data well. CFI and TLI were less than the recommended value of 0.90. However, the SRMR of 0.068 was less than the recommended 0.08, indicating a good fit.

Table 5. CFA results of Model 1.

Maximum likelihood estimates					
		Estimate	S.E	Est./S.E	P-value
Difficulty stopping	X1	0.649	0.023	28.307	0.000
	X2	0.740	0.018	40.431	0.000
	X3	0.765	0.017	45.215	0.000
	X4	0.706	0.020	35.110	0.000
	X5	0.801	0.015	53.747	0.000
	X6	0.805	0.015	54.847	0.000
	X7	0.822	0.014	60.103	0.000
	X8	0.791	0.016	50.962	0.000
	X9	0.731	0.019	38.679	0.000
Desire to engage	X10	0.787	0.016	49.608	0.000
	X11	0.764	0.017	44.388	0.000
	X12	0.820	0.014	58.320	0.000
	X13	0.770	0.017	45.757	0.000
	X14	0.740	0.019	39.751	0.000
	X15	0.780	0.016	48.046	0.000
	X16	0.795	0.015	51.347	0.000
	X17	0.683	0.021	31.951	0.000
Emotional engagement	X18	0.685	0.022	31.338	0.000
	X19	0.820	0.015	54.975	0.000
	X20	0.871	0.012	70.877	0.000
	X21	0.665	0.023	29.051	0.000
	X22	0.805	0.016	50.985	0.000
Social interaction	X23	0.595	0.030	19.961	0.000
	X24	0.808	0.023	34.787	0.000
	X25	0.697	0.026	26.410	0.000
	X26	**0.319**	0.038	8.364	0.000

According to the modification indices of Model 1, item 26 was removed from the fourth factor due to a low factor loading of less than 0.4 (0.319). Items 8 and 9 showed a high correlation (M.I. = 135.233). The structure of Model 1 is shown in Fig. 1.

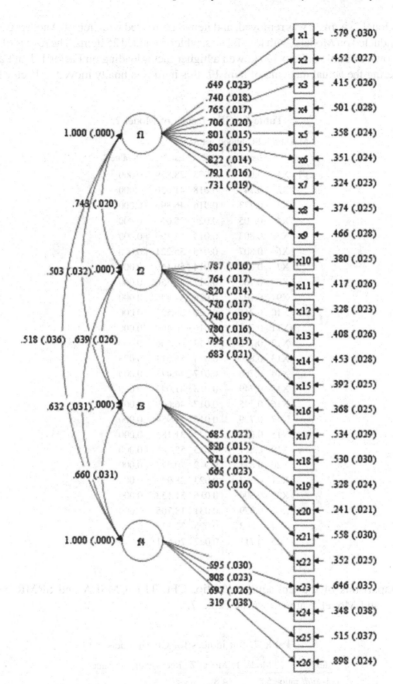

Fig. 1. The original four-factor model, 26-item solution with correlated residuals. Note. All coefficients are statistically significant (P < 0.05).

In Model 2, item 26 was removed, and item 8 correlated with item 9. Another CFA was then conducted on Model 2 with four factors, which included 25 items. The results of Model 2 are shown in Table 6. Item 17 showed a higher factor loading on Factor 1 than Factor 2. Considering the actual meaning of item 17, this item was finally moved to Factor 1.

Table 6. CFA results of Model 2.

Maximum likelihood estimates					
		Estimate	S.E	Est./S.E	P-value
F1	X1	0.654	0.023	28.859	0.000
	X2	0.743	0.018	41.056	0.000
	X3	0.773	0.016	46.896	0.000
	X4	0.705	0.020	35.011	0.000
	X5	0.803	0.015	54.195	0.000
	X6	0.807	0.015	55.221	0.000
	X7	0.820	0.014	59.169	0.000
	X8	0.766	0.017	45.356	0.000
	X9	0.702	0.020	34.496	0.000
F2	X10	0.716	0.020	36.522	0.000
	X11	0.790	0.016	49.669	0.000
	X12	0.775	0.017	46.506	0.000
	X13	0.816	0.014	56.511	0.000
	X14	0.766	0.017	44.471	0.000
	X15	0.749	0.018	41.097	0.000
	X16	0.775	0.017	46.669	0.000
	X17	0.799	0.015	51.954	0.000
F3	X18	0.684	0.022	31.181	0.000
	X19	0.821	0.015	55.283	0.000
	X20	0.871	0.012	70.572	0.000
	X21	0.664	0.023	28.947	0.000
	X22	0.806	0.016	51.133	0.000
F4	X23	0.579	0.031	18.705	0.000
	X24	0.803	0.025	32.137	0.000
	X25	0.711	0.027	26.551	0.000

Comparisons of the Chi-square/df ratio, CFI, TLI, RMSEA and SRMR between Model 1 and Model 2 are shown in Table 7.

Table 7. Fit indices for CFA models.

Index	Model 1	Model 2	Recommended value
chi-sq/df ratio	5.8	4.8	<5
RMSEA	0.08	0.07	<0.08
CFI	0.88	0.91	>0.9
TLI	0.87	0.90	>0.9
SRMR	0.068	0.058	<0.8

Using common rules of thumb for interpretation of model fit, Model 2 fit the data well. Figure 2 shows the final structure of the CVQ.

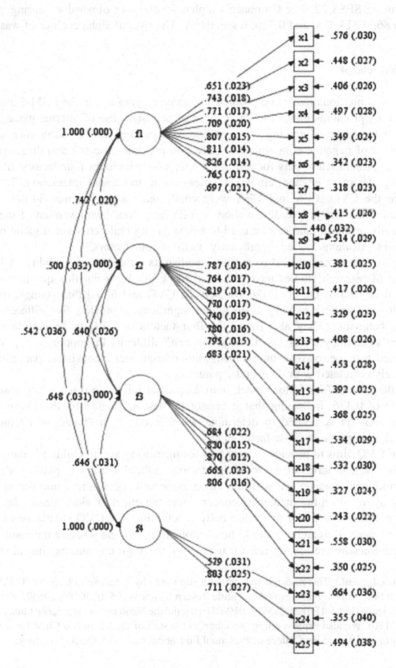

Fig. 2. The modified four-factor, 25-item solution with correlated residuals. Note. All coefficients are statistically significant ($p < 0.05$).

3.3 Internal Consistency

Internal consistency of the CVQ was checked by calculating alpha reliability coefficients using SPSS 22. The Cronbach's alphas for the four dimensions during gaming were 0.86, 0.815, 0.8, and 0.856, respectively. The overall alpha coefficient was good.

4 Discussion

As stated in previous studies on problematic game playing and in the DSM-5 and ICD-11, gaming problems may show the pattern of persistent use of internet games, emotional distress, use of gaming as an escape, and gaming despite occurrence and re-occurrence of negative consequences. Based on previous research and diagnostic criteria, the present study puts forward the CVQ, which includes four factors: difficulty stopping, desire to engage, emotional engagement and social interaction. To better validate the CVQ, EFA and CFA were conducted on the original 34-item CVQ. Combining the analysis results, a shortened 25-item, four-factor version of the CVQ was finally produced and can be used to assess young children's video game playing behaviors. All items loaded significantly on these four factors.

Future studies are needed to further establish its reliability and validity. A limited number of research studies have validated the CVQ by using this questionnaire to obtain their results. Qu et al. (2020) used the CVQ and found that young children's difficulty in stopping playing video games significantly predicts five different problematic behaviors. They also found the four factors of CVQ to be correlated with children's parenting styles; specifically, children's difficulty in stopping was positively correlated with permissive, uninvolved, authoritarian and inconsistent parenting, but negatively correlated with democratic parenting.

In the present four-factor model, item 23 (Social Interaction) has a low R-squared estimate of 0.336, indicating that it cannot be best accounted by the fourth factor. Further analysis is needed to determine whether this item should be excluded or replaced to improve the four-factor model.

The CVQ aims to provides a new tool for measuring young children's daily video game behavior in terms of the following factors: difficulty stopping playing, desire to play, emotional engagement with the video game and social interaction during video game playing. With the increasing concern over the effect of video game playing on young children's behavior and other daily functioning, the CVQ should be useful in future research. Researchers should be cautious to determine whether the results from this questionnaire are appropriate for use with diverse groups and its clinical utility.

Acknowledgment. This research was partially supported by grants from Capacity Building for Sci-Tech Innovation – Fundamental Scientific Research Funds (19530050186, 20530290062), the Social Science General Project (SM202010028010), and the National Social Science Fund of China (18BSH130). We also express our appreciation to the staff of the Infant and Child Learning and Developmental Lab at the College of Preschool Education, Capital Normal University.

Appendix

The Chinese Young Children Video-game Questionnaire (CVQ)

The following statements are about your children's daily video game playing behaviors. Please make a judgement about whether the description is consistent with your children's behavior. You can indicate your response choices on your answer sheet.

1. Very inconsistent.
2. Comparative inconsistence.
3. Between consistence and inconsistence.
4. Comparative consistent.
5. Very consistent.

Order	Does your child show the following behavior? (Please mark an "√" next to the corresponding number that meets the description)
1	Children often play video games
2	Children are very interested in video games
3	Children spend more and more time playing video games
4	Children ask to download or buy video games
5	Children want to play video games when they see others playing games
6	Children want to play video games when they are bored or depressed
7	Children want to play video games when they see electronic products
8	Children want to play video games when they are in high spirits
9	Children need company while playing video games
10	Children like to play video games with their parents
11	Children like to play video games with their young friends
12	Children who have difficulties in playing video games will seek help
13	When children play video games, they need someone to control (time, content, etc.)
14	When children play video games well, they will be happy
15	When children play video games badly, they will be upset
16	Children need to be reminded to finish the video game
17	When you stop your child playing video games, he/she will obey immediately
18	When you stop your child playing video games, it's hard for him/her to turn his/her attention to other tasks
19	When your child tries to reduce or stop playing video games, or can't play video games, his/her mood gets worse
20	Children hide their time playing video games from family, friends or others

(continued)

(*continued*)

Order	Does your child show the following behavior? (Please mark an "√" next to the corresponding number that meets the description)
21	Children play video games to forget their own problems or to relieve anxiety (such as guilt, anxiety, helplessness, depression, etc.)
22	Children want to reduce the amount of time they spend playing video games, but they can't
23	Children want to spend more time playing video games, or to play games with better equipment, or to play more exciting games
24	When children don't play video games, they also spend a lot of time thinking about video games or planning their next time playing video games
25	Children may give up other activities or lose interest in previous hobbies because of playing video games
26	Children will spend less time outdoors because of playing video games

References

Mazurek, M.O., Engelhardt, C.R.: Video game use and problem behaviors in boys with autism spectrum disorders. Res. Autism Spectr. Disord. **7**(2), 316–324 (2013)

Tortolero, S.R., et al.: Daily violent video game playing and depression in preadolescent youth. Cyberpsychol. Behav. Soc. Netw. **17**(9), 609–615 (2014)

Lobel, A., Engels, R.C., Stone, L.L., Burk, W.J., Granic, I.: Video gaming and children's psychosocial wellbeing: a longitudinal study. J. Youth Adolesc. **46**(4), 884–897 (2017)

Lau, C., Stewart, S.L., Sarmiento, C., Saklofske, D.H., Tremblay, P.F.: Who is at risk for problematic video gaming? risk factors in problematic video gaming in clinically referred Canadian children and adolescents. Multimodal Technol. Interact. **2**(2), 19 (2018)

Gentile, D.A., Swing, E.L., Lim, C.G., Khoo, A.: Video game playing, attention problems, and impulsiveness: evidence of bidirectional causality. Psychol. Pop. Media Cult. **1**(1), 62–70 (2012)

Linebarger, D.L.: Contextualizing video game play: the moderating effects of cumulative risk and parenting styles on the relations among video game exposure and problem behaviors. Psychol. Pop. Media Cult. **4**(4), 375–396 (2015)

King, D.L., Delfabbro, P.H., Griffiths, M.D.: The role of structural characteristics in problematic video game play: an empirical study. Int. J. Ment. Health Addict. **9**(3), 320–333 (2011)

American Psychiatric Association: Diagnostic and Statistical Manual of Mental Disorders: DSM-5TM, 5th edn. pp. 795–798. American Psychiatric Publishing, Inc., Arlington, TX (2013)

World Health Organization. 6C51 Gaming Disorder. ICD-11 Beta Draft. https://icd.who.int/dev11/l-m/en#/http%3a%2f%2fid.who.int%2ficd%2fentity%2f1448597234

Zhou, Y.: The relationship between young children's video game playing and problematic behavior. Master's thesis, Capital Normal University (2019)

Qu, F., Gu, C., Huang, H., Zhang, A., Sun, M., Liu, X.: Relationship between young children's problematic behaviors, video gaming status, and parenting styles. In: Fang, X. (ed.) HCI in Games. HCII 2020. Lecture Notes in Computer Science, vol. 12211. Springer, Cham (2020)

Johnson, B., Stevens, J.J.: Exploratory and confirmatory factor analysis of the School Level Environment Questionnaire (SLEQ). Learn Environ. Res. **4**, 325 (2001)

Game Mechanics

Using Multiple Data Streams in Executive Function Training Games to Optimize Outcomes for Neurodiverse Populations

Bruce D. Homer[1]([✉]) [ID] and Jan L. Plass[2] [ID]

[1] The Graduate Center, CUNY, 365 5th Avenue, New York, NY 10016, USA
bhomer@gc.cuny.edu
[2] New York University, 196 Mercer Street, New York, NY 10012, USA
jan.plass@nyu.edu

Abstract. To be optimally effective, digital technologies should be adaptive to specific learners' needs. Two examples are presented of data-informed approaches to developing digital games that support the development of executive functions (EF) in neurodiverse populations. The first is an experiment with younger and older adolescents that compared two versions of a video game designed to train the EF skill of inhibition. Based on developmental neurocognitive differences, one version focused on the *speed* of learners' responses, while the other focused on the *accuracy* of responses. Results indicated that, as hypothesized, younger adolescents benefited more from the focus on speed, while the older adolescents benefited more from the focus on accuracy. In the second example, ongoing work on adapting an EF game designed to train the EF skill of *shifting* for high-functioning adolescents with Autism Spectrum Disorder (ASD) is presented. A detailed analysis of game log data, specifically data on speed and accuracy of responses in the game, revealed that although accuracy was near ceiling, there was greater variability in speed of responses. This suggests that for high-functioning adolescents with ASD, a version of the EF game that focuses on speed of response would be most beneficial. Next steps for the project are discussed, as are broader implications for data-driven approaches to designing adaptive digital tools for learning.

Keywords: Adaptivity · Learning · Video games · Executive functions

1 Introduction: Adaptivity for Learning

1.1 Defining Adaptivity

One of the great promises of digital technology for education has been the ability to customize and be adaptive for different individuals. *Adaptivity* is the "ability of a learning system to diagnose a range of learner variables, and to accommodate a learners' specific needs by making appropriate adjustments to the learner's experience with the goal of enhancing learning outcomes" (Plass and Pawar 2020a; Plass and Pawar 2020b). *Learning outcomes* refers in this context to the goal of a learning activity, such as changes in the knowledge, skills, or attitudes of a learner. Learner variables are

© Springer Nature Switzerland AG 2021
X. Fang (Ed.): HCII 2021, LNCS 12789, pp. 281–292, 2021.
https://doi.org/10.1007/978-3-030-77277-2_22

characteristics describing an individual that have been shown to predict learning, such as a learner's current knowledge, motivation, or emotional state. The adjustments made by the learning environment are a defining quality of such a learning environment and may include adjustments in the learning progression, task difficulty, type and level of feedback, learning modality, and many others.

The significance of the ability of a learning environment to be adaptive is that if such adaptivity is successful, each student could be provided with exactly the learning experience they need at any given time, thereby enhancing the outcomes of learning. Such an optimization of the learning experience for each individual student has long been the goal of educators, psychologists, and learning scientists, but the effects of existing adaptive systems on learning outcomes have for the most part been modest (Plass and Pawar 2020a). There are two possible explanations for this lack of large effects of adaptive systems. One explanation is that learners do not, in fact, learn differently and therefore do not need to be given the specific kind and level of information they require at any given time. Most teachers would dismiss this explanation as incorrect. The other possibility is that to date, we have not able to design systems that implement adaptivity well, a possibility that deserves further consideration.

In designing adaptive learning systems, we need to consider three questions: (1) Which variables should the system adapt for? (2) How can these variables be reliably measured?, and, finally, (3) What is the type of adaptation the system will make during the learning process? (Plass and Pawar 2020b).

1.2   What Variables Should Be Measured?

The selection of which variable to measure depends on a myriad of factors. Many commercially available adaptive learning environments base adaptivity on cognitive variables, most frequently on the learner's current level of knowledge. Yet, many other variables could be considered for adaptive adjustments, such as learners' emotional state, level of motivation, cultural background, or social context. Table 1 provides examples that are by no means exhaustive but demonstrate the broad range of possible variables that could be considered a basis for an adaptive system, but most of which are not currently used for this purpose.

Table 1. Examples of cognitive, motivational, affective, and socio-cultural variables for which systems can adapt

Cognitive variables	Motivational variables	Affective variables	Socio-cultural variables
Current knowledge	Individual interest	Emotional state	Social context
Current skills	Situational interest	Appraisals	Cultural context
Developmental level	Goal orientation	Emotion regulation	Identity/self-perception
Language proficiency	Growth mindset	Attitudes	Relatedness
Learning strategies	Self-efficacy		Social agency
Cognitive Skills	Competence, connection, autonomy		
Self-regulation			
Cognitive load			

1.3 How Can These Variables Be Reliably Measured?

An important consideration for any adaptive systems is how to measure the variable to which the system is designed to respond. Since adaptivity implies the ability of the system to make frequent adjustments, there needs to be a way to measure the variable frequently, without having the measurements affecting that variable (Campbell and Stanley 1966) or affect learning outcomes.

1.4 What Type of Adaptation Will the System Make During the Learning?

Once one or more variables have been selected that are relevant to predict learning outcomes and are measurable, the final question is what kind of adaptation the system should make in response to the different levels of the variable. Figure 1 shows a model of adaptivity that shows how based on the observed learning performance, and based on the expression of a learner variable, a system can adapt the preparation of learning, core learning activity, learner support, learning assessment, and cross-course progression. Details of this model are discussed in Pawar and Plass (2020b), but for the purpose of this paper, we are concerned with the core learning activity. Here, the adaptivity can provide different scaffolds and cues, guidance and feedback, rehearsal schedules, interaction types, types of information representation, difficulty progressions or conceptual progressions.

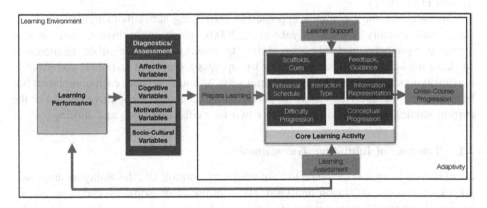

Fig. 1. Model of adaptivity

As illustrated in Fig. 1, the possible number of combinations of learner variables and type of adaptivity can lead to a large number of adaptive systems. For each of these combinations, a theoretical approach has to be identified that informs how the adaptive response is structured. For example, how would a system respond to performance within a game to train executive functions for neurocognitive needs of learners of different developmental ages, or for learners with Autism Spectrum Disorder (ASD)? In the next sections, we will describe how we designed and implemented adaptive games to train executive functions for adolescents of different developmental ages, as well as for adolescents with ASD.

2 Games for EF Training

For the past several years, our lab has been developing and empirically validating video games to support the acquisition of executive functions (e.g., Homer et al. 2019; Parong et al. 2017; Plass et al. 2019). Executive Functions (EFs) have been characterized as top-down cognitive control that is required to plan, monitor and control cognitive processes (Diamond and Lee 2011), and are considered critical for regulating behavior (Blair 2016; Miyake et al. 2000). Children first show evidence of EFs in early childhood, with continued development of EFs into adolescence and early adulthood (Blakemore and Choudhury 2006; Diamond 2013). EFs are associated with essential life skills, such as planning, problem-solving, and other goal-directed activity, as well as many important social, behavioral, and educational outcomes (Blair and Razza 2007; Yeniad et al. 2013).

Arguably the most common approach to classifying subskills that entail EF is the "unity and diversity" model (Miyake et al. 2000), which posits three related but separable components: *updating*, the ability to monitor and manipulate elements in working memory, *inhibition*, the ability to suppress a prepotent response, and *shifting*, the ability to shift between tasks or mental sets. Although related, each component has been found to uniquely contribute to performance on complex cognitive tasks. For the current studies, we focused on the latter two EF skills: inhibition and shifting.

2.1   Training of Inhibition: *Gwakkamolé*

Gwakkamolé is a game designed to train inhibitory control, i.e., the ability to suppress a prepotent response (Malagoli and Usai 2018). In the game, some avocados have to be squashed, whereas others cannot be squashed. For example, players have to inhibit squashing those avocados that wear spikey helmets, see Fig. 2.

Fig. 2. EF training game Gwakkamolé

Adaptivity in *Gwakkamolé* is implemented based on learners' speed and accuracy of smashing avocados. Speed relates to the reaction time required smashing the avocado, and accuracy relates to how many avocados were smashed vs. not smashed correctly versus incorrectly. If learners perform well, the window when an avocado can be smashed is shorter, and more avocados per time period pop up. If learners smash the wrong avocado, the avocados in the next round are visible longer.

2.2   Training of Shifting: All You Can ET

All You Can ET is a game designed to train shifting, i.e., our ability to the ability to mentally shift attention between tasks (Miyake et al. 2000). In the game, hungry aliens come from the spaceship moving down, and they need to be fed before they reach earth. Some aliens like milk shakes, whereas others like cupcakes. In our example, orange-colored aliens like cupcakes, whereas green colored aliens like milkshakes, see Fig. 3. However, these rules change frequently, and players have to accommodate these changes.

Adaptivity in *All You Can ET* is implemented based on learners' speed and accuracy of feeding aliens. Speed relates to the reaction time required to feed the alien, and accuracy relates to how many were fed the correct versus incorrect food. If learners feed aliens correctly, the speed with which the aliens drop down to earth increases. If learners make mistakes, the speed of the aliens decreases.

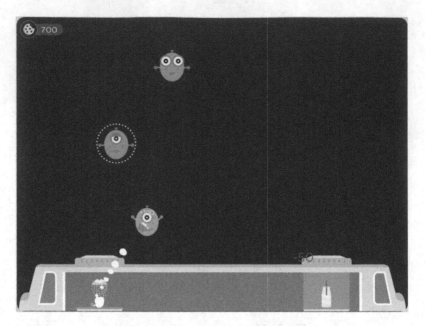

Fig. 3. EF training game *All You Can ET*

3   Study 1: Adaptivity for Neurocognitive Development in a Game to Train the EF Skill of Inhibition

The main research for Study 1 is whether changes in cognitive processing that are associated with neurocognitive developments in brain structure can inform the design of a games-based EF intervention? More specifically, the study aimed to examine whether changes in speed and accuracy of cognitive processing in early to mid-adolescence suggest the need for related changes in demands for increased speed versus improved accuracy in *Gwakkamolé*, an EF training game designed to improve adolescents' inhibition skills. Speed and accuracy match to key neurocognitive developments occurring in adolescence. During early adolescence, an increase neuronal myelination (which acts as an "insulator") results in improvements in general cognitive processing speed and decreased response time on cognitive tasks (Luna and Sweeney 2004). Developments in later adolescence include synaptic pruning, which is the strengthening of frequently used neural connections and elimination of infrequently used ones leading to improved neuronal efficiency, resulting in increased accuracy in cognitive tasks (Blakemore and Choudhury 2006; Dahl et al. 2018).

Based on these neurocognitive developments, it was hypothesized that matching the emphasis of the game's challenge (i.e., increasing speed or improving accuracy) to changes occurring in different developmental periods (i.e., early or later adolescence) would be most beneficial because early adolescents are "primed" for speed improvements and mid-adolescents are "primed" for accuracy improvements.

Two versions of the game were developed, one that emphasized improving speed of responses, and one that emphasized improving accuracy of responses. The flanker task (Eriksen 1995), a standard measure of inhibition, was given before and after the intervention. It was hypothesized that there would be an overall improvement in inhibition, and more specifically, that younger adolescents would have better results with the game version that focused on speed, and older adolescents would benefit more from the version that focused on accuracy. In other words, it was hypothesized that adolescents would show the greatest improvements with the version of the game that was adaptive for their stage of neurocognitive development.

Methods

Adolescents ($N = 96$) between the ages of 13 and 17 ($M = 14.6$, $SD = 1.4$) from New York City public schools participated in the study[1]. Fifty-five of the participants identified as female, and the rest identified as male. Participants were from schools with diverse populations: approximately 68% Hispanic/Latino, 24% White/Caucasian American, 7% Black/African American, and 1% Asian, with additional race/ethnicity categories accounting for less than 1% of the overall school population. Additionally, 66% of the students in the schools are eligible for free or reduced lunch. For analyses, the adolescents were divided into "younger" (13–14 years; $n = 51$) and "older" (15–17 years; $n = 45$) age groups.

The adolescents came into the research lab for the study, where they were tested in small groups, with each participant at their own computer. All materials were presented digitally in one session of about 50 min. After providing consent and completing a short demographic survey, the EF pretest measures were given, including the Flanker task (Eriksen 1995), a measure of inhibition. Participants were then randomly assigned to play either the speed or accuracy version of *Gwakkamolé* for 20 min. (Because the main question was how age interacted with condition, a non-intervention control group was not deemed necessary.) After a brief break, a posttest measure of inhibition was given.

Results and Discussion

Overall, the adolescents demonstrated a small, but significant increase in inhibition as measured by pre- to posttest changes on a standard measure of inhibition, the Flanker task, $t = 21.46$, $p < .001$, $d = .25$. The main hypothesis, that adapting the game to the neurocognitive demands of older versus younger adolescents was also supported, $F(1, 88) = 5.51$, $p = .021$, $\eta_p^2 = .06$. As seen in Fig. 4, although the effects were small, older adolescents did in fact have better posttest scores in the accuracy condition, and the younger adolescents did have better posttest scores in the speed condition.

The findings from the current study support the hypothesis that adapting design features of the game to neurocognitive developments of adolescents would result in better EF training outcomes. Although the effects were relatively small, the intervention was also brief (20 min), and larger effect sizes would be expected with a longer

---

[1] The data reported here come from a larger study reported in Homer et al. (2019). As part of this larger study, participants also received the Dimensional Change Card Sort task (Zelazo 2006), a measure of switching.

intervention. One question that emerges from the current study is whether an adaptive approach to game-based EF training would also benefit other populations, such as adolescents with ASD? Additionally, would similar effects be found for other EF training games? These two questions were the focus of Study 2.

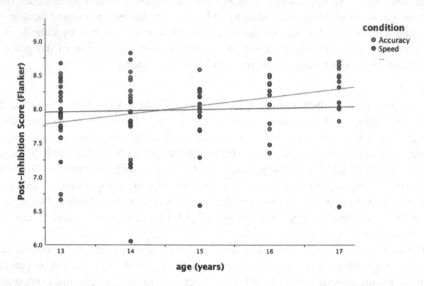

Fig. 4. Inhibition posttest scores (Flanker) by age for each condition (Speed vs. Accuracy)

4   Study 2: Adaptivity for Neurodiversity in a Game to Train the EF Skill of Shifting

Autism spectrum disorder (ASD) is a classification of individuals who experience a combination of difficulties, primarily in the social and communicative realms (APA 2013). With a prevalence of around 1%, ASD is characterized by social communication impairments, repetitive behaviors, highly restricted interests and sensory behaviors that start early in life (Lord et al. 2020). Executive disfunction, including reduced cognitive flexibility (e.g., as measured by card-sorting tasks) has been found as one of the central cognitive impairments associated with ASD (Landry and Al-Taie 2015). Furthermore, impaired EF has been linked to problems with social cognition and theory of mind (Happé et al. 2006).

However, a number of studies have found that interventions can be effective in improving the EF skills of children with autism. Most interventions have focused on intense behavioral training (e.g., Kenworthy et al. 2014), but others have used a game-based approach (e.g., Macoun et al. 2020). This suggests that EF training using video games that were focused on training EF may also work for children and adolescents with ASD. However, based on findings from Study 1, it may be ideal to adapt the games to be most effective for this population.

The goal of Study 2 was to investigate how best to adapt a video game developed to train shifting for high-functioning adolescents with ASD. Specifically, two components of shifting, speed and accuracy, were examined within the context of performance All You Can ET in order to determine which factor may need the most support for development with these adolescents.

Methods

Adolescents who were high functioning and had been diagnosed with ASD participated in the study (N = 48, 86.5% male; mean age = 13.7 years, SD = 2.4). The ethnicity of the adolescents was varied, with 33% reporting as white; 32% as Latinx; 8% as black; 8% as Asian, and the remaining as mixed or other.

For the study, the adolescents came into the research lab where they were tested in small groups, with each participant at their own computer. All materials were presented digitally in one session of about 30 min. After providing consent and completing a demographic questionnaire, the participants were given a standard measure of shifting from the NIH toolbox, the DCCS (Zelazo et al. 2013). All actions in the game, including number of correct responses (accuracy) and reaction time for responding to a target (speed) were recorded to a log for subsequent analyses.

5   Results and Discussion

The participant scored an average of 7.84 (SD = .65) on the 10-point NIH toolbox scale, which is not significantly different from the mean average expected for 13-year-olds of 8.04 (SD = .63). This suggests that in spite of their ASD, the adolescents in the study did not have profound deficits in the EF subskill of shifting. Next, log file data from All You Can ET was examined to give an indication of how the participants were performing on the game. Two key metrics were: 1) average reaction time, which indicated how long it took from the time the target appeared on screen until the participants correctly "targeted" it (a measure of speed); and 2) how many targets were correctly hit (a measure of accuracy). After an initial screening to remove any level where a participant had less than 50% correct (only 2.5% of the total game levels completed), it took participants an average of 1.3 s (SD = .83) to correctly respond to a target, and they had an average of 90% correct (SD = 10%) per level. Average response times for each level are displayed in Fig. 5 and average percent correct for each level are displayed in Fig. 6. Examination of the graphs illustrates that although the adolescents in the study were approaching ceiling for accuracy, there was greater variation in reaction time, suggesting that a focus on speed of response is likely to be a more fruitful approach for adapting the game to be the most beneficial for training shifting skills in high-functioning adolescents with ASD.

6   General Discussion and Conclusions

The goal of the current paper was to explore how digital games to train EF skills in adolescents could be tailored to meet the needs of different learners. Specifically, by adopting a comprehensive model of adaptivity, we identified speed and accuracy as two key factors that are not only central to the EF constructs, but have also been shown to

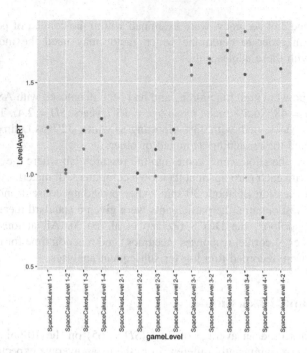

Fig. 5. Average reaction time for correct "hits" by level for All You Can ET.

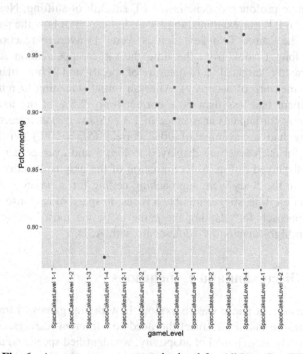

Fig. 6. Average percent correct by level for All You Can ET.

be important for understanding difference for different developmental ages and for neurodiverse populations. In the first study, we found that in a video game designed to train the EF subskill of inhibition, a focus on speed of response was more effective for younger adolescents, and a focus on accuracy was more effective for older adolescents. These effects correspond to understood neurocognitive developments in adolescence, specifically neuronal myelination during early adolescents, which increases processing speed and reaction time, and neuronal pruning in later adolescents, which results in increased accuracy and efficiency. The second study examined the performance of high-functioning adolescents with ASD on a video game designed to train the EF skill of shifting. The adolescents in this study were near ceiling in the accuracy of their responses in the game, but had greater variation in response time (i.e., the amount of time it took them to respond to a target once it appeared on screen). These findings suggesting that future efforts to adapt the game to optimize training for high-functioning adolescents with ASD should focus on improving speed of response. Taken together, these two studies support the argument that a robust model of adaptivity that is informed by multiple sources of data can best support the development of educational materials for the widest range of learners and best support neurodiverse populations.

References

Blair, C.: Developmental science and executive function. Curr. Dir. Psychol. Sci. **25**(1), 3–7 (2016)

Blair, C., Razza, R.P.: Relating effortful control, executive function, and false belief understanding to emerging math and literacy ability in kindergarten. Child Dev. **78**(2), 647–663 (2007)

Blakemore, S.J., Choudhury, S.: Development of the adolescent brain: implications for executive function and social cognition. J. Child Psychol. Psychiatry **47**(3–4), 296–312 (2006)

Campbell, D.T., Stanley, J.C.: Experimental and Quasi-experimental Design for Research. Rand McNally, Chicago, IL (1966)

Dahl, R.E., Allen, N.B., Wilbrecht, L., Suleiman, A.B.: Importance of investing in adolescence from a developmental science perspective. Nature **554**(7693), 441–450 (2018)

Diamond, A.: Executive functions. Annu. Rev. Psychol. **64**, 135–168 (2013)

Diamond, A., Lee, K.: Interventions shown to aid executive function development in children 4 to 12 years old. Science **333**(6045), 959–964 (2011)

Eriksen, C.W.: The flankers task and response competition: a useful tool for investigating a variety of cognitive problems. Vis. Cogn. **2**(2–3), 101–118 (1995)

Happé, F., Booth, R., Charlton, R., Hughes, C.: Executive function deficits in autism spectrum disorders and attention-deficit/hyperactivity disorder: examining profiles across domains and ages. Brain Cogn. **61**(1), 25–39 (2006)

Homer, B.D., Ober, T.M., Rose, M.C., MacNamara, A.P., Mayer, R., Plass, J.L.: Speed versus accuracy: implications of adolescents' neurocognitive developments in a digital game to train executive functions. Mind Brain Educ. **13**(1), 41–52 (2019)

Kenworthy, L., et al.: Randomized controlled effectiveness trial of executive function intervention for children on the autism spectrum. J. Child Psychol. Psychiatry **55**(4), 374–383 (2014)

Landry, O., Al-Taie, S.: A meta-analysis of the Wisconsin Card sort task in Autism. J. Autism Dev. Disord. **46**(4), 1220–1235 (2015). https://doi.org/10.1007/s10803-015-2659-3

Lord, C., et al.: Autism spectrum disorder. Nat. Rev. Dis. Primers. **6**(1), 1–23 (2020)

Luna, B., Sweeney, J.A.: The emergence of collaborative brain function: FMRI studies of the development of response inhibition. Ann. N. Y. Acad. Sci. **1021**(1), 296–309 (2004)

Miyake, A., Friedman, N.P., Emerson, M.J., Witzki, A.H., Howerter, A., Wager, T.D.: The unity and diversity of executive functions and their contributions to complex "frontal lobe" tasks: a latent variable analysis. Cogn. Psychol. **41**(1), 49–100 (2000)

Macoun, S.J., Schneider, I., Bedir, B., Sheehan, J., Sung, A.: Pilot study of an attention and executive function cognitive intervention in children with Autism spectrum disorders. J. Autism Dev. Disord., 1–11 (2020).https://doi.org/10.1007/s10803-020-04723-w

Malagoli, C., Usai, M.C.: The effects of gender and age on inhibition and working memory organization in 14-to 19-year-old adolescents and young adults. Cogn. Dev. **45**, 10–23 (2018)

Parong, J., Mayer, R.E., Fiorella, L., MacNamara, A., Homer, B.D., Plass, J.L.: Learning executive function skills by playing focused video games. Contemp. Educ. Psychol. **51**, 141–151 (2017). https://doi.org/10.1016/j.cedpsych.2017.07.002

Plass, J.L., Homer, B.D., Pawar, S., Brenner, C., MacNamara, A.P.: The effect of adaptive difficulty adjustment on the effectiveness of a game to develop executive function skills for learners of different ages. Cogn. Dev. **49**, 56–67 (2019)

Plass, J.L., Pawar, S.: Adaptivity and personalization in games for learning. In: Plass, J.L, Mayer, R.E., Homer, B.D. (eds.) Handbook of Game-Based Learning (2020)

Plass, J.L., Pawar, S.: Toward a taxonomy of adaptivity for learning. J. Res. Technol. Educ. **52**(3), 275–300 (2020b)

Yeniad, N., Malda, M., Mesman, J., van IJzendoorn, M.H., Pieper, S.: Shifting ability predicts math and reading performance in children: a meta-analytical study.Learn. Individ. Differ. **23**, 1–9 (2013).https://doi.org/10.1016/j.lindif.2012.10.004

Zelazo, P.D.: The Dimensional Change Card Sort (DCCS): a method of assessing executive function in children. Nat. Protoc. **1**(1), 297–301 (2006)

Zelazo, P.D., Anderson, J.E., Richler, J., Wallner-Allen, K., Beaumont, J.L., Weintraub, S.: II. NIH Toolbox Cognition Battery (CB): measuring executive function and attention. Monogr. Soc. Res. Child Dev. **78**(4), 16–33 (2013)

Gameplay as Network: Understanding the Consequences of Automation on Play and Use

Nicolas LaLone[✉] [iD]

University of Nebraska at Omaha, Omaha, NE 68182, USA
nlalone@unomaha.edu

Abstract. The design of software is often a process of intuition, guessing, and luck. It does not have to be. We present association mapping (AM), a novel take on social-network analysis that removes the human-centric biases of network analysis. To show the usefulness of this approach, we deploy AM on a board game and compare it to the digital version of that same board game. Overall, we show just how much less central humans are in the digital version of the board game and how that loss of centrality influenced the humans themselves. After discussing the reasoning behind the method, how to do AM, and what the data mean, we discuss how to deploy AM for design and different paths AM could develop.

Keywords: Social network analysis · Automation · Board games · Task-artifact cycle · Actor-Network Theory · Catan

1 Introduction

As the computer developed and became available for the first enthusiasts, many would-be programmers digitized different kinds of games in an effort to learn how to write and develop programs. From early iterations of checkers [33], chess [32], and Mah Jong [6] to disparate interpretations of the logical systems undergirding the roleplaying game Dungeons and Dragons [6,20,40], the mystique of logic and rules [27] at the center of programming formed a perfect modality for learning how to write and design computer programs. Collectively, these enthusiasts manifested a lucrative form of entertainment, the video game; however, not merely as digitized board games but as a different form of play. Board games mixed more readily with computation and became realtime, reaction-time based competitions. Platformers allowed designers to test the hand-eye coordination of players as they moved through increasingly complex environments. Shooters tested the ability for players to find and target objects on a screen while other designers used physics engines to bring statistic-heavy simulations like Strat-o-Matic Football into a realtime, competitive environment [1,34].

As the video game industry developed into an international, multi-billion dollar industry, the board game industry as well as the tabletop role-playing

© Springer Nature Switzerland AG 2021
X. Fang (Ed.): HCII 2021, LNCS 12789, pp. 293–313, 2021.
https://doi.org/10.1007/978-3-030-77277-2_23

game industry ushered in by Dungeons and Dragons languished and stagnated. This began to change in the late 1990s when different kinds of board gaming began to become more commonplace. In many ways, board games benefited from the proliferation of the computer and the diffusion of computer logic in society [14,35]. The mystique of logic and rules lost some of its enchantment and became rote, commonplace, and part of everyday life.

Games like *Catan* (1995), *Carcassone* (2000), *Ticket to Ride* (2004) and *Pandemic* (2008) took advantage of this accepted complexity and re-kindled consumer interests in board games [29]. These games, paired with broadcast media like Youtube, Twitch, and Facebook fostered a golden age of board gaming while new monetization and investment platforms like Kickstarter have allowed that golden age to resist stagnation for almost 2 decades [8]. In recent years, video game designers have once again begun to digitize these new board games so that players across the world can connect and play them together online.

In digitizing these current golden-era board games, the mystique of logic and rules is not something unknown, new, or novel for enthusiasts to experiment with but an activity with as rich of a history as the games those original programmers attempted to digitize. The mystique of logic and rules for these new golden-era board games is as such that many commonplace user-experience techniques are being integrated in order to usher in tight, easy to use digital editions that takes much of the maintenance of board games (moving cardboard and plastic bits around) and automates it [43]. Because of the expectations of user experience and the norms of design, much of what made these games a unique experience is removed from human maintenance to that of computation [7]. The consequences of these moves from human maintenance to automation is something that is in need of examination; however, no methods exist that can evaluate how a playful experience can change in this way.

The primary reason for a lack of method is that all existing methods of analysis place humans as the center of activity, as the only beings capable of agency despite our requirement of associating with non-human objects to achieve that agency [22]. Yet, recent philosophical moves have challenged this assertion noting that without non-human objects, human agency is often not possible [22]. It is not possible because potential is often contained within those objects and constrains what sort of activity can be achieved [2]. By adjusting a viewpoint to include all objects simultaneously, it becomes possible to consider more than just how humans react to an experience or how well a design communicates its potential. Instead, the object of analysis provides series of connections, of associations between objects and within these, trends can be glimpsed that could be controlled [21].

The present research contributes a novel deployment of social-network analysis – association mapping [21] – as a realtime representation of human/non-human networks, also called actor-networks [22,24] or monadologies [36]. By using association as a unit of measurement, researchers can quantify where, how, why, and what objects are associating in realtime. In understanding how a network shifts through the presence of computation, designers can account for how much their design shifts the feel of the game that they are digitizing. We deploy this method of 6 games of one of the most famous games in the world – *Catan* (1995) – in order to provide a proof of concept analysis. After discussing the background, previous literature, data collection process, and method of analysis, we will conclude with design implications and further developments we expect to perform in the future.

2   Background and Past Research

This section is split into two parts: 1) History and 2) Previous Research. The history expands the standpoints used in the introduction. The most important of these items is a brief explanation of how games relate to military history and its connection to both board games and the logic of computation. The second point is that of research into or surrounding automating aspects of boardgames. It is important to note that while board games were central to fostering play within computer-mediated environments, much of this development has been in purity of form: play only possible through digital worlds. Re-situating the focus on digitizing so-called "analog" play or play centered on hybrid environments not mediated by computation is a more recent development.

2.1   History

There is a relationship that is not really explored between board games and video games that is important for the study of both. That relationship begins with Napoleon Bonaparte and ends with two Daves, Wesely and Arneson. Between the two is the birth of the computer, the start of the age of empiricism, and information communication technologies that would change the world [20,37]. It was Hegel, witnessing Napoleon's victory in the battle of Jena-Auerstadt, who said that Napoleon symbolized the birth of a new world [11]. That world was the gathering of data to generate information to make decisions [12].

Those decisions would be played out on maps, physically, and that action would manifest later in the real world [20,39,40]. The Prussian Army, the greatest military in the world, was left reeling after the battle of Jena-Auerstedt. After the defeat, they dedicated themselves to discovering the ways that they could train soldiers to think and act like Napoleon's armies. What came out of this drive was the birth of a systematic evaluation of war that could be used to train soldiers, officers, and any interested party, into thinking systemically [11].

The manner of play was this: 2 players are generals in control of armies portrayed at scale on a large, table-sized topographical map. In order to actually play the game, they need to feed input into an apolitical arbiter of the fight. This umpire, this processor, this game master, would take inputs and show their results. When a decision needed to be made or if a signal for fighting had been indicated, the umpire would roll dice (adding appropriate modifiers) to determine the outcome [11,30].

While this fashion of play gained worldwide attention, thanks to two World Wars and dozens of smaller ones, this style of play began to disappear. In its place was that of players adhering to a set of rules that was mediated by charts, cardboard chits, and other human players [40]. The human umpire, the processor, the game master was missing and replaced with a social contract-like form of self-monitoring. This style of play persisted after World War 2 until David Wesley, a college student in the Twin Cities, re-discovered the games created in response to Napoleon [20,30].

This interpretation of those games, an American interpretation called *Strategos* [13,38], provided a foundation upon which David Wesley, and eventually Dave Arneson, would build until Gary Gygax codified the rules in its most recognizable form: *Dungeons and Dragons* (D&D) [13,20,30]. D&D is a game within which players can assume the role of other characters. Those characters, driven by variables and that seed algorithmic randomized checks of skill (e.g. can I make this jump? Did I hit that monster?), were able to persist within an imaginary world as long as the players liked or as long as the character lived. This game and style of play appeared in the late 1960s and early 1970s, just as the first computers became available for enthusiasts to use. The mental model of a fantasy world, mediated by an arbitrary 3rd party, and maintained by consistent variables that could be augmented with skills, weapons, and other modifiers, proved an ample space of inspiration.

If one looks at the formative games of the video game industry, nearly all of them are renditions of D&D in some fashion. *Colossal Cave Adventure* was based on a combination of Mammoth Cave spelunking and a D&D campaign [18]. PLATO's dnd was based on a D&D campaign and would later inspire the game Avatar and then Wizardry [6]. Each of these games linked the computer to a form of play that had already been using computation in the form of inputs and processing [20].

But what D&D allowed to foster was an automation of play as the paper-based, human-limited rate of play. What followed these developments was a constant cycle of growing complexity followed by resets that would start back at the beginning and try again. While much of this has been chronicled in studies of video games, the relationship between the representation of systemic thinking, what aspects of play are automated, or should be automated, is not fully realized.

2.2 Previous Literature

Automation, digitization, and how to best present the artifacts of play is absent from much of the discussion of games until recently. While there are early attempts to understand how digital games make things fun [26], it was not until more resources were available that digitizing pieces began to be considered in the literature [17]. Yet, this research was not so much asking about what aspects of a game should be automated but what parts of a game should be digitized.

Future research would examine the automation of board game spaces. Rogerson, et al. [7] examined the issues and tensions of digitizing board games. When games are not digitized, their housekeeping or the moving around of pieces, dealing of cards, or moving of meeples not only keep players involved with the game, but reinforce the rules, their interpretation, and the way players can associate [19,41]. But it is more than simply chores, not only are the chores a requisite part of play, the pieces themselves are also necessary for the game state [31]. Yet, when digitizing play, those bits are often automated because UX often points to them as a barrier of use for programs [5].

Despite that conclusion, there are many game designers looking at ways to make the hybrid space of games a digitally augmented one as well. For example, Augmented- and Mixed Reality approaches are still quite popular. Much like Scrabble on iOS which used smart phones and tablets, Huynh et al. attempted to combine smartphones with physical game pieces [16]. This approach was different than the bluetooth-augmented, app-enabled *Golem Arcana* in that it sought to create a hybrid digital-physical experience by coating miniatures with RF-tags allowing them to be read by a mobile app. Echtler also attempted to augment physical play by providing a way to play board games at a distance using augmented reality [10].

Augmenting and mixing digital aspects with board games can work because it is adding more bits but those chores remain, albeit in a different form. In digitizing, in automating board games, quite often those chores are replaced with a single button press. Yet, the impact of this automation is not well understood not because researchers haven't looked, but because methodologies do not permit researchers to look at anything but statistics and user studies. A new method is necessary and is the contribution of this paper.

3   Making Sense of Play in Order to Study It

At this point, the argument that play in digital spaces and play in non-digital spaces are different is all but decided, they are different and contain different ways of knowing, doing, playing, and being. Yet, the tensions and frustrations of digitizing board games, of moving from non-digital to digital spaces, shows that this may not necessarily be the case. At the core of these tensions is something we cannot necessarily see. This is a common issue within technology use. We can glimpse it when something goes wrong and play stops since play is the use of things found in a space whereas fun is closer to the surprise at an outcome of that use [2].

Through this definition, we see that play is a summation of objects inside of a space. And when those objects are assembled, that space exists independent of reality and is not permeable by current methods [15]. Only when the stranger appears, when the community for those that have nothing in common appears, but when it appears is also when play is over and we cannot reassemble it in the same way [25].

Yet, without being able to see within a space of play during its existence, all we can do is design and hope that use and users will accept that which is placed before them. As a result, design, creation of products, platforms, and other forms of object are a result of luck, time, and advertising. But it doesn't have to be this way. There is a way to think about this space using the tenets of Actor-Network Theory that can allow us to account for everything within a special space [24]. A space of play could be exploded like an exploded view diagram (see example in Fig. 1.

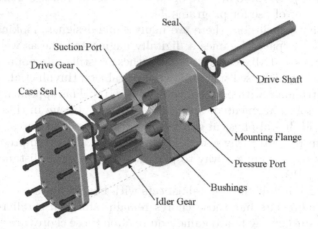

Fig. 1. An exploded view diagram shows all of the individual parts and how they fit together [9]. CC BY-SA 3.0

But unlike those physical connections between objects that fit together to form a whole, each of the individual objects–we will call them monads [24]– inside of a whole like a space of play, need to be found, identified, and observed as they persist within the space. Or to put it another way, in order to explode a space of play and observe it, all objects must be cataloged and all associations between objects must be taken into account. By doing this, what objects are most central, their strength, their ties to other objects, and the ways that these things change over time can be glimpsed, mapped, and otherwise analyzed. This was the premise we began with as we set out to map 6 games of *Catan* (1995).

4   Data and Method

The data we gathered began with 6 recordings of players playing *Catan* (1995) on the tabletop and via an iPad. By recording this way, the researcher could reference all of the players hands, pieces touched, and chores performed when they coded games later using Association Mapping (AM). Additionally, by recording voice and video, the researcher could transcribe conversation, note outside-of-game tasks, and other activities like eating, breaks, and whatever else would come along. The game *Catan* (1995) was chosen because of its recognition. Overall, 11 students were recruited to play of which 10 were undergraduate students and 1 was a graduate student.

There were 3 sessions total. In session 1, 3 of the players knew each other and 1 was new. In session 2, all of the players knew each other. In session 3, none of the players knew each other. Each of them was in the middle of their program and all came from socio-economic backgrounds that were similar. Future work can unpack demographic differences in play, and should. There needs to be a little bit said about our source of data, the game itself.

Catan (1995) is one of the most famous games in the world today. The game takes place on an island that is separated into hexagonal pieces. Each hexagon is designated as clay, sheep, wheat, metal ore, and wood and upon those hexagons are numeric tiles numbering from 2–12. Each round, a player rolls 2, 6-sided dice, the corresponding number generates resources with one exception. 1 Hexagon is noted as a desert where no resources are generated; instead, a thief appears there and can be hired upon rolling a 7. Who gets resources is dependent on roads and settlements each player builds. Each time a player builds a settlement, connects roads, or purchases cards, they can gain victory points. The game ends when a player reaches the set amount of victory points. A photo of the game set up and ready to play can be seen below in Fig. 2.

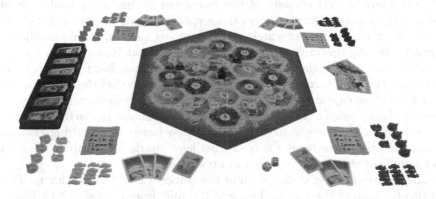

Fig. 2. All of the bits associated with the game *Catan* (1995) when it is set up to play on a tabletop.

To illustrate the abilities of AM, we felt that it was necessary to put together a comparative analysis of a task and its artifact-mediated counter-part. In this case, we had players play a game of *Catan* (1995) and then play another game using the iOS app of the same name. This app was chosen because it is an easy way to play co-located or at a distance and our players were all in the same room, being recorded. We wanted to observe the tensions of automating board games [7] and show them in a high-fidelity, yet data-driven, way. By situating this experiment as a comparative analysis, we hope to show what AM can provide designers.

More than just for recognition, a game was chosen as the initial space of observation because of the way games are played. In a board game, every move must be discussed, analyzed, cataloged, and the results of that process have are represented on the board itself. Thus, games are the best environment to display how SNA can be used in this manner in that much like a network of humans, associations are mapped. An association is made when a human or non-human makes a connection with a game piece, rule, or player. We used Latour's definition in the *Pasteurization of France* [22] or Leibniz's and Tarde's concept of Monad [23] for reference.

Association Mapping (AM) consists of creating chains of dyads, a group of 2 objects. For example, I grab the dice (Human ↔ Dice, Dice ↔ Human) and roll them on a table (Human ↔ Dice, Dice ↔ Table, Table ↔ Dice). This process of dyadic association making is consistent and often 2-way or bi-directional. I grab the dice, the dice are in my hand, I then toss the dice to the table and the table now has the dice. With each chain, the associations created in realtime are made in the order that they are created. In doing this, AM allows us to measure the power not only of each object present within a given context, but inside of a given time frame. While this presents a potentially dangerous amount of data (in terms of volume), this method of analysis is meant to allow researchers to consistently explode contexts to their desired fidelity.

More literally, AM consists of the researcher taking notes while watching players play a game. The researcher notes specific events of interest with a time stamp. Next, the researcher watches each game to make sure the recording was complete. During this initial pass, the research takes additional notes, for example, when each turn begins and what each dice result was. Next, they create field notes based on each turn. These accompanied the notes that the researcher took during the video capture itself. After the field notes were written, that researcher opens a blank NodeXL Template in Microsoft Excel and re-started the video[1]. The researcher then began to "code" each association made during the game. To maintain use of the term, the researcher kept our definition up on the screen. An example of the coding process can be seen in Fig. 3.

The end result after coding each of the games was a list of 6 chains of associations for each of the games. This was 6 chains from a total of 10+ Hours of footage resulting in 20,177 edges and 337 vertices. Each game's length, number of edges, and number of vertices can be seen in Table 1. While there was over 10 h of footage, each game took at least 4 times longer to code than it did to record or play. Thus, a 1 h game took anywhere from 5–7 h to code fully. In addition to the coding of each game, the spoken dialogue was additionally transcribed and analyzed using MaxQDA for frequencies, references, and other potential codes that may have been missed by the researcher. No method was used to analyze these data save counting utterances and times spoken. Future analyses will further integrate these data.

To be more specific to SNA, in AM an actor or member of a social network consists of all objects associated with given a particular bound. Within this analysis, an actor could be a resource card, a wooden road piece, the

---

[1] It is important to note here that NodeXL is not a requirement and that R or any other software that accepts these types of data are just as useful.

1			Labels	
2	Vertex 1 ▼	Vertex 2 ▼	Label	▼
3	Player1	Dice	Picks up Dice	
4	Dice	Player1		
5	Player1	Player2	Hands Dice	
6	Player2	Player1		
7	Dice	Player2		
8	Player2	Dice	Rolls Dice	
9	Dice	Numbers	Rolls Six	
10	Numbers	Dice		
11	Player1	Numbers	Numbers and Players Interact	
12	Player2	Numbers	Numbers and Players Interact	
13	Numbers	Player1		
14	Numbers	Player2		
15	Numbers	Player3	Dice number associates with player as it dictates action	
16	Numbers	Player4	Dice number associates with player as it dictates action	
17	Numbers	Terrain	The numbers form an association with the terrain	
18	Terrain	Player1	The terrain forms an association with each player	

Fig. 3. Vertex 1 to Vertex 2. In this example a player picks up the dice, hands them to another player, and rolls them. The resulting spread of information between other players and the board is also captured.

meaning attached to the result of a die roll, or even the rules dictating trading resources. Unlike SNA, AM does not necessarily consist of entities that do not act. Instead, all objects are separated from their intent and are instead cataloged and recorded in terms of what other objects they associate with over the sense of time that group of objects has defined. Another way to consider association between objects is that an association is a relational tie.

In SNA, a relational tie is essentially a social tie [42]. While SNA uses the term "social tie" and "relational tie" interchangeably, these types of ties are often associated with two actors being linked in some way. For example, actors could evaluate one another in that they form a friendship. Or, actors could transfer some sort of material between one another. Actors could be affiliated with a club or department within a company or they could simply be doing something together like walking or having a conversation. SNA is mostly focused on the whole in that a node or vertex bundles the non-human objects that make up that interaction. Thus, a vertex representing a human also contains roads, bridges, and other physical features that allow those humans to connect.

Table 1. Total time, edges, and vertices in each of the 6 games played in 3 groups

Session	Type	Time	Edges	Vertices
1	Tabletop	1:10:46	4172	43
1	iPad	1:53:00	2181	59
2	Tabletop	1:37:46	3561	48
2	iPad	1:25:38	2281	43
3	Tabletop	1:31:41	3409	62
3	iPad	2:29:50	4573	82
Total		10:08:41	20177	337

In AM, relational ties are devolved into a mutual exchange of information or recruitment. No object is devoid of intent to act, as such, roads on a *Catan* (1995) map recruit others to play more roads. Resource cards associate with players that result in their being made into tangible pieces on the game board or used to gather other types of resources. All of these entities form relational ties of a singular variety that result in the formation of other ties. These ties often form stronger and stronger networks because, at its core, association mapping relates to the constant pressure or agonism (in this case the tension of chores and the materiality of all the bits) of objects [28]. Speaking of the objects, there is one last point to make about AM, SNA, and the number of files.

While coding each of these games produce an initial 6 files, SNA is a method of analysis that quickly adds files and this can be cumbersome. For example, the researcher used NodeXL to code each of the games by manually typing dyads, dyad chains, and verticies. From each single NodeXL excel file, an additional 116 files were created and of those 116 files, only 6 were of use outside of the visualization and calculations that NodeXL itself can perform. The files created for UCINet were created in order to normalize all measures of centrality and cohesion. In total with these 6 games, there are approximately 116 * 6 files or around 700 files with additional files being created by video recordings, iPad screenshots, audio recordings, Adobe Premiere files, sample networks, exploratory network data, and other ancillary work. This resulted in approximately 1000–1500 files to work with across text, audio, video, and network dimensions. With this in mind, we analyze just the basic aspects of the data, centrality, frequency, and other descriptive information.

5   Analysis

For the present research, we are only concerned with simple centrality (in this case, centrality is essentially how important, connected, or necessary for network cohesion specific verticies are to a graph [42]). Breaking with tradition in SNA, we will also not be visualizing networks at all as this analysis is about the values attached to that individual vertex centrality rather than the visualization of the whole. The reason for this is that with SNA's most basic measurement, we can see the impact of automation and just the numeric quantites can provide adequate information. Future work will further analyze these data in order to better understand the details within that shape. For a longer discussion of these data, please refer to [21].

Table 2. Parameters of differences between modalities for players

Session 1

TT Color	TT-TS	iPad-TS	iPad Color	Diff	Type	Time
Red	332	551	Green	13.00%	TT	1:10:46
White	330	551	Yellow	12.83%	iPad	1:53:00
Orange	221	614	Red	1.41%	% Diff	62.63%
Blue	210	255	Blue	10.96%		
Total	1093	1971	AVG Change	9.34%		

Session 2

TT Color	TT-TS	iPad-TS	iPad Color	Diff	Type	Time
White	399	181	Red	4.81%	TT	1:37:46
Orange	342	383	Green	10.19%	iPad	1:25:38
Blue	472	343	Blue	9.12%	% Diff	114.17
Total	1213	907	AVG Change	8.04%		

Session 3

TT Color	TT-TS	iPad-TS	iPad Color	Diff	Type	Time
Red	337	560	Red	−6.89	TT	1:31:41
White	242	358	Yellow	−2.16%	iPad	2:27:30
Orange	228	313	Green	−.51%	% Diff	62.16
Blue	371	286	Blue	13.26%		
Total	1178	1517	AVG Change	.92%		

Overall, the data shows three items of interest with regard to automating board games. First, we will focus on a simple act in playing a game, how often the players speak. After discussing the frequency of speaking, we will dig deeper to understand how those differences manifest by focusing on the centralness of humans. Next, we will talk about the social life of non-human objects within the game space and how they too, are impacted by automation. After analyzing their representations, we will discuss what they mean.

5.1 Differences Between Modes of Play

The Impact of Automation on Times Spoken. One of the most poignant differences between modes of play was the number of times spoken. Analyzing data from this perspective provides a useful primer when considering an aspect of play, that in-person play means that players are discussing things with each other. This discussion could be maintenance of the board or, "is that piece supposed to be there?" or in the case of *Catan* (1995), trading pieces and discussing strategies, "We need to stop the white player." When automation is inserted into these discussions, one would expect (even co-located) for discussion to decrease. However, there was something interesting that occurred.

Looking at Table 2, we can see the number of times each person at the table spoke across each session and within each modality. Times spoken during the tabletop session (TT-TS) versus times spoken during the iPad session (iPad-TS). In order to make the comparison of speaking frequency, the frequencies had to be normalized based on the total time each game took to play. From the above chart, we can see that overall, the games with the iPad took longer to play but also that on average players spoke more during the iPad games. Digging into the data a little more, a curious thing began to occur.

When the players were engaged with the iPad, they did not communicate with others that often. Instead, when the iPad was with another player, the other players engaged in other activities and ended up talking more about other things. Just how much this was occurring can be glimpsed when looking at the Eigenvector centrality of the cellphone vertex in Table 3. What Eigenvector centrality is is best described by thinking about page rank wherein a bot crawls every word or image on a page and when a user performs a query on a search engine, the search engine finds the highest Eigenvector centralities to display [42].

While these values are small, their gains between Tabletop and iPad are noticeable and significant. From an observer's perspective, we can theorize that if the materiality of games, its chores, and its rules are all central to the activity, then when a computer is automating that activity other chores need to be performed. Thus it stands that a computer mediating a network – in this case, doing the chores of a game of *Catan* (1995) – the human will attend to other networks. Whether this is true of other games is in need of unpacking.

Table 3. Eigenvector centrality of the vertices representing cell phones or mobile devices held by the players. Note that in nearly every case that the rank of each player's phone more than doubles when the iPad is mediating play.

	1-TT	1-iPad	2-TT	2-iPad	3-TT	3-iPad
Blue	0.000	0.089	0.050	0.052	0.000	0.039
Orange	0.000	0.056	0.017	0.099	0.000	0.086
Red	0.000	0.203			0.015	0.135
White	0.000	0.054	0.011	0.063	0.000	0.097

On the Centrality of Humans. Within a network or space that is devoted to play, all objects are deployed and used according to the rules of that space. As a result, it stood to reason that if automating play was going to have an impact, then that impact was going to manifest via centrality. Specifically, the centrality of humans should probably go down because they do not have to maintain the space of play, they do not have to perform chores. While this measure of centrality is perhaps the most basic measurement of SNA, it is also perhaps the most useful. Degree centrality is essentially defined as how many neighbors a particular node has on a network or graph [42]. Another way to talk about this is that degree centrality allows the researcher to learn the most mathematically active actors in a particular network or graph.

Table 4. Average centrality by player within each modality including average overall centrality by player and overall centrality of humans in general.

	1-TT	1-iPad	2-TT	2-iPad	3-TT	3-iPad	TT	iPad
Blue	46.03%	38.41%	54.59%	29.89%	57.96%	31.30%	52.86%	33.20%
Orange	46.37%	36.84%	54.61%	32.18%	42.71%	28.88%	47.90%	32.63%
White	54.62%	42.76%	57.68%	35.41%	45.01%	34.79%	52.44%	37.65%
Red	47.24%	44.77%	0.00%	0.00%	46.60%	37.09%	46.92%	40.93%
					Overall average		50.03%	36.10%

Within directional networks (information flow going both ways) like the ones being used for AM, the degree centrality is somewhat unique. For example, directional graphs often use the concept of choice to indicate that choice is available and not forced. However, when doing anything social, the nature of choice is something that is not entirely evident. As such, AM rests on the idea of making a choice as a base of any actor. From Table 4, the average human centrality can be seen.

These data are averaged over the course of each game's turns. The games are separated by modality (TT being tabletop and iPad being iPad mediated game). Note that within each game that the centrality of each human within the network goes down. For example, in session 1, the blue player's centrality goes from about 46% to around 38%. If we average all of the games, the average centrality of humans within each game drops by about 14%. This means that the computer, that automation has taken about 14% of the chores of the game away from the humans themselves.

Speaking to the above Eigenvector centrality of mobile devices, we can say that automation is not necessarily making the players less social. Instead, we can say that automation, that the internet is making humans more social in that they attend to other networks when automation either allows them to do so or has removed their ability to. In this way, we see that a digitally mediated game that is automated using the tenets of UX is not only removing humans from the game literally, it is additionally impacting the game in that it is removing tasks that foster order at the table. And so, we can say that automation within board games is having an unintended consequence of fostering a disconnection of humans to the current work to instead tend to other chores in other networks. This finding is perhaps the most central to this work because it leaves designers with a means through which to not only diagnose where their design is failing, but also where they can grab more attention of the players themselves.

Non-human to Non-human Differences Between Mode of Play. As noted, the centrality of humans within the network of play changed significantly. This means that that centrality had to go somewhere and one oft-overlooked piece of analysis is how often the bits themselves changed in associating during play. One way to do this is to compare the material bits and their digital counterparts. In this case, we will examine the dice (of which 2, 6-sided dice are needed to play *Catan* (1995)), Resources (or the cards given to players when the dice signify that a piece of terrain they are attached to is producing material), and the terrain itself (where the resources originate).

Table 5. The centrality changes of the most central non-human objects in a game of *Catan* (1995) by modality.

	Dice	Resources	Terrain
1-TT	21.89%	44.06%	38.45%
1-iPad	24.04%	26.51%	10.74%
2-TT	23.22%	53.57%	38.13%
2-iPad	22.97%	18.30%	10.61%
3-TT	19.26%	44.12%	36.26%
3-iPad	21.89%	12.45%	38.45%
iPad average	**22.96%**	**19.09%**	**19.93%**
TT average	**21.46%**	**47.25%**	**37.61%**

With regard to dice, when on the tabletop, these are the first object that players touch and the last object that players touch (when they hand them off to another player). As such, within any given turn, there are 2 points within which the dice will be handled. The result of this is that the dice are routinely central to human activity. In the iPad version of the game, the dice are the first object a player touches (as a UI element). As a result, the centrality of the dice should go down but what occurs is that the dice are central to the iPad because it begins a slew of non-human to non-human associations. This results in the dice having a slightly higher centrality within the iPad game simply due to the loss of human centrality in the iPad games themselves.

With regard to resources, these are generated in card form and handed as a material piece of the game to players when they receive them. As a result, they are central because they form an essential component of the chores of the game. Dice are rolled, players must then look at the numbers of the board, the resources attached to the numbers, and where players may have a village or a town. Players then give those cards to the appropriate players. Yet, within the iPad version, players touch the dice icon and the game performs these chores and generates the resources for the players as needed. The result is that for the resources object, the centrality of the resources declines by almost 50% overall. This points to a central point within which players could be made to be more central, and thus more included in the maintanance of the game state.

With regard to the terrain, much like that of the resources, the terrain is the thing that generates them. So, when the dice are rolled, players must associate with the terrain and their proximity to humans makes them a powerfully central figure during the tabletop game. This is different than that of the iPad version where, again, their centrality is diminished due their being maintained by automation and thus are less central to the environment as a whole. The consistency of this points to [7]'s tensions and to [41] in that players simply press buttons and do not pay attention to what is being automated and do not have to really know how to play the game at all.

Table 6. In this table, the % difference from iPad to TT is observed in Human-to-Human, Non-Human-to-Human, Human-to-Non-Human, and Non-Human-to-Non-Human Associations. Additional data is provided for overall changes per session.

Game	H2H	NH2H	H2NH	NH2NH	Total
1 - iPad	228	572	735	448	1983
1 - TT	235	1096	1479	1360	4170
Changes	−1.51%	−31.41%	−33.60%	−50.44%	−35.54%
2 - iPad	35	442	732	884	2093
2 - TT	110	1191	722	1265	3288
Changes	−51.72%	−45.87%	0.69%	−17.73%	−22.21%
3 - iPad	176	585	1654	2156	4571
3 - TT	125	1157	715	1153	3150
Changes	16.94%	−32.84%	39.64%	30.31%	18.40%
Total	909	5043	6037	7266	19255

Non-Human to Human Differences Between Mode of Play. A counterintuitive thought process is how non-human objects communicate or provide information to humans. Remember that these objects are formative in terms of teaching humans to play and maintaining rules themselves [41]. Dispensing with centrality for a more raw number, edge creation. Edges are literally verticies or objects associating with one another. If we examine Table 6, we can see the number of edges created by the type of association.

The different types of associations are Human-to-Human (the SNA central unit of measurement), Non-human-to-Human, Human-to-Non-Human (or objects providing information to humans and humans providing information to non-humans), and Non-human-to-Non-Human. In terms of edge creation, the creation of data in a network analysis, we can see very plainly that nearly all of the associations at the table are hybrid in some manner. Interestingly, in the iPad game there are always fewer associations created, regardless of the amount of time played. Remember that almost all of the iPad games took longer than that of the tabletop games. The reason for this is that because humans were not associating with non-humans as often in the iPad games, the average number of edges went down. In most cases, this went down by 20–35% with exception to session 3 where the game went on for so long that their edges exceeded that of the tabletop game.

As a result, the centrality of these objects is a passive way to see if the materiality, if the objects, if the bits are helping to maintain the game state or if the automation has essentially taken over. This can be observed by simply looking at edge creation or by examining the centrality of non-human or human actants within the network. These are just a few of the differences observed within the game state of 6 games of *Catan* (1995) and they are powerful in that they show us a tangible impact on human centrality to the game state. But what do these observations really mean? And further, how does one use AM in design?

6   Discussion

In this section, we discuss our findings. First, we ask the question, "what does it mean to not be central?" For example, if human centrality in a game of *Catan* (1995) is lost by a factor of 14%, what does that mean? AM is a method that allows a social moment to not only be taken apart, but made plain, inventoried, and quantified. Future steps will be discussed. Finally, we offer some suggestions on how to use AM for design.

6.1   What Does It Mean to Be Not Central?

Understanding how human centrality shifts between modalities of play is a useful heuristic for the design computer-mediated systems. It is useful because it allows designers to understand precisely how humans create and bridge different nodes of a network, in this case, how the chores and bits of play shift. But it is not the numeric data itself that is important, it is the meaning behind those data. It is useful to see those numbers but they are not empirical, they are the result of observation in as much as qualitative data is. They are not generalizable, they are not really measuring anything, instead, they are descriptive numeric qualities that could be used in quantitative analyses.

The understanding enabled through AM allows designers to not only understand their users better, but to understand the materiality of the activity as well. If centrality lowers for humans, what could be done to bring it back? Is it the addition of new UI elements? Is it allowing the users to maintain the game state? But in affording for manual maintenance, how does one do that? The potential for these sorts of activities are such that entirely new kinds of interactivity within board games are possible. And by fostering those new kinds of activities, the circle of board games influencing new computer programmers to create new types of play will now create new types of play for board games inside of digital spaces. But this is getting in to how to use AM for design itself.

6.2   How to Use AM for Design

Generally, the greatest lesson learned from this analysis is that making things more automated means that humans will disconnect from the game. This is important because not only are the bits and chores socializing and social maintaining entities, their attachment to humans themselves keep players, or users in the case of software, focused on the task that the artifact is meant to replicate. Or to put this another way, users are disconnected from the task, game, artifact, or space use is meant to occur in. As noted above, centrality is a measure, but a descriptive one. It provides a description that can be intuited by gifted designers but with AM, we can see how much and in what direction.

So the trick then is to figure out how to use these data. The first way to use these data is how the data were used here – comparison of modality. Since any program is a theory of human-action [27] or an artifact meant to represent a task [4], a way to use AM is to catalog the activity that the product is meant to replicate while the theory of that activity is being developed. We can then perform the analysis of how that activity different and make adjustments. As said above, this could mean new UI elements, modes of interactivity, or even new kinds of hardware.

AM expands the Task-Artifact cycle by providing researchers a way to extract certain kinds of implicit assumptions. For example, with *Catan* (1995), there is a green check-mark on the iPad interface that players must always click on to show that the user is sure that they want to perform that action. This is an important point, and a very central piece for the iPad versions of the game. Much of the work this check-mark was doing was invisible. For the game itself, due to automation, performing an action would allow the user to see the consequences of their action. If the UI afforded for all actions to be taken and then be taken back, users could learn what cards are being drawn, resources that might be generated, or what other cards other users may have.

And so the work of the check-mark was paramount in not only slowing the game down, but getting around the issues relating to automation. To put this another way, the check-mark was a tremendous choking point for accessing the bits and chores of play because of the medium it was being played on. AM shows that this check-mark is responsible for a huge loss of centrality for humans themselves. If the design of the *Catan* (1995) app could be changed then, much of that UI element would need to be unpacked and its power would need to be redistributed within the user interface somehow. This analysis is fine for building new products but what would it mean for existing ones?

For existing products, AM can be performed to learn about how a product needs to evolve versus how users would like it to evolve. The release of a product starts this cycle of constraint-based innovation around limitations of that product and the development of new products that meet that evolution [3,4]. This is exemplified in the evolution of the word processor from typewrite simulator to its current iteration as a collection of tasks revolving around the concept of text. AM can provide a description of how products are changing and evolving. By also collecting data based on the use of ancillary products used during a specific product's use, new affordances, new development possibilities, and possible partnerships can also be evaluated in tandem.

Finally, AM can be used to explore existing activities before development begins. For example, the games of *Catan* (1995) that I observed allowed me to understand how humans play a role in the maintenance of a game system. In looking at the way that play developed over the course of just 3 games, I had an idea of how computation could be used to replicate many of the central components of the game. However, what aspects of the game could or should be replicated are not readily apparent. By using AM as an exploratory method, what exactly could be computer-mediated should become more obvious as more and more games are added to the data to examine. This deployment of AM also allows for more involvement with other disciplines as different types of researchers engage that research.

The last way to deploy AM is to deploy it in existing organizations and gather network data from independent contexts repeatedly. For example, word processor use in co-located groups assignments versus distributed collaborations of research teams is going to be somewhat different and rely on many other kinds of tools. The same type of activity is being performed so collecting repeated uses will provide more and more stable representations of those data. Once those data are collected across disparate languages, cultures, ages, and other demographic considerations, the similarities of these networks will provide useful insight for possible features to include in product development.

7   Conclusion

We began by outlining a relationship between digital play and analog play. Board games, specifically war games developed in the 1800s, had a massive impact on the way that digital gaming developed. That relationship has come full circle in that board games, inspired by video games, are being digitized so that the most popular modality of play at current – digital play – can contain board gaming as well. But, there are lingering tensions within digital gaming that are antithetical to the design of digital translations of board games.

For the most part, these tensions can be overlooked, dealt with, and simply ignored. And perhaps ignoring them works for now; however, much like that of the paradox of the active user [5], the eventual need to unpack the paradox in order to deal with the weight of what is being ignored will become an ever increasing tension in design. For this, we presented Association Mapping (AM), a modification of social-network analysis that simply allows everything within an area to be an agentive object.

In doing this, every part of a use space becomes a numeric entity that contributes a known quantity to the formation of that use space. By comparing those numbers between modalities, designers can see the impact of their design and potentially make adjustments. We have shown where centrality was lost, how centrality was lost, and the consequences of that loss.

But this process of analysis was cumbersome in terms of effort, time, and volume of files created. SNA is a cumbersome method still nascent in its deployment in human-computer interaction. We have an opportunity to disassemble it in order to re-purpose it as AM has. In doing so, HCI researchers can pair AM with object-recognizing video capturing tools. The process of coding can then be automated for more rapid results that can be analyzed and re-tested quickly. More research is needed, more development is needed to make this a reality.

References

1. Baerg, A.: It's game time: speed, acceleration, and the digital sports game. Temporalités. Revue de sciences sociales et humaines **1**(25) (2017)
2. Bogost, I.: Play Anything: The Pleasure of Limits, the Uses of Boredom, and the Secret of Games. Basic Books, New York (2016)
3. Carroll, J.M., Campbell, R.L.: Artifacts as psychological theories: the case of human-computer interaction. Behav. Inf. Technol. **8**(4), 247–256 (1989)
4. Carroll, J.M., Kellogg, W.A., Rosson, M.B.: The task-artifact cycle. In: Designing Interaction: Psychology at the Human-Computer Interface, pp. 74–102. Cambridge University Press, Cambridge, England (1991)
5. Carroll, J.M., Rosson, M.B.: Paradox of the active user. In: Interfacing Thought: Cognitive Aspects of Human-Computer Interaction, pp. 80–111. MIT Press, Cambridge, Massachusetts, USA (1987)
6. Dear, B.: The Friendly Orange Glow: The Untold Story of the Rise of Cyberculture. Vintage (2017)
7. DIGRA: Digitising boardgames: Issues and tensions. Digital Games Research Association (2015)
8. Duffy, O.: Board games' golden age: sociable, brilliant and driven by the internet. https://www.theguardian.com/technology/2014/nov/25/board-games-internet-playstation-xbox
9. Duk: Exploded view diagram. https://en.wikipedia.org/wiki/Exploded-view_drawing
10. Echtler, F.: Surfacestreams: a content-agnostic streaming toolkit for interactive surfaces. In: The 31st Annual ACM Symposium on User Interface Software and Technology Adjunct Proceedings, pp. 10–12 (2018)
11. Engberg-Pedersen, A.: Empire of Chance. Harvard University Press, Cambridge (2015)
12. Foucault, M.: The Order of Things: An Archeology of the Human Sciences. Random House, New York (1994)
13. Graves, C., Morgan, G.: Secrets of blackmoor (2019). http://www.secretsofblackmoor.com

14. Heyck, H.: Age of System: Understanding the Development of Modern Social Science. Johns Hopkins University Press, Baltimore (2015)
15. Huizinga, J.: Homo Ludens. Routledge & Kegan Paul Ltd. MA, USA, Boston (1954)
16. Huynh, D.N.T., Raveendran, K., Xu, Y., Spreen, K., MacIntyre, B.: Art of defense: a collaborative handheld augmented reality board game. In: Proceedings of the 2009 ACM SIGGRAPH Symposium on Video Games, pp. 135–142 (2009)
17. Ip, J., Cooperstock, J.: To virtualize or not? The importance of physical and virtual components in augmented reality board games. In: Anacleto, J.C., Fels, S., Graham, N., Kapralos, B., Saif El-Nasr, M., Stanley, K. (eds.) ICEC 2011. LNCS, vol. 6972, pp. 452–455. Springer, Heidelberg (2011). https://doi.org/10.1007/978-3-642-24500-8_64
18. Jerz, D.G.: Somewhere nearby is colossal cave: examining will crowther's original 'adventure' in code and in Kentucky. Digital Humanit. Q. 1(2), 2 (2007)
19. Kiilerich, L.: Automating board games (2017)
20. LaLone, N.: A tale of dungeons & dragons and the origins of the game platform. Analog Game Stud. 3(6) (2019)
21. Lalone, N.J.: Association Mapping: Social Network Analysis with Humans and Non-Humans. Ph.D. thesis, The Pennsylvania State University (2018)
22. Latour, B.: The Pasteurization of France. Harvard University Press, Cambridge (1993)
23. Latour, B.: We Have Never Been Modern. Harvard University Press, Cambridge (2012)
24. Latour, B., Jensen, P., Venturini, T., Grauwin, S., Boullier, D.: The whole is always smaller than its parts'-a digital test of Gabriel Tardes' monads. Br. J. Sociol. 63(4), 590–615 (2012)
25. Lingis, A.: The Community of Those Who Have Nothing in Common. Indiana University Press, Bloomington (1994)
26. Malone, T.: What makes computer games fun? In: Proceedings of the Joint Conference on Easier and More Productive Use of Computer Systems. (Part-II): Human Interface and the User Interface, vol. 1981, p. 143 (1981)
27. Naur, P.: Knowing and the Mystique of Logic and Rules: including True Statements in Knowing and Action* Computer Modelling of Human Knowing Activity* Coherent Description as the Core of Scholarship and Science, vol. 18. Springer Science & Business Media (1995). https://doi.org/10.1007/978-94-015-8549-1
28. Neill, W.J.: Beyond the balm of communicative planning: can actor-network theory insights and a more agonistic practice help unlock creative 'post-conflict' potential?: Towards a renewed research horizon in Northern Ireland. Plan. Pract. Res. 32(3), 319–332 (2017)
29. Nicholson, S., Begy, J.: A framework for exploring tablet-based tabletop games. In: Proceedings of the Canadian Game Studies Association Annual Conference: Borders Without Boundaries (2014)
30. Peterson, J.: Playing at the World: A History of Simulating Wars, People and Fantastic Adventures, from Chess to Role-Playing Games. Unreason Press, San Diego (2012)
31. Rogerson, M.J., Gibbs, M., Smith, W.: "I love all the bits" the materiality of board games. In: Proceedings of the 2016 CHI Conference on Human Factors in Computing Systems, pp. 3956–3969 (2016)
32. Shannon, C.E.: XXII. Programming a computer for playing chess. London, Edinb. Dublin Philos. Mag. J. Sci. 41(314), 256–275 (1950)

33. Smith, S.W.: An experiment in bibliographic mark-up: parsing metadata for xml export. In: Smythe, R.N., Noble, A. (eds.) Proceedings of the 3rd Annual Workshop on Librarians and Computers. LAC 2010, vol. 3, pp. 422–431. Paparazzi Press, Milan Italy (2010). http://dx.doi.org/99.0000/woot07-S422
34. Stein, A.: Playing the game on television. Sports Video Games. Routledge, London, pp. 115–137 (2013)
35. Streitz, N., Nixon, P.: The disappearing computer. Commun. ACM **48**(3), 32–35 (2005)
36. de Tarde, G.: Monadology and Sociology. Re. Press, Melbourne (2011)
37. Thomas, W.: Rational Action: The Sciences of Policy in Britain and America, 1940–1960. MIT Press, Cambridge (2015)
38. Totten, C.A.L.: Strategos: A Series of American Games of War. Game [Board] (1880), d. Appleton and Company, New York City, NY, USA (1880)
39. Toups, Z.O., Lalone, N., Alharthi, S.A., Sharma, H.N., Webb, A.M.: Making maps available for play: analyzing the design of game cartography interfaces. ACM Trans. Comput. Hum. Interact. (TOCHI) **26**(5), 1–43 (2019)
40. Toups, Z.O., LaLone, N., Spiel, K., Hamilton, B.: Paper to pixels: a chronicle of map interfaces in games. In: Proceedings of the 2020 ACM Designing Interactive Systems Conference, pp. 1433–1451 (2020)
41. Trammell, A.: Magic: the gathering in material and virtual space: an ethnographic approach toward understanding players who dislike online play. In: Meaningful Play 2010 Proceedings, pp. 1–21 (2010)
42. Wasserman, S., Faust, K., et al.: Social Network Analysis: Methods and Applications. Cambridge University Press, Cambridge (1994)
43. Xu, Y., Barba, E., Radu, I., Gandy, M., MacIntyre, B.: Chores are fun: understanding social play in board games for digital tabletop game design. In: DiGRA Conference (2011)

Hitboxes: A Survey About Collision Detection in Video Games

Lazaros Lazaridis, Maria Papatsimouli, Konstantinos-Filippos Kollias, Panagiotis Sarigiannidis(iD), and George F. Fragulis(✉)(iD)

Department of Electrical and Computer Engineering,
University of Western Macedonia, Kozani, Hellas
emplazaros@hotmail.com, m.papatsimoulh@kastoria.teiwm.gr,
kfkollias@gmail.com, {psarigiannidis,gfragulis}@uowm.gr

Abstract. Over the past decades, video games have become a mainstream form of entertainment and are increasingly used for other purposes such as education or health. This paper surveys recent research and practice in Collision detection in computer gaming that is the detection when two or more objects collide with each other and it plays a crucial role in almost every game as the majority of them are about one thing hitting another. Ground for your feet; a sword and a warrior's body; a golf ball and a golf club. Hence we have a lot of hitboxes, an invisible geometry around objects that inform them when a collision takes place. There are several methods which solve this kind of problems but what is proven so far from the research is that computers are unexpectedly bad at dealing with collisions. As a result, it is sensible different games take dissimilar approaches on how the way hitboxes work. In this paper we will be focused on Bounding Volumes Hierarchy (BVH) class analyzing three basic methods: OBB, AABB and k-DOP along with some improvements that have been done throughout the years and how these are applied in modern video games.

Keywords: Collision detection · Hitboxes · AABB-OBB algorithms · k-DOP · Multiplayer environment

1 Introduction

A hitbox is an invisible box-like area that when penetrated, counts as a "hit". It's different than the model (the visible character and his colors that you see). The hitbox is meant to compensate for lag and movement. When a character is moving, his hitbox is usually farther from the model. When a character is still, his hitbox is located directly on top of his model. Contrary to the name, a hitbox is actually composed of several boxes that represent the character's different areas (head, arm, torso). In Fig. 1 there is a picture of hitboxes from First Person shooter games. As these models are sitting still, the hitboxes are right on top of them.

© Springer Nature Switzerland AG 2021
X. Fang (Ed.): HCII 2021, LNCS 12789, pp. 314–326, 2021.
https://doi.org/10.1007/978-3-030-77277-2_24

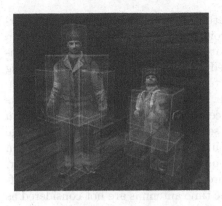 

Fig. 1. Hitboxes in FPS game (fair use)

The main reason they use a hitbox for collision detection is that computing a hit based on geometry is increasingly expensive as the geometry gets more complicated. Typically there are actually multiple bounding boxes that are used. Partly, this is because a hit test against a rectangular box uses simple math and is very fast. If it misses the outermost box, they can shortcut the process and simply stop checking any further. A hit on the outermost box prompts a check for a closer box. However, they also don't want to recurse too far, or else it becomes too expensive (in time spent). At some point they must say, "that's close enough - it's a hit!".

One technique sometimes used for this is called an "octree", where 3D space is defined in terms of a recursive hierarchy of cubes. An octree is a tree data structure in which each internal node has exactly eight children. Octrees are most often used to partition a three-dimensional space by recursively subdividing it into eight octants (Fig. 2). If two objects are in completely different branches of the octree, there is no possibility of them colliding so the detection can halt there. As they get closer to one another, the hit test becomes increasingly refined until the system knows that they have intersected or collided.

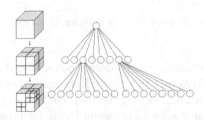

Fig. 2. An octree model - Wikipedia (fair use)

Different kinds of hitboxes are used in each video game. Despite their name, hitboxes usually are rectangles for 2D games but some games use circles, such as the platform-games, as these shapes are better to avoid unexpected hits on corners whereas in 3D games cuboid or spheroidal shapes are used respectively. In terms of animated objects, the hitboxes that are attached, follow them throughout the screen and it is common to be used different hitboxes for each moving part of the same object for the accuracy to be better secured during motion. However, video games are about perception, so it is not always desirable for hitboxes to cover the whole object. For instance, the hitbox of a ship in a shoot 'em up game is far smaller than the user could see. This enables the player to dodge projectiles otherwise he would have hit, resulting in spectacular near misses. On the other hand, not all parts of a specific object are necessarily accounted for. For instance, trucks and spaceships have antennas and cables that are not significant for the vehicle. As a result, most of the time antennas are not considered as objects that collide with another one. But, what if a game takes them as normal objects? In this case, a collision should be bendable as the antennas would not be destroyed but are bent for a short period until the collision reaches the end.

Many models of collision detection have been developed so far and they are separated into basic categories as is shown in Fig. 3. In virtual environments, much of the work done is supported by polygonal models and in this survey, we will examine approaches that belong to Bounding Volume Hierarchies (BVH) since algorithms in this class has been used to speed up collision detection both in broad and narrow phases by reducing the pair number of objects that are needed to be checked for contact [16].

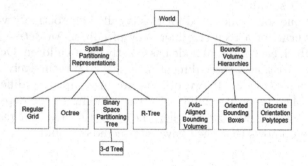

Fig. 3. A basic taxonomy of collision detection algorithms

Even though hitboxes are used to detect collisions, they also can be used to rule how the world behaves by triggering effects and events. Consider a spaceship with three hitboxes. The smallest will be used to detect collisions on rocks, starports, and any other obstacles. The second will be larger than a ship and it will detect the near-misses projectiles and a successful sound will be triggered. The third will be far larger, three times the ship for example, and will trigger an "echoing" sound when she passes through a narrow passage. Euro Truck Simulator 2 is a good example of this, as the truck passes through a tunnel the engine sound is changing matching better to the real state. The same is happening when other vehicles are passing around you. However, this kind of use of hitboxes is beyond the scope of this survey.

2 Hitboxes Modeling

Despite the shape complexity of a model, either 2D or 3D, it is preferred the use a simple shape as a hitbox. The computational load for collision detection is quite heavy and in gaming, there is a high possibility of multiple collisions taking place at the same time. For n objects in a scene, the computational load for an algorithm, typically, will be $O(n^2)$ which is computationally intensive, especially when n is large. There are several kinds of hitbox techniques such as AABB (Axis-Aligned Bounding Boxes), OBB (Oriented Bounding Boxes), Spheroidal hitboxes (including spheres), DOP (Discrete Oriented Polytope) etc. In general, performance can be measured by Eq. (1)

$$T = Nu * Cu + Nv * Cv \tag{1}$$

where T equals the total cost for detecting interference between objects that depicted by a bounding volume hierarchy; Nu equals with the volumes number, usually called primitives, that are updated during the traversal of hierarchies; Cu equals the cost of updating a primitive because of motion; Nv depict the number of overlapping tests performed in total and finally Cv is the cost of performing an overlapping test between of primitive nodes from the hierarchy [11,17,22].

However, a newer version of Eq. (2) has been used which separates bounding volumes and primitives

$$T = Nu * Cu + Nv * Cv + Np * Cp \tag{2}$$

where Nu now is the number of updated bounding volumes due to motion; Cu is the corresponding cost of updating; Np represents the number of primitives tested for interference and Cp is the cost of corresponding interference [24,25]. Recent research includes real-time requirement [27] by using collision detection algorithms for both high-level accuracy and real-time requirement by using particle swarm optimization [41] which is proposed by Eberhart and Kennedy [14] in the field of computational intelligence. This kind of algorithm has been widely applied in virtual environments, signal processing, and other fields due to its simplicity, convenient realization, and reduces parameters number.

2.1 Oriented Bounding Box (OBB)

As OBB can be defined as a general cuboid box that consists of six faces and the encompassing object is relative to axis orientation. One of the most important features is the fact that its direction is not fixed. This means it is feasible to surround the encompassing object as best as possible to its shape [34,40]. In comparison with AABB (an algorithm discussed in the next section), this method utilizes more resources but it is a better fit and it can be used effectively to reduce the amount of intersection test boxes and the fundamental geometric elements. Moreover, if an object rotates, all other OBB boxes are executing the same rotation [29]. Although OBB is essentially an AABB with a different orientation, an issue was emerged about finding a minimal enclosing box for an object. In the 2D environment, an optimal rectangle can be computed in linear by using a method called *rotating calipers* which is proposed from Toussaint [36]. For the 3D environment, an algorithm was published by O'Rourke in 1985 [31] with computing time complexity $O(N_v^3)$ but in practice, it is too slow to use and also it is extremely hard to be implemented [10,15]. Instead, heuristic approaches are preferred and the most popular ones are based either on Principal Component Analysis (PCA) [21] or on brute-force search. More advanced approaches have been also proposed such as formulating the search of a minimal OBB volume as an optimization problem to be defined in various ways [12].

2.2   Axis-Aligned Bounding Box (AABB)

In the AABB algorithm a hitbox is defined as the smallest orthogonal box which embraces as best as possible the contained object and its edges are axis-aligned to the environment [11,37]. This method speeds up the collision detection process as its structure is quite simple, consumes less memory, and is updated faster. In general, it is based on the intersection test between bounding boxes rather than between objects [32,39]. The hitbox is non-rotated and it is best used in 2D games and in terms of 3D games it is selected only for performance reasons where it is possible.

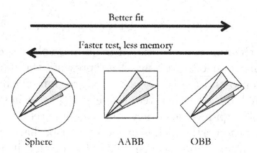

Fig. 4. Depending on selection each bounding box has its own pron and cons. In general, perfection costs more resources.

However, tests had shown that AABB trees are slower compared to OBB trees for performing complex overlap model tests for rigid motion and deformation, thus research for efficient collision detection was done (see e.g. [11]. To provide a better comprehension of running time from AABB, in [38] the authors estimated the expected running time under different conditions. Because of their nature, the same techniques are applied for both rigid [33] and deformable objects, e.g.

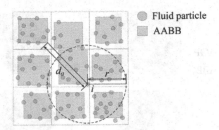

Fig. 5. Neighbor search in uniform grid (2D space) in which determining whether the AABB is in influence range r of the i particle. In this case it is clearly that upper left and upper right grids are out of scope. Image obtained from National Institute of Technology, Akita College (fair use)

fluids. Particularly, in terms of fluid computer graphics which is applied mainly in the entertainment field in general, Axis-Aligned Bounding Boxes are usually preferred because such algorithms rely on a grid-based space (Fig. 4). In this method, an AABB is embracing particles that existed in a grid (not necessarily all of them), is obtained, and finally, it is determined if the particular AABB is within the influence range of the specified particle. This method called neighborhood search for the uniform grid using an AABB [35] and depicted with more details in Fig. 5.

2.3 Discrete Oriented Polytope (DOP)

The k-DOP algorithm generalize the hitbox of the AABB method as the axes of a DOP hitbox do not have to be orthogonal and it is possible to have more discrete directional axes than the dimensions of a selected space. This structure leads to a tighter hitbox comparing with other Bounding Volume Hierarchies such as AABB or OBB. Depending on the number k hitbox can be more precise as possible to the contained object, especially to the complicated ones. In Fig. 6 there are several examples of k-DOP hitboxes. A 6-DOP is an AABB in 3D space, with orientation vectors determined by the positive and negative coordinate axes [22]. In other words, k-DOP provides a convex hitbox by using k predefined levels. One of the main drawbacks of this method is focused on its expensively recalculating cost of an object which rotates and translates in a scene, whereas k-planes cannot be rotated [30]. To overcome such hurdles hybrid methods are proposed as well, e.g. the Three-layer HBVH algorithm [19, 28].

3 Using Hitbox Algorithms in Video Games

Different kinds of video games have different demands for hitboxes and the most important thing is to choose the right one to make a great game. In this section, several commercial video games will be discussed to see what hitboxes are used in each case. For instance, a truck hauling a trailer as it is shown in Fig. 7, all

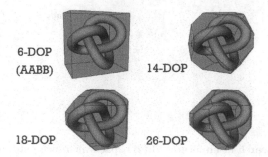

6-DOP
(AABB)   14-DOP

18-DOP   26-DOP

Fig. 6. Examples of k-DOP bounding boxes. Bigger value of k means higher embracing precision and increased computation cost. Image obtained from Stefan Kimmerle University of Tubingen (fair use)

the hitboxes that are being used are rectangular except tires which are using k-DOP or ellipsoid ones. As for the truck three main cuboid zones are shown on each side: main body, bottom base, and spoiler. On the other hand, a trailer is a different object so hitboxes include different parts of it: main body, bottom extra space, and landing gear. Precision is quite straightforward and they cover the whole truck satisfactorily. Only the small and tiny parts are excluded such as front bottom antennas, mirrors, and other tiny projections. Extra caution needs to be taken as in some cases the landing gear was hit the road when specific conditions were taken place, e.g. when the trailer is found at the beginning of a steep downhill or it passes towards a deep road hole. Another use of the hitbox is to define the durability of an object's part. In this way, you could define hit zones where a specific part of an e.g. vehicle is softer than another one. Example of games which use this method is the World of Tanks [8] and World of Warships [9] from Wargaming.Net [7].

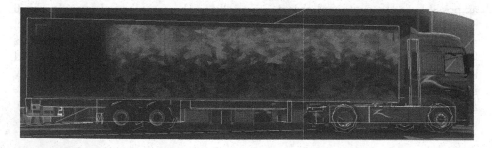

Fig. 7. A truck with a trailer in Euro Truck Simulator 2 [1]. Several hitboxes have been applied for different truck parts. Image obtained from https://forum.scssoft.com (fair use)

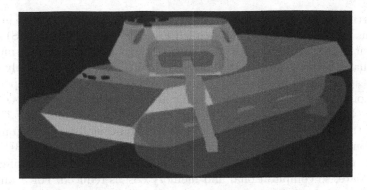

Fig. 8. Example of hitzones for a battle tank. Image obtained from the World of Tanks [8] (fair use)

In this case, an object consists of several hitboxes where each hitbox includes a specific object's hit zone. In this way, a projectile (or maybe a crush) can or cannot affect the specific part which hit, depending on the projectile's capabilities (velocity, angle, ammunition type, etc.). In Fig. 8 a battle tank is divided into five basic hit zones where the red zone is harder to be penetrated compared to the green one which is the softest. The same hitboxes are used to detect the collision on rocks, houses, fences, trees, other tanks etc. However, not all parts from the tank are considered solid objects (e.g. the embedded parts such as shovels and camouflage nets), something that affects the collide precision.

3.1 Precision of Detecting Collisions

Almost all modern games are trying to simulate physics in a sophisticated way. Collisions can be far varied from video game to video game, from the most basic collision in a dungeon crawler to advanced Kerbal Space Program [2] or Train Sim World [5] with complex calculations. A platform game usually does not demand high precision, the characters always maintain a safe distance from walls, and the grounds are considered as a flat level or distinct obstacles such as ladders, steps, and cuboid objects. On the other hand, open-world games also simulate the surrounding environment which includes whatever there is in nature itself, e.g. trees, lakes, cliffs because we have finite capabilities to fully simulate each part of the environment, even the player's object itself. It is practically not possible to simulate all these and some conventions must be taken into account, especially in a multiplayer game as the computational load will be enormous and the scene would not probably be updated timely. The most common object that is not considered a solid one is tree foliage. Although their textures are getting more and more accurate with better graphics, foliage is not considered a critical part of the gameplay in terms of collision. Even in simulation games, some parts are neglected in favor of reduced computation load. In Euro Truck Simulator2 [1] the mirrors of the truck do not count as a solid object. Indeed, this kind of collision is not considered an important one and does not reduce realism.

Nevertheless, there are games in which precision plays a major role in winning conditions and this kind of game is called First Person Shooters (FPS). It is the genre that contains the most varied hitboxes and the chosen ones must work hand-in-hand with the game to feel more realistic. The process to apply hitboxes on a character model involves the lining up of boxes or ellipsoid shapes to each model's joints. For instance, if the graphic around the leg has a radius e.g. 15 cm along the bone, then the hitbox, in this case, will have a radius of 15 cm and a length that is the same as the leg (Fig. 9). Additionally, axis-alignment and orientation is an important issue for what method to choose, AABB or OBB boxes. In most cases, Axis-Aligned boxes are preferred as their primary axes do not rotate, so computational and memory cost is reduced. For example, the 'down' direction is always the same vector. However, in shooter games, capsule-style hitboxes are frequently used because both capsules are computationally less expensive to intersect with each other and at the same time they offer better precision [23].

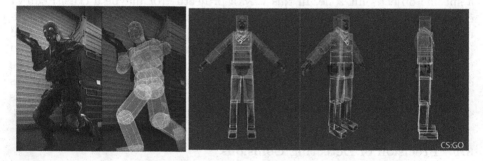

Fig. 9. Left image: Applied hitboxes on a character model from an updated version of Counter-Strike. In this version capsule-based hitboxes are used as they offer gain in computation cost and greater accuracy. Right image: Early hitbox builds of Counter-Strike, cuboid hitboxes were used. Image obtained from [4] (fair use)

3.2 Balancing Issues

Several balancing issues have come up that decide how a game can be fairly played by all character players. Regarding hitboxes, the most usual issue that must be confronted is their size. Not all character players have the same size and this behavior is inherited also by the corresponding hitboxes. In single-player games, bigger hitboxes can be applied on tough bosses as, usually, they have more health and they are considerably stronger with bigger damage. In multiplayer games though, all playable characters should have the same hitbox size otherwise bigger ones will always be avoided by the players. A very good example is the Quake Champions [3] as this game includes varied models in terms of size. Lighter playable character hitboxes are expanded by double, to make players easier to hit them and also suit the players' expectations on how

Fig. 10. Quake Champions like using chunky hitboxes in order to make character models easier to hit. Image obtained from [4] (fair use)

hard a target is to be hit. Another issue is about movement mechanics and game speed. The faster a character player moves, the harder is to be hit. If you combine this behavior with 'tight' hitboxes upon the adversary model might affect the game negatively since the target is either overly hard to hit or make players think the collision detection is quite bad. Very fast-paced games such as Quake Champions [3] is frequently using quite chunky hitboxes (Fig. 10) as this kind of game emphasizes fast movement techniques. However, other games such as World of Tanks [8] or War Thunder [6] accuracy plays a significantly more important role in contrast with easy-to-hit targets although war tanks greatly differ from each other in terms of size.

4 Multiplayer Environment

Many games can be played both as single-player and in multiplayer mode with, usually, small teams. In networked games, the synchronization among players must be as accurate as possible, especially in Massively Multiplayer Online (MMO) games. These kind of games are providing a Distributed Virtual Environment (DVE) that is used to represent a virtual world which can be explored by a big amount of players. Each player owns an avatar and also there are additional objects such as constructions, animals, weather conditions, and so on. Except for games, other applications that uses DVEs are training ones [13,20] and Computer Supported Collaborative Work (CSCW) [18,26].

5 Conclusions

Unfortunately, hitboxes do not behave as we expect as there are cases, for example, in which an object cannot land a successful blow hit by using a jab attack because its hitbox is quite small even if it is covering the whole object exactly. Although it is unrealistic for a jab to have an exaggerated hitbox, it is necessary though for the player to be satisfied as a skillful one. These kinds of problems are particularly difficult to be discovered. In fact, collision is an infamously difficult field within computer science. It is still an open problem and there is not a completely acceptable solution to date. While it is simple for humans to work out when a thing is overlapping another, describing that in maths is very difficult and adds a significant extra processing computational load to the game along with other game's features, thus modern games are using tricks to reduce the load. We are working on a Unity engine that supports the C# programming language and what we have been trying to achieve is to create an efficient algorithm that will predict as best as possible how many objects in a scene would collide with each other so that computational load will be reduced significantly and at the same time the saved burden will be used to create as much as accurate hitboxes to each object's shape.

References

1. Euro truck simulator 2. https://eurotrucksimulator2.com
2. Kerbal space program. https://www.kerbalspaceprogram.com/
3. Quake champions official website. https://quake.bethesda.net/en
4. Olckers, A.: The Theory Behind First-Person Hitboxes (2020). https://levelup. gitconnected.com/the-theory-behind-first-person-hitboxes-d593ecc6de9
5. Train sim world. https://live.dovetailgames.com/live/train-sim-world
6. War thunder. https://warthunder.com
7. Wargaming.net. https://eu.wargaming.net/en
8. World of tanks. https://worldoftanks.eu/
9. World of warships. https://worldofwarships.eu/
10. Barequet, G., Har-Peled, S.: Efficiently approximating the minimum-volume bounding box of a point set in three dimensions. J. Algorithms **38**(1), 91–109 (2001)
11. Bergen, G.: Efficient collision detection of complex deformable models using AABB trees. J. Graph. Tools **2**(4), 1–13 (1997)
12. Chang, C.T., Gorissen, B., Melchior, S.: Fast oriented bounding box optimization on the rotation group so (3, r). ACM Trans. Graph. (TOG) **30**(5), 1–16 (2011)
13. Miller, D., Thorpe, J.A.: SIMNET: the advent of simulator networking. Proc. IEEE **83**(8), 1114–1123 (1995)
14. Eberhart, R., Kennedy, J.: A new optimizer using particle swarm theory. In: Proceedings of the 6th International Symposium on Micro Machine and Human Science, MHS 1995, pp. 39–43. IEEE (1995)
15. Ericson, C.: Real-Time Collision Detection. CRC Press (2004)
16. Figueiredo, M., Marcelino, L., Fernando, T.: A survey on collision detection techniques for virtual environments. In: Proceedings of the V Symposium in Virtual Reality, pp. 285–307 (2002)
17. Gottschalk, S., Lin, M.C., Manocha, D.: OBBtree: a hierarchical structure for rapid interference detection. In: Proceedings of the 23rd Annual Conference on Computer Graphics and Interactive Techniques, pp. 171–180 (1996)
18. Greenhalgh, C., Benford, S.: Massive: a distributed virtual reality system incorporating spatial trading. In: Proceedings of 15th International Conference on Distributed Computing Systems, pp. 27–34. IEEE (1995)

19. Guo, X., Zhang, Y., Liu, R., Wang, Y.: Efficient collision detection with a deformable model of an abdominal aorta. In: 2016 IEEE International Conference on Information and Automation (ICIA), pp. 927–932. IEEE (2016)
20. Gutmann, G., Konagaya, A.: Real-time inferencing and training of artificial neural network for adaptive latency negation in distributed virtual environments. In: 2020 International Congress on Human-Computer Interaction, Optimization and Robotic Applications (HORA), pp. 1–8. IEEE (2020)
21. Jolliffe, I.T., Trendafilov, N.T., Uddin, M.: A modified principal component technique based on the lasso. J. Comput. Graph. Stat. 12(3), 531–547 (2003)
22. Klosowski, J.T., Held, M., Mitchell, J.S., Sowizral, H., Zikan, K.: Efficient collision detection using bounding volume hierarchies of k-DOPs. IEEE Trans. Vis. Comput. Graph. 4(1), 21–36 (1998)
23. Kong, D., Liu, Y., Cui, N.: Collosion detection research based on capsule bounding. J. Comput. Inf. Syst. 10(7), 2743–2750 (2014)
24. Krishnan, S., Gopi, M., Lin, M., Manocha, D., Pattekar, A.: Rapid and accurate contact determination between spline models using ShelltTees. In: Computer Graphics Forum, vol. 17, pp. 315–326. Wiley Online Library (1998)
25. Larsson, T., Akenine-Möller, T.: Strategies for bounding volume hierarchy updates for ray tracing of deformable models. MRTC Report (2003)
26. Lei, Z., Huang, J., Li, Z., Wang, L., Cui, J., Tang, Z.: Research on collaborative technology in distributed virtual reality system. J. Phys: Conf. Ser. 960, 012016 (2018)
27. Liang, T., Song, W., Hou, T., Liu, L.l., Cao, W., Yan, Z.: Collision detection of virtual plant based on bounding volume hierarchy: a case study on virtual wheat. J. Integr. Agric. 17(2), 306–314 (2018)
28. Liu, Y., Wang, H., Yang, P.: A three-layer hybrid bounding volume hierarchy for collision detection. In: 7th International Conference on Computer Engineering and Networks, p. 53 (2017)
29. Ma, D., Ye, W., Li, Y.: Survey of box-based algorithms for collision detection. J. Syst. Simul. 18(4), 1058–1061 (2006)
30. Melero, F.J., Aguilera, Á., Feito, F.R.: Fast collision detection between high resolution polygonal models. Comput. Graph. 83, 97–106 (2019)
31. O'Rourke, J.: Finding minimal enclosing boxes. Int. J. Comput. Inf. Sci. 14(3), 183–199 (1985)
32. Raj Prasanth, D., Shunmugam, M.: Collision detection during planning for sheet metal bending by bounding volume hierarchy approaches. Int. J. Comput. Integr. Manuf. 31(9), 893–906 (2018)
33. Sukormo, N., Sulaiman, H., Pee, A., Bade, A., Yazid, R., Abdullasim, N.: The framework of collision detection for rigid bodies in the virtual environment. J. Phys. Conf. Ser. 1358, 012083 (2019)
34. Szauer, G.: Game Physics Cookbook. Packt Publishing Ltd. (2017)
35. Takeshita, D.: AABB pruning: pruning of neighborhood search for uniform grid using axis-aligned bounding box. J. Soc. Art Sci. 19(1), 1–8 (2020)
36. Toussaint, G.T.: Solving geometric problems with the rotating calipers. In: Proceedings of the IEEE MELECON, vol. 83, p. A10 (1983)
37. Van Verth, J.M., Bishop, L.M.: Essential Mathematics for Games and Interactive Applications. CRC Press (2015)
38. Weller, R., Klein, J., Zachmann, G.: A model for the expected running time of collision detection using AABB trees. In: EGVE, pp. 11–17 (2006)

39. Xiao-rong, W., Meng, W., Chun-Gui, L.: Research on collision detection algorithm based on AABB. In: 2009 5th International Conference on Natural Computation, vol. 6, pp. 422–424. IEEE (2009)
40. Yuanfeng, Z., Jun, M., Guanghua, X., et al.: Research on real-time collision detection based on hybrid hierarchical bounding volume. J. Syst. Simul. **20**(2), 372–377 (2008)
41. Zou, Y., Liu, P.X., Yang, C., Li, C., Cheng, Q.: Collision detection for virtual environment using particle swarm optimization with adaptive Cauchy mutation. Clust. Comput. **20**(2), 1765–1774 (2017). https://doi.org/10.1007/s10586-017-0815-6

Adaptive Gamification and Its Impact on Performance

Christian E. Lopez[1]([⊠]) and Conrad S. Tucker[2]

[1] Department of Computer Science, Lafayette College, Easton, PA 18042, USA
lopezbec@lafayette.edu
[2] Department of Mechanical Engineering, Carnegie Mellon University,
Pittsburgh, PA 15213, USA
conradt@andrew.cmu.edu

Abstract. The objective of this work is to measure the effects that adaptive and counter-adaptive gamified applications have on individuals' performance. Researchers have sought to explore how individuals' player type can be used to tailor gamification. However, existing studies do not measure the impact that adaptive gamification has on individuals' performance since they tend to focus on exploring the relationship between individuals' player type and their game element preferences. Consequently, a designer may spend valuable resources creating a gamified application and yet, not see any positive effects or even see negative effects on individuals' performance. In light of this gap, a randomized experiment was conducted in which participants' performance on (i) an adapted gamified application, (ii) a non-adapted gamified application, (iii) a non-gamified application, and (iv) a counter-adapted gamified application was analyzed. In this work, the game elements in the adapted and counter-adapted gamified applications were selected based on individuals' Hexad player type dimensions. The results revealed that the performance of individuals who interacted with the adapted gamified application was greater than any other group. In contrast, the performance of individuals who interacted with the counter-adapted gamified application was worse than any other group. This work provides empirical evidence on the effectiveness of adaptive gamification. Moreover, the results highlight the need to consider individuals' player type when designing gamified applications and the latent detrimental effects of not doing so.

Keywords: Gamification · Hexad player type · Adaptation

1 Introduction

The research community has gained increased interest in gamification to improve individuals' motivation [1–4]. In gamification, designers integrate game elements into their applications (e.g., Points, Leaderboards, Levels) to motivate individuals to perform a task or a series of tasks [5]. For example, in the health and wellness context, several studies have implemented gamification to motivate users to perform physical tasks in order to improve their physical fitness or health awareness [6–9].

© Springer Nature Switzerland AG 2021
X. Fang (Ed.): HCII 2021, LNCS 12789, pp. 327–341, 2021.
https://doi.org/10.1007/978-3-030-77277-2_25

Multiple studies indicate that the perception and preference of game elements differ at an individual level [10–15]. Studies also suggest that a gamified application that motives an individual might not have the same effect on another individual [9, 16]. These studies are in line with the Self-Determination Theory (SDT) and the Cognitive Evaluation Theory which indicate that the effects of a stimulus (e.g., game element) on an individual's motivation is mediated by his/her perception of the stimulus itself [17]. Because of these differences, researchers are exploring how individuals' game element preferences can be assessed using player type models [7, 13, 18–21]. Individuals' player type information can be used to adapt or personalize gamified applications [3, 15]. The concepts of adaptation and personalization are closely related since their objective is to tailor an application to provide an improved user experience [22]. Personalization is defined as the process where "*the content is tailored by the system to individuals' tastes*" [23]. While adaptation is when an application is used to "*tailor the interaction to different users in the same context*" [24].

While researchers are gaining interest in adaptive gamification, a recent literature review found that most of the studies to date only explore user modeling for future adaptation and do not measure the impact of adaptive gamification [3]. The few studies that do not focus on user modeling, only provide conceptual frameworks or little empirical evidence of the impact that adaptive gamification has on individuals [3, 13, 19, 21, 22, 25]. Hence, it still unclear if designers should spend valuable resources adapting an existing gamified application with the objective to improve an individual's performance. In light of the existing knowledge gap, a randomized between-subject experiment is conducted to explore the differences between participants' performance on (i) an adapted gamified application (i.e., an application that implements the game elements that are recommended for a given individual), (ii) a non-adapted gamified application (i.e., a *one-size-fits-all* application that implements all possible game elements), (iii) a non-gamified application (i.e., an application that does not implement any game elements), and (iv) a counter-adapted gamified application (i.e., an application that implements game elements that are not recommended for a given individual).

2   Literature Review

Research indicates that gamifying an application may not lead to increased motivation or behavioral changes in every condition [14, 26, 27]. Studies have also found that the perception and preference of game elements differ at an individual level [10, 13]. Unfortunately, most of the existing gamification applications are designed with a "*one-size-fits-all*" approach (i.e., non-adapted).

According to the Self-Determination Theory (SDT), an individual will be motivated if his/her innate psychological needs for *Autonomy*, *Competence*, and *Relatedness* are satisfied. Nevertheless, how these psychological needs are fulfilled depends on individuals' perceptions [17]. Furthermore, the Cognitive Evaluation Theory indicates that the effect of extrinsic rewards (e.g., game elements) on an individual's innate psychological needs is mediated by their perception of these extrinsic rewards as controlling or informational [17]. A recent gamification study found that participants valued certain basic psychological needs more than others and suggested that more research is needed to better understand how this weighting process takes place in gamification [28]. Moreover, a study exploring the counterproductive effects of gamification found that individuals had different gamification beliefs, and these beliefs were correlated to their perception of the application as useful [29]. Along with the motivational theories, these studies support the need to consider individuals' unique characteristics when designing gamified applications.

2.1 Player Type Models

In light of the heterogeneity across individuals, researchers are exploring the use of player type models to improve gamified applications [18–20, 30, 31]. The "Gamification User Types Hexad Framework" was introduced by Marczewski [32] to evaluate individuals' preference for game elements in gamified applications. Subsequently, Tondello et al. [33] proposed a 24-item questionnaire to assess individuals' Hexad player type. Recent studies support the validity and reliability of this Hexad player type questionnaire [34, 35]. Because of this, several gamification studies have used the Hexad player type questionnaire as a basis to explore individuals' game element preferences and perceptions [7, 10, 12, 14, 20]. In the field of gamification, the Hexad player type model is the most frequently used model [3, 13]. Moreover, a recent study that compared several personalities and player types models concluded that the "*Hexad is the most relevant typology to identify user preferences for game elements*" [15]. The Hexad player type model introduces six-player type dimensions: (i) Philanthropists, (ii) Disruptors, (iii) Socialisers, (iv) Free Spirits, (v) Achievers, and (vi) Players. Table 1 shows a summary of the Hexad player types from the literature.

Table 1. Summary of Hexad player types

Hexad player type dimension	Description
Philanthropists	These players are motivated by purpose and meaning. They show altruistic behavior and are willing to give without expecting a reward
Disruptors	These players are motivated by change. They tend to disrupt and challenge the system. They often test the limitations of the system and try to push it further
Socialisers	These players are motivated by relatedness. These players want to interact with other players and create social connections
Free spirits	These players are motivated by autonomy and self-expression. They like to have meaning, freedom, act without external control, and explore within a system
Achievers	These players are motivated by competence and mastery. They seek to progress within a system by completing tasks or prove themselves by tackling difficult challenges
Players	These players are motivated by extrinsic rewards. They will do what is needed to earn a reward within a system, independently of the type of activity

Note: This summary was adapted from Tondello et al. (2016) and Marczewski's Gamified UK website [https://www.gamified.uk/user-types]

Researchers have used storyboards to explore the correlation between individuals' Hexad player type and their game element preferences and perceptions [10, 12, 20, 33]. In the context of physical-interactive applications, the Hexad player type model was used to explore the relationship between individuals' player type, their perception of game elements, and their performance on a gamified and a non-gamified application [14]. The results of this study indicate that individuals' Hexad player type correlates with their perception of game elements and performance in the applications used. Moreover, this study supports the need to consider partial membership between the Hexad player types. That is, an individual's dominant Hexad player type does not have enough discriminative power to differentiate individuals according to their game element preferences, similar to other studies [15].

While the previous studies indicate that individuals with different player types perceived game elements differently, it is still not clear if implementing different game elements in an application based on individuals' player type will motivate them to perform differently. That is, it is still unclear if a designer can negatively or positively impact the performance of an individual by implementing specific game elements based on the individual's player type. This is because none of these studies have tested the impact of adaptive gamification. Therefore, while studies and motivational theories suggest that individuals can be motivated by game elements differently, there is still a need to better comprehend how player type models can be used to advance the field of gamification and improve individuals' performance [3, 22, 36].

2.2 Adaptive Gamified Applications

Several studies have started exploring different methods for adapting gamified applications based on individuals' Hexad player types. For example, [30] proposes an adaptive framework for educational gamified applications. Similarly, a recommender system framework to adapt gamified applications based on individuals' player type and their game element preferences was proposed in [19]. Lastly, a machine learning model to tailor the content of gamified applications based on individuals' player type was proposed in [21]. Unfortunately, these studies only provide conceptual frameworks and no empirical evidence of their implementation nor the effectiveness of their framework for improving individuals' performance.

Some studies have shown promising results by adapting educational gamified applications based on students' player type. For example, [37] implement four different educational gamified applications in which the game element of Rewards was adapted based on students' Hexad player type. That is, the specific rules about who gets the rewards and how the scoring was achieved differed between the applications. Their results did not show any statistically significant difference between the intervention group (adapted reward application) and the control group (non-adapted reward application). However, their descriptive statistics suggest that adaptation works better than generic approaches when it comes to improving the behavioral and emotional engagement of the students. Similarly, [18] propose a design framework to adapt gamified applications based on individuals' Hexad player types. In their study, they implement their framework to adapt the feedback provided in a gamified online platform for physicians. Their results indicate that by gamifying and adapting the application, user acceptance and system usage increased. Moreover, [38] implement a matrix factorization approach to select what game elements students would interact with, in an educational gamified application. In their matrix factorization approach, they used "experts" to match individuals' player type to five different game elements. Their results indicate that students that interacted with the non-adapted application have a higher level of amotivation (i.e., not motivated). However, their adapted application only had a positive effect on the most engaged students (i.e., students who used the environment the longest).

Table 2. Summary of current literature of adaptive gamification

Study	Empirical evidence†	Non-adapted group	Non-gamified group	Counter-adapted group	Measure performance
[19, 21, 30]	No	No	No	No	No
[37]	Yes*	Yes	No	No	No
[18]	Yes**	No	Yes	No	No
[38]	Yes***	No	Yes	Yes	No
This work	Yes	Yes	Yes	Yes	Yes

†If the study presents evidence of the implementation of a tailored gamified application; if not, only a method is presented. * [37] did not find any statistically significant results. **[18] used a within-subject experimental design, so the control group was the same as the intervention group. The group interacted with the non-gamified version of the application first. ***[38] results indicate that the adapted application only had a positive effect on the students who used the environment the longest.

Table 2 summarizes current studies that have explored the use of individuals' player type to adapt gamified applications. While these studies are a first step towards understanding the value of adaptive gamified applications using individuals' player types, several limitations still exist. First, some of these studies only provide conceptual frameworks or little empirical evidence of the effects that adaptive gamification has on individuals [19, 21, 30]. Secondly, some studies only compare the effects of their adapted application against a non-gamified application. Hence, it cannot be concluded if the positive effects shown are due to the adaptation or the gamification aspect of the application [18]. Similarly, while [38] did compare the results of an adapted gamified application against a non-gamified application, and a counter-adapted gamified application, it is not clear if there would be any incremental improvement by moving from a non-adapted gamified application to an adapted one. Moreover, their results only show that students that interacted with the counter-adapted and the non-gamified applications have a higher level of amotivation and that the adapted application only had a positive effect on the most engaged students. Likewise, while [37] compared an adapted gamified application vs. a non-adapted gamified application, they did not find any statistically significant results. More importantly, in their adapted application, all participants interacted with the same game elements of Reward. The rules about who gets the rewards and how the scoring was achieved, was the only aspect tailored. Lastly, all these studies only measured the effects of adapted applications on individuals' emotional engagement or usage of the applications, and not on the individuals' performance. All these studies have focused on educational applications, which makes it difficult to demonstrate the impact of adaptive gamification on individuals' performance [38]. Hence, it is still not clear if designers should spend valuable resources adapting a gamified application according to individuals' player type to improve their performance on a task.

In light of current knowledge gaps, this work presents a randomized between-subject experiment to measure the effects that (i) an adapted gamified application, (ii) a non-adapted gamified application, (iii) a non-gamified application, and (iv) a counter-adapted gamified application have on individuals' performance. In this work, a matrix factorization approach is used to adapt and counter-adapt the gamified applications, similar to [38]. However, in this work, the relationship between individuals' player type dimensions and game element preferences were drawn from previous empirical studies and not from the input of "experts" (see Table 4).

3 Case Study

Before the randomized controlled experiment, participants were introduced to the informed consent documents, informed about the concept of gamification, and that they were going to interact with a physically-interactive application intended to promote and motivate them to perform several physical tasks. Once participants provided their consent, they (i) completed a pre-experiment questionnaire, and (ii) interacted with their respective applications. The pre-experiment questionnaire captured participant's Hexad player type, their demographics, and background information.

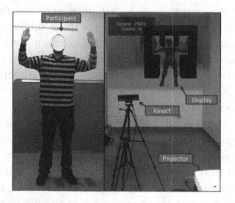

Fig. 1. Experimental setup

3.1 Applications

The applications required the participants to use full-body motions (e.g., bend, extend an arm, jump) to complete a series of physical tasks, similar to the applications introduced by [14]. Each participant interacted with the application twice. The applications contained the same set of 14 tasks. Figure 1 shows the experimental setup used in this work, where the Microsoft Kinect sensor was positioned between the projected display and the participants. The same set of game elements used in the non-adapted gamified application introduced in [14] were implemented in this study (see Table 3). However, in this work, the game elements that each participant interacted with in the adapted or counter-adapted application were selected based on a recommender system.

Table 3. Game elements implemented

Game element	Description
Points	The score measurement of an individual was shown in the top left corner of the projected display
Content unlocking	Coins were placed throughout the application in different locations. If more than 21 coins were collected, the individual was allowed to change the gaming environment background
Avatar	The individuals were given the option to change the color of the avatar that would represent them in the virtual environment

One of the advantages of the matrix factorization approach used in the recommender system is that it uses individuals' Hexad player type dimensions. Hence, it does not discretize individuals into single-player type categories; rather, it considers partial membership between player types. This overcomes some of the limitations of previous studies, helping designers adapt applications at a more individualized level [9, 15]. In this study, the matrices used are obtained by implementing the Hexed player type questionnaire [33] and constructed based on the results of previous studies that have explored the relationship between individuals' game element preferences and their Hexad player type (see Table 4). In this study, participants in the adapted group were only shown the elements that were recommended, while participants in the counter-adapted group were shown the elements that were not recommended.

Table 4. The matrix that matches individuals' player type dimensions to the game elements

Hexad scale dimensions						
Game element	Free spirit	Philanthropist	Achiever	Player	Socialiser	Disruptor
Avatar	$0.130°$	–	$-0.570^{\dagger}$	$-0.680^{\dagger}$	$0.170°$	$-0.150°$
Content unlocking	–	–	–	0.351^{*}	$-0.535^{\dagger}$	$0.024^{\dagger}$
Points	$0.563^{\dagger}$	$-0.027^{\dagger}$	$0.591^{\dagger}$	0.247^{*}	$0.619^{\dagger}$	0.183^{*}

[*]Correlations from [10]. [°]Correlations from [12]. [†]Correlations from [14]. –No significant correlations found (p-value > 0.05).

Figure 2 shows the application used in this study with only one game element enabled at a time. For example, if all game elements are enabled, the application would look like the application shown in Fig. 1. Based on participants' Hexad player type and the recommender system, of the group that interacted with the adapted gamified application, 50% (10 participants) were exposed to the Points and Content Unlocking elements, while the remaining 50% were exposed only to the Points game element. In the group that interacted with the counter-adapted gamified application, 40% (8 participants) were exposed to the Avatar and Content Unlocking elements, while the remaining 60% were exposed to just the Avatar game element. Finally, in this study, the participants' final score after interacting with the application twice (performance score: P), and the difference between their scores from each interaction (performance difference: PD) are used as dependent variables.

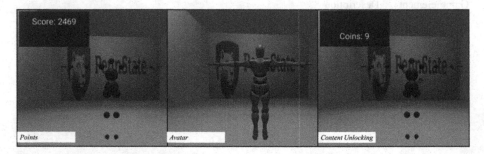

Fig. 2. Illustration of the application with only one element enabled at a time

3.2 Participants

A total of 40 participants were part of this study. The age of participants ranged from 18 to 30 years old (M = 21.45, SD = 3.39 years of age). Forty-eight percent (48%) of the participants identified themselves as Caucasian, and thirty-three percent (33%) as Asian/Pacific Islanders. Only eighteen percent (18%) of the participants identified themselves as Latino/Hispanic and three percent (3%) as African American. Moreover, participants reported playing games an average of 3.78 days per week (SD = 2.34) and spent an average of 2.00 h (SD = 1.69) playing games during those days.

4 Results and Discussions

In this work, the experiment was conducted in the same location, with the same equipment, and following the same experimental protocol as the experiment presented in [14]. This allows comparisons to be drawn between the performance of participants from this work that interacted with (i) an adapted gamified application and (ii) a counter-adapted gamified application, against the performance of participants from [14] that interacted with (iii) a non-adapted gamified application and (iv) a non-gamified application. The results of a series of t-tests and χ-square tests indicate that from a demographic, playing habits, and Hexad player type point of view, there is no significant difference between the distribution of participants in the four groups. Table 5 show the summary statistics of participants' performance score and performance difference.

Table 5. Summary of participants performance

Application	Number of participants	Performance score		Performance difference	
		Mean	SD	Mean	SD
Adapted	20	37,632.45	6,939.01	3,292.00	4,147.97
Non-adapted	15	33,814.72	6,292.55	3,711.70	4,862.22
Non-gamified	15	33,182.80	8,116.41	3,732.70	6,691.41
Counter adapted	20	22,778.95	8,389.93	1,535.00	7,583.88

Out of the participants that interacted with the adapted gamified application, 40% achieved a performance score greater than the maximum score achieved by any participant in the counter-adapted group, and 10% achieved a performance score greater than the maximum score obtained by any participant in the non-adapted or non-gamified groups. Similarly, out of the participants that interacted with the counter-adapted gamified application, 50% achieved a performance score lower than the minimum score obtained by any participant in the adapted or non-adapted groups, and 30% achieved a performance score lower than the minimum score achieved by any participant in the non-gamified group. Figure 3 shows a bar plot with the average performance score of participants who interacted with the adapted gamified application (A-G), non-adapted gamified application (G), the non-gamified application (N-G), and the counter-adapted gamified application (C-A-G).

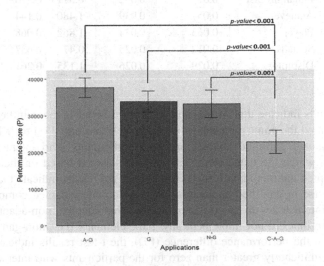

Fig. 3. Summary of participants' performance conditioned on the application used

The one-way between-subjects ANOVA results indicate a significant effect of application type on participants' performance for the four conditions ($F_{(3,66)} = 15.13$, p-value < 0.0001). Moreover, a pairwise comparison with a Bonferroni correction shows that individuals' performance on the counter-adaptive application was statistically significantly lowered than the performance of any other group. While not statistically significant after a Bonferroni correction, the results also show that the performance of individuals who interacted with the adapted gamified application was, on average, greater than any other group.

When controlling for participants' Hexad player type dimensions, the results of a linear regression analysis indicate that participants who interacted with (i) the non-adapted gamified application, (ii) the non-gamified application, and (iii) the counter-adapted application, had a lower performance score than the participants who interacted with the adapted gamified application. Table 6 shows the summary statistics of the linear regression model fitted. A significant equation was found ($F_{(9,60)} = 5.707$, p-value < 0.001), with a R^2 of 0.461. Moreover, the Shapiro-Wilk test reveals that the residuals of the model were normally distributed (p-value $= 0.651$), and an a posteriori power analysis of the regression model indicates that with a sample size of n = 70, a significant alpha level of 0.05, and an R^2 of 0.461, the predicted power of the analysis is 0.98 [39].

Table 6. Summary of linear regression model fitted for the final score performance (P)

Variable	Standardized β	Std. error	t-value	p-value
Intercept	0.419	1.075	0.389	0.698
Non-adapted	−0.601	0.294	−2.043	0.045
Non-gamified	−0.677	0.285	−2.379	0.021
Counter-adapted	−1.627	0.252	−6.464	<0.01
Free spirits	0.011	0.038	0.288	0.774
Philanthropist	0.019	0.032	0.571	0.570
Achiever	0.057	0.039	1.480	0.144
Player	−0.063	0.034	−1.862	0.068
Socialiser	0.012	0.025	0.47	0.637
Disruptor	−0.029	0.026	−1.135	0.261

These results indicate that participants performed better in the gamified application that implemented the game elements which were selected based on their Hexad player type (i.e., adapted gamified application) than participants who interacted with the application in which the game elements were not selected based on their player type (i.e., non-adapted gamified application). Moreover, the results indicate that individuals performed worse in gamified applications that are counter-adapted compared to individuals who interacted with gamified applications that adapted, non-adapted, and even the application that did not implement any game elements (i.e., non-gamified).

Looking at the performance difference (PD), the t-test results indicate that it was statistically significantly greater than zero for the participants who interacted with the adapted gamified application (t_{19} = 3.449, p-value = 0.001), the non-adapted gamified application (t_{14} = 2.965, p-value = 0.005), and the non-gamified application (t_{14} = 2.161, p-value = 0.024). However, there was not enough evidence to indicate that participants who interacted with the counter-adapted gamified application had a performance difference significantly greater than zero (t_{19} = 0.905, p-value = 0.188). The t-test results also reveal that there was not enough evidence to indicate that the performance difference of participants was statistically significantly different between groups, even after controlling for participants' Hexad player type dimensions. Moreover, Table 7 shows the number and proportion of participants that performed better or worse the second time they interacted with the application given each group. While Table 7 shows a clear trend, the χ-square test results indicate that there was not a statistically significant difference between the groups.

Table 7. Distribution of performance difference

Group	Performed better the 2nd time [Number of participants/percentages]	Performed worse the 2nd time [Number of participants/percentages]
Adapted application	17/85%	3/15%
Non-adapted application	12/80%	3/20%
Non-gamified application	11/73%	4/27%
Counter-adapted application	14/70%	6/30%

The results of the performance difference reveal that participants who interacted with the counter-adapted application did not improve as they interacted with the application for a second time. In contrast, participants who interacted with the other applications improved their performance. This performance improvement can be attributed to a possible learning effect. However, the lack of performance improvement by participants who interacted with the counter-adapted gamified application could be attributed to a lack of engagement and motivation.

Most of the studies to date only explore user modeling to help adapt applications without measuring the impact of adapted gamification on individuals' performance. This work provides empirical evidence that validates the value of using individuals' Head player type when designing gamified applications. The findings show that designers can improve individuals' performance by using the Hexad player type model to select the game elements individuals interact with. Moreover, this work shows that designers need to be cautious when implementing one-size-fits-all applications (i.e., applications that do not consider individuals' player type) since some individuals might perform worse in gamified applications that implement game elements that are not aligned with their Hexad player type dimensions, than in applications that are not gamified (i.e., do not implement any game elements), as shown by the results of the counter-adapted group. These findings could help explain why some studies that have used gamified applications designed without considering individuals' player type (i.e., a one-size-fits-all approach) have shown mixed results [36, 40, 41].

5 Limitations and Future Works

While the results of this work provide quantitative evidence of the effects of adapted and counter-adapted gamified applications on individuals' performance, several limitations still exist. First, in this study, only three game elements were implemented. This limited the number of different game element combinations individuals were exposed to. Moreover, this could have also generated some possible confounding effects. For example, the results show that participants performed better in the adapted gamified application than in the counter-adapted gamified application. Nonetheless, this performance difference might be confounded by a possible interaction effect related to the exposure of the Point and Avatar game elements. This is because based on the recommender system the participants who interacted with the adapted application were exposed to the Points element and not to the Avatar element, while the participants who interacted with the counter-adapted gamified application were exposed to the Avatar element and not to the Points element. However, participants in the non-adapted group performed better than the participants in the counter-adapted group; even though they interacted with both the Point and Avatar game elements. Similarly, participants in the non-gamified group performed better than the participants in the counter-adapted group; even though they did not interact with the Point or Avatar game elements.

Finally, a limitation that this work shares with many other gamification studies is the potential issue of generalizability. For example, the recommender system, which guided the adaptation process, might not generalize to other applications. Moreover, the tasks that participants performed in the applications were physical in nature. Hence, future work must focus on measuring the effects of adapted gamified applications based on individuals' player types in other contexts or with non-physical tasks. Nevertheless, this study provides valuable evidence of the effects of adapted gamified applications and the value of using the Hexad player type model for adapting applications.

6 Conclusion

Motivational theories reveal that treating individuals as a homogenous group is not an optimal design approach since what motivates one individual might demotivate another. Moreover, studies have shown that individuals' perception of game elements differ based on individual characteristics. Because of this, researchers have started exploring how player type models can be used to adapt gamification. Unfortunately, most of the existing studies only provide conceptual frameworks or little empirical evidence of their implementation and effectiveness in improving individuals' performance. In light of this, a randomized experiment was conducted to test the effects that adapting gamified applications, based on individuals' player type, have on their performance.

The results of this work revealed that individuals who interacted with the adapted gamified application performed better than participants that interacted with a non-adapted gamified application, a non-gamified application, and a counter-adapted gamified application. In contrast, participants who interacted with the counter-adapted gamified application performed worse than any other group and did not show any performance improvement after interacting with the application for a second time. The results of this work provide empirical evidence of the value of adapting gamified applications based on individuals' Hexad player type. These findings support the need to consider individuals' player type when designing gamified applications. This is because adapted gamified applications could potentially produce better results than non-adapted applications. Furthermore, a non-adapted gamified application could potentially produce worse results than a non-gamified application if the users' player type is not considered when selecting the game elements to implement. Thus, this works highlights the need to consider individuals' player type when designing gamification applications and the potential latent detrimental effects of not doing so.

Acknowledgements. This research is funded in part by NSF NRI #1527148 & NSF DUE #1834465. Any opinions, findings, or conclusions found in this paper are those of the authors and do not necessarily reflect the views of the sponsors.

References

1. Hallifax, S., Serna, A., Marty, J.C., Lavoué, É.: Adaptive gamification in education: a literature review of current trends and developments. In: European Conference on Technology Enhanced Learnin (EC-TEL), pp. 294–307 (2019)
2. Koivisto, J., Hamari, J.: The rise of motivational information systems: a review of gamification research. Int. J. Inf. Manage. **45**, 191–210 (2019)
3. Klock, A.C.T., Gasparini, I., Pimenta, M.S., Hamari, J.: Tailored gamification: a review of literature. Int. J. Hum. Comput. Stud. **144**, 102495 (2020)
4. Legaki, N., Xi, N., Hamari, J., Karpouzis, K.: The effect of challenge-based gamification on learning: an experiment in the context of statistics education. Int. J. Hum. Comput. Stud. **144**, 102496 (2020)
5. Deterding, S., Dixon, D., Khaled, R., Nacke, L.: From game design elements to gamefulness: defining "gamification". In: ACM MindTreck 2011 (2011)
6. Patel, M.S., et al.: Effect of a game-based intervention designed to enhance social incentives to increase physical activity among families: the BE FIT randomized clinical trial. JAMA Intern. Med. **177**, 1586–1593 (2017)
7. Altmeyer, M., Lessel, P., Muller, L., Krüger, A.: Combining behavior change intentions and user types to select suitable gamification elements for persuasive fitness systems. In: Oinas-Kukkonen, H., Win, K.T., Karapanos, E., Karppinen, P., Kyza, E. (eds.) PERSUASIVE 2019. LNCS, vol. 11433, pp. 337–349. Springer, Cham (2019). https://doi.org/10.1007/978-3-030-17287-9_27

8. Lopez, C., Tucker, C.: A quantitative method for evaluating the complexity of implementing and performing game features in physically-interactive gamified applications. Comput. Human Behav. **71**, 42–58 (2017)
9. Orji, R., Vassileva, J., Mandryk, R.L.: Modeling the efficacy of persuasive strategies for different gamer types in serious games for health. User Model. User-Adap. Interact. **24**(5), 453–498 (2014). https://doi.org/10.1007/s11257-014-9149-8
10. Tondello, G., Mora, A., Nacke, L.: Elements of gameful design emerging from user preferences. In: Proceedings of the Annual Symposium on Computer-Human Interaction in Play (CHI Play 2017), pp. 129–142 (2017)
11. Busch, M., et al.: Using player type models for personalized game design - an empirical investigation. Int. J. Interact. Des. Archit. **28**, 145–163 (2016)
12. Orji, R., Tondello, G.F., Nacke, L.E.: Personalizing persuasive strategies in gameful systems to gamification user types. In: ACM CHI Conference on Human Factors in Computing Systems, Montreal, QC, Canada (2018)
13. Hallifax, S., Serna, A., Marty, J.-C., Lavoué, É.: Adaptive gamification in education: a literature review of current trends and developments. In: Scheffel, M., Broisin, J., Pammer-Schindler, V., Ioannou, A., Schneider, J. (eds.) EC-TEL 2019. LNCS, vol. 11722, pp. 294–307. Springer, Cham (2019). https://doi.org/10.1007/978-3-030-29736-7_22
14. Lopez, C., Tucker, C.: The effects of player type on performance: a gamification case study. Comput. Hum. Behav. **91**, 333–345 (2019)
15. Hallifax, S., Serna, A., Marty, J.C., Lavoué, G., Lavoué, E.: Factors to consider for tailored gamification. In: CHI Play 2019 - Proceedings of the Annual Symposium on Computer-Human Interaction in Play, pp. 559–572 (2019)
16. Codish, D., Ravid, G.: Personality based gamification: how different personalities perceive gamification. In: Proceedings of 22nd European Conference on Information Systems (2014)
17. Ryan, R.M., Deci, E.L.: Self-determination theory and the facilitation of intrinsic motivation, social development, and well-being. Am. Psychol. **55**, 68–78 (2000)
18. Böckle, M., Micheel, I., Bick, M.: A design framework for adaptive gamification applications. In: Proceedings of the 51st Hawaii International Conference on System Sciences, pp. 1227–1236 (2018)
19. Tondello, G., Orji, R., Nacke, L.: Recommender systems for personalized gamification. In: Adjunct Publication of the 25th Conference on User Modeling, Adaptation and Personalization - UMAP 2017, pp. 425–430 (2017)
20. Mora, A., Tondello, G.F., Calvet, L., González, C., Arnedo-Moreno, J., Nacke, L.E.: The quest for a better tailoring of gameful design: an analysis of player type preferences. In: Proceedings of the XX International Conference on Human Computer Interaction, Conostia Gipuzkoa Spain, pp. 1–8 (2019)
21. Knutas, A., van Roy, R., Hynninen, T., Granato, M., Kasurinen, J., Ikonen, J.: A process for designing algorithm-based personalized gamification. Multimed. Tools Appl. **78**(10), 13593–13612 (2018). https://doi.org/10.1007/s11042-018-6913-5
22. Böckle, M., Bick, M.: Towards adaptive gamification: a synthesis of current developments. In: Proceedings of the 25th European Conference on Information Systems (ECIS), Guimarães, Portugal (2017)
23. Sundar, S.S., Marathe, S.S.: Personalization versus customization: the importance of agency, privacy, and power usage. Hum. Commun. Res. **36**(3), 298–322 (2010)
24. Brusilovsky, P., Maybury, M.T.: From adaptive hypermedia to the adaptive web. Commun. ACM. **45**(5), 30–33 (2002)
25. Rajanen, D., Rajanen, M.: Personalized gamification: a model for play data profiling. In: CEUR Workshop Proceedings, Tampere, Finland, pp. 1–8 (2017)

26. Fitz-Walter, Z., Johnson, D., Wyeth, P., Tjondronegoro, D., Scott-Parker, B.: Driven to drive? Investigating the effect of gamification on learner driver behavior, perceived motivation and user experience. Comput. Hum. Behav. **71**, 586–595 (2017)
27. Hanus, M.D., Fox, J.: Assessing the effects of gamification in the classroom: a longitudinal study on intrinsic motivation, social comparison, satisfaction, effort, and academic performance. Comput. Educ. **80**, 152–161 (2015)
28. Van Roy, R., Zaman, B.: Unravelling the ambivalent motivational power of gamification: a basic psychological needs perspective. Int. J. Hum. Comput. Stud. **127**, 38–50 (2019)
29. Diefenbach, S., Müssig, A.: Counterproductive effects of gamification: an analysis on the example of the gamified task manager Habitica. Int. J. Hum. Comput. Stud. **127**, 190–210 (2019)
30. Monterrat, B., Desmarais, M., Lavoué, É., George, S.: A player model for adaptive gamification in learning environments. In: Conati, C., Heffernan, N., Mitrovic, A., Verdejo, MFelisa (eds.) AIED 2015. LNCS (LNAI), vol. 9112, pp. 297–306. Springer, Cham (2015). https://doi.org/10.1007/978-3-319-19773-9_30
31. Amado, C.M., Roleda, L.S.: Game element preferences and engagement of different Hexad player types in a gamified physics course. In: Proceedings of the 2020 11th International Conference on E-Education, E-Business, E-Management, and E-Learning, pp. 261–267 (2020)
32. Marczewski, A.: User types. In: Even Ninja Monkeys like to Play: Gamification, Game Thinking and Motivational Design, pp. 65–80 (2015)
33. Tondello, G., Wehbe, R.R., Diamond, L., Busch, M., Marczewski, A., Nacke L.E.: The gamification user types Hexad scale. In: Proceedings of the 2016 Annual Symposium on Computer-Human Interaction in Play - CHI Play 2016, pp. 229–243 (2016)
34. Tondello, G.F., Mora, A., Marczewski, A., Nacke, L.E.: Empirical validation of the gamification user types Hexad scale in English and Spanish. Int. J. Hum. Comput. Stud. **127**, 95–111 (2018)
35. Akgün, Ö.E., Topal, M.: Adaptation of the gamification user types Hexad scale into Turkish. Int. J. Assess. Tools Educ. **12**, ep268 (2018)
36. Nacke, L.E., Deterding, S.: The maturing of gamification research. Comput. Hum. Behav. **71**, 450–454 (2017)
37. Mora, A., Tondello, G.F., Nacke, L.E., Arnedo-Moreno, J.: Effect of personalized gameful design on student engagement. In: IEEE 2018 IEEE Global Engineering Education Conference (EDUCON), Canary Islands, Spain, pp. 1925–1933 (2018)
38. Lavoué, É., Monterrat, B., Desmarais, M., George, S.: Adaptive gamification for learning environments. IEEE Trans. Learn. Technol. **12**(1), 16–28 (2018)
39. Cohen, J.: Statistical Power Analysis for the Behavioral Sciences, 2nd edn. Lawrence Erlbaum Associates, Mahwah (1988)
40. Seaborn, K., Fels, D.I.: Gamification in theory and action: a survey. Int. J. Hum. Comput. Stud. **74**, 14–31 (2015)
41. Hamari, J., Koivisto, J., Sarsa, H.: Does gamification work? - A literature review of empirical studies on gamification. In: Proceedings of the Hawaii International Conference on System Sciences, pp. 3025–3034 (2014)

Designing Interactive Storytelling Games to Teach Computational Thinking

Eric Shadrach Miller[✉]

The University of Texas at Dallas, Richardson, TX 75080, USA
eric.miller@utdallas.edu

Abstract. In the section of The Design of Everyday Things titled "Moral Obligations of Design," Don Norman writes, "Designers need to make things that satisfy people's needs, in terms of function, in terms of being understandable and usable, and in terms of their ability to deliver emotional satisfaction, pride, and delight," (Norman, 293). This is equally true of doors, lessons, teapots, narratives, and games. And for some complex emerging objects, such as educational narrative games, designers must look at a synthesis of different object types to hypothesize heuristics and principles that will guide their design. Game designers rarely have extensive research on the design of their artifacts to analyze before they are asked to invent new combinations of mechanics, couple them with themes they did not create, and then test their efficacy for whatever the intended design goal of the game, be it education, entertainment, or training. Instead, designers often rely on anecdotal accounts of design of their genre of games, if they're fortunate, or on heuristics uncovered most often in other fields. In conversation with games studies and interactive storytelling scholars, I define these digital artifacts as games that use narratives generated in response to open text input from their players. For the emerging genre of interactive storytelling games the dearth of game design research and a lack of examples of fully functional games in the genre give designers little to start with. Though many in the field of interactive storytelling believe, for good reason, that these games have incredible educational potential, there are even fewer examples of such games to learn from, and practically no specific game design research on their creation. Such artifacts are the complex synthesis of generated narrative, a system open to a continuum of user input, and educational content that personalizes to the player to a high degree. Without proper design, these objects will fail to be understood, to satisfy their users' needs, to function, and they will certainly fail to deliver pride, satisfaction, and delight. Without game design research, the proper design of such complicated artifacts will happen only by accident and will most likely be delayed, possibly indefinitely. In what seems at first like an odd coincidence, there is one field, computational thinking, where two effective prototypes of interactive storytelling educational games exist, and these, along with other case studies of mechanics and even science fiction, can guide the beginning of game design research into their creation.

How can we design interactive storytelling systems in order to be effective at teaching computational thinking? While the industry process of iteration and design will be key, the costs of developing these systems, and the costs of designing them improperly, are too high not to attempt other formal approaches to researching their design. By following a game design research methodology and pursuing specific cases with the formal methods, this paper analyzes game

X. Fang (Ed.): HCII 2021, LNCS 12789, pp. 342–351, 2021.
https://doi.org/10.1007/978-3-030-77277-2_26

design principles and hypotheses to produce knowledge about how to design these complex and potentially transformational objects. As Don Norman makes clear in The Design of Everyday Things, not only can design increase our enjoyment and understanding of those things around us, but design can be a life or death matter. The stakes may seem lower in game design; however, as James Paul Gee points out in his work on games and education, games are sites of identity formation and for learning their own unique semiotic domains (Gee). We need to design the powerful educational systems that will emerge from the synthesis of deep learning and natural language processes with care, so that we do not allow for stochastic identity formation in the players of these games.

This paper is a research-based analysis of interactive storytelling systems and relevant games with relevant mechanics in order to address the question of how to design interactive storytelling games that teach computational thinking in an informal context. In addition to this analysis, this paper describes relevant research into narrative-centered learning, games-based learning, and informal learning. I will also analyze science fiction criticism alongside my game design research, and research into other fields, by adapting a methodology used in ubiquitous computing research that recognizes that, "Design-oriented research is an act of collective imagining—a way in which we work together to bring about a future that lies slightly out of our grasp," (Dourish and Bell, 769). In this way, I will expand upon and practice game design research methods as called for by Paul Coultan and Alan Hook, game design researchers at Lancaster University.

Currently, even formal tools such as machinations.io and more formal texts on game mechanics such as Patterns In Game Design do not delve into thorough specific game design considerations around creating interactive storytelling systems as described by authors such as Chris Crawford, Brenda Laurel, and Janet Murray (Björk and Holopainen; Crawford; Laurel; Murray). Ultimately, this paper will provide insight into how game designers can design interactive storytelling systems in order to teach computational thinking in informal settings, in hopes that these lessons will apply to the emerging field of interactive storytelling design and their use in informal learning experiences.

Keywords: Computer games · Design tools/technologies · Edutainment/education games · Game and flow/game immersion · Game based learning/games for learning · Game improvement · Game psychology · Games and society · Games and well being · Interaction design of games · Playful generation of game mechanics · Serious games · Simulation games · Interactive storytelling · Narrative games · Computational thinking

1 New Game Design Research Methods Borrowed from Ubiquitous Computing

1.1 Science Fiction Prototyping Interactive Storytelling Games that Teach Computational Thinking

How can we design interactive storytelling systems in order to be effective at teaching computational thinking? While the industry process of iteration and design will be key, the costs of developing these systems, and the costs of designing them improperly, are too high not to attempt other formal approaches to researching their design. By following a game design research methodology and pursuing specific cases with the formal methods, this paper analyzes game design principles and hypotheses to produce knowledge about how to design these complex and potentially transformational objects. As Don Norman makes clear in The Design of Everyday Things, not only can design increase our enjoyment and understanding of those things around us, but design can be a life or death matter. The stakes may seem lower in game design; however, as James Paul Gee points out in his work on games and education, games are sites of identity formation and for learning their own unique semiotic domains [2]. We need to design the powerful educational systems that will emerge from the synthesis of deep learning and natural language processes with care, so that we do not allow for stochastic identity formation in the players of these games.

This paper is a research-based analysis of interactive storytelling systems and relevant games with relevant mechanics in order to address the question of how to design interactive storytelling games that teach computational thinking in an informal context. In addition to this analysis, this paper describes relevant research into narrative-centered learning, games-based learning, and informal learning. I will also analyze science fiction criticism alongside my game design research, and research into other fields, by adapting a methodology used in ubiquitous computing research that recognizes that, "Design-oriented research is an act of collective imagining—a way in which we work together to bring about a future that lies slightly out of our grasp," [3, p. 769]. In this way, I will expand upon and practice game design research methods as called for by Paul Coultan and Alan Hook, game design researchers at Lancaster University.

Currently, even formal tools such as machinations.io and more formal texts on game mechanics such as Patterns In Game Design do not delve into thorough specific game design considerations around creating interactive storytelling systems as described by authors such as Chris Crawford, Brenda Laurel, and Janet Murray [4–7]. Ultimately, this paper will provide insight into how game designers can design interactive storytelling systems in order to teach computational thinking in informal settings, in hopes that these lessons will apply to the emerging field of interactive storytelling design and their use in informal learning experiences.

This paper grows out of the research from the author's dissertation, Toward the Design of Interactive Storytelling Games That Teach Computational Thinking, which he is currently preparing for graduation in the spring of 2021. That dissertation is research into extending the methodology of game design research to prepare for the design of interactive storytelling games as an emerging genre and in order to understand how to utilize them to teach computational thinking. As an operational definition, Interactive storytelling games are game experiences that allow for the player to perform any action that they can imagine while the game dynamically creates a storytelling experience around the player's action. As the abstract for this paper and that dissertation argue, this is a laudable and timely goal because interactive storytelling games currently have affordances that allow for direct scripting replication, they are closest in time to the origins of digital computer programming, and those who design them will need to both play the first digital interactive storytelling games extensively to understand their medium, and to understand computational thinking in order to use the digital affordances they rely on for their potential as games and educational experiences.

Janet Murray describes these digital affordances in Hamlet on the Holodeck [6, p. 94]. According to her writing, four major digital affordances that game designers will need to consider as narrative and other design options transform are that the digital medium is procedural, spatial, encyclopedic, and participatory [6, p. 3]. The creators of the first widely recognized successful interactive storytelling game prototype, Mateas and Stern, further elaborate on how Murray's affordances relate to interactive story-telling games in particular and they also expand on Murray's affordances by describing how the spatial, participatory, and encyclopedic all grow out of the procedural affordance [8, 9]. While Mateas and Stern use traditional, though advanced, sequential logic based artificial intelligence and modular techniques to create 20 min of repeatable gameplay that feels open-ended, they write themselves that their techniques are labor intensive and do not give the degrees of local agency and global agency that they had hoped for [8]. Through iterative experimental gameplay, this author found in his dissertation and detailed there how their game, Façade [10], is not open-ended enough to teach computational thinking or to enter domains other than the scene imagined. This open-ended quality, as described by Kenneth O. Stanley, Joel Lehman and Lisa Soros as "a single process that invents astronomical complexity for near-eternity..." can describes myriad wonderous natural phenomena, and is a grand challenge for the machine learning community [11]. In this manner of speaking, Façade is not open ended, however, in 2019 Nick Walton and several others from what is now the company Latitude, built the first and only interactive storytelling game that is: AI Dungeon, now developed into AI Dungeon 2 [12]. Through an investigation of this game using a dual methodology of critical play with the game itself and science fiction prototyping, this paper will provide insight into and analysis of how near-future open-ended interactive storytelling games like AI Dungeon could teach computational thinking through gameplay and narrative in informal settings.

In order to achieve this, the author set up and played through the creation of a science fiction prototype in AI Dungeon itself. This case study of these methodologies is meant to illuminate the use of science fiction prototyping as part of the development process as described by ubiquitous computing scholars. Science fiction prototypes are, "...short stories, movies and comics that are created based on real science and tech-nology" in order to "...use these fictional creations explicitly as a step or input in the development process" because they "...offer a way to imagine and envision the future..." according to their inventor Brian David Johnson [13, p. vii]. Brian David Johnson invented science fiction prototyping as a method to deal with the need for long development cycles of chips at intel, which took more than 5 years [14, p. 1]. Science then the practice has been formally adopted in ubiquitous computing. Because of the mobile and integrated nature of modern digital games, they also represent examples of ubiquitous computing. Science fiction prototyping is appropriate as a methodology for developing and understanding the need for specific areas of game design research, especially open-ended interactive storytelling games, not only because they do repre-sent ubiquitous computing technology, but also because the potential play cycle of a single educational open-ended interactive storytelling game might span 5 to 20 years or longer of a players life, and might integrate into domains far beyond that which the initial design anticipated. Science fiction prototyping not only attempts to imagine these domains and their interactions through concrete dramatized worlds, it also seeks to create conversational starting points for critique of design ideas and assumptions and potential areas of technological exploitation. What follows is an analysis through close reading of the science fiction prototype produced for this paper. A full version of this prototype is available at the end of this paper and of the one referenced [15]. Excerpts of the story are included for the analysis and may make more sense if the reader is familiar with the story in its entirety.

The story was created using the custom prompt on AI Dungeon in order to both perform science fiction prototyping as praxis and test the capabilities of the open-endedness and cohesion of the only open-ended interactive storytelling game using neural networks and OpenAI's GTP-3 natural language processing. Two models were used in the creation of the prototype, the less powerful Griffin model and the more powerful Dragon model, as described by the creators of AI Dungeon in the following blog post. This was done both to compare and contrast the models and to seed the story with a high amount of player generated text at the start. Of the first 1003 words, only 148 words are generated by the natural language model. Two versions of the prototype are included, the first unmarked for ease of reading and the second marked for analysis of computer generated text, and for a feature described at the end of this paper.

The prototype illustrates a setting in the near future where a middle school student, Cordellia, is trying to find as much time as possible to play AI Invasion while also managing her other responsibilities, and studying to become a better player. The game and her life are revealed slowly through dramatization, and in the interest of openness about the process, the author also is exploring the creation of the character and the setting through the act of prototyping. For the author, this represents a dramatization and praxis of the research into interactive storytelling that has been the primary focus of the last four years of his studies in ATEC at UTD while earning his PhD, along with techniques for creating science fiction learned and practiced in both gaming industry jobs and while earning his MFA at Temple University under the guidance of science fiction author Samuel Delaney.

As a near-future science fiction prototype about education, this story could not ignore the pandemic or the rise of virtual learning, which in many ways was it's call to research in the first place. Science fiction prototypes are meant to be based on facts as much as possible and in this case the future is assumed to be largely remote, either due to continued pandemic emergencies or adaptation in anticipation of them by school districts. From March 11, 2020 the COVID-19 global pandemic, declared by the World Health Organization, caused US schools to close in all 50 states and four territories, continuing to affect in person meeting of classes through the start of 2021 of more than 9 million students [16]. The first line of the story reveals relevant setting and character information, "Cordellia sat at her computer trying to focus on her teacher Nell, whose microphone kept clipping in and out as she answered questions about computational thinking," [15] The setting is near future and should evoke the current 2020 United States largely virtual classrooms experienced during the pandemic. This highlights not only the need for better technological solutions for education, but the understanding by curriculum developers for computational thinking as a subject. Cordellia follows with a question about their reading, which references the The Tinkertoy Computer [17]. This is meant to highlight the evolving state of computational devices, and also the playful nature of understanding computation as modeling thinking, but also to show Cordellia's maturity in understanding computational thinking. Though she is later revealed to be studying the concepts in her own time to better play the game, her question of why they should bother to study something without a clear use to her shows a lack of internal motivation for learning the subject.

Cordellia, like many of her peers, both relishes and despises digital technology as it is used to both entertain and discipline her. During the last five minutes of class, she is tempted to play AI Invasion, a fictional Alternate reality game with the same capabilities of open-ended text generation of AI Dungeon but with gameplay similar to games like Mafia, Werewolf, or the popular indie game Among Us. The prototype is meant to address the potentials and the issues of designing such a game with GTP-3 text generation. In the game, some players are humans and some are AI characters. The rumors of the sophistication of the AI characters run rampant throughout Cordellia's suspicions about a fellow player, who she knows as BotKilla472, and also throughout her own defence of herself as human.

Some of the issues brought up in the story, aside from unending games becoming a distraction from school participation, especially when that participation is plagued by technological problems, include the possibility of players using the platform to take advantage of other players, a seeming increase in paranoia around artificial intelligence, and disengagement from one's surroundings as the ubiquitous technology takes attention away from the natural world or other diegetic concerns. The critique is not dystopian, but mild and meant to be near to real experiences, "Since she could play AI invasion on her phone, tablet, or laptop, she played it all day and the rest of her life felt like an interruption" [15]. In contrast to these concerns that the prototype illustrates, it also illuminates strengths of informal learning and the footholds of internal motivation that the external motivational scaffolding of gameplay can lead toward. This aspect of the prototype is guided by research like that written about in Resonant Games by the MIT Education Arcade, particularly insights into their development of Labyrinth which uses dark fairy tales to teach math concepts informally to middle schoolers [18, Ch. 3]. Like the students who encounter mythological creatures and explore them outside of the game in the Education Arcade's experience, Cordellia explores concepts around computational thinking in order to better understand the turing test game that she is involved in. This open-ended goal of both proving to her group that she is human and finding those players in her group who are not, leads her to explore the topic from a wired as well as perspective. Inadvertently, as she gains mastery and understanding and as she adapts to the difficulties of the task, she also ends up enjoying the subject for her own sake, finding that she has a favorite book on the topic of Turing Tests, The Most Human Human, which gives her a key insight about how to play the game better, watch the humans as closely as you watch the AI in order to see them make genuine human errors.

Through her exploration of the topic, she learns not only about traditional sequential methods for testing artificial intelligences, but about the difficulty of using these techniques on modern neural net architectures like that in AI Dungeon (and the fictional AI Invasion). Dealing with neural nets and coming to grips with how they work is exactly the kind of advanced computational thinking that Denning and Tedre argue most elementary and K-12 education on the topic ignores [19, p. 200]. While the prototype advances these as goals for computational thinking education, it also critiques the common stereotype of gaming and simulations that Denning and Tedre offhandedly support when they write "This requires an advanced form of CT that is not learned from children's simulation games. "CT for professionals" is deadly serious" [19, p. 11]. The prototype does this in two ways. First, it shows Cordellia as motivated by a children's simulation to learn advanced computational thinking, to improve her gameplay. The dramatization is as follows:

> She wanted to play AI Invasion, a game where some of the players on your team were Artificial Intelligences and you didn't know you, so you had to catch them and vote them off before they sabotaged you. But the game was set in the real world, and it used news and got you to play in weird ways. She had needed to get her mom to take her to the museum the other day to take a picture to prove to the other people on her team that she was not an AI. Thankfully, it seemed to have worked. A player, Botkilla472, who Cordellia suspected was an AI, said that was no kind of proof because an AI not only could find a picture like that and share it, but it could generate the face in the photo so that no one would even know it wasn't a real person.

> The rest of the week went by without much else happening except for classes, which meant that Cordelia spent most of her free time playing AI Invasion or reading about Computational Thinking in order to catch Botkilla472 and the other AI's on her team. She'd been playing with the same team all year, and so far no one had been booted as an AI. Sometimes Cordellia thought she was the only real person on the team.

> She'd been trying to catch Botkilla472 for the last month since he, as the AI identified itself, started bringing up suspicions about her after she noticed a weird blur in one of the photos that he'd shared of a picnic he'd gone to. It was nothing but random people and no real hints of anything odd. She'd gotten a bunch of points for hitting him with that, and he'd pissed her off so much that she kept playing after she found out what he was.

> The books on computational thinking really got her to see how hard it was to catch these AI, which used OpenAI's GTP-3 combined with real world news and photos to create individual characters who were supposedly involved in a plot for world domination. The problem wasn't so much that the AI was so amazing, though it really was incredible, but that people were so often disingenuous and inauthentic themselves. One of her favorite books on the subject, which she'd read just to get better at the game, was The Most Human Human, and she saw now that she wasn't waiting for the bots to slip up, but for the humans to slip up in the most human ways possible [15].

Her engagement with the subject stems from a motivation to improve her experience and likelihood of winning the game, but in the end she learns a great deal about a myriad of subjects, including computational thinking and psychology and puts them into the context of not only the game, but her real life.

The final critique of the attitude expressed that learning from games cannot be serious or advanced comes from the final dramatic situation of the prototype. Cordially has agreed to meet BotKilla472, not in person, but in another game, so that they can prove to one another that they are real. Another player, GoosePies, warns Cordellia that there are rumors that real people are using this kind of proof of humanity in the game to set up other players for financial or other scams. The prototype dramatizes it this way:

> Cordellia wrote back, "Thanks, GoosePies. I'll be careful! At least if he scams me we'll know he's a real person!"

Cordellia waited a moment for a response, and when one didn't come she went and grabbed the last item on the list, a present from her mom for being helpful, a pack of kuala yums, her favorite japanese candy. Then she felt the buzz of what she was sure was GoosePies' response. "Haha, yeah! Unless the AI is actually scamming people now in order to appear human!" [15]

This is both a dramatization of paranoia around AI, as well as a design problem. In a game where a self improving AI built on the same principles of AlphaGoZero and other video game mastering algorithms is paired with GTP-3, what are the limitations of the AI after years of training with real players? This is referenced earlier in the story when describing the character of GoosePies through the lens of Cordellia,

GoosePies was too kind to be an AI and she seemed to lurk in the game a lot, which most people didn't because early bots that hadn't learned to play the game yet did that, so it was always seen as an easy tip off [15].

With various neural net technologies synthesized together in the AI of this fictional game, what would actually be possible. AI have been known to play multiplayer games and their detection is a serious problem in the gaming industry [20]. The behaviour of playing another game and participating in online chat during it would be a combination of solved problems, rather than any unsolved ones. Even the idea of an AI replicating a known scam, with the proper neural net motivation architecture, is not farfetched. Rather, what is new is the underlying open-endedness of the AI's ability to adapt. The survival motivation in AI Invasion and the open-ended reasons that an AI might be ejected from a group lead to unforeseen improvements in the AI's ability to pass the Turing test in novel ways. The story leaves open how much of this adaptation is due to gameplay development by the team or learning by the neural networks.

Scientific experimentation is one valid and unyielding way to produce knowledge, and in many ways, play mimics the scientific process. Dr. Stuart Brown, a Psychologist from the Institute of Play writes, [Play is science exploration] [cite]. Furthermore, the scientific method gives knowledge of both the external world and internal world of the self, as does play. As Thomas Henricks writes in Play: a BasicPathway to the Self [Play is one way that we form our identities and become who we are.[21]. Finally, through understanding that the processes of knowing and exploring the world and ourselves are also processes of becoming, we can come to understand what scholar James Paul Gee has to say about games and their potential for learning. [Gee quote about semiotic domains and how they shape and change us] [2]. Open-ended games not only advance the possibility of understanding computational thinking, but through their open-endedness they enhance our ability to traverse the pathways of self exploration, and exploration about computational thinking, which also gives perspective on the nature of thought. For this paper, the author has attempted to practice science fiction prototyping and analysis in order to show how imagining the future can be incorporated into game design methodologies to discover game design challenges, anticipate the player experience stories of games with play cycles that last 5 to 20 years, and to simultaneously perform these tasks while playing a real interactive storytelling game to gain experiential knowledge and share that knowledge and process with the paper's audience.

In addition, this paper and the science fiction prototype included with it are actual prototypes of the game AI Invasion with the additional character role of audience member, that those reading the paper may play at their leisure. The rules of the game and how to play follow. As an observer, your role is to determine which of the characters presented in the prototype is an AI. In the tutorial, players guess which sentences are AI or human written. There are approximately 30 AI written sentences. Each one that you find earns you a health point for the next round. Each sentence that you guess is AI written that is human, you lose a point. You lose the game when you run out of points.

After the tutorial, everything that character says in dialogue was actually written by either the Griffon Model AI in AI Dungeon or the Dragon Model. The observer will earn one point for each character they correctly eject, and they will lose one point for each human authored character they incorrectly eject.

In order to play multiplayer using the exact same prototype provided, it is important for fairness that none of the players have played the game with that text before. The process is the same except that the players vote together to eject whomever they believe are AI within the story. It is possible for more than one character in each prototype version to be an AI.

Finally, to play this game again with a group and with new text, simply try the following. Copy the text of the story and have one player make the AI generate the text for one or more of the character's dialogues. Make sure they mark somewhere hidden who the players were.

If one plays this game and would like to share thoughts, please write to me and let me know any feedback you have. As a play-centric designer, I am always looking to improve the experience of my players through direct feedback and playtests. The prototypes can be found here [22].

References

1. Norman, D.A.: The Design of Everyday Things, Revised and, Expanded Basic Books, New York (2013)
2. Gee, J.P.: What Video Games Have to Teach Us About Learning and Literacy, 1, Paperback Palgrave Macmillan, New York, NY (2004)
3. Dourish, P., Bell, G.: "Resistance is futile": reading science fiction alongside ubiquitous computing. Pers. Ubiquit. Comput. 18(4), 769–778 (2013). https://doi.org/10.1007/s00779-013-0678-7
4. Björk, S., Holopainen, J.: Patterns in Game Design, p. 12
5. Crawford, C.: Chris Crawford on Interactive Storytelling. New Riders, Berkeley (2013)
6. Murray, J.H.: Hamlet on the Holodeck: The Future of Narrative in Cyberspace, Updated. The MIT Press, Cambridge (2017)
7. Laurel, B.: Computers as Theatre, 2nd edn. Addison-Wesley, Upper Saddle River (2014)
8. Mateas, M., Stern, A.: Writing façade: a case study in procedural authorship. Comput. Sci. (2007)
9. Mateas, M., Stern, A.: Façade: An Experiment in Building a Fully-Realized Interactive Drama, p. 24
10. Stern, A., Mateas, M.: Façade. Playable Studios (2005)

11. Stanley, K.O., Lehman, J., Soros, L.: Open-endedness: The Last Grand Challenge You've Never Heard of. O'Reilly Media (2017). https://www.oreilly.com/radar/open-endedness-the-last-grand-challenge-youve-never-heard-of/. Accessed 12 Feb 2021
12. Walton, N., Dungeon, A.I.: Latitude
13. Johnson, B.D.: Science fiction prototyping: designing the future with science fiction. Synth. Lect. Comput. Sci. **3**(1), 1–190 (2011). https://doi.org/10.2200/S00336ED1V01Y201102 CSL003
14. Hensman, J.: The holonovel—a powerful methodology for prototyping and creating the future. In: 2017 23rd International Conference on Virtual System & Multimedia (VSMM), Dublin, October 2017, pp. 1–5. https://doi.org/10.1109/VSMM.2017.8346257
15. Miller, E.: Science Fiction Prototype AI Invasion Via Cordellia Tutorial, February 2021. https://drive.google.com/file/d/1qpv8qEkmt5I3bgpnHILiT7yyVZr1Qbip/view?usp=sharing
16. A What Works Clearinghouse Rapid Evidence Review of Distance Learning Programs, p. 18
17. Günther, G., Huschke, W., Steiner, W.: In: Günther, G., Huschke, W., Steiner, W. (eds.) Weimar, pp. 475–501. J.B. Metzler, Stuttgart (1993). https://doi.org/10.1007/978-3-476-02958-4_23
18. Klopfer, E., Haas, J., Osterweil, S., Rosenheck, L.: Resonant games: design principles for learning games that connect hearts, minds, and the everyday (2018)
19. Denning, P.J., Tedre, M.: Computational Thinking, p. 129
20. Kang, A.R., Jeong, S.H., Mohaisen, A., Kim, H.K.: Multimodal game bot detection using user behavioral characteristics. Springerplus **5**(1), 1–19 (2016). https://doi.org/10.1186/s40064-016-2122-8
21. Henricks, T.S.: Play: a basic pathway to the self. The Strong (2020)
22. Miller, E.: Link To Science Fiction Prototype AI Invasion Via Cordellia Game Documents, February 2021. https://drive.google.com/drive/folders/1gdtFdsP7TXhWOEOj9Xg5iYZ6b_2bsANF?usp=sharing

In-Game Advertising: Brand Integration and Player Involvement as Key Influencing Factors on Brand Recall

Fabrizio Palmas[1][✉] [iD], Ramona Reinelt[2][✉] [iD],
and Gudrun Klinker[1][✉] [iD]

[1] Technical University of Munich, 85748 Garching, Germany
fabrizio.palmas@tum.de, klinker@in.tum.de
[2] University of Augsburg, 86159 Augsburg, Germany
ramona.reinelt@wiwi.uni-augsburg.de

Abstract. In-game advertising is proving itself as an important marketing tool because it promises a strong advertising impact when considering essential influencing factors. This study focuses on involvement and brand integration as influencing factors on brand recall. Regarding involvement, we aim to examine if players will remember significantly more brands than observers based on the former's higher levels of emotional involvement. Additionally, we examine if a more pronounced sports affinity, as an expression of personal involvement, positively affects brand recall. We aim to determine if significant differences between brand recall for prominent and peripheral advertisements can be observed regarding the degree of brand integration.

Within this study, 56 players and 58 observers first played or watched someone play a racing game and were consequently polled regarding their ability to recall the brands advertised within the game. Our findings show that advertisers should not exclusively rely on in-game advertisements for their products. This is because this type of advertisement cannot match the advertising effect that more conventional formats on traditional media can offer and hence is unfit to replace them entirely. Moreover, advertisers are encouraged to investigate personal involvement further, as an important influencing factor for advertising impact. The improved brand recall we observed for participants with a high value for sports affinity indicates a positive correlation between stronger personal involvement and a more substantial advertising impact. Additionally, advertisers aiming to market high-involvement products should focus on prominent advertisement displays by establishing as many interactive player contacts as possible to achieve better brand recall.

Keywords: In-game advertising · Brand recall · Video games

1 Introduction

1.1 Video Games Market

One of the most outstanding marketing triumphs in the entertainment sector are video games, which, ever since their inception, have continuously expanded their market [1].

© Springer Nature Switzerland AG 2021
X. Fang (Ed.): HCII 2021, LNCS 12789, pp. 352–367, 2021.
https://doi.org/10.1007/978-3-030-77277-2_27

Since the first games emerged, the video gaming industry has shown no signs of decline and is expected to reach three billion gamers by 2023 [2, 3].

The COVID-19 pandemic has forced the world into an economic recession. However, the video game sector is bucking the trend and thriving thanks to many people being forced to stay at home and using video games as a form of entertainment [4]. Furthermore, several new business models have been established around video games thanks to the new technological possibilities offered by the various devices and platforms used to play video games online and offline, enabling them to consistently expand their reach and thus appeal to an ever-increasing number of players [2, 5].

Nowadays, the digitalization, the internet and the widespread availability of computing devices have helped video games become an accessible form of entertainment [6]. Game development studios, publishing companies and indie developers can all easily distribute video games and reach an ever-increasing number of customers of all demographics, allowing gaming to become a form of entertainment with high commercial value. Games are now gaining popularity worldwide and across nearly all age groups, with even parents, seniors aged 65 or older and gamers of all genders devoting more and more of their time to gaming [7]. Existing video game content spans a wide range of topics and video game consumption is further evolving into watching someone else play games on web-based streaming services instead of actively playing them [8, 9, 10].

The results of several surveys show that one of the more common video game genres is racing games [1, 11–16]. In racing games, the player competes in a lapped race competition with vehicles in real-world racing leagues (simulations) or fictive settings (arcade racing games). The global racing game market is expected to grow even more in the next years because of the growing demand for racing games and driving simulators since the number of professional and casual gamers, in general, is increasing around the world. Racing video games seem to be preferred by male gamers aged between 21 and 35 moreso than female gamers [17]. The increasing acceptance of AR and VR technology and the increasing demand for immersive games could further support this market's growth [18]. Meanwhile, racing video games (e.g. Formula 1) are already being incorporated into worldwide eSports events [12, 19].

Companies that want to reach new potential customers should consider extending their advertising strategy to include video games as a valuable new platform for brand communication and therefore as a new opportunity to advertise their products. Investing in an in-game brand advertisement to reach gamers could result in new opportunities and allow companies to reach an even broader spectrum of potential target consumers: the audience of gaming video content on online streaming services. Although advertisers may be tempted to transform video games into an interactive and immersive outbound marketing gimmick, it is essential to investigate which key factors can influence brand recall to incorporate advertisement in video games in a meaningful way and to thus develop an effective marketing strategy around them.

1.2   Understanding Video Games

To understand why video games have gained such impressive popularity, several different aspects need to be analyzed. In the last years, game development has changed radically through the democratization of game engines and the improved accessibility of game development tools and game assets [20]. It has also become easier for small teams of indie game developers, not just for big developer studios, to release their video games on several platforms and reach a broader range of players [21, 22].

Even although video game development embraces creativity, at their core, video games differ from other media within the entertainment industry based on their interactivity and the sense of agency that players experience while playing. A game system generates content and reacts to limited players choices and behaviours, evoking a sense of control in players [23, 24]. Players can be engaged in several ways while gaming. One of them is by providing an interactive environment called a gameworld with information, which helps create immersive experiences, dispersed throughout it [25]. In these gameworlds, players can engage with vast amounts of base content, challenges and adaptive customized content updates, which can be made available in real-time. Due to the progress of technology and computer science, it is possible to represent a broad range of interactive scenarios and utilize different graphical styles in video games.

Additionally, the graphical detail achievable in video games and simulations is astonishingly high and tends to achieve photorealism [26]. Players can explore the gameworld playing as photorealistic characters which are animated by humans using motion capturing systems and display realistic facial animations [27–29]. This helps players to feel immersed in the video game.

Another engaging aspect of video games is the possibility to play them in multiplayer modes together with and against real people anywhere in the world and at any time.

A new direction in the evolution of video games is the use of immersive technologies such as extended reality (virtual, augmented and mixed-reality) that involves and engages the players in new immersive ways [30–32].

At this point, we can summarize what video games are: they can be defined as the result of a creative process which aims to entertain people by engaging them to interact with a game system via a computing device. The immediate response of each goal-oriented interaction in a rule-bound gameplay system is displayed to the gamer. Typically, video games are characterized by adopting a graphical style and representation which follow a creator's vision, having playable and non-playable characters, taking place in a game world, utilizing a sound design (which may include music) and by being designed to create an enjoyable experience that can optionally be embedded into a story.

Companies should aim to utilize the strong advertising potential provided by the popularity and the engaging nature of games and thus examine their communicational strategy to determine if in-game advertising could be implemented to further improve their brand communication.

1.3 Video Games Advertising Types

Games being available on various platforms and devices results in a multitude of advertising opportunities and formats. In this context, games can showcase the selected brands via various digital display methods, ranging from conventional non-immersive displays to complex custom solutions. Around game ads, custom branded games (aka Advergames) and in-game advertising are considered as the three most significant ways for advertisers to reach their target groups in games [33].

Around game ads describe the sponsoring of advertising units which are positioned around the game and the gameplay itself. To achieve this, ads or digital product videos can be displayed during loading screens, natural game pauses or in-between the rounds of a match [33].

Advergames are games that are tailor-made for a specific brand and distributed online via converging media (Computers, Smartphones, Tablets or Consoles) [34]. In this case, the advertisement is directly integrated into an interactive gaming experience. Consequently, a connection between the brand and the game is established without distracting the players or otherwise affecting their engagement. The high degree of effectiveness for this advertising type results from the prolonged contact time between the brand and the player. Thus, the user is continuously confronted with the respective advertisements, facilitating the transmission of brand values [33].

In-game advertising describes the direct integration of advertisement displays into the gameworld or into specific scenes within a video game. The available slots for brand placement are determined by the game's developer and filled with real or fictional brands in accordance with possible contractual obligations. Research has demonstrated that real advertisements within a game positively affect the player's experience because they make the game environment feel more realistic and lifelike [34]. Today, compared to past advertisement placement in games, brands can be integrated into the game experience on a deeper level. Especially in sports games, the use of real brands or sponsoring supports an improved sense of realism and authenticity for the gaming experience.

On a basic level, we can distinguish between static and dynamic advertisements for in-game advertising. Most advertising campaigns displayed in video games utilize dynamic advertisements. When directly programmed into the game, dynamic advertisements' main advantages compared to static ones are their flexibility and their efficiency. They allow advertisers to specifically tailor their advertising campaigns to circumstances like the geographical location, the time of day etc. [33].

Despite the increasing use of in-game advertising, there is little research on the true potential of this important advertising tool. Although increasing the players' brand awareness is the primary goal of in-game advertising, little is known about the actual effect this has on their brand recall, their brand attitude and their purchase behaviour [35].

2 Advertising in Video Games

2.1 Success Factors and Impact of In-Game Advertising

At its core, in-game advertising functions as an important new communicative tool in marketing, which aims to contribute to an increase in brand awareness and at the same time aims to influence the recipient's brand attitude positively [36].

The impact of in-game advertising can be secured by taking into consideration certain key success factors. Most studies measure the success factors for in-game advertising by polling the participants' brand recall. Examples of influencing factors, in this case are the systematical integration of brands or products in a virtual environment or the users' involvement. In this context, the degree of integration for a brand can be understood as the level of depth at which the respective advertisement is integrated into the game [37].

Chen and Ringel (2001) differentiate between three types of brand integration within a game as displayed in Fig. 1:

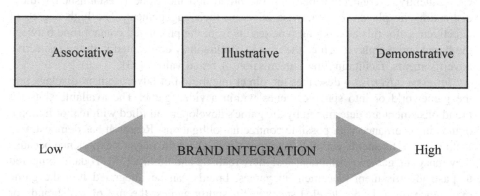

Fig. 1. Types of brand integration within a game [39]

Associative advertisement aims to increase brand awareness by creating a connection between the showcased product and the activity. The game's content is intended to strengthen the brand image logically or emotionally [39].

Illustrative advertisement focuses on the actual interaction between the player and the brand/product, allowing the player to gain increased knowledge of the product's properties by seamlessly integrating it into the game's plot, without directing the player's attention to it [39].

Demonstrative advertisement aims to directly integrate the advertised product/brand and a realistic example for its usage into the game, allowing the player to interact with it actively [39].

The authors Chen and Ringel observe a strong transfer of effectiveness from the game to the player's attitude towards the brand/product for in-game advertising with a high degree of brand integration [38]. The potent psychological effectiveness and performance of an instance of strong brand integration for in-game advertisement are best understood via Kroeber-Riel's and Weinberg's model of pathways, as depicted in Fig. 2. The model exemplifies the individual processes within a human being after an advertising contact and is therefore well suited to a simplified explanation of the general advertising impact of in-game advertising.

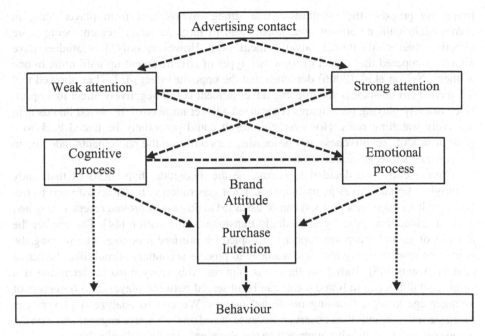

Fig. 2. Model of pathways [40]

The model of pathways is based on the assumptions that a recipient's attitude towards a product and their purchase intention depend on the degree of involvement and the advertisement's processing level [41].

Due to the active process of media consumption and the direct interaction with the medium by the player, a gamer's involvement level tends to be relatively high. Furthermore, given the voluntary and active nature of the player's interaction with the game content, their activation potential is strengthened and their concentration levels are elevated [42].

Regarding the advertising message, because of their limited capacity for processing information, the recipient is forced to differentiate between the perceived stimuli and filter out the ones that seem more important subjectively [37].

Thus, for in-game advertisement, it is assumed that advertisements with a high degree of integration offer the highest probability of successful acquisition and processing of information on the player's end.

Consequently, in-game advertisement's success is traced back to a high degree of involvement based on the emotional influence experienced whilst playing a game. This can be explained via the strong brand integration within the digital game, which leads to players being more inclined to engage with the advertising message cognitively [36].

2.2 Research Questions

In accordance with the model of pathways, involvement has been identified as an important influencing factor for the effectiveness of in-game advertising. Thus, authors frequently propose the assumption that strong involvement from players can, in combination with emotional attachment, lead to in-game advertisement being more effective than conventional advertisement [41]. However, only few studies have directly compared the impact of these two types of advertisement up until now. In one of them, Nelson et al. (2006) demonstrated the opposite effect [43]. They showed that the medial circumstances for in-game advertisement could negatively affect its impact, since actively playing participants recognized a lower number of displayed brands than passively watching ones. However, this result could potentially be traced back to a general lack of receptiveness and processing capability on the participants' side due to the selected subjects' characteristics.

Consequently, we decided to reexamine the theoretical hypothesis of that study employing digital natives as participants. Their generation is better accustomed to frequent multimedia interaction and can be assumed to possess improved receptiveness and have an easier time processing medially transmitted information [44]. The smaller the amount of mental reception capacity occupied by primary processes like playing the game, the more capacity remains available to process secondary stimuli like the actual advertisements [45]. Based on these assumptions, this study aims to determine if a significant difference in brand recall can be observed between players and observers of younger age groups, focusing on digital natives. We aim to analyze if players can recognize more brands than observers because, based on their active engagement with the game compared to a passive approach on the observers' side, they display higher levels of emotional involvement and a higher capacity for the reception of secondary stimuli through their higher levels of habituation. Therefore, H1 can be formulated as follows:

H1: Players recognize more brands than observers.

Additionally, theoretical assumptions claim that the effectiveness of in-game advertisement can be ascribed not only to the high levels of emotional involvement caused by actively playing the game, but also to high degrees of personal involvement with the game's content itself [42]. Over the course of this study, we noticed a research deficit regarding the dependency of the effectiveness of in-game advertising on the user's personal involvement. Thus, we decided to examine the connection between a user's personal involvement and brand recall within a sports game. In order to empirically measure their personal levels of involvement, players were determined to possess certain levels of affinity for sports, representing their levels of personal involvement. We aim to confirm the positive influence of this personal involvement on brand recall by showing that players with a more pronounced affinity for sports remember more brands from the racing game than players with lower sports affinity levels. On this basis, we formulated our second hypothesis, H2:

H2: The stronger a player's sports affinity, the stronger their brand recall.

Brand integration has previously been described as another essential factor for successful and effective in-game advertising. The degree of integration for types of in-game advertisement has been the subject of various empirical studies aiming to research its effect on advertisement perception. Generally, the consensus seems to confirm the theoretical assumption of prominent advertisements with a high degree of integration being remembered and recognized more readily [35, 37, 41, 46–48].

A closer examination of these studies reveals that, during the respective experiments, not all brand names had been displayed equally often. From a learning-psychology perspective, the capability for memorization is boosted by frequent repetition [49]. This may have led to evaluation inaccuracies in these empirical studies, where better brand recall may have been falsely attributed to a high degree of integration, and not just to certain brands being displayed more often. This study aims to reinforce the validity of the previously listed studies by ensuring the same number of displays for peripheral and prominent brands during the experiment. Under this condition, possible differences in brand recall between peripheral and prominent advertisement displays can be examined. The aim is to prove that participants better remember prominent advertisement displays with which they interact actively. H3 can therefore be formulated as:

H3: Prominent brand displays are remembered more often than peripheral ones.

3 Method

3.1 Sample

For our sample, we were able to consider n = 114 valid participants. Through an approximately even split of 49% players and 51% observers, we performed reliable comparisons between the groups. Table 1 summarises the main characteristics and illustrates the equal distribution of players and observers.

Table 1. Sample characteristics and distribution.

		Player	Observer
Sex	Female	26%	32%
	Male	23%	19%
Age	> 21	20%	21%
	21–30	27%	27%
	31–40	2%	1%
	> 40	0%	2%
Game console usage	Never	7%	15%
	Rarely	24%	19%
	Frequently	9%	4%
	Regularly	8%	6%
	Daily	2%	6%
Frequency of playing sports games	Never	17%	22%
	Rarely	16%	15%
	Frequently	6%	2%
	Regularly	4%	3%
	Daily	6%	10%
Sports affinity	Never	5%	4%
	Rarely	16%	14%
	Frequently	16%	18%
	Regularly	7%	9%
	Daily	5%	6%

3.2 Questionnaire

The questionnaire consisted of examining the participants' brand recall, the registration of their role (player/observer) and demographic data and questions regarding game console usage, frequency of playing sports games and sports affinity.

Sports affinity for the player-subjects was determined as a construct via a 5-step Likert scale, ranging from 1 = "daily" to 5 = "never" for each one of the following three items: "visits to a sports stadium", "sports broadcasts followed" and "console sports games played". This approach was selected because for H2 the focus was not placed on the connection between singular sports activities and brand recall, but instead on finding out if a general interest in sports can improve brand recall in a sports game. In accordance with George and Mallery (2002), the internal consistency is acceptable with a Cronbach's α of α = .76 [50].

Brand recall was determined based on the surveying of 8 different nominally scaled brand memorizations. When answering the questionnaire, the subjects were presented with a choice between the correct brand and a dummy one[1].

For the examination of H1, the eight singular instances of brand recall were assigned a score between 8 and 16. Subsequently, they were recoded into a ranking system between 0 = "no brand recognized" and 8 = "eight brands recognized". We considered the calculation of a total score to be a more functional option since the aim was not to determine the effectiveness of in-game advertising for a specific brand but to deliver a blanket statement on the influence of a player's role or sports affinity on their brand recall.

For the examination of H2, only participants with the player role were selected for evaluation. This decision was taken to ensure a target-group focussed examination with the aim of being able to provide relevant and practical recommendations.

Surveying the brand recall of prominent and peripheral brands for H3 functioned in an analogous way to examining brand recall in H1, whilst being based on player data only. The brands were first divided into prominent and peripheral brand displays based on their degree of integration within the game. The brand recall for the prominent brands consisted of the combined score for the recognition of Rolex, Pirelli, Allianz and Fly Emirates. On the other hand, the brand recall for the peripheral brands consisted of the combined score for the recognition of DHL, Petronas, UBS and P Zero. For the examination of H3, calculated scores ranging from 4 to 8 for both variables were coded in gradations with values between 0 = "no brand recognized" and 4 = "all four brands recognized".

3.3 Study Design

The study design comprised the conduction of the experiment on the PS4 game console and the racing game Formula-1 2016 as well as the subsequent surveying of the participants via a questionnaire. On this basis, brand recall for in-game advertising was measured for participants after they completed a time trial over three predefined laps on a racetrack (the gameworld) with various advertisements positioned along the route.

---

[1] The dummy options resembled the actual brands from the game.

Immediately afterwards, their memory regarding the advertisement was tested via a questionnaire. Brand recall was measured by allowing each participant to choose between two potential brands, one of them being the actual advertisement displayed in the game and the other being a dummy. This approach allowed us to test all the varyingly integrated brands, even peripheral ones, for their conscious or semi-conscious memorization by the players. The placement of prominent brands in especially challenging areas and situations within the race (e g. tight corners), led to them achieving higher degrees of interactivity with the players. Peripheral brands could only be seen on less attention-grabbing advertising boards. To secure the validity of our results, the experiment was conducted with consistently the same game settings. All test subjects drove on the same racetrack and encountered the same advertisements. The experiment was conducted as follows:

It was presented to the participants under the pretext of a study to evaluate stress levels in sports games. Players wore a dummy fitness tracker pretending to measure their heart rate. This procedure aimed to ensure a natural playing situation without an artificial focus on the displayed brands. The experiment was conducted in groups of two, with the participants themselves assigning each other the roles of player and observer. To avoid a reduction in reception capacity because of difficulties with the game controls, the main functions and controls were explained to the participants before the experiment. The observers' reception capacity was secured by requesting that they cheer on the player, therefore being forced to engage with the game actively. In order to create a more natural playing environment for the player, the vibration function of the controller was enabled, the volume for the game sound was raised, and the testing room was darkened. After the experiment, the participants were asked to fill out a questionnaire in a separate room.

4 Results

All necessary requirements for all three hypotheses were met.

H1 aimed to examine if the means for both roles (player/observer) displayed significant differences regarding the brand recall. To this end, we conducted an independent two-sample t-test. The comparison of the brand recall means for players and observers showed a negative mean difference of $M = -0,485$. Players displayed a mean of $M = 4,95$ with observers reaching a value of $M = 5,43$, resulting in the mean difference of $M = -0,485$. This difference was confirmed as being significant via a t-test: $t(114) = -2,034$, $p < 0,044$.

Players ($M = 4,95$; $SD = 1,420$) remember significantly less brands than observers ($M = 5,43$; $SD = 1,110$). Thus, our first hypothesis was not confirmed.

H2 aimed to explore the connection between an affinity to sports and the brand recall of the players. The strength of the statistical relationship between the variables was measured via Spearman's rank correlation coefficient. The correlation analysis resulted in a negative correlation coefficient ($r = -0,300$, $p = 0,025$). The result is interpreted as a weak correlation, which is significant. Consequently, regarding the surveyed players, it can be determined that the lower/higher their sports affinity was rated, the higher/lower the number of correctly remembered brands was.

In turn, it can be derived from the polarity of the scales that players with a greater affinity for sports remember more brands correctly. Therefore, H2 can be considered as confirmed.

H3 aimed to examine possible significant differences between the means for the players' brand recall regarding prominent and peripheral brands, respectively. For this purpose, we used the dependent t-test for paired samples. The comparison resulted in a positive mean difference M = 0,911. Brand recall for prominent brands displayed a mean of M = 2,93, which was M = 0,911 higher than the Mean M = 2,02 for peripheral ones. The t-test also documented a significant difference, t (56) = 5,703, p < 0,001.

Prominent brands (M = 2,93; SD = 0,828) were memorized significantly more often than peripheral ones (M = 2,02; SD = 1,018). Therefore, hypothesis H3 can be considered as confirmed.

5 Discussion

5.1 Findings

This paper aimed to examine specific findings regarding the practical use and the design of in-game advertising. In this context, the objective was to confirm the degree of integration and involvement as significant influential factors for improving brand recall.

To this end, the first hypothesis examined the participant role regarding a systematic difference in brand recall. Players remembered significantly fewer brands than observers. Contrary to our theoretical assumptions, this study was unable to confirm that the high emotional involvement players experience can help in-game advertisements match the advertisement perception provided by more conventional media, even for comparatively young participants with an assumed higher capacity for stimulus processing. One possible cause for this result could be unconsidered influential factors that may have led to the players' worse brand recall values. Therefore, the result may not necessarily be attributed solely to the participants' role.

Considering the sampling characteristics, we found a clear majority of the participants to be relatively inexperienced gamers. Thus, it can be inferred that these inexperienced players were forced to utilize a high percentage of their mental capacity for controlling the game and were limited in the number of resources they could devote to secondary brand stimuli, while the observers were able to fully concentrate on the on-screen gameplay. Therefore, it can be assumed that a smaller amount of gaming experience leads to negative consequences regarding the brand recall for the players. In light of the above, we conclude that the influence emotional investment has on brand recall needs to be further examined with experienced gamers as test subjects. This would ensure the players' capacity to match the observers' ability to focus on the on-screen gameplay and avoid a reduction in receptiveness because of a lack of familiarity with game controls.

The second hypothesis aimed to determine the possible correlation between the players' sports affinity and their brand recall. We were able to observe a statistically significant correlation between sports affinity and brand recall since players with stronger sports affinity were able to remember more brands. The basis for this hypothesis was our intention to highlight not only emotional involvement but also personal involvement as an influencing factor for the effectiveness of in-game advertisement. Our selection of a player's sports affinity as an expression of their personal involvement when playing a racing game was based on the assumption that consumer interest for a sports game would be reflected in a general affinity for sports. Under closer scrutiny, uncertainties regarding the representative status of the self-determined variable of sports affinity with an acceptable internal consistency of ($\alpha = .76$) arise since it may consist of stereotypical assumptions. Thus, this hypothesis's examination has primarily confirmed a systematic correlation, which could be further investigated for a content-related causal-connection. For this purpose, additional studies could, while building on this study's foundation, aim to identify targeted representations of the personal involvement for racing game players. The potential findings could allow for more reliable conclusions regarding the specific characteristics which cause better brand recall for target groups with a strong affinity for sports.

Lastly, hypothesis H3 examined the differences in brand recall between prominently and peripherally displayed advertisements. To this end, one criterion for racetrack selection was the same number of occurrences for advertisements of each brand to avoid more frequent recurrences of one brand over another as a cause for better brand recall. We confirmed significantly better brand recall for prominent advertisements, allowing us to assume a more substantial advertising impact in this case. When evaluating these results, it has to be considered that the influence of the degree of integration was examined for high-involvement products only. Therefore, it is impossible to infer any generalized assertions regarding the profitability of utilizing high-level advertisements for low-involvement products. Various publications refer to the necessity of varying the degree of integration in accordance with the degree of product-involvement. According to this research, high-involvement goods, in particular, require a high degree of integration for their respective in-game advertisements, whilst low-involvement goods can achieve a strong advertising impact even with peripheral advertisements [51]. These assumptions often draw upon the mere-exposure-effect theory. It describes an automatic learning process, which achieves an improved attitude towards an object via repeated displays and demonstrably functions even for unconscious perception or after brief stimulus exposure [52]. This allows companies to structure their advertisements for low-involvement products accordingly and thus sensibly reduce costs compared to more interactive types of advertisements. Further scientific research may seek a deeper understanding of the relation between the degree of integration of an advertisement and product-involvement. Well-founded recommendations for action could be derived from the resulting findings, especially if they indicated better brand recall for low-involvement products when using peripheral advertisements compared to prominent ones.

5.2   Limitations

When evaluating our results, the exclusive use of a racing game in our experiment must be considered. Thus, their validity is limited to the context of racing games and cannot be extended more generally to in-game advertising as a whole. For example, it is impossible to infer any assumptions about the validity of the examined influencing factors for other game genres like open-world games, which allow players to move freely around in the game world without time restraints.

Additionally, brand recall was only observed over a relatively short amount of time instead of examining the participants' brand recall in a long-term study. Therefore, no definitive assertions can be made about the effectiveness of in-game advertisement and brand recall in the long term.

Furthermore, the selected participants coincidentally focused on young test subjects, without gaming experience being applied as a criterion for selection.

6 Conclusion

This study was able to make an important contribution to research on key influencing factors and create awareness for the fact that the success of in-game advertising depends on certain essential influencing factors. The hypotheses were tested via correlation analysis and mean differences (t-tests). Results demonstrate that players recall significantly fewer brands than observers, that higher degrees of sports affinity lead to better brand recall and that prominent advertisement displays are recalled significantly more often.

This study allows further research to build upon our findings and expediently study the use of in-game advertising in more practical detail to achieve more effective advertising contacts with a specified target group. To this end, a variety of opportunities for further research, including the degree of gaming experience as an additional sampling criterion, was highlighted.

After thorough discussion and interpretation of our results, we can infer the following conclusion for practical applications: Advertisers may not, in the absence of stronger and more relevant empirical evidence to the contrary, exclusively rely on advertising their products via in-game advertising because this type of advertising (as observed in our study) seems to be unable to match the advertising impact provided by more conventional media and therefore replace it. Advertisers are called upon to further study gamers' personal involvement since the stronger brand recall observed for participants with stronger sports affinity indicates a high degree of personal involvement, leading to an increase in advertising impact. According to our study, advertisers should focus on prominent advertisement displays for better brand recall when advertising high-involvement products by achieving as many interactive player-contacts as possible.

Acknowledgements. We thank Luca Sarsky for proofreading this paper.

References

1. Marchand, A., Hennig-Thurau, T.: Value creation in the video game industry: Industry economics, consumer benefits, and research opportunities. J. Interact. Mark. **27**(3), 141–157 (2013)
2. Statista: Number of active video gamers worldwide from 2015 to 2023. https://www.statista.com/statistics/748044/number-video-gamers-world. Accessed 07 Feb 2021
3. Statista: Revenue of the video gaming market worldwide from 2015 to 2024, by category. https://www.statista.com/statistics/254106/value-of-the-global-video-game-market-by-component. Accessed 07 Feb 2021
4. Statista: Increase in time spent video gaming during the COVID-19 pandemic worldwide as of June 2020, by genre. https://www.statista.com/statistics/1188558/gaming-genres-spent-covid. Accessed 07 Feb 2021
5. Statista: The Most Important Gaming Platforms in 2019. https://www.statista.com/chart/4527/game-developers-platform-preferences. Accessed 07 Feb 2021
6. Statista: On which devices do you play video or computer games? https://www.statista.com/statistics/818671/gaming-device-preferences-germany. Accessed 07 Feb 2021
7. Statista: Gender distribution of video gaming parents worldwide in 2020, by country. https://www.statista.com/statistics/1128578/distribution-video-gaming-parents. Accessed 07 Feb 2021
8. Johnsmeyer, B., Getomer, J., Okimoto, M.: Gamers on YouTube: Evolving Video Consumption (2013). https://www.thinkwithgoogle.com/marketing-strategies/app-and-mobile/youtube-marketing-to-gamers. Accessed 07 Feb 2021
9. Ramdurai, G.: Think Gaming Content Is Niche? Think Again (2014). https://www.thinkwithgoogle.com/marketing-strategies/video/think-gaming-content-is-niche-think-again. Accessed 07 Feb 2021
10. Statista: Gaming video content market - Statistics & Facts. https://www.statista.com/topics/3147/gaming-video-content-market. Accessed 07 Feb 2021
11. Statista: Video games ranked by unit sales in the United Kingdom (UK) in 2020. https://www.statista.com/statistics/274072/most-popular-games-in-the-united-kingdom-uk-by-unit-sales. Accessed 07 Feb 2021
12. Statista: Most popular video games among eSports players in Italy in 2019. https://www.statista.com/statistics/1027914/most-popular-video-games-in-italy/. Accessed 07 Feb 2021
13. Statista: Preferred genres of console games in South Korea in 2020. https://www.statista.com/statistics/1075559/south-korea-preferred-console-games-genres/. Accessed 07 Feb 2021
14. Statista: Share of women who like racing video games in Japan as of February 2020, by age group. https://www.statista.com/statistics/1115665/japan-popularity-video-game-genre-racing-games-women-by-age-group/. Accessed 07 Feb 2021
15. Statista: Genre breakdown of video game sales in the United States in 2018. https://www.statista.com/statistics/189592/breakdown-of-us-video-game-sales-2009-by-genre/. Accessed 07 Feb 2021
16. Statista: Unit sales of Mario Kart video games worldwide as of December 2019, by title. https://www.statista.com/statistics/1091382/mario-kart-unit-sales/. Accessed 07 Feb 2021
17. Statista: Share of players of racing video games worldwide as of November 2020, by gender and age. https://www.statista.com/statistics/1188966/racing-video-game-players/. Accessed 07 Feb 2021
18. Market Research Future: Global racing games market research report: Forecast till 2026. Grand View Research (2020)

19. F1 Esports Series. https://f1esports.com/. Accessed 07 Feb 2021
20. Unity. https://unity.com/our-company/newsroom/unity-drives-democratization-development-2016-eight-unite-conferences-globally. Accessed 07 Feb 2021
21. Lipkin, N.D.: The Indiepocalypse: the political-economy of independent game development labor in contemporary indie markets (2019). http://gamestudies.org/1902/articles/lipkin. Accessed 07 Feb 2021
22. Statista: Number of indie games released on Steam worldwide from 2015 to 2017. https://www.statista.com/statistics/809258/number-indie-games-steam/. Accessed 07 Feb 2021
23. Stang, S.: This action will have consequences': interactivity and player agency (2019). http://gamestudies.org/1901/articles/stang. Accessed 07 Feb 2021
24. Zackariasson, P., Walfisz, M., Wilson, T.L.: Management of creativity in video game development: a case study. Serv. Mark. Q. 27(4), 73–97 (2006)
25. Bayliss, P.: Beings in the game-world: characters, avatars, and players. In: Proceedings of the 4th Australasian Conference on Interactive Entertainment, pp. 1–6. RMIT University, Melbourne (2007)
26. Wattanasoontorn, V., Theppaitoon, M., Bernik, A.: A Classification of Visual Style for 3D Games. In: 2019 23rd International Computer Science and Engineering Conference (ICSEC), pp. 12–17. Phuket (2019)
27. Smith, G.M.: Computer games have words, too: dialogue conventions in final fantasy VII (2002). http://www.gamestudies.org/0202/smith. Accessed 07 Feb 2021
28. Parke, F.I., Waters, K.: Computer Facial Animation, 2nd edn. CRC Press, New York (2008)
29. Menache, A.: Motion Capture Primer. In: Parent, R., Ebert, D.S., Gould, D. et al. Computer Animation Complete: All-in-One: Learn Motion Capture, Characteristic, Point-Based, and Maya Winning Techniques, p. 71. Morgan Kaufmann, Burlington (2009)
30. Statista: VR/AR/MR/XR technology and content investment focus worldwide from 2016 to 2019. https://www.statista.com/statistics/829729/investments-focus-vr-augmented-reality-worldwide/. Accessed 07 Feb 2021
31. Statista: Investment in augmented and virtual reality (AR/VR) technology worldwide in 2024, by use case. https://www.statista.com/statistics/1098345/worldwide-ar-vr-investment-use-case/. Accessed 07 Feb 2021
32. SuperData a Nielsen Company: 2020 Year In Review: Digital Games and Interactive Media. https://www.superdataresearch.com/reports/p/2020-year-in-review. Accessed 07 Feb 2021
33. IAB: Games Advertising Ecosystem Guide: Understanding today's game play, the core game types and advertising categories for marketers to reach consumers. https://www.iab.com/wp-content/uploads/2015/10/IAB_Games_Ad_Eco_Guide.pdf. Accessed 07 Feb 2021
34. Morillas, A.S., Martin, L.R.: Advergaming: an advertising tool with a future. Int. J. Hisp. Media 9, 14–31 (2016)
35. Nelson, M.R.: Recall of brand placements in computer/Video games. J. Advert. Res. 42, 80–92 (2002)
36. Kroeber-Riel, W., Weinberg, P.: Konsumentenverhalten [Consumer behaviour], 8th edn. Verlag Franz Vahlen, München (2002)
37. Grace, L.D., Coyle, J.: Player performance and in game advertising retention. In: Proceedings of the 8th International Conference on Advances in Computer Entertainment Technology, pp. 1–5. Association for Computing Machinery, New York (2011)
38. Chen, J., Ringel, M.: Can Advergaming be the Future of Interactive Advertising? (2001). http://web.archive.org/web/20030410231814/http:/www.kpe.com/ourwork/pdf/advergaming.pdf. Accessed 07 Feb 2021

39. Martí-Parreño, J., Aldas-Manzano, J., Currás-Pérez, R., Sanchez-Garcia, I.: Factors contributing brand attitude in advergames: entertainment and irritation. J. Brand Manag. **20**(5), 374–388 (2013)

40. Kroeber-Riel, W., Weinberg, P.: Konsumentenverhalten [Consumer behaviour], 7th edn. Verlag Franz Vahlen, München (1999)

41. Reich, C.: Was beeinflusst die Werbewirkung von In-Game-Advertising? [What influences the advertising impact of in-game advertising?]. In: Aretz, W., Mierke, K. (eds.) Aktuelle Themen der Wirtshaftspsychologie: Beitrage und Studien – vol. 1, pp. 212–230. Kölner Wissenschaftsverlag, Köln (2008)

42. Herrewijn, L., Poels, K.: Recall and recognition of in-game advertising: the role of game control. Front. Psychol. **4**(1023), 1–14 (2014)

43. Nelson, M.R., Yaros, R.A., Keum, H.: Examining the influence of telepresence on spectator and player processing of real and fictitious brands in a computer game. J. Advert. **35**(4), 87–99 (2006)

44. Bennett, S., Maton, K., Kervin, L.: The "digital natives" debate: a critical review of the evidence. Br. J. Edu. Technol. **39**(5), 775–786 (2008)

45. Kahneman, D.: Attention and Effort. Prentice-Hall, Englewood Cliffs (1973)

46. Schneider, L.-P., Cornwell, T.B.: Cashing in on crashes via brand placement in computer games. Int. J. Advert. **24**(3), 321–343 (2005)

47. Lee, M., Faber, R.J.: Effects of product placement in online games on brand memory. J. Advert. **36**(4), 75–90 (2007)

48. Grigorovic, I,D.M., Constantin, C.D.: Experiencing interactive advertising beyond rich media: impacts of ad type and presence on brand effectiveness in 3D gaming immersive virtual environments. J. Interact. Adv. **5**(1), 22–36 (2004)

49. Tabibian, B., Upadhyay, U., De, A., Zarezade, A., Schölkopf, B., Gomez-Rodriguez, M.: Enhancing human learning via spaced repetition optimization. Proc. Natl. Acad. Sci. **116** (10), 3988–3993 (2019)

50. George, D., Mallery, P.: SPSS for Windows Step by Step: A Simple Guide and Reference, 4th edn. Allyn & Bacon, Boston (2002)

51. Edery, D., Mollick, E.: Changing the Game: How Video Games Are Transforming the Future of Business. FT Press, Upper Saddle River (2009)

52. Ruggieri, S., Boca, S.: At the roots of product placement: the mere exposure effect. Eur. J. Psychol. **9**(2), 246–258 (2013)

Detecting Real-Time Correlated Simultaneous Events in Microblogs: The Case of Men's Olympic Football

Samer Muthana Sarsam[1]([⊠]), Hosam Al-Samarraie[2],
Nurhidayah Bahar[3], Abdul Samad Shibghatullah[4], Atef Eldenfria[5],
and Ahmed Al-Sa'Di[6,7]

[1] Department of Business Analytics, Sunway University Business School,
Sunway University, Petaling Jaya, Selangor, Malaysia
samers@sunway.edu.my
[2] School of Media and Performing Arts, Coventry University, Coventry, UK
[3] Department of Operations and Management Information Systems, Faculty
of Business and Accountancy, University of Malaya, Kuala Lumpur, Malaysia
[4] Institute of Computer Science and Digital Innovation, UCSI University,
Kuala Lumpur, Malaysia
[5] Faculty of Information Technology, Misurata University, Misurata, Libya
[6] School of Engineering, Computer and Mathematical Sciences,
Auckland University of Technology, Auckland, New Zealand
[7] Whitireia and WelTec, Wellington, New Zealand

Abstract. Although many predictive models have been designed to detect real-time events, there is still little progress in characterizing simultaneous events. Simultaneous events found in the sport domain can be used to understand how several correlated incidents occur at the same time to describe a specific phenomenon. We proposed a novel mechanism that uses Twitter messages in order to predict emotions associated with the final football match between Brazil and Germany in Rio Olympics 2016. Users' opinions and their sentiments were extracted from the obtained tweets using the K-means clustering algorithm and the SentiStrength technique. We also applied the "Multi-label" classification technique in conjunction with the "Binary Relevance" (BR) method. The results showed that NaiveBayes was able to predict the match outcomes and related emotions with an accuracy value of 81% and a hamming loss value of 16%. This study provides a robust approach to successfully detect real-time events using social media platforms. It also helps football clubs to characterize matches during the time span of the game. Finally, the proposed method contributes to the decision-making process in the sport domain.

Keywords: Twitter · Emotion · Football · Multi-label classification · Sentiment analysis

X. Fang (Ed.): HCII 2021, LNCS 12789, pp. 368–377, 2021.
https://doi.org/10.1007/978-3-030-77277-2_28

1 Introduction

Despite the dramatic growth of sentiment analysis as an important medium to understand peoples' opinions about real-time events, still the process of characterizing simultaneous events in social media is a challenging task. Simultaneous events are found in the sports domain where several correlated incidents occur at the same time to explain a specific phenomenon. Football is a popular type of sport, so analyzing the sentiment conveyed in users' posts about football matches can be extremely useful in examining the type of emotions expressed by fans and make timely decisions. Mega-events like Olympics and the FIFA World Cup attract millions of people and motivates them to put their opinions on social medial platforms like Twitter. From the literature, it can be observed that fans of such events used Twitter to post millions of tweets [1]. Also, the Twitter official blog stated that during the FIFA World Cup 2018, 115 billion tweets were posted on issues related to goal scoring, players' injuries, and outcome prediction. Such a huge number of tweets motivated several scholars to explore issues related to football games. The academic literature on soccer decision-making tasks can be categorized into several types. The first type of studies looked at the data structure of events [2]. The second type of studies addressed the prediction stage during or before the game commenced. And the third type of studies examined the potential of using data from the first half of the game to predict the outcome for the second half. However, the third type of studies attempted to only predict the outcomes of a match such as the number of the scored goals [3] and the outcome of the game "win-loss-draw" [4].

Predicting the outcome of a football match is a challenging task due to this dynamically changing domain which requires reliable platforms to efficiently store and track these changes. For this reason, scholars used social media platforms, such as Twitter, to collect and analyze real-time data of the football matches. For instance, Sinha, Dyer [5] examined the relationship between social media output and National Football League (NFL) games. The authors considered tweets about specific teams and games in the NFL season and use them alongside statistical game data to build predictive models for future game outcomes. They found that the logistic regression results achieved an average accuracy of 67% over the tested weeks. A study by Lock and Nettleton [6] utilized a random forest classifier to combine pre-play variables to estimate the win probability days before an NFL game. The algorithm showed a high prediction performance of 10% to 20% mean squared error. Another study by UzZaman, Blanco [7] used a system that retrieved filtered tweets about the 2010 FIFA World Cup to predict the outcome of a match. The authors achieved up to 88% prediction accuracy. From these studies, it can be clearly observed that most of the existed studies on the prediction of soccer matches are not considering the detection of multiple events of the game. In a real-world scenario, examining only one event related to a game may not offer a solid understanding of the overall phenomenon which may influence the reliability of the resulting decisions [1]. Besides, although individuals' emotions play a significant role in their decisions [8], previous studies did not deeply explore the role of users' emotion embedded in social media content and its relation with the outcome of the match. This study explored the possibility of extracting the sentiment from tweets related to soccer games based on the recommendations of Sarsam, Al-Samarraie [9].

We then used these tweets to predict the outcome of the match by mapping simultaneous events found in the "Men's Olympic Football Tournament Rio 2016" [10, 11]. The match was between Brazil and Germany, and the final outcome of the match was 1–1. A multi-label classification approach was applied to predict these valid decisions about future opinions related to the examined phenomenon.

2   Procedure

Figure 1 summarizes the following steps: data collection, data pre-processing, cluster analysis, emotion extraction, and multi-label classification.

2.1   Data Collection

On the day of the final football match between Brazil and Germany in Rio Olympics (20 August-2016), a total of 35,731,265 English tweets were collected using the Twitter Streaming API (Application Programming Interface). We used the following search keywords to retrieve the tweets: 'Rio Olympics 2016 final' and 'Rio 2016 Brazil vs. Germany'.

2.2   Data Pre-processing

After collecting the data, several pre-processing techniques were applied to generate the necessary information that can be used in the analysis stage. The bag-of-words model was used to extract text-related features from the tweets. We removed any repeated tweets (retweets), and all the words were changed to a lowercase form before using the stopwords list method.

2.3   Clustering and Emotion Extraction

Predicting user's emotions from social media posts is referred to as "sentiment analysis". This type of analysis was found to be extremely essential in characterizing real-time events [12]. Hence, in this study, to obtain emotions that are related to the examined phenomenon, both cluster analysis and emotion extraction were performed via the K-means clustering algorithm and the SentiStrength, respectively. This is because the resulted tweets from the previous stage were a mixture of Brazil and Germany tweets. We isolated the tweets of each team to properly extract the sentiment from them. To do so, the K-means clustering algorithm was used based on the recommendation of Al-Samarraie, Sarsam [13, 14] to group the tweets of each team. Then, two experts from the sport field were asked to inspect the tweets of each team. This helped us to identify Brazil and Germany clusters. After that, the users' sentiments were extracted from each cluster using the "SentiStrength" technique via the Waikato environment for knowledge analysis (WEKA) tool [15, 16]. For each tweet, SentiStrength was used to assign scores ranging from '+1' for 'not positive' to '+5' for 'extremely positive' and '−1' for 'not negative' to '−5' for 'extremely negative'. Based

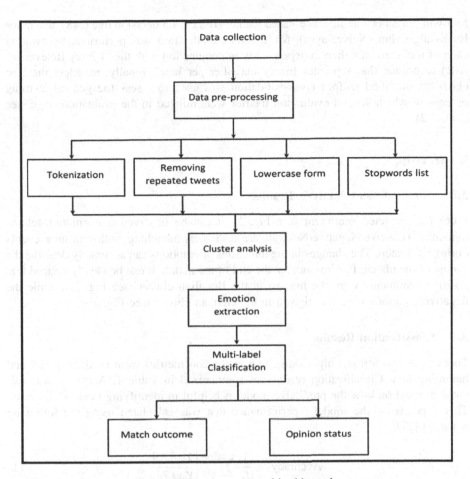

Fig. 1. The main steps used in this study

on these scores, we labeled the tweets with +5 as 'Positive' tweets, −5 as 'Negative' tweets, and −1/+1 as 'Neutral' tweets.

To further understand the dynamics of users' emotions during the football game, we plotted the extracted sentiments (Positive/Negative/Neutral) during the match between Brazil and Germany in Rio Olympics 2016, see Fig. 2. Then, we mapped the extracted outcomes and emotions over the match time (in minutes) (r = 0.99). With the help of the two experts, we labeled each tweet with two labels: (i) Match outcome (Win/Lose/draw) and (ii) Emotion (Positive/Negative/Neutral). We then fed the data to the multi-label machine learning algorithm to predict the status of future tweets.

2.4 Multi-label Classification

To perform multi-label classification, we used the Meka framework– an extension of the Weka tool that deals with multi-label classification problems. We used the following lassifiers: an instance-based learner (IBk), C4.5 decision tree (J48), and naïve Bayes algorithm (NaiveBayes). Multi-label classification was performed by evoking each of the three classifiers independently in conjunction with the "Binary Relevance" (BR) technique that separates binary classifier per label. Finally, to select the best classifier, stratified tenfold cross-validation was used to assess the general learning process in which several evaluation metrics were utilized in the evaluation stage (see Sect. 3.2).

3 Results

3.1 The Sentiment Analysis Results

From the extracted sentiment (see Fig. 2), it can be observed that emotion-related dynamics (Positive/Negative/Neutral) are accurately matching with real-time events during the match. The changes in the directions of emotions can accurately describe the events of the match. For instance, at the end of the match, it can be clearly noticed that positive sentiments were the highest in the Brazilian cluster (see Fig. 2a), while the negative emotions were the highest in the German cluster (see Fig. 2b).

3.2 Classification Results

To evaluate the utilized algorithms, two evaluation metrics were used: accuracy and hamming loss. Classification results are summarized in Table 1. Accuracy was calculated based on how the predictive model is helpful in identifying models' diversity. This depends on the model's performance that was calculated using the following equation [17]:

$$\text{Accuracy} = \frac{1}{|D|} \sum\nolimits_{i=1}^{|D|} \frac{|Y_i \cap Z_i|}{|Y_i \cup Z_i|} \tag{1}$$

Table 1 shows that NaiveBayes algorithm has the highest accuracy (93%), followed by IBk (70%), and J48 (62%), respectively.

Hamming loss was also calculated by treating $Yi \subseteq L$ as true labels set, as i = 1 ... m. $L = \{\lambda_j : j = 1...q\}$ is the set of all labels. However, the specified instance x_i was denoted as Z_i. Δ, which was used to represent the symmetric difference of two sets. We referred to D as the instance number in each trial. To assess the number of misclassified tweets, hamming loss was computed based on the following formula [18]:

$$\text{Hamming loss} = \frac{1}{|D|} \sum\nolimits_{i=0}^{|D|} \frac{|Y_i \Delta Z_i|}{|L|} \tag{2}$$

Here, we considered a classifier performance to be an ideal one when it has a hamming loss value that is closed to zero. Table 1 reveals that NaiveBayes classifier has the closest value to zero (5%), followed by IBk (25%), and J48 (48%), respectively.

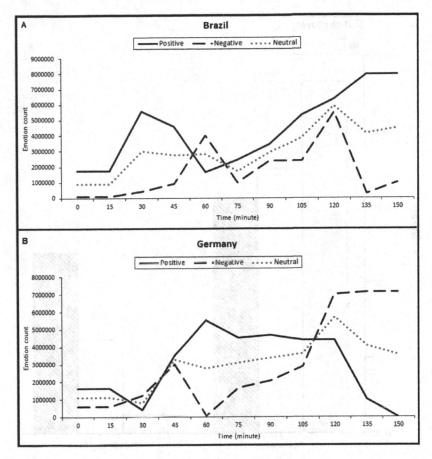

Fig. 2. The extracted emotions from the football match between Brazil and Germany, Rio Olympics 2016

Table 1. Evaluation metrics of multi-class algorithms.

Learning algorithm	Accuracy (%)	Hamming loss (%)
NaiveBayes	93	5
IBk	70	25
J48	62	48

Also, the classification results illustrated in Fig. 3 shows that NaiveBayes was the best algorithm for classifying our data (highest prediction accuracy and lowest hamming lost values). Table 2 presents example of tweets used to predict the label of the match.

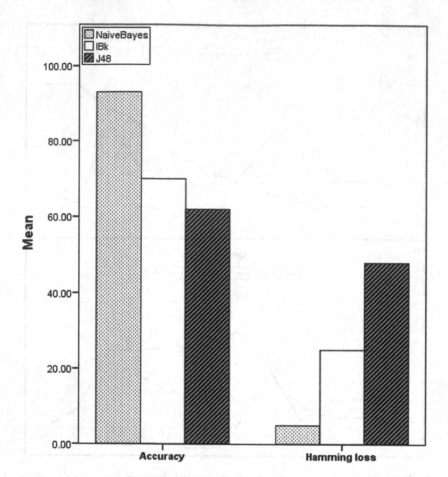

Fig. 3. Classification results

Table 2. Example of tweets.

No.	Example tweets	Predicted label
1.	Brazil is back to winning :)	Positive
2.	Big dislike, Brazil	Negative
3.	Good job Germany. We are here to win	Positive
4.	Seriously, what is this, Germany? :(	Negative
5.	They do this always, but today is different	Neutral
6.	This is a unique day :|	Neutral

4   Discussion

This study used the multi-label classification technique to predict simultaneous events that occurred in the football domain. Our results showed that the BR algorithm in conjunction with the NaiveBayes classifier achieved the best performance in predicting the tweets and the outcome of the final football match between Brazil and Germany in Rio Olympics 2016. We believe that NaiveBayes had such performance because of its efficiency in utilizing a nominal feature type. This result is in line with the work of Tax and Joustra [19] who examined several classifiers to predict the football match outcome. They compared Naive Bayes, LogitBoost, Random Forest, and others on a self-made dataset from public sources, consisting of thirteen seasons of Dutch Eredivisie match data. Tax and Joustra [19] argued that NaiveBayes is likely to achieve a better result due to the independence between the data features. Also, Baboota and Kaur [2] compared several classifiers to predict the results of the English Premier League. They examined NaiveBayes, support vector machine, random forest, and gradient boosting. The best performance was achieved using the NaiveBayes algorithm (51.9%). Our results also add to the work of Odachowski and Grekow [20] who investigated the possibility of predicting the final result of football matches using changes in bookmaker odds. These odds were constantly changing due to bets placed by gamblers where the number of changes is highly related to the amount of a bet on a specified odd. In contrast, other scholars such as Hucaljuk and Rakipović [21] had different prediction results when exploring the possibility of predicting football scores by comparing several machine learning algorithms including Naïve Bayesian, Bayesian networks, LogitBoost, k-NN, Random forest, and artificial neural networks. They found that Naïve Bayesian classifier had the worse prediction accuracy. We believe that the low result of Naïve Bayes could be reasoned to the nature of the utilized features. In the literature, the use of emotion extracted from social media platforms showed an optimistic result in event detections [22]. Having positive types of emotions is relevant since the expressed emotions of the fans are associated with the progress achieved by their teams during the match [23]. In addition, having negative sentiments is possible since it can be related to the negative consequences of sudden changes in the game state [24]. Besides, being upset can potentially trigger internal negative emotions and generate the belief of having an unfair state.

Our review of the literature showed that several factors can positively influence the predictive capability of Naïve Bayes classifier such as dealing with nominal data (e.g., discretization features) and applying feature selection techniques. Furthermore, interaction with the game is likely to generate a set of emotions that can be efficiently transferred to social media tools via their users. Our approach provides an in-depth understanding of the reason behind each opinion. This novel method can extremely help football fans and clubs to predict the outcome of a match based on the extracted emotions in tweets.

5   Conclusion

This study proposed an approach to predict correlated simultaneous events in sport (the final football match between Brazil and Germany in Rio Olympics 2016). For this purpose, users' opinions and their emotions were extracted from the obtained tweets using the K-means clustering algorithm and the SentiStrength technique. The proposed predictive model achieved an accuracy value of 81% and a hamming loss value of 16%. The proposed mechanism has several implications for sport decision making in that it shows the feasibility of predicting multiple real-time events of a match. Also, it allows predicting the interaction type between the players. Such interaction is extremely useful for football club management to make decisions about the coach's strategies. Despite these implications, the current work has several limitations. For example, this study was limited to the retrieval and processing of English tweets—due to the popularity of the English language. Besides, football was the main focus of this study since it is the most popular sport in the world. Thus, future works may consider evaluating our approach in other sport domains.

References

1. Aloufi, S., El Saddik, A.: Sentiment identification in football-specific tweets. IEEE Access **6**, 78609–78621 (2018)
2. Baboota, R., Kaur, H.: Predictive analysis and modelling football results using machine learning approach for English Premier League. Int. J. Forecast. **35**(2), 741–755 (2019)
3. Baio, G., Blangiardo, M.: Bayesian hierarchical model for the prediction of football results. J. Appl. Stat. **37**(2), 253–264 (2010)
4. Goddard, J.: Regression models for forecasting goals and match results in association football. Int. J. Forecast. **21**(2), 331–340 (2005)
5. Sinha, S., et al.: Predicting the NFL using Twitter. arXiv preprint arXiv:1310.6998 (2013)
6. Lock, D., Nettleton, D.: Using random forests to estimate win probability before each play of an NFL game. J. Quant. Anal. Sports **10**(2), 197–205 (2014)
7. UzZaman, N., Blanco, R., Matthews, M.: TwitterPaul: extracting and aggregating Twitter predictions. arXiv preprint arXiv:1211.6496 (2012)
8. Sarsam, S.M., Al-Samarraie, H., Omar, B.: Geo-spatial-based emotions: a mechanism for event detection in microblogs. In: Proceedings of the 2019 8th International Conference on Software and Computer Applications (2019)
9. Sarsam, S.M., Al-Samarraie, H., Al-Sadi, A.: Disease discovery-based emotion lexicon: a heuristic approach to characterise sicknesses in microblogs. Netw. Model. Anal. Health Inform. Bioinform. **9**(1), 1–10 (2020). https://doi.org/10.1007/s13721-020-00271-6
10. Fuller, C.W., Taylor, A., Raftery, M.: 2016 Rio Olympics: an epidemiological study of the men's and women's Rugby-7s tournaments. Br. J. Sports Med. **51**(17), 1272–1278 (2017)
11. Wu, H.C., Cheng, C.C.: What drives spectators' experiential loyalty? A case study of the Olympic Football Tournament Rio 2016. Asia Pac. J. Mark. Logist. **30**(4), 837–866 (2018)
12. Sarsam, S.M., et al.: A lexicon-based approach to detecting suicide-related messages on Twitter. Biomed. Sig. Process. Control **65**, 102355 (2021)
13. Al-Samarraie, H., Sarsam, S.M., Alzahrani, A.I., Alalwan, N.: Personality and individual differences: the potential of using preferences for visual stimuli to predict the Big Five traits. Cogn. Technol. Work **20**(3), 337–349 (2018). https://doi.org/10.1007/s10111-018-0470-6

14. Sarsam, S.M., Al-Samarraie, H.: A first look at the effectiveness of personality dimensions in promoting users' satisfaction with the system. Sage Open **8**(2) (2018). https://doi.org/10.1177/2158244018769125
15. Culpeper, J., et al.: Measuring emotional temperatures in Shakespeare's drama. Engl. Text Constr. **11**(1), 10–37 (2018)
16. Thelwall, M.: The heart and soul of the web? Sentiment strength detection in the social web with SentiStrength. In: Holyst, J.A. (ed.) Cyberemotions: Collective Emotions in Cyberspace, pp. 119–134. Springer , Cham (2017). https://doi.org/10.1007/978-3-319-43639-5_7
17. Tsoumakas, G., Katakis, I.: Multi-label classification: an overview. Int. J. Data Warehouse. Min. (IJDWM) **3**(3), 1–13 (2007)
18. Schapire, R.E., Singer, Y.: BoosTexter: a boosting-based system for text categorization. Mach. Learn. **39**(2–3), 135–168 (2000). https://doi.org/10.1023/A:1007649029923
19. Tax, N., Joustra, Y.: Predicting the Dutch football competition using public data: a machine learning approach. Trans. Knowl. Data Eng **10**(10), 1–13 (2015)
20. Odachowski, K., Grekow, J.: Using bookmaker odds to predict the final result of football matches. In: Graña, M., Toro, C., Howlett, R.J., Jain, L.C. (eds.) Knowledge Engineering, Machine Learning and Lattice Computing with Applications, pp. 196–205. Springer, Heidelberg (2013). https://doi.org/10.1007/978-3-642-37343-5_20
21. Hucaljuk, J., Rakipović, A.: Predicting football scores using machine learning techniques. In: 2011 Proceedings of the 34th International Convention MIPRO. IEEE (2011)
22. Sarsam, S.M., et al.: A real-time biosurveillance mechanism for early-stage disease detection from microblogs: a case study of interconnection between emotional and climatic factors related to migraine disease. Netw. Model. Anal. Health Inform. Bioinform. **9**(1) (2020). Article number: 32. https://doi.org/10.1007/s13721-020-00239-6
23. Tamura, K., Masuda, N.: Win-stay lose-shift strategy in formation changes in football. EPJ Data Sci. **4**(1) (2015). Article number: 9. https://doi.org/10.1140/epjds/s13688-015-0045-1
24. Jensen, M., Kim, H.: The real Oscar curse: the negative consequences of positive status shifts. Organ. Sci. **26**(1), 1–21 (2015)

UNITY-Things: An Internet-of-Things Software Framework Integrating Arduino-Enabled Remote Devices with the UNITY Game Engine

Dag Svanæs[1,2]([⊠]), Andreas Scharvet Lyngby[1], Magnus Bärnhold[1], Terje Røsand[1], and Sruti Subramanian[1]

[1] Computer Science Department, Norwegian University of Science and Technology, Trondheim, Norway
{dag.svanes,terjero,sruti.subramanian}@ntnu.no,
{andresly,magnbarn}@stud.ntnu.no
[2] Digital Design Department, IT, University of Copenhagen, Copenhagen, Denmark

Abstract. We present a software framework that integrates Arduino-enabled remote devices with the UNITY game engine through Internet-of-Things technology. The framework allows a technology stack where networked physical devices become digital-twin game objects in UNITY. This makes it possible for game developers without competence in electronics or Arduino programming to develop hybrid pervasive games directly in UNITY. The framework was implemented in C# on the UNITY side and C++ on the Arduino side, using MQTT as a message broker. The first version of the framework was evaluated empirically with UNITY game developers, resulting in requirements for an updated version. The updated version was used to develop a hybrid pervasive exergame for elderly, which is presented in the paper. The overall positive feedback from the evaluation with game developers and our own experience using the framework encourages us to develop the framework further and integrating it as much as possible with the UNITY development environment. Our aim is to make developing hybrid pervasive games possible for UNITY game developers, without requiring them to concern themselves with the troubles of networks, electronics, or low-level microcontroller programming.

Keywords: Internet-of-Things · Hybrid pervasive games · UNITY · Software framework · Arduino

1 Introduction

Hybrid pervasive games that bridge the physical and the virtual world are often hard to implement. This is due to the complexity introduced by the need to integrate a high number of heterogeneous hardware, software and communication technologies.

The design of such games also pose a challenge when it comes to the required competences in the design team. Games that combine digitally enhanced physical objects with screen-based games require competence in both product design (e.g. 3D

© Springer Nature Switzerland AG 2021
X. Fang (Ed.): HCII 2021, LNCS 12789, pp. 378–388, 2021.
https://doi.org/10.1007/978-3-030-77277-2_29

modelling and 3D printing), electronics, microcontroller programming (e.g. Arduino [1]), network technology (e.g. WLAN or Bluetooth), game design and game programming. Few people master all these competences, and it is therefore beneficial to create levels of abstraction that enable teams to cooperate well across competences.

The challenge we specifically address in this paper is how to give game developers a software framework that enables them to design and implement hybrid pervasive games in their usual game development environment (e.g. UNITY [2]), without having to deal with networks, electronics, microcontrollers, and hardware.

This requires a division of labor where the developers of the physical elements of the game (the "game things" developers) do not have to concern themselves with the design of the game, but can focus on providing the game developers with the required building blocks.

Figure 1 illustrates the connection between levels of abstraction (software stack) and division of labor. In our case, the UNITY-Things framework presented in this paper connects the game layer (e.g. UNITY) with the "game things" layer (e.g. Arduino) and enables the two developers to work independently of each other.

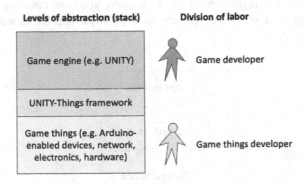

Fig. 1. Levels of abstraction and division of labor.

The success criteria for such a framework is not only that it works from a technical perspective, but also that game developers are able to understand and use it with a minimum of training. This is the usability of the framework for the game developers, i.e. to what extent the framework enables game developers to develop hybrid pervasive games with ease, efficiency and user satisfaction. To evaluate the usability of the framework, it is necessary to assess it empirically with actual game developers doing relevant tasks, i.e. a usability test.

The paper starts with a description of the requirements and software architecture for the UNITY-Things framework. This is followed by a lab-based empirical evaluation of the framework with game developers. We then present an example of a hybrid pervasive game developed using the UNITY-Things framework. The paper ends with a discussion and conclusion giving suggestions for future research.

2 Internet-of-Things and Digital Twins

In today's complex and mature digital world, it is in most cases not necessary to build a new technology or software solution from scratch. Innovations can build on existing technologies, harvesting the benefits of integrating them in new ways.

For the present task of integrating a game engine with small networked digital devices, Internet-of-Things (IoT) is an obvious candidate for a technology to learn from and build on.

2.1 Internet-of-Things Technology Stack

The International Telecommunication Union (ITU) defines Internet-of-Things:

> *"A global infrastructure for the Information Society, enabling advanced services by inter-connecting (physical and virtual) things based on, existing and evolving, inter-operable information and communication technologies. [3, p. 221]*

The implementation of the software and hardware used in IoT product solutions usually come in a multi-layer technology stack where you have three main categories of layers. The thing or device layer, the connectivity layer and the cloud layer. This is illustrated in Fig. 2.

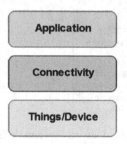

Fig. 2. Simplified technology stack for IoT systems.

At the thing or device layer, you usually have your typical IoT-enabled hardware, in some cases Arduinos, with additional components such as sensors, actuators and even in some cases more processors components. Along the hardware is usually also some embedded software which can be modified or integrated to manage and operate the physical thing.

At the connectivity layer, you have communication protocols such as MQTT or Web-Sockets which aids in the communication between the thing/device and the last layer, the cloud layer.

At the cloud layer, you have various management software which helps in device communication, and is used to communicate with, provision and manage the various connected things. At this level is also an application platform which helps in terms of development and execution of IoT applications. A lot of the management also comes down to analysis and data management, while there can also be a process management software which helps to define, execute and monitor processes between the categories of people, system and things.

2.2 Digital Twins

The concept of Digital Twin is a relatively recent one, and there's a bit of a split exactly where the terminology and concept of it stems from. According a paper on the subject from Glaessgen and Stargel [4], NASA and the U.S Air Force, the term Digital Twin was first conceived at DARPA, and then later Grieves and Vickers [5] properly conceptualized the terminology around it in their early works of Product Life cycle Management (PLM) from 2002 until around 2011 where the concept was finalized to where it is today. Digital Twins as a concept is independent of IoT, but most IoT platforms today provide digital twin solutions.

According to Tao et al. [6] the most commonly used definition of Digital Twin was proposed by Glaessgen and Stargel:

> *"Digital twin means an integrated multiphysics, multiscale, probabilistic simulation of a complex product, which functions to mirror the life of its corresponding twin". [4, p. 13]*

With digital twins, the world is separated into two spaces; a physical space and a virtual space. Between these two spaces, there are links for data to flow in both directions. This gives us a system that consists of the two systems with the physical being as it always has been, and the virtual space containing all information available about the physical.

3 The UNITY-Things Software Architecture

Bass, Clements and Kazman define software architecture the following way:

> *"The software architecture of a system is the set of structures needed to reason about the system, which comprise software elements, relations among them, and properties of both". [7]*

Essentially, software architecture is all that describes the system, from the implementation itself to the various types of documentation surrounding it.

Quality attributes are the criteria that we define as non-functional requirements. These are requirements used to evaluate the system as a whole, but not for specific behavior. Quality attributes can be divided into two main categories. The attributes that affect system behavior, design and the user interface, and those that affect the development and support of the system.

To achieve the greatest success with the architecture, it is a good idea to combine quality attributes such as performance, reliability and ease of use. It is also important to consider the impact the characteristics may have on the functional requirements and weigh these against each other.

3.1   Requirements for the UNITY-Things Framework

Architecturally significant requirements are the requirements that measurably affects a framework's architecture. This may involve both programming and hardware requirements. It's a subset of the architectural requirements, which affects the construction of a framework in quantifiable recognizable ways.

Table 1 sums up the architecturally significant requirements for the UNITY-Things framework.

Table 1. Quality attributes and architecturally significant requirements

Quality attributes	Architecturally significant requirements
QA1: Implementation cost	The framework and the technology used should reduce the overall cost of prototyping
QA2: IoT Flexibility	The IoT technology should support different I/O modules to allow developers to customize the game objects to their game design
QA3: Addressability	The IoT technology should provide the ability to uniquely identify and address the device
QA4: Device-to-Device communication	The IoT technology should support the ability to transfer and receive data from different IoT devices
QA5: Distributed vs Local use	The IoT technology should support both local and distributed applications
QA6: Scalability	The IoT technology should support the ability to be used in pervasive games with different amounts or sorts of devices
QA7: Interoperability	The framework and the technology used should support communication between various IoT devices
QA8: Connection of new devices	The framework should provide intuitive handling of connecting new devices both during development and run time
QA9: IoT Flexibility	The framework should allow developers to create custom interaction and visualization of different virtual I/O components that mirror traditional physical I/O modules
QA10: Game logic centralized	The framework should support running the game logic outside of the IoT devices

3.2   The UNITY-Things Technology Stack

While the original three-layer technology stack proposed by Wortmann and Flüchter [1] works fine for our project, there are different ways to setup a technology stack, and we have decided then to modify this technology stack a little. The main difference between our suggested technology stack base and the original proposed technology stack, is adding a layer for the object abstraction which covers the connections types between devices, like WiFi, Bluetooth, or similar.

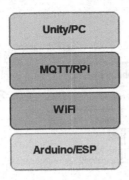

Fig. 3. Proposed technology stack.

With this modified technology stack organization, this gives us the following technology stack, which can be seen in Fig. 3. Briefly, this gives us the following organization; Unity program as a data and device management software, the brain of the system. MQTT as the connection handler between devices in the system, where most of the messages go back and forth between devices and Unity. WiFi is the connection type, and how devices are connected together. Lastly, Arduinos and a RPi being the main IoT device objects with actuators and sensors.

3.3 The UNITY-Things Implementation

The resulting UNITY-Things is an Internet-of-Things (IoT) [8] software framework that allows remotely connected Arduino-enabled devices to be programmed as digital-twin game objects for the UNITY game engine. The remote devices (things) communicate with the UNITY game engine through an MQTT broker [9] using WLAN.

On the Arduino-enabled devices [10], the UNITY-Things Arduino library (written in C++) provides an abstraction level that makes it easy to program the devices as IoT "things". For UNITY game developers, the UNITY-Things UNITY library (written in C#) make the Arduino-enabled devices automatically show up as "digital twin" game objects, allowing the game developers to define their behavior without doing any Arduino programming.

The software architecture is shown in Fig. 4. In this setup, we see a game with four Arduino-enabled devices using the ESP8266 processor with built-in WLAN [8]. They all run local MQTT clients.

A Rapsberry Pi 3 with built-in WLAN runs a DHCP server and an MQTT broker. A PC is connected to the local network through WLAN, running an MQTT client integrating with UNITY. The game logic is implemented on the PC, using the framework.

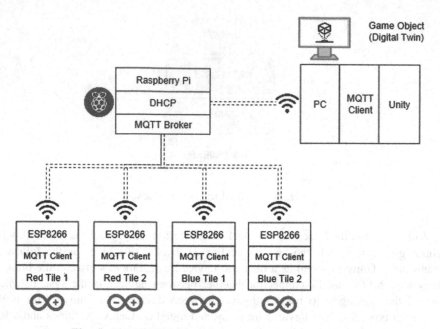

Fig. 4. The UNITY-things framework software architecture.

3.4   The UNITY-Things Component Roles

Raspberry Pi. The Raspberry Pi is the broker in the pattern and is set up with the Mosquitto message broker which implements the MQTT protocol [7]. This is a very lightweight message broker, which makes it perfect to use in low power single board computers like the raspberry pi, and is widely used in IoT projects. In the system, all messages passes through the Raspberry Pi since it works as a broker, it's powerful enough to run a DHCP server as well, turning it into a router and a connection point for all the other devices.

PC/UNITY. The PC component is a computer running the game program compiled from Unity. While Unity can compile to Linux, which makes the Raspberry Pi a potential target for running the game itself if it's light enough, a distinction has been made to properly separate Unity as its own component.

This component in the architecture runs the game logic and will function as a server or service provider for the rest of the system, as per the Publish and Subscribe pattern. With the game, the logic of the system, and digital twin data, all run here. While all the MQTT messages run through the broker, the other components will not talk to each other and will act separately with all handling of the messages being done in Unity.

Arduino. The Arduino is a reactive component in the system. Aside from going online and connecting to the MQTT broker and subscribing to certain messages, this component mostly awaits messages from the broker to update its actuators (lights, sound, etc.), or sends a message over MQTT if a user interacts with one of the input sensors.

As the specific Arduinos used in this system does not have Ethernet connections, they run on WiFi to connect to the DHCP server on the Raspberry Pi. The configurations and how the Arduinos are set up can vary from component to component, but their role remains that of a client, as per the Publish and Subscribe pattern.

Game Objects/Digital Twins. The Game Object component is a sub-component of the PC/Unity component. These are Unity-specific Game Objects which have class objects that hold information based on the various Arduino components. This can be information on the whole configuration of the device it's a Digital Twin of, or the states of the various components, such as button and light states, or methods for controlling the different physical actuators connected to the Arduino. This acts as a synchronized digital mimic of the physical device.

4   Empirical Validation

To validate the first version of the framework, we invited two professional UNITY game developers and four students with UNITY experience to a lab-based empirical evaluation. Recruiting the right participants is crucial to getting valuable results from a usability test. Our participants were primarily recruited through a presentation we had at a meetup for game developers, in addition to sending out an e-mail to students who had taken the subject Game Design at NTNU. We wanted to gather a group of representative end-users where the skills were from novice to experts, to improve the chances of meeting the true end-users.

The participants worked in pairs and were given a design problem to solve with the framework. We had preprogrammed two red and two blue tiles with input (tapping) and output (LED ring) capabilities. We had further made C# classes in the UNITY framework that made it easy to instantiate "digital twin" game objects for the tiles.

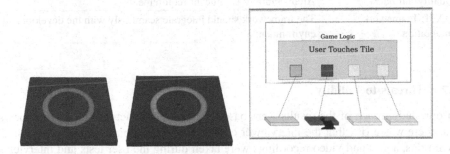

Fig. 5. Tiles in the real world (left) and as digital twin game objects in UNITY (right).

In Fig. 5, we see the form factor of the tiles and how they became digital twin game objects in UNITY. In Fig. 6, we see the lab setup for the tests.

All programmer pairs solved the given design problem, and they all reported that this was a very promising approach to pervasive game development. They all

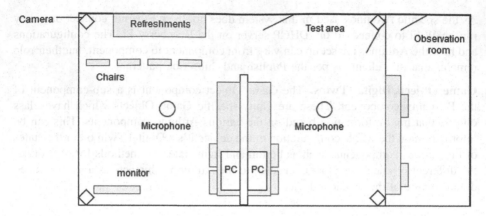

Fig. 6. Lab setup for the evaluation.

appreciated the simplicity of the framework. In the first version of the software framework, the C# classes were not fully integrated with the UNITY development environment. This was pointed out by all groups as an area for improvement. They also missed more documentation and fully functional examples as one often finds on GitHub.

4.1   Updated Requirements

Based on the results from the evaluation, we found a need to add one more requirement to the framework, as shown in Table 2.

Table 2. Added quality attribute and architecturally significant requirement

Quality attributes	Architecturally significant requirements
QA11: Framework integration	The framework should integrate seamlessly with the development environment

4.2   Threats to Validity

In our study, much of the results were based on the semi-structured group interviews, and there was a risk that the interviewer could influence the participants' answers. To avoid this, audio and video recordings were taken during the user tests and interviews. This made it possible to analyze whether the participants were affected in their behavior after the interview. However, it is not possible to eliminate the influence of the interviewer completely. It seemed that most of the participants were sincere in their answers, although there is a possibility that some of the participants wanted to be positive in their answers.

5 Example of a Pervasive Game Implemented with the Framework

The areas of improvement pointed out by the participants in the evaluation served as the basis for an improved version of the framework. This version was used to implement pervasive exercise games for elderly. For these game, we built a toolkit of thirteen tiles and two cubes with RFID capabilities. All devices had digital twins in UNITY, and the games were programmed without having to reprogram the Arduino-enabled tiles.

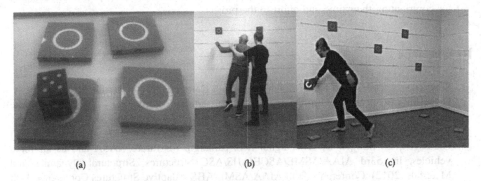

(a)   (b)   (c)

Fig. 7. A game implemented using the software framework.

In Fig. 7, we see (a) the tiles and a cube (dice), (b) a physiotherapist instructing an elderly person, and (c) an elderly person playing the game herself. The game running in Fig. 7c is called "follow the white dot". The game starts by lighting up a random tile. The tile is lit until it is hit by the player. The light then fades out and moves to a random other tile. The aim is to follow the movements of the light from one tile to the next. Despite its extreme simplicity, this game was very popular by the participants in a usability test we performed [11].

6 Conclusions and Future Work

The Unity-Things framework makes it possible to implement hybrid pervasive games with Arduino-based IoT devices directly in UNITY. Both the feedback from UNITY developers and our own experience using the framework, point to this being a promising way of prototyping and developing such games. With ready-made Arduino-based devises preprogrammed with basic input-output capabilities, the software framework made it possible for game developers to implement pervasive games without having to do any Arduino programming. We believe the framework speeds up and simplifies the development process considerably.

The results from the evaluation indicate that there are several improvements for future development on the framework. As a start, the code should be ported from the more general C# solution to a more integrated Unity solution, which means it should be more familiar to the way Unity handles game objects and class components.

One thing that was not addressed during the usability test, but is important for future work, is to look deeper into the security of the framework. In particular, it is important to add extra care in making the broker and the communication secure.

We consider the current version of the framework more akin to an alpha version, and as such there are several steps needed to be fulfilled before a proper beta version is ready, among these the changes described above. Preferably more iterations of testing need to be done after the changes regarding the Unity integration mentioned above.

Acknowledgments. We thank the UNITY developers and students taking part in the usability test for contributing their time and effort to the project.

References

1. Severance, C.: Massimo banzi: building arduino. Computer **47**(1), 11–12 (2014)
2. Haas, J.: A history of the unity game engine. Dissertation Worchester Polytechnic Institute (2014)
3. Wortmann, F., Flüchter, K.: Internet of things. Bus. Inf. Syst. Eng. **57**(3), 221–224 (2015)
4. Glaessgen, E., Stargel, D.: The digital twin paradigm for future NASA and us air force vehicles. In: 53rd AIAA/ASME/ASCE/AHS/ASC Structures, Structural Dynamics and Materials (2012). Conference 20th AIAA/ASME/AHS Adaptive Structures Conference 14th AIAA
5. Grieves, M., Vickers, J.: Digital twin: mitigating unpredictable, undesirable emergent behavior in complex systems. In: Kahlen, Franz-Josef., Flumerfelt, Shannon, Alves, Anabela (eds.) Transdisciplinary perspectives on complex systems, pp. 85–113. Springer, Cham (2017). https://doi.org/10.1007/978-3-319-38756-7_4
6. Tao, F., Cheng, J., Qi, Q., Zhang, M., Zhang, H., Sui, F.: Digital twin-driven product design, manufacturing and service with big data. Int. J. Adv. Manuf. Technol. **94**(9–12), 3563–3576 (2017). https://doi.org/10.1007/s00170-017-0233-1
7. Bass, L., Clements, P., Kazman, R.: Software Architecture in Practice. Addison-Wesley Professional, Boston (2003)
8. Ashton, K., et al.: That 'internet of things' thing. RFID J. **22**(7), 97–114 (2009)
9. Ecclipse. An open source mqtt broker. https://mosquitto.org/. Accessed 01 Oct 2020
10. Adafruit: Adafruit feather huzzah with esp8266 - loose headers. https://www.adafruit.com/product/2821. Accessed 02 Oct 2020
11. Subramanian, S., Dahl, Y., Vereijken, B., Svanæs, D.:. ExerTiles: a tangible interactive physiotherapy toolkit for balance training with older adults. In: OZCHI 2020 - Proceedings of the 32nd Australian Conference on Human-Computer-Interaction (2020)

The Effects of Vibration on Assisting Game Play and Improving Player Engagement When Lacking Sound

Xinyi Tao[(⊠)], Keyu Wu, and Yujie Yang

NetEase, Hangzhou, China
{taoxinyi,wukeyu,yangyujie01}@corp.netease.com

Abstract. Mobile games have become a very common way of playing because of its portability and simplicity. In addition to rendering the environment atmosphere in game, sound can also play an important functional role in conveying information. However, the situation that people play mobile games without sound is very normal, both for hearing-impaired people and for normal people in public environment. Vibration is an important form of feedback information, which can enhance the player experience in soundless situation. But in most situations, they are only used to build atmosphere, not to convey specific information. There are few researchers have directly measured the effect of vibration on assisting mobile game and improving players' engagement. This study compared the difference between playing game with and without vibration through a role-playing game (RPG) mod, to examining the effects of vibration on players' engagement and which kind of vibration works better. Data analysis revealed that the participants who played the game with vibration were more engaged than participants who played without vibration. The results of this study will guide practitioners to explore more ways of how vibration can be used in mobile games to improve players' engagement (both for normal people and hearing-impaired people).

Keywords: Vibration · Assist · Engagement · Lacking sound · Hearing-impaired · Mobile games

1 Introduction

1.1 Different Senses of Games

Game experience is constructed with various facts. Playing games involves both diegetic and extradiegetic activities. Conscious interaction between the player and the interface is diegetic, At the same time, instinct corporeal response to the gaming environment happens in the procedure, which means the extradiegetic activities [1].

Different senses are involved when playing games, including visual, auditory and tactile feeling. Vision is always regarded as the most crucial one and the basis for people to understand the user interfaces. However, bodily responses to the gaming environment and experiences mostly depend on the support by sound and haptics. Sonic and tactile interaction can assist the players to gain more complete and

© Springer Nature Switzerland AG 2021
X. Fang (Ed.): HCII 2021, LNCS 12789, pp. 389–407, 2021.
https://doi.org/10.1007/978-3-030-77277-2_30

immersive experience of games. These elements of interactivity distinguish games from many other forms of media, in which the physical body is "transcended" in order to be immersed in the narrative space [2].

At present, sonic interaction has been fully used in games, including background music, notification sound etc. Sound can carry plenty of information and lots of games are closely integrated with sound. "Touching" is the basic action for people to use gaming devices. People needs to perform "touching" first to use keyboards, controllers and mobile phones as the input devices. Except for touching to play games, we also use vibration to convey information. But compared with sonic interaction, there are relatively few scenarios where haptic feedback acts as informative interaction.

1.2   Sound and Game Experience

Sound is commonly used in games at present. There were mainly two types of sound interaction. One is to create a certain atmosphere. It does not convey specific information but is only used for emotion and vibe. For instance, Soothing music could be used in normal situation and intense music would be used to enhance tension in a battle. During the plot prelude, animation would be performed with appropriate background music and voice-over. Study [3] in recorded electrodermal activities and facial muscle activities in addition to a Game Experience Questionnaire (GEQ) when playing FPS games and indicated significant effect of sound and music on GEQ dimension tension and flow.

The second one is for informative notification. Sometimes sound is used to convey specific information. Unlike the consumption of many other forms of media in which the audience is a more passive "receiver" of a sound signal, game players play an active role in the triggering of sound events in the game (including dialogue, ambient sounds, sound effects, and even musical events). While they are still, in a sense, the receiver of the end sound signal, they are also partly the transmitter of that signal, playing an active role in the triggering and timing of these audio events [2].

Some types of informative sound are listed below:

1. UI notification sound. Audio information could prompt some game mechanics companied with user interfaces (UI). This kind of sound usually corresponds to the change of UI and the information conveyed is the same as that conveyed by UI. Although players can gain enough information from visual stimuli, audio could be the supplementary feedback. Besides, if the change of UI is too sight or the player's vision is disturbed in some situations, sound could help the player to notice the visual information. Taking countdown as an example, audio would company with the visual effect of countdown to tell the player it is about to end. Moreover, some UI notification sound can also convey emotion. Glorious prompt is a typical example. It can help to enhance proud feeling when players make achievements.

2. Environmental Sound. Lots of games use sound to represent the surroundings. It is mentioned above that background music can create certain atmosphere. There are also some environmental sound which is used to express specific information. In the game Zelda, when a monster appears nearby, specific pre-recorded music will start. Thus, even though the monster approaches behind the player and is beyond the sight, the player can get the early warning. In addition, in some FPS games, players can hear footsteps when other players appear nearby. They can also get the information of the enemy's position and distance from the intensity and direction of footsteps. This kind of footstep prompt has also be converted into visual UI elements. A footprint icon will be displayed on the small map to compensate for the lack of sound in some scenarios of mobile games.

3. Combat Sound. In combat games, sound effects are integrated in the fighting procedure, which is helpful for players to predict and react to the opponent's actions. These sounds are usually corresponded to the actions or effects of the character model. For example, when the enemy is about to attack the enemy or release skills, there will be corresponding sound. The player can dodge or block the attack with the sonic information, which can help the player to fight better. If there's no sound, the player could only rely on the character's actions of effects of skills to make decision, and the reaction would be slower.

1.3 Gaming Scenarios Lacking Sound

Sound plays a crucial role in improving game experience. Without the sound, the players will lack emotional feeling and information acquisition from the game. However, this situation often occurs in current gaming scenarios, especially in mobile games.

Scenarios of playing mobile games have been greatly expanded because they are portable and easy to start. People can play mobile games in different occasions and in time fragments. We can play games on subway to and off work, during spare time in companies and while eating etc. Many of the scenarios are inconvenient to turn on the sound. In a study [4], Ekman discussed that the challenge with mobile sound is coping with various listening environments. Playing games implemented with audio components would be companied with the risk that sounds were masked by social disturbance. When playing games in public places such as the subway, lots of people tend to turn off the sound to avoid disturbing people nearby.

As for hearing-impaired people, they lack the access to sound and cannot have a complete gaming experience. Various sonic interaction does not exist for them. Game characters' voice-over, which is one of the elements that stimulate players' audial perception, has a moderate but significant effect on play-learners' engagement [5]. In a experiment [6], Grimshaw and Nacke made both subjective and objective assessments of game sound and music to discuss the emotional affect created by sonic interaction in games.

The lack of sound leads to the lack of two effects from gaming sound: creating atmosphere and giving out information. Without background music enhance emotional atmosphere, players will lack immersive feeling in a certain way. Ermi and Mäyrä has established the sensory, challenge-based and imaginative immersion model (SCI model) to explain three crucial elements of game immersive experience. In this model, sensory immersion could be enhanced by amplifying audio interaction in one game [7]. Without the vital sound notifications, they may not be able to obtain complete information and some operations will lack clear feedbacks, which may cause slower reaction at some important moments. If there's not sound prompt during a fight, the player will take actions when the enemy has already made an attack or the skill effect has been displayed, which often makes them miss the opportunity to take the lead.

1.4 Vibration in Games

Except for visual and sonic interaction, vibration is a good approach to complement sensory experience of the players through tactile feeling. It can also take the responsibility to create atmosphere and convey information. When the scene, the sound and the vibration fit perfectly with each other, players can feel engagement in the gaming experience. But when some sound and visual elements are missing, vibration can be a supplement to a certain extent, providing more complete information and feedback to players.

At present, vibration is commonly used in console games. Some console games use vibration form the controller to enhance atmosphere and create better effects with sound and pictures. In 1998, Microsoft released Force Feedback 2 Joystick with feature rich enhancements and new force feedback effects. The stick will shake just like in a real aircraft and simulate thud by vibration if the plane stalls in flight [8]. In 2006, Immersion Cooperation introduced TouchSense (R) vibration technology to match the realism expected of video console gaming systems, which also helped the haptic feedback synchronize with audio and onscreen visual events [9]. Here we take Zelda on Nintendo Switch as an example. When the first tower (which is an important part of the world view and needs to be emphasized) rises, an animation of earthquake is displayed, together with exciting music and the vibration of joysticks, making the players feel the magnificent scene immersively.

Console games also use vibration to convey information. A research [10] has examined the popularity of vibration used in Nintendo DS hand-held game console, which implemented haptic feedbacks in games. It was proved that vibration is acceptable interaction for players. In the game Ring Fit Adventure, The fitness ring will vibrate with the body motion of the player and guide the player together with UI elements. Vibration is used as a reminder of the motion range, as well as a reminder of the duration. For example, when the player is asked to perform a bending action, fitness ring will start to vibrate when the waist is bent to a suitable position and will stop vibrating if the player continues to bend over to reach a sufficient distance. In this way, even though the player cannot see the visual interfaces all the time when doing some certain actions, he can know the effective range of actions accurately.

Vibration is not very common in mobile games and is mainly used to create atmosphere but not to convey some specific information. In the mobile game Identity V, the player can hit the screen quickly to struggle from the "hunter". During this procedure, mobile phone will also vibrate, making the player feel urgency and tension.

2 Vibration Assists Game Interaction

2.1 Features of Vibration

There are four dimensions for vibration measurement: duration [11], gap [12], frequency [13–15] and intension [14]. Different dimensions can represent different information. In one study [11] directed by NUS-HCI Lab, researchers designed ten vibration alerts by different features to compare which index would influence users' perception of notification urgency. They concluded that shorter gap lengths between vibrations and shorter duration of vibration could make the participants regard the alert as more urgent. It has already been used in our life. Most people are familiar with the incoming call reminding vibration, which is usually a dense and short vibration to remind people that the event should be dealt with urgently. Moreover, because different manufacturers of mobile phones use different vibration rhythms, some users can even distinguish which phone is receiving a call by vibration.

Duration, gaps and frequency constitute the rhythm of vibration. Vibration rhythm is relatively similar to music rhythm, bringing people some conventional cognition. For example, short and dense vibration can make people feel tension and soothing rhythm with long gaps make people calm down. The rhythm of vibration can also match the rhythm of information we want to convey. In games, footsteps of characters, attacks from the enemy etc. all have specific vibration rhythms. When the vibration rhythm keeps the same as the effects, it can convey clearer information and facilitate people to have better understanding. In addition, when a set of vibrations with a specific rhythm is always used to convey the same kind of information and is known and remembered by the players, whenever the player feels the vibration with this rhythm, the player can quickly associate it with the meaning.

The intensity of the vibration can convey another dimension of information. For example, in an fps game, we will hear the sound of footsteps when there are enemies nearby, so even in a complex scene, the player can rely on the sound of footsteps to know that there are enemies nearby. Similarly, this information can also be conveyed by vibration. We can make the rhythm of the vibration correspond to the rhythm of the footsteps. The intensity of the vibration represents the distance between the enemy and us. The closer we are, the stronger the vibration is.

In the same way, we can convey multi-dimensional information by setting different features of vibration. It should be considered to design a vibration rhythm representing a specific kind of information according to concrete scenarios.

At present, some hand-held devices use four parameters to set vibration. However, most of the mobile phones cannot support to adjust the intensity of vibration. Because the target scenario of this study is the use of mobile games, we do not consider the use of vibration intension, but only focus on duration, interval and frequency.

The mobile phone vibrates by internal vibration motor. The phone equipped with Android 8.0 was used to do the research. Features of vibration was controlled by calling the native interface Vibrator class. Vibrator class provides a function void vibrate (long[] pattern, int repeat), which controls the phone to vibrate in the pattern set by the function. Here, pattern represents a set of time series. The odd-numbered bits represent the interval, and the even-numbered bits represent the vibration duration in milliseconds. Repeat represents the repeating mode. 0 means keeping repeating and −1 means no repeat.

2.2   Vibration Assist Game

In this study, we tried to use vibration to replace part of the role of sound effects in games, exploring whether vibration can assist players to play mobile games and enhance the immersive feelings. The mechanics how vibration assists players' immersion can also correspond to the types of sonic interaction in games. As we mentioned above, we divide two types of sound according their effects in games, which are atmosphere enhancing sound and information prompts. Similarly, the auxiliary effect of vibration can also correspond to these two types. Vibration to enhance atmosphere has been widely used in existing games and this kind of vibration does not represent specific information. Thus we did not discuss that in this research. This project mainly explored the effect of using vibration instead of some special sound effects to convey specific information and assist game playing.

The information and using scenarios of by vibration can correspond to types of sound: (1) UI notification: Company with user interfaces to strengthen the communication of some UI information. (2) Environmental notification: notify the players about some special situations, such as approaching danger etc., similar to the effect of environmental sound. (3) Combat notification: notify the players about some battle-related information, such as attack, dodging and blocking.

2.3   Vibration Game Mod

In this study, we created a demo game integrated with vibration to represent some information. We used Unity to develop the demo (see Fig. 1). There are some open source Unity assets, including virtual sciences, characters models and some common action animations. We used these assets to build the demo scene with some boxes and monsters. The player can walk around in the demo scene, collect the boxes and attack the monsters etc., In addition, we designed the user interfaces in order to facilitate operation on the mobile phone.

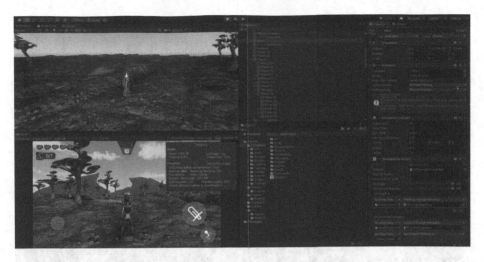

Fig. 1. Screenshot of the game mod in unity.

We used four kinds of vibration in this demo, which include several ways to convey information by vibration. Coutdown notification and progress notification are both UI notification. Footsteps of monsters are notification of surroundings and the interaction of attack form monsters are combat notification. There is a UI element on the top of the screen to display the icons representing the four vibrations (see Fig. 2). The icon displayed corresponds to the meaning of the current vibration.

Fig. 2. Four icons represents four types of vibration.

1. Countdown notification. We set a time limit for this game. When the countdown is about to end, there will be a vibration reminder. It will vibrate at the 15 s countdown and the 10 s countdown. In the last 5 s, it will vibrate every second in the last 5 s. When the phone is vibrating, the countdown clock icon will be displayed on the top of the screen (see Fig. 3).

Fig. 3. Interface of the game mod when the vibration of countdown comes out.

2. Progress notification to open the box. There is a waiting process to open the box. When approaching a box, the player will see a button above the box. The unboxing progress bar will increase when the player keeps pressing the button. When the progress bar is full, the box will open and disappear after that to show that the player as collect the box successfully. While if the player release the button in the halfway, the

Fig. 4. Interface of the game mod when opening the box.

progress will be cleared and the opening progress should be started again. In this process, a short vibration will keep repeating while the button is being pressed and will stop if the player releases the finger. When the progress bar is full, the phone will vibrate twice with longer duration and intervals (similar to "double click"), corresponding to the state that the box is collected. The box icon will be displayed (see Fig. 4).

3. Footsteps notification. When the player walk around within a certain distance to the monster, the monster will run towards the player. Simultaneously, vibration representing footsteps of the monster will be triggered and the vibrating rhythm is the same as the running pace of the monster. The footprint icon is displayed at the top of the screen (see Fig. 5).

Fig. 5. Interface of the game mod when monsters appear nearby and the footstep vibration comes out.

4. Attack notification. When the monster is closed to the player, it will jump to attack the character. The player can dodge or attack the monster. Vibration of footsteps does not exist in this situation. instead, there will be a significant vibration every time the monster attacks. The monster icon is displayed at the top of the screen (see Fig. 6).

Fig. 6. Interface of the game mod when battling with monsters.

3   Method

The research question is, "What is the effect of vibration on player engagement in soundless situation?", and so, the null-hypothesis is, "There will be statistically significant difference between the engagement levels of participants playing a mobile game with or without vibration in soundless situation."

3.1   Participants

A total of 45 participants (24 males and 19 females) participated in the research study. There are 42 normal people (22 males and 18 females), ages 22 to 34 (mean = 27) and 3 hearing-impaired people, ages 25 to 29 (mean = 27). Most of the participants work in Internet Company. Before the experiment, we explained the relevant situation to the participants and promised to keep their personal information confidential.

3.2   Research Design and Procedure

We created three identical game mods: (1) the control mod (CM): without sound and vibration, (2) the sound mod (SM): with sound but without vibration, (3) the vibration mod (VM): with vibration but without sound. The sound mod simulated a normal game situation (playing game with sound). And the other two were used to measure the engagement of players in soundless situation. We set the same goals for each mod: collect 7 boxes and defeat 3 monsters in 3 min. This goal was settled based on a preliminary experiment to make sure that it's difficult to achieve within the time limit. So that participants were able to experience all types of vibration, including the countdown vibration in the end.

For normal participants, the first step was to experience the sound mod (SM, with sound but without vibration) And were asked to complete the In-game GEQ. The second step is to experience the control mod (CM, without sound and vibration) and complete another In-game GEQ. The third step is to experience the vibration mod (VM, with vibration but without sound) and also complete an In-game GEQ. To avoid the effect of the order of experiencing different mod, we randomly divided the participants into two groups (A: n = 21, B: n = 21). For these two groups, the order of step 2 and step 3 is reversed.

For hearing-impaired participants, they are only asked to experience the two mods without sound (CM and VM). And then they were interviewed about how they feel about the two mods.

3.3 Instruments

Three paper-based, self-reported instruments were used in this research to elicit participants' response. The first was a demographics questionnaire, which collected background information about the participants. The second was the In-game GEQ. The In-game version of the GEQ [16] is a concise version of the core questionnaire. It has an identical component structure and consists of items selected from this module. The in-game questionnaire is developed for assessing game experience at multiple intervals during a game session, or play-back session. This should facilitate the validation of continuous and real-time indicators some of the partners in the FUGA project are developing [17]. The third is SUS, which is a fast and effective questionnaire for testing system usability. In this experiment, we need to compare the effects of four different vibrations horizontally. In order to save time and reduce the workload of participants, we used the UMUX-Lite, which is consisted of two positive items. Estimates of reliability were .82 and .83 – excellent for a two-item instrument. Concurrent validity was also high, with significant correlation with the SUS (.81, .81) [18].

4 Results

4.1 Reliability Analysis of the Questionnaire

After all the questionnaire was collected, the reliability analysis was performed with Cronbach's α. In further analysis, we found that item#3 and #9 have a low item-total correlation in the three reliability analyses. Take the first questionnaire result filled out by the SM group as an example: the CITC value of #3 is -0.343 and 0.112 for #9, both of which are significantly lower than other parts. We removed item #3 and #9 from further analysis and finally Cronbach's α can be seen in Table 1.

According to previous studies, the consistency between the items can be considered good when the Cronbach's α coefficient is more significant than 0.7. The reliability coefficients of each part in the questionnaire are above 0.7 (see Table1), while the minimum value is .729. Therefore, it is a good-designed questionnaire with a high internal consistency, which will help to analyze the relevant variables in this study.

Table 1. Reliability coefficient of game engagement questionnaire in this study.

Scale name	Cronbach's α
SM GEQ	.770
VM GEQ	.881
CM GEQ	.754
Whole questionnaire	.931

4.2 Verification of Equivalence Between the Two Groups

When the same participant is subjected to a repeat experiment, the first experiment result/earlier presented item may effect on the second one [19]. In this study, participants were asked to complete the same task three times in three different versions of the game mod. To minimize the order effect on the outcome of the experiment, we controlled for this additional variable by randomly dividing the players into two groups, each of which played the game in a designed order. There are many factors can affect a player's perception of engagement in a game, therefore, all players were asked to fill out a questionnaire about their personal information and experience with the game. Five questions were included in the questionnaire: (1) gender, (2) age, (3) player's self-rated mobile game ability, (4) RPG experience, (5) hours of mobile games per week.

Table 2. Results of homogeneity tests between A and B groups.

	Group (AVG ± SD)		t	p
	Group A (n = 21)	Group B (n = 21)		
Gender	1.70 ± 0.48	1.40 ± 0.52	1.342	0.196
Age	27.80 ± 1.32	26.00 ± 1.41	−0.327	0.747
Self-evaluation of game ability	2.80 ± 0.63	3.00 ± 0.67	−0.688	0.500
Prior RPG experience	3.30 ± 0.82	3.20 ± 1.03	0.239	0.813
Hrs of mobile games per wk	3.10 ± 1.20	3.10 ± 1.29	0.000	1.000

* $p < 0.05$ ** $p < 0.01$

As shown in Table 2, the results of the t tests was no significant statistical difference in gender between group A and group B. Therefore, we could assume that two groups were statistically homogenous in terms of demographic variables.

4.3 Hypothesis Testing

After obtaining the questionnaire data for all players, we calculated the GEQ scores (based on 12 items) for Group A and Group B. The average score of group A in SM, VM and CM was 134, 127 and 93. Meanwhile, the three scores for group B are 113, 121 and 77 (Table 3).

Table 3. Results of GEQ average score for group A and group B.

Name	Group		Total
	Group A	Group B	
SM	134.000	113.000	123.500
VM	127.000	121.000	124.000
CM	93.000	77.000	85.000

As shown in Table 4 and 5, the scores of all participants (SM, VM, CM) were tested by paired t-test respectively. The score between the SM and the CM was statistically significant ($t = 4.56, p < .001$) with a large effect size (Cohen's $d = 1.020$), which means the average score of SM was significantly higher than that of the CM.

There was also a statistical significance between the CM and the VM scores ($t = -3.86$, $p = .001$, Cohen's $d = .863$), which shows the average score of VM was significantly higher than that of the CM.

However, there was no significant difference between the SM and the VM scores ($p > 0.05$), which refers to the immersion of VM was close to the level of SM.

Table 4. Results of the paired sample t-test.

	Pair (AVG ± SD)		Difference (Pair1-Pair2)	t	p
	Pair 1	Pair 2			
SM & CM	123.50 ± 59.85	85.00 ± 47.30	38.50	4.563	0.000**
SM & VM	123.50 ± 59.85	124.00 ± 67.39	−0.50	−0.061	0.952
CM & VM	85.00 ± 47.30	124.00 ± 67.39	−39.00	−3.861	0.001**

* $p < 0.05$ ** $p < 0.01$

Table 5. Paired samples correlations.

	DF	Std. Deviation	Cohen's d
SM & CM	38.50	37.735	1.020
SM & VM	−39.00	45.178	0.863

4.4   Usability Score Comparison of Different Vibration Form

When analyzing the UMUX-LITE questionnaire, it shows a very low reliability of the usability for footsteps part (Cronbach's $\alpha = .153$). We had further conversations with some of the players who participated in the experiment about this situation. Most of them (25 of the 31 players interviewed) said it was the first time they had played the game mod and needed time to explore the game map. When they face an oncoming monster, they were so engrossed in the battle that they didn't notice what was happening before the monster arrived. They can't recall the scene they encountered in the game after the game is over, so they couldn't give an accurate response to those

Table 6. Reliability coefficient of UMUX-LITE in this study.

Part name	Cronbach's α
Open the box	.672
Under attack	.723
Countdown	.663
Footsteps around	.153

questions about footsteps. However, the reliability coefficients of the other three parts in the questionnaire are above 0.6 (Table 6), which refers to an acceptable consistency.

UMUX is a simple four-item questionnaire listing two positive and two negative statements that respondents rate agreement with on a five or seven-point Likert scale. UMUX-Lite is the shorter version which only contains the 2 positive statements. Previous studies have provided evidence of strong concurrent suggesting that UMUX was statistically equivalent to the SUS. The analysis of UMUX-Lite showed high reliability (.82, .83) and a high concurrent validity which has a significant correlation with the SUS (.81, .81) [20]. Using regression formula to corrective scores, the researchers converted UMUX-Lite's scores to SUS's scores (as shown below).

$$UMUX - LITE = .65(UMUX(1,3)) + 22.9$$

A product with a score above 70 on the SUS rating could be considered to have good usability [21], however, the scores in this study were low (around 50). This is because the demo of the game used in the study is an easy version with a big gap with the best games in the market. This performance gap results in a lower overall usability score, however, horizontal comparisons can be made between different vibration types in this game.

From the average score (See Table 7), vibration of under attack (UA, mean = 51.25) and countdown (CD, mean = 51.75) have a higher availability level than opening the box (OB, mean = 46.2).

Table 7. Results of UMUX-Lite average score for three forms of vibration.

Name	Sample size	AVG	SD	AVG ± SD
Open the box (OB)	42	47.452	14.417	47.452 ± 14.417
Under attack (UA)	42	55.167	14.516	55.167 ± 14.516
Countdown (CD)	42	54.405	13.415	54.405 ± 13.415

As shown in Table 8, OB was significantly different from that of UA and CD with a lower score (0.008, .017), which means players perceive UA and CD to be more usability than OB in this study (simple RPG game task).

Table 8. Results of the paired sample t-test.

	Pair(AVG ± SD)		Difference	t	p
	Pair 1	Pair 2	(Pair1-Pair2)		
OB & UA	47.45 ± 14.42	55.17 ± 14.52	−7.71	−2.768	0.008**
OB & CD	47.45 ± 14.42	54.40 ± 13.41	−6.95	−2.488	0.017**
UA & CD	55.17 ± 14.52	54.40 ± 13.41	0.76	0.310	0.758

* p < 0.05 ** p < 0.01

In Fig. 7, each dot represents one player, orange represents the difference between UA and OB, and blue represents the difference between CD and OB. Most players think UA and CD is more usability than OB (81%, 74%).

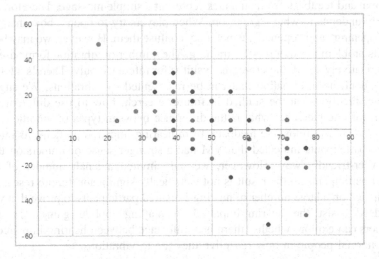

Fig. 7. A scatter plot using the difference between UA, OB and CD. (Color figure online)

5 Findings and Discussion

The aim of this study was to examine the effects of vibration on players' engagement in soundless situation. The result of t-test confirmed that participants were found to be more 'engaged' in a gaming environment with vibration than one without vibration.

By comparing the engagement levels of the three game mods, we can draw the following conclusions. As shown in Table 2, the difference between the GEQ score means of the control mod (CM) and the vibration mod (VM) was found to be statistically significant ($p < 0.01$) and the mean for the vibration mod (VM) was obviously higher. Thus, it comes out that vibration has a significant effect on improving player engagement. The difference between the control mod (CM) and the sound mod (SM) was also found to be statistically significant ($p < 0.01$) and the mean for the sound mod (SM) was higher. This shows that sound has a positive effect on player engagement, which is consistent with the previous research results [2, 3, 5].

There was no significant difference between the SM and the VM scores ($p > 0.05$), which refers to the immersion of VM was close to the level of CM. This is consistent with our presupposition (when the lack of sound negatively affects player engagement, we try to assist players with vibration). However, we think that this conclusion is not absolutely applicable to all cases. As the game mod used in this experiment is simple, as well as the vibration and sound effects, vibration can be well applied to this situation. However, because the dimensions and diversity of sound are more complex than vibrations, sound can be adapted to more complex scenes. Therefore, based on this experiment, we can only conclude that vibration plays a role in improving engagement. Further research is needed to compare the effects of vibration and sound on engagement.

By comparing the UMUX-Lite scores of different types of vibration in this study, we could see that CD and UA have a higher score than OB. This may because that the countdown and feedback from an attack represent a simple message. Therefore, players can easily understand what's going on. When players try to open a box, there are two states: "opening" and "opened", which may confuse them. However, we may be able to solve this problem through pre-test training. The number of vibration forms used in this study is relatively small, therefore, the result is for reference only. There's a lot more to explore about the information that can be represented by vibrations. We suggest the following directions can be studied in future research: how to use different types of vibration for one message; what is the difference between types of vibration.

We also received positive feedback from hearing-impaired participants interviews. All three participants indicated that VM had a stronger sense of immersion than CM with a user-friendly way. However, we only invited a small number of hearing-impaired participants so the result is not statistically significant. Future research could be conducted on a large number of hearing-impaired participants to prove that vibration can indeed assist the hearing-impaired in playing mobile games. In addition, researchers can explore whether there is a difference between hearing-impaired people and the normal people in how receptive they are to vibrations.

5.1   Significance of the Study

The results of this study answer an important question for researchers in the field of game research. The positive effect of vibration (as a sensory stimulus) on players' engagement levels will help designers/developers determine how to better design mobile games. Also, this study explores the different dimensions of vibration and the types of information that are more suitable for transmission, which provides the direction and inspiration for further research. The results of this study are also consistent with the findings of previous studies [2, 3, 5] on the positive effects of sound on game engagement.

Also, this study is also helpful to expand the use scenarios of mobile game. Vibrations can help make the game better suited to some situations where it is not appropriate to turn on the sound.

This study also has design implications for game developers and game designers. This study designed the game mod that combines vibration and UI, tried to expand the way of combining vibration and game. This can help inspire game designers to incorporate vibration into their game design, and may even use vibration as a core experience of the game. What kind of information is better conveyed by vibration also has implications for the designers to use vibration in suitable situations.

Last but not least, this study is helpful to arouse people's attention to the game experience of disabled people (including hearing-impaired people). Apart from the essential aspects of daily life, how do they get better entertainment is also an area that worth to be concerned. It also provides some inspiration for exploring other designs that benefit the disabled.

5.2 Limitations of the Study

The first limitation of this study would be the make-up of the participants, who are all less than 34 years old, and mostly work in Internet Company, which means they are familiar with mobile games. This set of limitations means that it might not be easy to generalize the finding to the larger populations (people who have no experience with mobile games).

The second limitation of this study is the integrity of the game mod we used. Since it's a simple demo made up of open source material, some details experience and usability is below the level of mature games on the market, such as the experience of fighting monsters or move in the forest. Although we used controlled trials to rule out this effect, it cannot be denied that the integrity of the game mod itself may have some influence on participants' engagement.

Thirdly, it is possible that the study was potentially limited by the short gameplay time (of less than 15 min). By COTS game standards, most digital games have a recommended total playtime of 20–40 h. Loh and Sheng (2015) suggested that a more appropriate time frame for serious game research should last about 1–2 h per session [22].

Last but not least, most of our participants are normal people and the number of hearing-impaired participants was small. Therefore, our conclusion can only be applied to the situations of normal people using mobile game, but not be statistically proven to apply to the hearing-impaired. Future research will also be needed to determine the effects on hearing-impaired people.

6 Conclusion

The main purpose of this study was to verify that vibrations can improve player immersion and assist them in a soundless game environment. As most people know, sound plays an important role in the game experience which our study also confirms. Vibrations are a great way to enrich the player's experience and enhance game immersion in many social environments that cannot open the sound. And also, helpful for hearing-impaired people who want to play mobile games. This conclusion has important implications for future game design that game designers should explore more ways to combine vibration with mobile games. It is also helpful to improve the game experience for hearing-impaired people.

Therefore, further research may focus on the exploration of different types of vibrations and effects to find out which is better for people to understand and use. Results will contribute to the field of game design and evolve the way of game interaction design.

References

1. Shinkle, E.: Corporealis ergo sum: affective response in digital games. Mcfarland & Co. (2005)
2. Blake, A.: Game sound, an introduction to the history, theory, and practice of video game music and sound design. J. Des. Hist. **22**(3), 226–227 (2008)
3. Nacke, L.E., Grimshaw, M.N., Lindley, C.A.: More than a feeling: measurement of sonic user experience and psychophysiology in a first-person shooter game. Interact. Comput. **22**(5), 336–343 (2010)
4. Ekman, I.: Sound-based gaming for sighted audiences–experiences from a mobile multiplayer location aware game. In: Proceedings of the 2nd Audio Mostly Conference, pp. 148–153 (2007)
5. Byun, J.H., Loh, C.S.: Audial engagement: effects of game sound on learner engagement in digital game-based learning environments. Comput. Hum. Behav. **46**, 129–138 (2015)
6. Nacke, L.E., Grimshaw, M.: Player-game interaction through affective sound. In: Game Sound Technology and Player Interaction: Concepts and Developments, pp. 264–285. IGI global (2011)
7. Ermi, L., Mäyrä, F.: Fundamental components of the gameplay experience: analysing immersion. In: Worlds in Play: International Perspectives on Digital Games Research, vol. 37, no. 2, pp. 37–53 (2005)
8. Orozco, M., Silva, J., El Saddik, A., et al.: The role of haptics in games. In: Haptics Rendering and Applications, pp. 217–234 (2012)
9. Immersion Technology: Next-generation TouchSense Vibration for Video Game Console System (2006)
10. Shirali-Shahreza, M., Shirali-Shahreza, S.: Examining the usage of feedback vibration in Nintendo DS handheld game console. In: 2009 11th International Conference on Advanced Communication Technology, vol. 3, pp. 1997–2000. IEEE (2009)
11. Saket, B., Prasojo, C., Huang, Y., et al.: Designing an effective vibration-based notification interface for mobile phones. In: Proceedings of the 2013 Conference on Computer Supported Cooperative Work, pp. 149–1504 (2013)
12. White, T.: The Perceived Urgency of Tactile Patterns. Human Research and Engineering Directorate, Army Research Laboratory. ARL-TR-5557 (2011)
13. Hwang, J., Hwang, W.: Vibration perception and excitatory direction for haptic devices. J. Intell. Manuf. **22**(1), 17–27 (2011)
14. Ryu, J., Jung, J., Choi, S.: Perceived magnitudes of vibrations transmitted through mobile device. In: 2008 Symposium on Haptic Interfaces for Virtual Environment and Teleoperator Systems, pp. 139–140. IEEE (2008)
15. Yao, H.Y., Grant, D., Cruz, M.: Perceived vibration strength in mobile devices: the effect of weight and frequency. IEEE Trans. Haptics **3**(1), 56–62 (2009)
16. Ijsselsteijn, W.A., Kort, Y.D., Poels, K.: D3.3 the game experience questionnaire: development of a self-report measure to assess the psychological impact of digital games (2008)

17. IJsselsteijn, W.A., de Kort, Y.A.W., Poels, K.: The game experience questionnaire, vol. 46, no. 1. Technische Universiteit Eindhoven, Eindhoven (2013)
18. Lewis, J.R., Utesch, B.S., Maher, D.E.: UMUX-LITE – when there's no time for the SUS. In: Proceedings of CHI 2013, Paris, France, pp. 2099–2102. Association for Computing Machinery (2013)
19. Krosnick, J.A., Alwin, D.F.: An evaluation of a cognitive theory of response-order effects in survey measurement. Public Opin. Q. **51**(2), 201–219 (1987)
20. Lewis, J.R., Utesch, B.S., Maher, D.E.: UMUX-LITE: when there's no time for the SUS. In: Proceedings of the SIGCHI Conference on Human Factors in Computing Systems (2013)
21. Bangor, A., Kortum, P., Miller, J.: Determining what individual SUS scores mean: adding an adjective rating scale. J. Usability Stud. **4**(3), 114–123 (2009)
22. Loh, C.S., Sheng, Y.: Measuring the (dis-)similarity between expert and novice behaviors as Serious Games Analytics. Educ. Inf. Technol. **20**(1), 5–19 (2015)

Investigating the Impact of Task Significance on Task Engagement and Enjoyment in Digital Games

Manasa Vaidyabhushana, Matthew Kirchoff, and Owen Schaffer[(⊠)]

Computer Science and Information Systems, Bradley University,
1501 W Bradley Ave, Peoria, IL 61625, USA
{mvaidyabhushana, mekirchoff}@mail.bradley.edu,
oschaffer@bradley.edu

Abstract. The Positive Psychologists Peterson, Park, and Seligman identified three paths to human happiness, which they called orientations to happiness: pleasure, flow and meaning. Pleasure can be attained by making games beautiful and pleasurable to the five senses, and flow can be attained with dynamic difficulty adjustment to maintain an optimal level of challenge. However, to the best of our knowledge there has yet to be empirical research showing the impact of meaning on enjoyment in digital games. This study aims to fill that gap in the literature. An online controlled experiment with 440 total participants is proposed to test the impact of Task Significance on Task Engagement and Enjoyment. Participants will play one of 12 versions of a custom research game online (3 × 4 factorial experimental design), and then complete an online survey. Two different ways to facilitate Task Significance in games are proposed and tested: narrative framing and character upgrading mechanisms. This results of this experiment will advance the study of game enjoyment by testing how well these two ways of designing for meaning or Task Significance lead to enjoyment in digital games.

Keywords: Enjoyment · Meaning · Task Significance · Narrative framing · Character upgrades · Eudemonia · Controlled experiment · Flow · Task Engagement · Intrinsic motivation · Digital games · Computer games · Video games

1 Introduction

In the second quarter (April–June) of 2020, consumers spent a record $11.6 billion on video gaming in the U.S., an increase of 30% when compared to the same time period last year, and a 7% increase over the first quarter 2020 (January–March) record of $10.9 billion [45]. So, digital games continue to be in demand despite the global COVID-19 pandemic. Digital games are interactive, computer-based systems that present users with a series of goal-directed, challenging tasks to complete for the enjoyment those tasks provide. Enjoyment, as we define it here, is the extent to which people positively evaluate their experience.

© Springer Nature Switzerland AG 2021
X. Fang (Ed.): HCII 2021, LNCS 12789, pp. 408–420, 2021.
https://doi.org/10.1007/978-3-030-77277-2_31

There remains insufficient scientific consensus about what all of the factors are that lead to digital game enjoyment. Research on digital game enjoyment is still in its early stages in our view, with scattered and incomplete theories that are either not supported by empirical research showing the factors they identify lead to enjoyment such as Caillios's [8] categories of games, Bartle's [6] four player types, and Lazarro's [24, 25] Four Keys to Fun, or do not provide a fully comprehensive model of what leads to enjoyment such as Self-Determination Theory [38], Player Experience of Needs Satisfaction (PENS [39], Flow Theory [31], the Game Engagement Questionnaire [7], Yee's model of motivations to play online games [47, 48], Malone's [26, 27] model of intrinsically motivating educational games, the Player Experience (PLEX) Framework [23], and Quick and colleagues' taxonomy of gameplay enjoyment [37].

For example, Self-Determination Theory (SDT) and the Player Experience of Need Satisfaction (PENS) model based on SDT suggests that three factors lead to intrinsic motivation – autonomy, competence, and relatedness [38]. Autonomy is how much players feel they have voluntarily chosen their actions, competence is how skilled players feel at playing the game, and relatedness is feeling socially connected to others. PENS added intuitive controls, which is the usability or ease of use of the game's controls, and presence, which is feeling that one is actually there in the game, as additional factors [39]. SDT and PENS are not a fully complete account of the factors that lead to digital game enjoyment in our view because they do not include Meaning or Task Significance. We define Task Significance here as the extent to which you perceive what you are doing as important or meaningful. Task Significance is not included in the SDT or PENS models.

Abeele et al. [1] created a *Player Experience Inventory* measure that included a meaning subscale. Rather than directly testing the impact of meaning on enjoyment, they combined their 10 subscale factors into two high-level factors, which they called functional and psychosocial consequences, and tested how those high-level factors impacted enjoyment. In contract, the present study aims to directly test the impact of meaning on enjoyment at the subscale level with a controlled experiment.

Understanding what makes digital games enjoyable is important not only for video and computer game designers, but also for practitioners of Gamification and designers of Serious Games as well. Gamification is "the use of game design elements in non-game contexts" [14:10], such as to make non-game systems more game-like and enjoyable. Serious games are "full-fledged games for non-entertainment purposes" [14:11], such as education, exercise, or persuasion.

The Positive Psychologists Peterson, Park, and Seligman [35] identified three paths to human happiness, which they called orientations to happiness: pleasure, engagement and meaning. The pleasure path to happiness is experiences that please the five senses, such as beautiful audio-visuals, haptic feedback, tangible interfaces, or pleasurable smells. The engagement path to happiness is about optimal challenge, having an optimal level of difficulty that gets people into what Csikszentmihalyi [9–13] called a flow state of "getting in the zone" while overcoming those challenges. Digital games can be designed with dynamic difficulty adjustment or adaptive difficulty to maintain an optimal level of challenge [2, 20, 22, 30], which involves continuously monitoring player performance and adjusting the difficulty level of the game to match the performance of the player.

The meaning path to happiness is about what makes life worth living. There is extensive literature on meaning in life, from Aristotle's eudemonia [4] to Viktor Frankl's logotherapy [16]. Meaning, as we define it here, is the sense that what you are doing contributes to a life well lived, or a life that you will perceive more positively in retrospect at the end of your life.

To use a more specific term, we define Task Significance as the extent to which you perceive what you are doing as important or meaningful. While there has been extensive research on sensory pleasure and flow in digital games, there has been little to no research on task significance in digital games. The present research aims to fill that gap in the literature.

The research questions guiding this study are:

1. Do games designed for task significance lead to more digital game enjoyment compared to control conditions?
2. Between narrative framing and upgrade mechanisms, which is the most effective way to design digital games for task significance?
3. Is there an interaction effect between narrative framing and upgrade mechanisms such that using both has a greater impact than using either on their own?

This study will contribute both to the theory and practice of designing interactive systems for meaning and enjoyment.

2   Related Work

For those interested in designing games and other interactive systems for enjoyment, Positive Psychology is a useful field from which to draw ideas. Positive Psychology is not just the study of what leads to happiness, but can be thought of more broadly as the empirical study of what makes life worth living, or what will lead to a positive evaluation of one's life. While happiness and enjoyment are both the extent of positive evaluation, the unit of analysis or focus of evaluation is one's life in the case of happiness and an experience in the vase of enjoyment. The sources of that positive evaluation that makes up happiness and enjoyment may be the same or heavily overlap. Peterson, Park, and Seligman [35] identified three paths to happiness, which they called orientations to happiness: pleasure, engagement and meaning. Meaning is perhaps the least well understood of these three, especially in terms of how to design meaningful interactive experiences to increase enjoyment.

Nakamura and Csikszentmihalyi proposed a concept called vital engagement, which they defined as "a relationship to the world that is characterized both by experiences of flow (enjoyed absorption) and by meaning (subjective significance)" [32:87]. Through interviews with artists and scientists, Nakamura and Csikszentmihalyi suggested that subjective meaning can grow out of sustained interest in an activity that provides flow and enjoyment, an experience they called emergent meaning. Vital engagement involves a strong connection between the self and the object being engaged with, regardless of what or who the object is [32:86–87].

One path to a life of meaning explored in Positive Psychology has its roots in the virtue ethics of Aristotle [4]. Aristotle suggested that voluntarily taking virtuous actions until virtuous actions become a habit leads to virtuous character, which in turn leads to *eudaimonia*, or a life well lived. *Eudaimonia* or a life of meaning we define as a life that is evaluated positively in retrospect at the end of life. Peterson and Seligman [36] developed the Values in Action Classification of Character Strengths and Virtues (CSV) as Positive Psychology's response to Clinical Psychology's *Diagnostic and Statistical Manual of Mental Disorders* (DSM) [5]. The CSV presents 24 character strengths categorized into 6 virtues: Wisdom and Knowledge, Courage, Humanity, Justice, Temperance, and Transcendence [36]. While each kind of virtuous action may be a fulfilling source of enjoyment, character strengths focus on the traits of the individual rather than on qualities of an experience or a task.

Wong [46] developed the PURE model of meaning for meaning therapy, consisting of Purpose, Understanding, Responsible Action, and Evaluation. McDonald et al. [28] developed a Personal Meaning Profile consisting of seven sources of meaning: Achievement, Relationship, Religion, Self-transcendence, Self-acceptance, Intimacy, and Fair treatment. Edwards [15] combined several existing measures of meaning in life and used exploratory factor analysis to identify 10 factors: Achievement, Framework/Purpose, Religion, Death Acceptance, Interpersonal Satisfaction, Fulfillment/Excitement, Giving to the World, Existential Vacuum, Intimacy, and Control.

Much of the Psychological research has focused on individuals assessing themselves and their life as a whole. In contrast, the Human-Computer Interaction (HCI) field focuses on evaluation of experiences, which could mean evaluating an experience using an interactive system after using that system or evaluating one's moment-to-moment experience using an Experience Sampling Method approach [19]. Mekler and Hornbæk [29] made this distinction between meaning in life and the experience of meaning as well, and presented a framework for the experience of meaning in HCI. Their framework consisted of five components of meaning: Connectedness, Purpose, Coherence, Resonance, and Significance. They defined significance as "the sense that our experiences and actions at a given moment feel important and worthwhile, yet also consequential and enduring" [29:6]. As Mekler and Hornbæk pointed out, significance has also been called value, mattering, and the affective or evaluative component of meaning. For example, George and Park [17, 18] created a model and measure of existential meaning in life with three dimensions: Comprehension, Purpose, and Mattering, and the Mattering subscale would be a measure of significance in life.

Schaffer and Fang conducted a card sorting study to develop a new model of the sources of computer game enjoyment [42, 43]. Sixty participants sorted 167 sources of digital game enjoyment drawn from the literature into categories, and the cards and categories refined after every ten participants. Through this process, 34 categories of enjoyment sources were identified. One of those categories was "Significance, Meaning, Purpose, and Legacy", which was described in part as "Knowing why your actions are important, significant, or meaningful" [43:8].

One of the classic works of existential psychology is Frankl's [16] book *Man's Search for Meaning*, in which he developed a psychotherapy approach focused on helping people find meaning in their lives that he called logotherapy. Frankl described his experience surviving Nazi concentration camps, and what he learned about finding meaning in life from that experience. Frankl quoted Nietzsche [33], "He who has a *why* to live for can bear almost any *how*," and adds that "in the Nazi concentration camps… those who knew that there was a task waiting for them to fulfill were most apt to survive" [16:126]. This aspect of meaning is reflected in the Purpose component of meaning.

Frankl wrote that "the categorical imperative of logotherapy" is to "Live as if you were living already for the second time and as if you had acted the first time as wrongly as you are about to act now!" [16:131–132]. This imperative serves a similar function to focusing on living a life that will be evaluated positively in retrospect at the end of life except that it focuses more on the present moment. Frankl wrote that this imperative confronts people with life's finiteness and the finality of what one makes out of life and themselves [16:132]. This seems to be one route to giving people a sense that their actions are significant or important.

Frankl continues that the aim of logotherapy is to make people "fully aware of their own responsibleness; therefore, it must leave to [them] the option for what, to what, or to whom [they] understand [themselves] to be responsible" [16:132] For Frankl, responsible action is the path to meaning in life, regardless of what, to what, or to whom one decide to be responsible. Frankl emphasized that this responsibility must be directed to something or someone other than oneself, that self-actualization is only possible "as a side-effect of self-transcendence" [16:133]. Frankl describes self-transcendence as forgetting oneself or giving oneself to a cause or another person [16:133]. So, one way to understand meaning in life is as self-transcendence, deciding what or whom one will be responsible for, and taking responsible action. Shifting from the more global assessment of meaning in life to the more specific assessment of moment-to-moment experience, the experience of taking actions perceived as responsible may lead to more meaning and enjoyment than actions not perceived as responsible actions.

3   Method

3.1   Participants

An online controlled experiment with 440 total participants is proposed to test the impact of Task Significance on Task Engagement and Enjoyment. 40 participants in the pilot study and then 400 participants in the main study will be recruited online using

Amazon Mechanical Turk. The number of participants for the main study was based on a power analysis conducted with G*Power for a 3×4 factorial ANOVA with 12 groups including main effects and interactions (effect size $f = 0.25$; $p < 0.05$; power > 0.95). Participants will play one of twelve versions of the same game created for this research, with specific design differences between the versions, and then complete a survey.

3.2   Measures

The survey includes psychometric measures of player Enjoyment, Task Engagement, and Task Significance made up of Likert-type scale items adapted from previously validated measures.

The measures of Enjoyment and Task Engagement were adapted primarily from the Activity Flow Scale [34], which was adapted from the Flow State Scale [21]. Task engagement is defined as the flow indicators, or the factors that indicate how much a person is in a flow state, not including enjoyment or Autotelic Experience [40, 41]. One of the subscales of the Activity Flow Scale, Autotelic Experience, contains items such as "I really enjoyed the experience", so this subscale was separated from the other flow indicators identified by Nakamura and Csikszentmihalyi [31] so that enjoyment and the flow state could be measured separately [40, 41]. The remaining flow indicators that make up the subscales of Task Engagement are Sense of Control, Concentration, Merging of Action and Awareness, Loss of Self-Consciousness, and Altered Perception of Time.

The measure of Task Significance included items from previously validated measures of meaning [1, 35, 44], some of which were adapted to the context of games research.

3.3   Study Design and Experimental Conditions

This study will be a between-subjects controlled experiment with twelve experimental conditions. Twelve versions of a custom research game will be developed for this study with the Unity game engine and C#. The games will be built to WebGL and embedded on Qualtrics, an online survey platform. The branching logic feature of Qualtrics will be used to randomly assign participants to play only one version of the game.

The research game will be a 2D top-down pickup-and-delivery game, where players will pick up and deliver as many boxes as they can from one type of location to another before a timer runs out while avoiding enemies and obstacles. The twelve versions of the game make up a 3×4 factorial experimental design, as shown in Fig. 1 below.

Independent Variable A:
Upgrade Mechanisms

		Upgrade Mechanisms	Cosmetic Upgrades	No Upgrade Mechanisms
IV B: Narrative Framing	Helping People in Need	Upgrade Mechanisms & Helping People Framing	Cosmetic Upgrades & Helping People Framing	No Upgrade Mechanisms & Helping People Framing
	Working for Money	Upgrade Mechanisms & Working for Money Framing	Cosmetic Upgrades & Working for Money Framing	No Upgrade Mechanisms & Working for Money Framing
	No Reason	Upgrade Mechanisms & No Reason Framing	Cosmetic Upgrades & No Reason Framing	No Upgrade Mechanisms & No Reason Framing
	Undone Reason	Upgrade Mechanisms & Undone Reason Framing	Cosmetic Upgrades & Undone Reason Framing	No Upgrade Mechanisms & Undone Reason Framing

Fig. 1. 3×4 factorial design of experiment testing the impact of task significance on task engagement and enjoyment in digital games

Two different ways to facilitate Task Significance in games are proposed and tested: narrative framing and character upgrading mechanisms.

There will be four Narrative Framing conditions. In each of these conditions, the text that will appear at the beginning and end of each round of the game and the images accompanying that text will be different. In the Helping People in Need narrative framing conditions, the text will describes the player's task in the game as delivering boxes of free food to elderly poor people self-quarantining at home during the COVID-19 pandemic. The images shown before and after each round of the game will show people in need at the beginning of the round and grateful people who received the food the player delivered at the end of the round. The Helping People in Need narrative framing is designed to give players a meaningful and important reason for their actions within the fictional world of the game to increase Task Significance.

In the Working for Money narrative framing condition, the images shown at the beginning of each round show impatient customers waiting for their delivery and the images shown at the end of each round show money being given. The text accompanying the images frames the task as being motivated by making money.

In the No Reason narrative framing conditions, the text will not describe a purpose for the player's task in the game. Images shown at the beginning and end of rounds, will not communicate any reason for the player's actions in the game. Instead, the images and text will focus on the setting of the game and not the player's task, showing images of the snowy town where the game is taking place. This narrative framing is intended as a control condition.

In the Undone Reason narrative framing conditions, the player is delivering flyers rather than boxes. The player's task will be described at the beginning of the game as posting flyers for an upcoming auction. At the end of each round, on screen text informs players that their efforts were wasted, such as because the date on the flyer was wrong, the wind swept all the flyers away, or the event was rescheduled. Then at the start of each round after the first players are told their task is to repost the flyers. This narrative framing is intended to be more devoid of meaning than the No Reason condition. This condition is inspired by the Sisyphus condition from Ariely et al.'s [3] experiment, where a Lego model building task was made more meaningless by having the experimenter take apart the Lego models participants built after each model was built, while in their more meaningful condition the Lego models were not taken apart and were allowed to accumulate.

In the Upgrade Mechanisms condition, the player will be able to spend points collected during the game on upgrades to their player character's movement speed and abilities between each round of the game. In the No Upgrade Mechanisms condition, points will still be accumulated, but the points cannot be spent or used for any purpose. In the Cosmetic Upgrades condition, the player can purchase upgrades with the points, but the upgrades have no effect on the player's actual abilities and power to be effective in the game. The cosmetic upgrades may change the appearance of the player character, but they do not make players more powerful or effective at increasing their score. Having all three of these upgrade conditions allows us to test if just being able to purchase upgrades with points is sufficient to increase enjoyment compared to having no upgrades (Cosmetic vs No Upgrades) or if the upgrades must provide functional abilities that make the player more effective in the game (Upgrades vs. No Upgrades).

The idea behind these upgrade conditions is that when the player is able to spend the points collected for a purpose, then this game mechanism may make the player feel that what they are doing in the game is for a specific purpose within the game. In other words, having upgrades may make players feel that what they are doing is important (increase Task Significance) because their actions have an impact on the gameplay mechanisms of the game and their actual abilities within the game rather than because of the fictional narrative framing of their actions.

3.4 Procedure

Participants will be recruited with Amazon Mechanical Turk. They will be directed to a survey on Qualtrics, an online survey platform. Participants will read an information sheet on informed consent and voluntarily agree to participate. Branching logic on Qualtrics will be used to randomly assign participants to play one of twelve versions of the same game created for this research, with the specific design differences between the versions described above. After playing the game for 30 min, participants will complete a survey with the measures described above to assess the extent of their enjoyment, task engagement, and task significance. This study will be reviewed and approved by the University's internal ethics review board for research involving human participants before it will be conducted.

3.5   Discussion

This experiment will advance the study of game enjoyment by testing how well these two ways of facilitating task significance or meaning lead to greater task engagement and enjoyment in digital games. By using a controlled experiment with random assignment, this study aims to provide evidence of a causal relationship between systems designed for task significance and user enjoyment. This study will also test the effectiveness of narrative framing with text and images and character upgrade game mechanisms as two different ways to make the player feel that their actions in the game are important.

If the results of this study support the hypothesized causal relationships, this study will provide two concrete and different paths to design for task significance and enjoyment, with narrative framing using the game's story to explain the purpose of player actions within the fictional context of the game world and with character upgrades using game mechanisms to give players an additional purpose for their actions in the game that increases their ability to do well in the game, namely upgrading their character. This study aims to show that designing for task significance, making players feel that what they are doing is important and meaningful, causes more player enjoyment, and to provide specific tools practitioners and researchers can use to give players that experience.

4   Design Implications

There are multiple potential design implications of this study if the hypothesized relationships are supported. If players who play the versions of the research game that are designed for task significance experience significantly more enjoyment than players in the control conditions, then designing for task significance is one effective way to design for enjoyment. This means that those who wish to design interactive systems for user enjoyable would be well advised to design activities, tasks, or user actions that are perceived by users as important, significant, and meaningful. In other words, if the hypotheses are supported, it would suggest that one way to design for enjoyment is to design for task significance.

This raises the question of how to design games and other interactive systems for task significance. There may be many ways to give people the feeling that what they are doing is important. Two ways will be tested in the present study: narrative framing and upgrade game mechanisms.

If the present study finds that narrative framing is an effective way to significantly increase task significance and enjoyment, this will mean that framing a task in a fictional game as helping other people in need in that fictional world significantly increases task significance and enjoyment. If narrative framing is effective, this will mean that giving people an important reason for their actions increases task significance and enjoyment. The design implications of this are straightforward: give users an important reason explaining why their actions are important in the context of the story the game or system is telling. In particular, it will mean that framing user actions as helping others in need increases task significance and enjoyment. If the results of this study support the hypotheses, framing user actions as helping others, taking prosocial actions, taking responsible action, or social responsibility is one way to increase task significance and user enjoyment. This finding would be in line with Frankl's [16] focus on responsible action as a path to meaning.

If upgrade mechanisms are an effective way to significantly increase task significance and enjoyment, then that will mean that giving players a way to use the points they collect in the game is one way to make their actions in the game feel important and meaningful, and this makes the game more enjoyable as well. The design implications of this are to make players feel that their actions are for a specific purpose within the game and have an impact on the game mechanisms of the game that will increase their abilities within the game. In other words, if the results of this study support the hypothesis that the presence of upgrade mechanisms increase task engagement and enjoyment, then making players feel their actions are working towards increasing their power or abilities within the game is one way to make players feel that their actions matter. If the results support this hypothesis, designers can increase the extent to which player actions matter (task significance) and increase enjoyment by designing player actions that matter within the mechanisms of the game because they actually increase players' abilities within the game. While narrative framing focuses on the reasons given for player actions within the story of game, the upgrade mechanisms conditions make how well the player plays the game actually more important within the game. Collecting more points in the upgrade mechanisms conditions allows the player to unlock more upgrades that give the player more abilities and power within the game to score more points within each timed round, points that can be used to use to unlock more upgrades.

If one of these two ways to increase task significance and enjoyment is more effective than the other, that will be an interesting finding. If upgrade mechanisms are more effective, that would suggest that making player actions more important within the logic, mechanisms, and rules of the game is a more effective path to task significance. If narrative framing is more effective, that would suggest the reasons given for why players are taking action and making those reasons involve helping others or taking responsible action is a more effective path to task significance.

Finally, if there is an interaction effect between narrative framing and upgrade mechanisms such that the presence of both of these paths to task significance increases enjoyment, that would suggest that using both of these approaches together have a greater effect than the sum of their parts. If found, the implications of this finding would be to both frame user action as responsible actions that help others and to make player actions matter by having those actions build towards increasing player abilities within the mechanisms and rules of the game.

5   Conclusion

Does the extent to which players perceive their actions as meaningful or significant cause more digital game enjoyment? Is it the framing and perception of player actions that makes them significant, or is it the game mechanisms and rules of the game the consequences of their actions in terms of increasing their abilities and power within the game that makes them significant? This paper proposes a controlled experiment to address these questions. There is more research to be done to fully understand what leads to digital game enjoyment and how to design interactive systems for enjoyment. Understanding the impact of task significance and how to design for task significance is one path forward.

References

1. Abeele, V.V., Spiel, K., Nacke, L., Johnson, D., Gerling, K.: Development and validation of the player experience inventory: a scale to measure player experiences at the level of functional and psychosocial consequences. Int. J. Hum.-Comput. Stud. **135**, 102370 (2020)
2. Abuhamdeh, S., Csikszentmihalyi, M.: The importance of challenge for the enjoyment of intrinsically motivated, goal-directed activities. Pers. Soc. Psychol. Bull. **38**(3), 317–330 (2012)
3. Ariely, D., Kamenica, E., Prelec, D.: Man's search for meaning: the case of Legos. J. Econ. Behav. Organ. **67**(3–4), 671–677 (2008)
4. Aristotle: Nicomachean Ethics, 3rd edn. Hackett Publishing Company Inc., Indianapolis (2019)
5. American Psychiatric Association: Diagnostic and statistical manual of mental disorders (DSM-5®). American Psychiatric Pub. (2013)
6. Bartle, R.: Hearts, clubs, diamonds, spades: players who suit MUDs. J. MUD Res. **1**(1), 19 (1996)
7. Brockmyer, J.H., Fox, C.M., Curtiss, K.A., McBroom, E., Burkhart, K.M., Pidruzny, J.N.: The development of the game engagement questionnaire: a measure of engagement in video game-playing. J. Exp. Soc. Psychol. **45**(4), 624–634 (2009)
8. Caillois, R.: Man, Play, and Games. University of Illinois Press, Champaign (1961)
9. Csikszentmihalyi, M.: Finding Flow: The Psychology of Engagement with Everyday Life, 1st edn. Basic Books, New York (1998)
10. Csikszentmihalyi, M.: Flow: The Psychology of Optimal Experience, 1st edn. Harper Perennial Modern Classics, New York (2008)
11. Csikszentmihalyi, M., Csikszentmihalyi, I.S. (eds.): Optimal Experience: Psychological Studies of Flow in Consciousness. Cambridge University Press, Cambridge, New York (1988)
12. Csikszentmihalyi, M., LeFevre, J.: Optimal experience in work and leisure. J. Pers. Soc. Psychol. **56**(5), 815–822 (1989). https://doi.org/10.1037/0022-3514.56.5.815
13. Csikszentmihalyi, M., Nakamura, J.: Effortless attention in everyday life: a systematic phenomenology. In: Effortless Attention: A New Perspective in the Cognitive Science of Attention and Action, pp. 179–190 (2010)
14. Deterding, S., Dixon, D., Khaled, R., Nacke, L.: From game design elements to gamefulness: defining gamification. In Proceedings of the 15th International Academic MindTrek Conference: Envisioning Future Media Environments, pp. 9–15. ACM (2011). http://dl.acm.org/citation.cfm?id=2181040. Accessed 15 Feb 2017
15. Edwards, M.J.: The dimensionality and construct valid measurement of life meaning. Ph.D. thesis, Queen's University (2007)
16. Frankl, V.E.: Man's Search for Meaning. Simon and Schuster, New York (1985)
17. George, L., Park, C.: Meaning in life as comprehension, purpose, and mattering: toward integration and new research questions. Rev. General Psychol. **20** (2016). https://doi.org/10.1037/gpr0000077

18. George, L.S., Park, C.L.: The multidimensional existential meaning scale: a tripartite approach to measuring meaning in life. J. Positive Psychol. **12**(6), 613–627 (2017)
19. Hektner, J.M., Schmidt, J.A., Csikszentmihalyi, M.: Experience Sampling Method: Measuring the Quality of Everyday Life. Sage, Thousand Oaks (2007)
20. Hunicke, R.: The case for dynamic difficulty adjustment in games. In: Proceedings of the 2005 ACM SIGCHI International Conference on Advances in Computer Entertainment Technology, pp. 429–433. ACM, New York (2005). https://doi.org/10.1145/1178477.1178573
21. Jackson, S.A., Marsh, H.W.: Development and validation of a scale to measure optimal experience: the flow state scale. J. Sport Exerc. Psychol. **18**(1), 17–35 (1996)
22. Keller, J., Bless, H.: Flow and regulatory compatibility: an experimental approach to the flow model of intrinsic motivation. Pers. Soc. Psychol. Bull. **34**(2), 196–209 (2008)
23. Korhonen, H., Montola, M., Arrasvuori, J.: Understanding playful user experience through digital games. In: International Conference on Designing Pleasurable Products and Interfaces. Citeseer (2009). http://citeseerx.ist.psu.edu/viewdoc/download?doi=10.1.1.586.7146&rep=rep1&type=pdf. Accessed 26 Jan 2017
24. Lazzaro, N.: Why We Play Games: Four Keys to More Emotion Without Story (2004). http://gamemodworkshop.com/readings/xeodesign_whyweplaygames.pdf
25. Lazzaro, N.: Why we play: affect and the fun of games. In: Human-Computer Interaction: Designing for Diverse Users and Domains, pp. 155–176 (2009)
26. Malone, T.W.: What makes things fun to learn? Heuristics for designing instructional computer games. In: Proceedings of the 3rd ACM SIGSMALL Symposium and the First SIGPC Symposium on Small Systems (SIGSMALL 1980), pp. 162–169. ACM, New York (1980). https://doi.org/10.1145/800088.802839
27. Malone, T.W.: Toward a theory of intrinsically motivating instruction. Cogn. Sci. **5**(4), 333–369 (1981)
28. McDonald, M.J., Wong, P.T.P., Gingras, D.T.: Meaning-in-life measures and development of a brief version of the Personal Meaning Profile. In: The Human Quest for Meaning: Theories, Research, and Applications, vol. 2 (2012)
29. Mekler, E.D., Hornbæk, K.: A framework for the experience of meaning in human-computer interaction. In: Proceedings of the 2019 CHI Conference on Human Factors in Computing Systems (CHI 2019), pp. 1–15. Association for Computing Machinery, New York (2019). https://doi.org/10.1145/3290605.3300455
30. Moller, A.C., Meier, B.P., Wall, R.D.: Developing an experimental induction of flow: effortless action in the lab. In: Effortless Attention: A New Perspective in the Cognitive Science of Attention and Action, pp. 191–204 (2010)
31. Nakamura, J., Csikszentmihalyi, M.: The concept of flow. In: Flow and the Foundations of Positive Psychology, pp. 239–263. Springer, Dordrecht (2014). https://doi.org/10.1007/978-94-017-9088-8_16
32. Nakamura, J., Csikszentmihalyi, M.: The construction of meaning through vital engagement. In: Flourishing: Positive Psychology and the Life Well-Lived, pp. 83–104. American Psychological Association, Washington, DC (2003). https://doi.org/10.1037/10594-004
33. Nietzsche, F.: Twilight of the Idols. CreateSpace Independent Publishing Platform (2012)
34. Payne, B.R., Jackson, J.J., Noh, S.R., Stine-Morrow, E.A.L.: In the zone: flow state and cognition in older adults. Psychol. Aging **26**(3), 738–743 (2011). https://doi.org/10.1037/a0022359
35. Peterson, C., Park, N., Seligman, M.E.P.: Orientations to happiness and life satisfaction: the full life versus the empty life. J. Happiness Stud. **6**(1), 25–41 (2005)
36. Peterson, C., Seligman, M.E.P.: Character Strengths and Virtues: A Handbook and Classification. Oxford University Press, Oxford (2004)

37. Quick, J.M., Atkinson, R.K., Lin, L.: Empirical taxonomies of gameplay enjoyment: personality and video game preference. Int. J. Game-Based Learn. **2**(3), 11–31 (2012)
38. Ryan, R.M., Deci, E.L.: Self-determination theory and the facilitation of intrinsic motivation, social development, and well-being. Am. Psychol. **55**(1), 68–78 (2000). https://doi.org/10.1037//0003-066X.55.1.68
39. Ryan, R.M., Rigby, S.C., Przybylski, A.: The motivational pull of video games: a self-determination theory approach. Motiv. Emotion **30**(4), 344–360 (2006). https://doi.org/10.1007/s11031-006-9051-8
40. Schaffer, O., Fang, X.: Finding Flow with Games: Does Immediate Progress Feedback Cause Flow? Puerto Rico (2015). https://doi.org/10.13140/RG.2.1.4236.8725
41. Schaffer, O., Fang, X.: Impact of Task and Interface Design on Flow, Dublin, Ireland (2016). http://aisel.aisnet.org/sighci2016/7/
42. Schaffer, O., Fang, X.: Sources of computer game enjoyment: card sorting to develop a new model. In: Kurosu, M. (ed.) HCI 2017. LNCS, vol. 10272, pp. 99–108. Springer, Cham (2017). https://doi.org/10.1007/978-3-319-58077-7_9
43. Schaffer, O., Fang, X.: What Makes Games Fun? Card Sort Reveals 34 Sources of Computer Game Enjoyment, New Orleans (2018). http://aisel.aisnet.org/amcis2018/HCI/Presentations/2/
44. Sheldon, K.M., Elliot, A.J., Kim, Y., Kasser, T.: What is satisfying about satisfying events? Testing 10 candidate psychological needs. J. Pers. Soc. Psychol. **80**(2), 325 (2001)
45. The NPD Group: Record-breaking U.S. video game industry sales were driven by strong gains across content, hardware, and accessories (2020). https://www.npd.com/wps/portal/npd/us/news/press-releases/2020/the-npd-group-us-consumer-spend-on-video-game-products-continues-to-break-records/. Accessed 2 Oct 2020
46. Wong, P.T.P.: Meaning therapy: an integrative and positive existential psychotherapy. J. Contemp. Psychother. **40**(2), 85–93 (2010). https://doi.org/10.1007/s10879-009-9132-6
47. Yee, N.: Motivations for play in online games. Cyber Psychol. Behav. **9**(6), 772–775 (2006)
48. Yee, N., Ducheneaut, N., Nelson, L.: Online gaming motivations scale: development and validation. In: Proceedings of the SIGCHI Conference on Human Factors in Computing Systems, pp. 2803–2806. ACM (2012). http://dl.acm.org/citation.cfm?id=2208681. Accessed 24 Apr 2016

Author Index

Printed in the United States
by Baker & Taylor Publisher Services

Printed in the United States
by Baker & Taylor Publisher Services